WOMEN'S HEALTH

Sue O'Sullivan came to London in 1963 and has been active in women's liberation groups since 1969. Her interest in feminism led to an involvement in women's health activities. She holds a Diploma in Health Education, and for many years taught health classes in Holloway Prison. A member of the *Spare Rib* collective from 1979 to 1984, she currently edits the magazine's health page. She was co-editor (with Michèle Barrett, Sue Bruley, Gail Chester, Maggie Millman, Amanda Sebestyn and Lynne Segal) of *No Turning Back: Writings from the Women's Liberation Movement, 1975–80* (Women's Press, 1981). Two of her articles in *Feminist Review*, where she is on the editorial collective, are reprinted in *Sexuality Reader* (Virago, 1987). Sue O'Sullivan lives in London and works part-time for Sheba Feminist Publishers.

Pauline King
Oct 99

WOMEN'S HEALTH
A SPARE RIB READER

EDITED BY
SUE O'SULLIVAN

London   New York

First published in 1987 by
Pandora Press (Routledge & Kegan Paul Ltd)
11 New Fetter Lane, London EC4P 4EE

Published in the USA by
Pandora Press (Routledge & Kegan Paul Inc.)
in association with Methuen Inc.
29 West 35th Street, New York, NY 10001

Set in Palatino 9/10pt
by Input Typesetting Ltd, London SW19 8DR
and printed in the British Isles
by The Guernsey Press Co Ltd
Guernsey, Channel Islands

Library of Congress Cataloguing in Publication Data

Women's Health.

   Bibliography: p.
   Includes index.
   1. Women—Health and hygiene.   2. Women—Medical care
—Social aspects.   3. Feminism.   I. O'Sullivan, Sue.
II. Ardill, Susan.
RA564.85.B63   1987   362.1'088042   87–9104

British Library CIP Data also available

ISBN 0–86358–218–4

For Pauline Bradshaw, my sister-in-law and much more, who died of cancer, aged 48, in 1984

CONTENTS

FIGURES

ACKNOWLEDGMENTS

For me, getting this anthology done was more difficult than I ever imagined, a process with many starts and stops. Since 'signing up' with Pandora I've left the *Spare Rib* collective, been unemployed, started working at Sheba Feminist Publishers, and reconnected with *Spare Rib* through editing its monthly health page.

First, I would like to thank all the contributors to the book. I'm only sorry that, for reasons of space, I've had to cut some articles, and haven't been able to include others. Every effort was made to contact all the contributors, by advertising in *Spare Rib*, when no address was available.

At each starting point on this book women have put in time to help me out. I hope they know how much their help meant to me, even if I didn't go on to finish the project off immediately. Jill Posener originally convinced me that a *Spare Rib* health anthology was a good idea and a logical extension of my work around health issues. In the beginning Lisa Saffron and Susan Hemmings looked through all the material and made suggestions about the structure of the book. Later members of the *SR* collective gave me feedback on suggested selections. Amanda Sebestyn offered opinions on several chapters and Jill Rakusen gave me support at particularly difficult times. Rosie Parker gave me advice on what became the chapter on emotional matters, and Ruth Wallsgrove took on the chapter on abortion and drafted an introduction to it. Sona Osman helped me with the resource section. Along the way, as I sorted both the book and myself out, the supportive friendship of Ruthie Petrie, Sona Osman, Karen Goldman, Janet Hadley and Pratibha Parmar sustained me and gave me much pleasure. My teenage children, Tom and Dan, and their father John have always accepted my separate life and welcomed me into theirs. Barbara Smith's editorial suggestions were valuable and her word processing skills a wonder, but I think her ability to make me laugh gets the gold star.

Finally, when the bloody thing still wasn't done, my dear friend Susan Ardill stepped in to haul me across the finish line. Without her collaboration in all aspects of the final version, I still might be languishing among the piles and piles of paper I'd amassed. Susan and I met while both working at *Spare Rib*; we have collaborated on writing projects before and I hope will do so again in the future. Certainly her involvement in this book was what made it possible to complete.

In the end I want to say that what makes sense of my life, my future and my dreams are the existence, no matter how frustrating at times, of the different, interconnected struggles for liberation being waged throughout the world at this very moment.

INTRODUCTION

Spare Rib is a women's liberation magazine which has appeared every month since 1972. For most of its 15 years it has been run as a collective, attempting in its structure to reflect the non-hierarchical, skill-sharing ideals of the women's liberation movement. As a popular magazine which also sees itself as political, *Spare Rib* has always balanced (or not) precariously between being the mouthpiece of already committed feminists and a vehicle for spreading the words of feminism to women not yet familiar with them.

Over the years the collective has varied in size from six to 12 members but has always represented more in its pages than the sum total of the collective at any one point. The women on *Spare Rib* have subscribed to a variety of feminisms, and this diversity has usually been reflected in the magazine's content. There is no one *Spare Rib* line, except for a loosely defined agreement not to publish material which is anti-women, anti-lesbian, anti-working class, anti-semitic or racist.

The magazine is both a part of, and separate from, the women's liberation movement, whatever that is at any given point. It is not accountable to any particular group of women except for what accountability it takes on itself, or is pressurized into taking on, by groups or circumstances outside. However, the internal workings of the collective, and the content of the magazine, have gone through many changes over the years, and these have often been linked to debates and upheavals within the wider women's liberation movement.

At times, particular women on the collective have prioritized certain sorts of articles and ways of approaching subjects. Pressure from 'outside' and internal disagreements led to two fierce and prolonged public battles on *Spare Rib*. The first centred on sexuality, and boiled down to accusations that lesbians were silencing heterosexual women, countered by accusations of anti-lesbianism. The second occurred when the collective was engaged in an attempt to become racially mixed. There were difficult splits, and at the same time some women outside were accusing the whole collective of being anti-semitic. At each point of conflict, the interests of different feminists outside both coincided and clashed with different groups of women on the collective. Each contention had at its core the aggrieved and angry assertions of groups of women who were fighting within the larger women's liberation movement for recognition, for a place of priority in that movement.

All these years of bitter talk, long discussions, and meetings with women outside the collective have had an impact on the content of the magazine. While not wishing to suggest that everything is roses now, it does seem that out of the chaos and unhappiness some positive lessons have been learned. Yet despite the changes, certain themes and styles have remained consistent throughout the years.

This potted history of *Spare Rib*, of its woes and workings, does have a connection with the present collection of articles on health. In the first place, the kind of articles which make up this collection could only have appeared in the numbers and with the consistency they have in a feminist magazine. What the magazine is, how it has changed, are part of what situates these articles, and raises themes and considerations which would never find a place in any other magazine, even when the same subject is being covered.

Secondly, health articles in *Spare Rib* have had the same problems as any others in the magazine, and there are absences, omissions and political problems in this collection which it would be wrong not to acknowledge and understand. There is no doubt that throughout most of the 1970s *Spare Rib* articles more often than not assumed that 'women' meant 'all women'. Yet Black women, lesbians, women with disabilities and older women have been largely absent. Their experiences have not been represented, they have not been present visually. Hopefully, this is changing in current articles. Now it would be hard to write a feature on contraceptives, for example, as if all women were heterosexual or heterosexually active. Now it would be difficult to write about abortion, for another example, without bringing in the experiences of Black women who have been urged, against their wishes, to have abortions. Reproductive rights have to take it both ways.

Of course, the *Spare Rib* collective has not only responded to attacks and criticisms: there has always been an eagerness to 'do the right thing'. But taking something on board also means coming face to face with the reality, the confusions, and going through a process in which everyone has to work in practice towards the changes desired. This cannot happen by goodwill alone.

The magazine is still catching up with its own changes. As far as health issues go, it needs more articles which draw out the specific concerns and experiences of the different groups of women so long excluded. It needs more articles which make an analysis of health, ill-health, and health care, enabling us to understand those different experiences, and the forces which both produce and perpetuate them.

Several themes run through many *Spare Rib* articles on health. One poses the question, 'what is health?', sometimes directly, at other times obliquely. And more specifically, what is it in relation to women? Popularly, it has been defined as the absence of disease, and, more than that, a sense of well-being. But this definition doesn't indicate that we all experience our healthiness or dis-ease within a social context and in various relationships.

Many western definitions of what constitutes health and ill-health have been constructed over the centuries within class-divided, white male-dominated societies, and have become incontrovertible 'fact'. It is no coincidence then, that the most important biological *events* in the lives of the majority of women – the onset of menstruation, pregnancy and childbirth, the menopause – have been regarded as pathological *conditions* in need of treatment. Since in a sexist and heterosexist world these events define what it means to be a woman, womanhood itself is often seen as the disease, and any deviation from that male-defined role is regarded as a *double* infirmity. So, for example, lesbians are *physically* 'diseased' because they are women, and *emotionally* 'dis-eased' because they refuse to fulfil their biological destiny. Or, for another example, women with disabilities are seen as subverting woman's traditional role as carer for others, because they may need care themselves. So much fear and hatred of the female body, so much guilt and confusion about sex and sexuality, so much pain and sadness in female psychology: all of it is assumed to be somehow part of a 'natural' condition or predisposition of women.

Traditionally in Britain, women in their roles as wives, housewives, mothers, daughters and lovers take on, or are expected to take on, certain health responsibilities which are then assumed to belong 'naturally' to those roles. Women have 'special' responsibilities for others – for 'proper' nutritious feeding, for the hygiene of the home, for bringing up healthy children, maintaining healthy men, looking after ill family members, but also knowing when to approach the medical system, and then how to follow doctors' directions.

Women also have less well-defined responsibilities connected to the health of others; they mediate the stress which waged work and education places on other family members, they calm away the strains of life 'outside' the home. In addition to all this expenditure of time and energy *for others*, women are still also expected to be available sexually for men, to make themselves attractive as heterosexual partners. They are supposed to find their fulfilment as women through these responsibilities and availabilities.

Added to that is the fact that women are usually expected to 'soldier on' in these male-defined roles, both because of and despite this female 'infirmity', and so we often find the situation where men think women are 'diseased' when we are not, and will not believe us when *we* say we are ill. The phenomenon of premenstrual tension is a case in point: our biology *does* incommode us on occasion, but by the same stroke it does not completely incapacitate us. We are no more *automatic* or perpetual victims of our biology than men.

And who takes care of the carer? Often she is also a waged worker, often in a low-paid service or caring sector of employment. She suffers from work hazards both at home and out of work, and is subject to all the stress factors any other worker comes up against.

The general infantilisation of women involves, amongst many other things, the notion of 'Father knows best', so information regarding our bodies is concealed from us by 'experts' because of our added 'infirmity' of mind. This has had the effect that many women are still largely fearful

3

and ignorant of their own body processes, let alone of what can happen when these processes break down or are disrupted by, for example, hormonal imbalances produced by contraceptive pills.

Access to information, and to *correct* information, is one of the vital prerequisites for women's physical and emotional health. One only has to think of the pill and thrombosis, the Dalkon shield and severe gynaecological disorders, thalidomide, and unnecessary caesarean sections, to see how crucial is the dissemination of medical knowledge.

Health is an intensely political issue. Feminist concern with health aims both to free women from notions of biological determinism and to turn upside-down accepted definitions of women's bodies, minds and emotions. We attempt to seize knowledge and understanding of these in order to have more control over our lives. Women's health roles and relationships are part of other social relations, and part of reinforcing and constructing those relations – in waged work, in sexual relationships, in the community. They are essential to the maintenance of things as they are, the status quo. However, there is no one universal status quo and an international perspective on women's health has to take this on board.

Spare Rib's emphasis on women's health from a feminist perspective has been one of the magazine's consistent strengths. Often, the experiential side of health came to the fore first – personal stories of childbirth, of reproductive health, sexuality, emotional distress, addiction. But along with the 'stories' came the attempt to criticise and agitate around the system which has such a powerful role in producing both our health and our ill-health. Questions of power, who holds it, who holds on to it, who creates it; questions of control, of institutions, wealth, the NHS; searches for information from alternative sources, from the medical establishment, from our own experiences; production of knowledge, for women away from the individualised 'woman'; all this and more became the aim of women active around health issues.

This multi-faceted approach necessitates an ability to take on contradictions and ambivalences. We have emphasised the importance of women's personal experiences in illness and health and of exploring alternatives to the cut-and-cure practices of the NHS. At the same time, the magazine has supported struggles within the NHS, be they of nurses, hospital workers or patients. We have to recognize that class and race determinants bring different priorities, different necessities to the fore in any particular instance.

But health issues and concerns can also bring many women together, across their differences. As feminists, we aim to see the connections between things, and it seems that almost any area of women's health throws up one, two, three, many connections. For instance, through a concern with how she and/or other women were individually treated at childbirth, it is possible for *one* woman to understand how *all* women suffer from living in a male-dominated society, and where the connections and differences are with other groups of oppressed people.

In radical tradition, the inequality of distribution of resources in the NHS has often been the main point of criticism and organising. Feminist critiques have also brought out the necessity of fighting for equality of concern. Even if all the resources of the NHS were distributed equally throughout the country (a highly unlikely occurrence), and even if the cutbacks were halted and more resources were equally available, this would still leave unchanged the way in which the medical profession treats women, Black people, working class people and homosexuals. When a middle-aged woman goes to her (male) GP, for example, studies have shown that she is likely to receive one-third the time a middle-aged man will receive.

Feminists have also questioned the *content* of so much of western medicine. Are the twin gods of drugs and technological intervention the unmitigated blessings they are made out to be? What about the quality of life? What about treating people as integrated beings, not a series of separate organs, limbs, systems to be dosed with drugs, cut off and maintained on machines. What are the long-term effects of many 'wonder' drugs, and what role do drug companies' insatiable thirst for profits play in their proliferation?

Women working around health issues can be involved in specific areas of health. Some feminists are particularly caught up in trying to save hospitals from closure, even as they try to organise pressure to change the way in which those same hospitals treat women and other people without power. Some are totally committed to exploring and making available to more women alternative forms of treatment and preventative health care – something sorely lacking in western medicine. Other women are mainly involved in women and health groups and classes, where issues and consciousness raising go hand in hand. And some feminists are concentrating on a critique of health care, patriarchy, capitalism and imperialism, which spells out their meanings and the ways they intersect with each other.

A feminist politics of health attempts to integrate all of these issues and segments, and provide ways of linking them up. Nurses working in the NHS can link up with women in the community organising to prevent their hospital closing. But further still, exploring alternative health, developing self-help techniques and groups, being concerned about nuclear disaster, supporting low-paid workers' demands, and taking a stand against the rampant heterosexism and racism of the medical profession are not mutually exclusive. They do have relevance to hospital workers, nurses, and doctors, as well as to those working outside medical institutions. Health is a wide umbrella, and it is possible to work on many fronts and make many links under it, ones which reach out to other structures and sites of oppression.

What remains, in a shadowed half-light, is the way in which certain sets of historical, economic and political determinants tug and twist to create women's contradictory view of themselves and others' view of

5

them. If women seem to spontaneously recognise their health responsibilities, it is absolutely vital for feminists to understand that their/our recognition comes about though particular constructions of femininity and womanhood. They are not eternal or unchanging, they have chinks, quirks and weaknesses, which are different through history, in different cultures, for different classes and races. But women do rebel, do question, do organise and demand, and sometimes these rebellions are at the heart of women's health concerns.

Now, mainstream women's magazines regularly go where *Spare Rib* dared to forge a path. The difference remains, however, in the basic perspective. Working or writing around sexual and reproductive health issues or about the medical system is not necessarily feminist in itself. The continuous absence of a lesbian presence, for example, in any mainstream women's magazine health article illustrates those magazines' inability or refusal to take on board the notion of heterosexism or their own homophobia. Ironically, many lesbian feminist health activists in Britain have been centrally involved in developing and expanding women's health knowledge and control in a way which benefits heterosexuals as much as, or more than, lesbians. Similarly, their refusal to deal with class or race leads them to criticisms without any bite.

Involvement in women's health becomes feminist and political when it isn't *only* about coping, finding alternative cures or sharing these things – important as they are. When a connection is made between ill-health and an oppressive society, and when that connection exposes and opposes the sexism, heterosexism, racism and exploitative class relations which run through our institutions and ourselves – that's when self-help becomes political and feminist.

CHAPTER 1

DOWN THERE

Understanding our bodies, taking back the initiative from doctors and 'experts', redefining the meanings of biology – all these have been central to the women's liberation movement in Britain.

Women's biology has traditionally been understood as the key to their destiny. It was the underpinning and justification for their inferior position and their 'otherness'. Whether women were labelled as hysterical, neurotic or suffering from premenstrual tension; it all stemmed from that 'special' female biology. If women were naturally suited to childcare because they bore the babies, they were also expected to find perfect 'human' fulfilment in this activity because of their biology.

Feminists don't deny biology or that men and women are different. Women are *not* exactly like men except for certain minuses and pluses 'down there'. Thank god. We have to take into account these differences and their definitions. How we experience our biology occupies a lot of our energies in a sexist society, but feminists also maintain that biology comes loaded with socially constructed meanings.

In order to break out of the rule of an oppressively defined female biology we have to understand it, politicise it *for ourselves* – it has already been politicised, although we are supposed to understand it as 'natural'.

The difficulty of this task is enormous; we are so steeped in the inevitability, the 'naturalness' of the biological imperative that to question it is to challenge deeply ingrained parts of ourselves. At the same time we are attempting to envisage and construct new ways of making choices, new possibilities, new relationships and ways of working. Sometimes we flounder.

Starting to understand our bodies and our emotions led to setting up self-help groups around women's health concerns, especially those which were most ignored or most oppressively treated by the (male) medical profession. Vaginal self-examination literally revealed what had been hidden from us. Its consciousness-raising effect was important, its practical significance for monitoring and understanding changes in our vaginas and cervices gave us the possibility for more control over our bodies.

Even talking about self-exam shook up a lot of women's fears of their sexual and reproductive organs. Touching or looking 'down there' can still produce anxiety in women. Distress and disgust vie with the knowledge that heterosexual intercourse is meant to be pleasurable.

Women organised self-help and discussion groups out of common suffering in order to share their experiences and advice, *and* to agitate for better treatment and research. They came together to discuss how age, disability, sexuality and class affect their health, their care, their concerns.

And women started the long process of analysing why we feel about our bodies the way we do, and how it's all connected with the subjugation of women.

Spare Rib has always represented self-help projects and discussions of reproductive and sexual health issues in its pages. Often these were the first occasions that women had access to printed information. For example, we published an article on herpes long before it hit the media. And a later article, 'Living with herpes' written together by a lesbian and a heterosexual woman, brought in such a deluge of letters, phone calls and desperate callers at the office that the Herpes Association was lifted off the ground out of pure necessity.

Down there – using speculums for self-examination
Sophie Laws
SR 108 July 1981

Self-exam stands the medical approach on its head: we observe *well women*, our normal states. Medical men have always looked first at the sick body and then at the well one. We start from our own needs as women, not from the position of the professional.

Writing this article we found ourselves casting around for solid medically-acceptable reasons for doing self-exam, somehow trying to justify our interest in it: they are hard to find. At the same time we should say that it *is* practically useful – you can learn to spot any change in yourself at an early stage, and it is a first step towards coping with a number of things ourselves – the treatment of some vaginal infections, birth control by observing natural cycles and self-insemination, for example. Some groups of women have gone further and have learnt to do early abortions by vacuum aspiration.

Woman's body in patriarchal culture is abnormal: we are all alienated from our physical selves by their inherent 'wrongness' – that is, their non-maleness. For us to observe our bodies in detail, to get familiar with what is right for us, gives us a picture which is missing from gynaecology textbooks, from young girls' upbringing, from the whole culture.

The technicalities of self-exam are so essentially simple that it may seem daft to be writing an article on it – but then why do so few women ever do it? A woman who has taught self-exam says:

Demonstrating self-exam to women with even the slightest, most tentative curiosity always surprises me. I'm careful not to pressure them into doing it in the group for fear they'll be nervous or embarrassed so I do it first and tell them to go home and try it privately. At first they crouch four feet away and peer down the tunnel of my vagina, nodding politely while I point out my cervix, my erosion and my os. But If I can coax them a little closer so they can actually see my cervix, then the spark of excitement is kindled. Before I've even taken my speculum out, they've got their knickers off, eager to be the next to do it.

I've been in many self-exam groups. Some women have had difficulties at first in finding their cervixes, and a few have found the speculum uncomfortable, but all have been pleased and excited when the cervix came into view. All it takes to begin to reclaim our bodies is a simple plastic speculum, a mirror and a light.

The difference between examining the cervix in a women's group and in a doctor's surgery is great. At best the doctor creates an atmosphere of cold clinical detachment, where our spare parts are analysed for possible malfunction. There, at worst, the disgust and contempt for women's bodies is out in the open. Our cunts are so shameful that often a piece of paper must be placed on the stomach to hide the pelvic region from the woman herself. Most doctors don't explain what they are doing with their cold mysterious instruments nor do they share with us what they have discovered except in ways designed to keep us in fear and dependence on them. Using words which are intimidating and unnecessarily technical, they give an impression of abnormality and unease.

What is important about self-exam is what it symbolises – a step away from male-controlled definitions of women and a step towards women-centred definitions and gaining control of our lives. Gynaecologists understand the threat to their power that self-exam represents and react aggressively. I was first given a speculum by a consultant who had perforated my uterus while inserting an IUD. He was so terrified that I would sue him that he gave me everything I asked for. Months later, I went to the health centre worried about thrush. I told the doctor that I had used a speculum and he hit the roof – 'Who gave you a speculum? Don't you realise how unhygienic it is? Those speculums are sterile and meant to be used only once. You could get all sorts of infections putting something unsterile in your vagina!' As I was leaving, I asked him whether boiling or roasting was the best way to sterilise a penis.

Self-exam starts with getting a mirror and having a proper look at your outer genitals – for many of us this is the hardest part. While we can't escape from the penises men draw on walls everywhere, many women nurture fearful fantasies about the abnormality of their genitals. Their appearance varies a lot from one woman to another – one may have lots of hair spreading down her legs and high up on her abdomen, and another just a little tuft over the pubic bone. The inner labia, the soft lips around the vagina, urinary opening and clitoris can be large and protruding or small and compact. The appearance of women's genitals seems to be an extremely well-kept secret – from women. Men, it seems, may look at them, but few little girls or even women get the reassurance they need that theirs are normal and as much like any other woman's as their nose is.

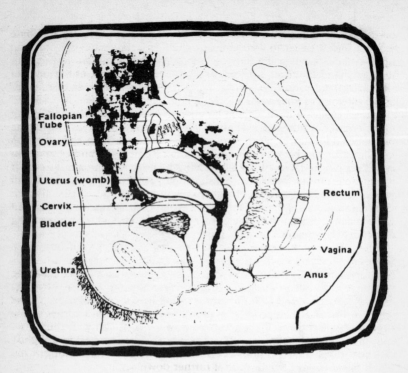

FIGURE 1 Female reproductive anatomy (*SR 108* July 1981)

First of all, have a good look at the speculum, practise opening and closing it and make sure that the ratchet will hold it open.

Then, settle yourself comfortably – there's nothing so certain to make self-exam impossible or painful as trying to hold yourself sitting up awkwardly while you put the speculum in. Obviously, if you need to, it's best to have a pee before you start. Find something to lean against – a wall, a bed or a friend – so that you can lean back a bit and relax your stomach muscles.

It's a good idea to reach in with your finger to feel where your cervix is so that you know the direction to point the speculum in – roughly, it will be towards the top of the crease of your bottom. The cervix feels like a firm, smooth, dome, quite a different texture from the rest of your vagina. A pregnant cervix from about eight to ten weeks on begins to feel soft and squashy, not firm as usual.

Now close the speculum completely, put some KY jelly (from the chemist) on it, and spread your labia open around your vagina with one hand so that you can insert the speculum. Don't use vaseline or *anything* oil-based like that. If you haven't any KY jelly, plain water is best. Some women find it easier to slide the speculum in turned sideways, turning up the handles when it's fully in before opening it, others to put it in with the handles turned up straight away. Point it, again, at the small of your back, and slide it in gently – after it's through the ring of muscles at the opening of your vagina it should go in quite easily.

Once it seems to have gone in far enough (for some women this is half of its length, for others the whole of it – you have to judge by the feeling of it) open it up slowly, a couple of notches. If you are tense, the speculum may tend to slip back closed again, so hold onto the handles and you won't get pinched. Now have a look with the torch and mirror. It's easiest if you hold one of these and get someone else to move the other until you've got the angle right. You can either shine the torch directly into the vagina or you can point it into the tunnel you've made. If you want to do it alone you can hold the mirror between your feet, or use a strong anglepoise lamp which will stand by itself.

You will see pink, crinkly vaginal walls and with luck your cervix will be visible straight away in the end of the speculum. If all you can see is folds of vaginal walls, don't despair – some times just coughing will bring it into view. The cervix, when it appears, may be pointing straight at you or it may be that you can only see the side of it at first because of the way the uterus is lying. If you can only see the side or a corner of the cervix, wiggle the speculum until you can see it properly. If there's no sign of it, take the speculum out and start again, pointing it in a slightly different direction. The most likely thing is that you're pointing it too much towards your head – turn it further down.

Always take a speculum out open – if you close it inside you you'll pinch yourself. Speculums should be washed in warm water and soap, rinsed well and let dry in the air – there's no need to sterilise them. The vagina is not a sterile environment.

If you have trouble finding your cervix, persist – some women find it always takes a while, but it does get easier as you get to know yourself.

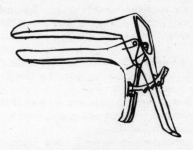

FIGURE 2 Speculum (*SR 108* July 1981)

Put lots of jelly on the speculum so that you don't get sore. Don't hold your breath in concentration – it doesn't help at all! Some women can push their cervixes into view by bearing down with their stomach muscles. the main thing seems to be not to abandon hope at the first setback. If you're in a group make sure that everyone is given the time they need.

Cervixes have been described in print as like a doughnut, like the end of your nose when you touch it with a finger, and like the tip of a penis!! Well it is hard to describe . . . none of these are terribly convincing! The cervix does not look or feel much like anything else. A non-pregnant womb is a solid muscle and the cervix is the bit of it you can feel at the end of your vagina. Looking at it with a speculum you can see that distinct from the wrinkly/foldy skin of the vaginal walls the cervix is smoother and round. You will also be able to see the os, the hole in the middle of the cervix which is the opening into the uterus. The os may be tiny as a pinhead and quite closed or it may be in the centre of a deep dip in the cervix, or in women who have had children it may be a long uneven slit.

The size, shape and colour of the cervix varies enormously from one woman to another and over the course of the menstrual cycle. A healthy cervix is shiny, smooth and even – the colour can vary from pale pink to much redder, getting a bluish tinge in pregnancy and in some women just before a period. Some women's are small and pointed, some larger and flat, and after childbirth, particularly if there was a tear or a cut, the cervix tends to be lumpy and very uneven in shape, harder to be sure what you're looking at until you get used to it.

If you have an IUD, you should be able to see the strings coming a little way out of the os – if you can't see it, look again on another day and if you still can't see it, go to the doctor or clinic to check if it's still there. If you can see or feel the plastic end of the IUD, it is on its way out and you should see a doctor straight away – a coil working its way out can be painful and they're best removed quickly.

Women have observed a large number of changes in themselves over the course of the menstrual cycle and many are using this understanding either to avoid getting pregnant or to conceive. At ovulation, around two weeks before your next period, the os opens and the secretion from it changes from being white, tacky and slight, to a clear, slippery thin mucous, which is often described as like raw egg-white. Some women say that they notice that their cervix is raised and the os open at ovulation, others get a distinct one-sided pain as the ovum is released. The mucous builds up gradually over a period of about five days, up until the wettest day, which is the day before you ovulate. Afterwards the mucous becomes scantier and whiter until you are quite dry again. The driest days are during and immediately after bleeding.

You can use these observations, along with taking your temperature, to practise birth control by avoiding intercourse with penetration during your fertile periods, but it is most important to be absolutely clear and disciplined about what you are observing. Write down your observations over several cycles and do not rely on the method until you are quite sure you can detect the run-up to ovulation. Read a thorough account of the method, and try to get advice from someone who is already practising it.

Women who have been in self-exam groups have observed other kinds of changes too – women with small cervical 'erosions', a ring of redness around the os, have seen them come and go with their cycles, and, over long periods of time, have seen that they seem to be linked to a number of other factors: the use of the pill, the coil, tampons for menstruation, even to hot weather. While doctors tend to declare a woman's uterus retroverted (turned to the back rather than to the front as the majority are) with an air of finality, we find that many women's seem to move and can be tilted backwards one week and tilted forward (anteverted) another.

VAGINAL DISCHARGE

All women have some vaginal discharge – the quantity varies a good deal from one woman to another, and through the menstrual cycle. Many women worry about whether their discharge is 'normal'. The real question is whether your discharge at the moment is normal for you. Doing self-exam and being aware of your menstrual cycle gives you a knowledge of the normal variations in your own secretions.

The discharge from the vagina is an accumulation of secretions: first of all, as you'll see with your speculum, the glands of the cervix put out mucous of different kinds and in different quantities depending on the hormones affecting them at that time of the month. This comes out of the os and passes down the vagina picking up dead cells off the vaginal walls and some fluid which oozes from the walls (sometimes very little, at other times, such as in pregnancy, much more). Then it may be joined by the juice produced by the glands at the entrance to the vagina when you get sexually excited.

Getting to know the smell and texture of your normal secretions is very useful so that you can spot any change. A peculiar smelling, or odd-coloured discharge is often an early sign of infection. For example, lots of white discharge looking like cottage cheese and smelling of yeast (like beer or bread baking) is a sign of thrush. If you think you have an infection, go to a doctor or a clinic and get a swab taken to be sure what it is.

Some infections do make one's discharge smell decidedly offensive, but many women hate their discharges, and find them very smelly and unpleasant though there is no infection. These attitudes come from our culture's making out that women's bodies are dirty, mysterious, oozing strange fluids – different from men's, therefore wrong. Advertising plays

13

on women's ignorance and insecurities to sell us products like vaginal deodorants and perfumed soap which quite often themselves cause irritation and allergic reactions in perfectly healthy women. Accepting our own smell is part of relearning to like our own bodies, our selves.

A RADICAL APPROACH TO REPRODUCTION

Reproduction: the fact is that women's bodies are the means by which humankind is reproduced: this is central to our oppression as women. Men control our bodies in very profound ways. The terrible trouble many of us have coping with the fact that we have genitals, that we have a sexuality, is a force maintaining the patriarchy, and separating women from one another, just as much as more overt violence against women is. One follows from the other: we cannot fight with our full power until we make our bodies our home ground.

In early 1981, Onlywomen Press published a pamphlet called Down There. *It introduces vaginal self-examination and explains in detail what to look for. Our article is written by the same woman and is based on their pamphlet. Information on how to order the pamphlet is included in the chapter references at the end of the book.*

More than one womb
Louise Marsden
SR 88 October 1979

For the first 31 years of my life, I thought I had a fairly good idea of what my body was like; it functioned 'normally', and since I had a paramedical education, having trained as a pharmacist, I thought that I was informed. Then for various reasons I decided to have a child. I am a woman, I can bear children, so it should be straightforward, I thought. (It couldn't be quite straightforward, I am a lesbian.) I was trying for a year, towards the end of which I began to think I was infertile. I suspect that friends wondered at my continued attempts to become pregnant, as infertility seemed more and more of a possibility. Then one month just when my period was due, I became sick with what seemed incredibly like German measles. It *was* German measles, and my period did not come that month, and I was pregnant. There was no question of whether or not to have an abortion: the effects of German measles on a foetus are usually ghastly. It was not too difficult to get an NHS abortion, although there was some delay, of course! In my anaesthetic haze after the abortion (or termination as they say), the doctor came around and told me that there had been 'scanty products' from the abortion. He looked sceptical and told me to come back in ten days. By then the results of the histology tests – the examination of the embryonic tissue – would be ready. He did not stay to explain. The ward sister assured me that at least one woman every week has scanty products from an abortion.

During the next ten days I tried to find out why there would be 'scanty products'. Perhaps the embryo had already died. This sometimes happens and if it is in the first three months our bodies can reabsorb the 'products'. Perhaps with the German measles it had not grown much anyway. Perhaps the whole pregnancy had been hysterical. I had been trying hard to get pregnant, and maybe I'd forced my body to pretend that it was. Confidence in my own judgment seeped away a little. Were these symptoms psychological?

Anyway, I waited, searching for information as usual. On the appointed day I went, they did not have the histology results, of course. However, I was examined and my uterus was still swollen. It was a different doctor and he decided to have a look around, or rather a feel around. Finally he found something: 'a vaginal septum perhaps', yes, a vaginal septum. Did I mind a student doctor having a look? No, but what are you looking at? He explained that I had a piece of flesh dividing my vagina into two, nothing else. He asked for another sample of urine and I was asked to return to see the consultant in two days and dismissed.

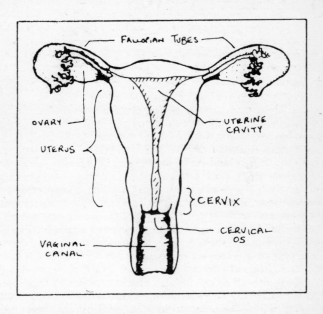

FIGURE 3 Average female reproductive organs: here is a diagram of what are called 'the female reproductive organs', but we'll call them average female reproductive organs' *Teresa Savage (SR 88* October 1979)

I immediately did a pregnancy test at home, it was still positive. Great! The consultant was very apologetic, another abortion immediately. But it may not be simple; he may have to cut the septum; he may not be able to remove the foetus without doing a caesarian type abortion, which means cutting me open. He didn't quite know, but it seemed that I had a double uterus. Well, the abortion was quite straightforward fortunately (we have to be thankful for small mercies); my uterus is completely divided into two, it's a uterus didelphys. From the outside I look like any woman does, there is one entrance to my vagina, but once inside a little, there is this tissue – septum – which divides the pathway into two, going up to two cervixes, then into the two uteruses. The pathway on the left is much narrower and until this abortion business, had never been discovered, although I had had countless internal examinations by doctors for one thing or another. What follows is what I've learned since. I want as many women as possible to know that these anomalies exist.

In the first 12 weeks when the egg is dividing into different cells (when it is called an embryo), two tubes form and they are called Mullerian

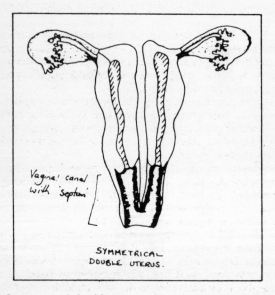

FIGURE 4 Symmetrical double uterus: here you get two uteruses, two cervixes. There is a fallopian tube attached to each uterus, so the usual number of fallopian tubes and ovaries. The duplication can continue down to the vagina. This is called a Uterus Didelphys
Teresa Savage (*SR 88* Ocrober 1979)

ducts. There is one on either side, and they come together to form one tube or vessel, and eventually, the uterus, cervix and upper vagina. If they do not join together completely, and fuse, then these variations on the theme of the female reproductive system develop. The urinary tract, the kidneys, urethras (tubes going down to the bladder) and bladder also form during this fusion of the Mullerian ducts. So if you get incomplete joining of those ducts, it is possible to have variations in that area too. I have a double lot of kidneys and urethras, but the urethras join together before getting to the bladder. Again they have never caused me any trouble, although some variations can.

It is not known why these things happen, they just do. These things are not passed on from mother to child, so they are not hereditary.

There are a number of possible variations in the uterus and vagina in the female reproductive system. You can have extra ovaries, but that seems to be extremely rare. You can be born without the top part of the vagina or with a very strong division across it.

THE PROBLEMS CAUSED BY THE DIFFERENT VARIATIONS

Infertility: there is complete infertility if the path to the cervix and vagina is blocked and there is relative infertility if the pathways are narrowed and there are divisions or septa in any of the paths. So with a Unicornuate uterus, one side is completely missing, including one ovary: this means fertility will be considerably reduced.

Miscarriage: miscarriage is more common because implantation of the fertilised egg can happen on a septum, and the septum is likely to have a weaker blood supply and will not be strong enough to support the growing egg (embryo). Also the space inside the uterus may be irregular, and this will prevent growth.

Premature labour and premature rupture of the membranes (waters): both of these happen for the same reasons as miscarriage happens. The foetus may not be able to position itself properly for birth, because of the shape of the uterus. So 'malpresentation' is more common. The baby may lie across the uterus, or upside down (breech).

Dystocia (abnormal labour): the uterine contractions may not be co-ordinated, also the non-pregnant side of the uterus can block the way of the baby. Placenta can remain in the uterus, again because of the unco-ordinated contractions, so it has to be removed by hand.

All of the above problems are to do with childbirth, but with a uterus which has a blind side, you can get a build up of menstrual blood because there is no way for it to come out. So periods can be very painful and eventually after some years, you can get a big lump which is made up of old menstrual blood and it falls down into the vagina. Its removal would have to be by surgery.

It is hard to find very much written on how often these variations occur; they are often not discovered at all because they are not always problematic. Ian Donald in *Practical Obstetric Problems* says that two out of every thousand women have a 'congenital deformity' that is bad enough to interfere with pregnancy. This is 0.2% and presumably he means that 0.2% of women have problems conceiving because of one of these variations. Belscher and Mackay in *Obstetrics and the Newborn* say, however, that the incidence of variation is approximately 1%, but if minor forms of duplication like a septate uterus are included, it could be close to 5%. So five women in every 100 have some variation, and this knowledge is kept in weighty medical tomes, hidden from us.

The gynaecology consultant whom I saw for the abortion said that he sees about one woman a year with some variation. I have spoken to midwives who have been practising for years, and who have seen only two or three – not surprising, really, as midwives deal with women who have successfully conceived, and not with women who are having problems.

Until I decided to get pregnant, my double uterus caused me no difficulties at all; most of the problems do seem to happen in pregnancy. If a lot go unnoticed, it's possible that they are trouble free. Ian Donald quotes that from 42 pregnancies where there were uterine variations, 19 ended in miscarriage, five in premature labour, eight with unstable presentation, that is breech or sideways, and in five the placenta had to be removed by hand. Out of the 23 pregnancies reaching labour, four babies died. He also says that the more minor the variation, then the more treacherous; for example, in some variations the growing foetus could lie with its head in one side, and body in the other, and this would be very dangerous. Since mine is completely separate, the problems are minimised.

That is all the technical information I have been able to find; there is not a lot written, just two or three pages in gynaecology books in chapters headed 'Congenital Anomalies/Abnormalities'. Are we not told much about the abnormalities of the female reproductive system because these women are not normal, possibly not reproductive, or is it a continuation of the mystification that prevents us from having control over our bodies and our lives?

In the past few months I have heard of other women with such variations, but as yet I have not met any others. It would be good to hear of other women's experience. I have not had a lot to do with doctors since the discovery. My GP was mildly amused and the consultant at the hospital objectively curious.

I am pregnant again now; it happened the first time I tried after the second abortion, clever body, so I have been to an antenatal clinic. I suspect that I am a curiosity there. I don't mind people learning from my parts; the more who know the better. But I think that I will have to undergo more examinations than usual for the sake of medical science and I also think that I will not be told what they are seeing or what they are thinking. I object to being seen as a medical specimen and not just as a variation. I am not sick. I do not feel any different from how I felt for the first 31 years of my life.

My present lover noticed ages ago that there were 'two ways that she could go' inside my vagina, and she often felt worried about it. Why don't we trust our own discoveries? The 'experts' have made us totally dependent. Now that I am pregnant, I feel less in control than I might otherwise have felt. I keep thinking that perhaps I should be doing things that other pregnant women don't need to do, I don't know quite what. I suppose I am feeling that I do have some deformity for which I am responsible. The feeling is not strong and I resist it, but it's there. I feel angry that some of my confidence has been taken from me. We should know that these variations are possible, but of course there is so much that we should know and we don't.

Neither the woman I am involved with nor I were shocked or horrified by the knowledge, only curious and we sought out as much information as we could, as quickly as we could. Other women have been shocked and thought it peculiar, but I think that reflects a standard acceptance of what is 'normal'. We're fighting the 'norms' of this society.

They say that these variations often go undetected, that is until they present a problem. But if we knew about them, some we could easily discover ourselves like double vaginas. We would not be taken by surprise and the possibility of thinking it 'odd' would at least be reduced.

Vaginal infections
Carol Smith
SR 168 July 1986 (Part I)
SR 169 August 1986 (Part II)

PART I

Time and time again women tell me they have 'tried everything' for vaginal infections, but when I ask them in detail what they did then it becomes clear why the treatment didn't work. Obviously there is no guarantee that these remedies will work for you, but at least it improves the chances if it's described and explained adequately. There is a real need for an ongoing critical appraisal of the benefits and relative effectiveness of whatever field of alternative medicine may be most effective for a particular woman, or a specific condition.

The ideas of 'alternative' or 'holistic' medicine are based on the principle of the 'whole body'; that our bodies, minds and spirits are all related and all affect each other. In other cultures this concept is commonplace, but in western Europe is relatively new. The fundamental basis of alternative medical practice is that our bodies contain within them the 'vital energy' or 'life-force' which, given a chance, has the potential for self-cure. The different sorts of treatment will variously see themselves as aiding the body's life-force (camomile tea as a herbal relaxant), or of re-balancing the body's energies (acupuncture), or of giving the body a physiological rest (via a restricted diet), and then using dietary methods to help the healing process – e.g. food high in vitamins A and E in the treatment of stomach ulcers.

A large percentage of people using alternative medicine are women, but we do need to consistently raise questions around whether it is necessarily better for us than western medicine. Do women go to alternative practitioners more frequently because they are more open to change, or does it reflect the pattern of western 'allopathic' medicine – that women have particular stress patterns which lead them to have a higher incidence of more common health problems? Women in particular have suffered bad treatment because of the failures and practice of western medicine, not only but especially in the field of gynaecology.

The development of current 'alternative' theory and practice unfortunately reflects prevailing ideas about women; i.e., that we're vaguely (or definitely) disgusting, or at the very least, a bit distasteful. When I was at college, to be into gynaecology was somehow a bit cranky, or because I was into 'women's lib'!! Male naturopaths who are interested in gynaecology are few and far between, and are generally considered to be dirty old men (which on reflection is probably correct!). I do have serious questions to ask of men who choose to specialise in gynaecology, and have a gut mistrust of their motives, which at best must be patronising. Tales abound of the kind of comments that are made by surgeons performing gynae operations, and presumably male alternative practitioners are engaged in a milder version of the same process.

This series is intended to be practical in orientation; I want to go through some of the more common gynaecological conditions including vaginal infections. I want to give some description of the condition and its process and treatment which I hope will enable women to understand how and why a particular remedy may work.

THRUSH

Thrush is not strictly a vaginal infection; it is caused by a yeast-like organism called *Candida Albicans*. It is one of the many bacteria which are naturally present in the vagina and the gastro-intestinal tract. These bacteria are symbiotic/good bacteria which help to maintain the acid/alkaline (pH) balance of the vagina. Thrush is not a serious vaginal infection, but it is a real nuisance physically and can have a very undermining effect on a women's self-image and sexuality. Thrush and other vaginal infections are very debilitating emotionally. Increasingly, thrush is a chronic long-term, recurrent problem – part of the blame for this must be laid at the door of the repeated use of antibiotics, and of antifungal pessaries and creams for the treatment of the thrush itself. These effectively destroy the 'good' bacteria as well as the 'bad' bacteria and therefore disturb the acid/alkaline balance within the vaginal walls. Most branches of alternative medicine would agree that these forms of treatment only serve to suppress the symptoms, for some women very effectively, but for most women only temporarily if at all.

The natural pH balance of the vagina is 4–5 which rises around menstruation because of the increased alkalinity of the blood. Since yeast thrives in warm moist conditions (as do other infections), women are more prone to these around menstruation. The walls of the vagina are naturally wet from the continuous fluid secretion which keeps the vagina clean and healthy and maintains the acidity of the vagina. The mucous secreted by the vagina contains glycogen (sugar) which is converted into lactic acid by the bacteria called lactobacilli in the vagina.

There are a number of different causes which affect the environmental flora of the vagina and thus create a breeding ground for the proliferation of yeast and of harmful bacteria. These causes include the pill, pregnancy (these two are associated with increased oestrogen levels in the blood), and also because pregnant women have a higher level of glycogen in the vaginal mucous, as do women with diabetes. The use of antibiotics is the most common cause of thrush; regardless of the type of infection they are prescribed for, antibiotics have the effect of killing off the good bacteria as well as the baddies – therefore the ecological balance of the vagina is disturbed and the pH level will be upset. Other causes include an increase or decrease in sexual activity which could be said to cause hyperactivity or stagnation respectively, in the vaginal fluid. The use of perfumed soap, bath oils, talcum powder and stress, particularly in conjunction with lack of sleep, are all significant. A poor diet high in sugar and refined carbohydrate can have quite a dramatic effect on the intestinal as well as the vaginal flora, and thus help to perpetuate a chronic condition.

Other causes include those which inhibit the circulation to the pelvic area, and which also keep the pelvis 'unaired'; for example tights, nylon underwear, tight jeans, and exercise or sports in synthetic clothes such as leotards or nylon shorts. Synthetic material does not allow the body to breathe, and the warm moist atmosphere which builds up is an ideal environment for the proliferation of the yeast.

Before I go into the treatment of thrush, I want to raise some of the other issues for women which are largely neglected in most discussions of vaginal infection. The way in which constant (or even one-off) vaginal infection affects our lives is rarely looked at. Chronic, long-term illness or disease of any sort is emotionally debilitating, but vaginal infection can have a very undermining effect on our self-image and our sexuality. We are brought up in a society which tells us that our bodies smell and we are inundated with advertising for products which will 'remedy' this. A particularly insidious example of this is the advent of vaginal deodorants about fifteen years ago. (Are these still on the market?)

Whilst we live in a world where men call us 'smelly cunts' as the worst insult they can think of, it is very difficult to separate our own feelings about vaginal infection from those we have already internalised about our body/bodies.

A bacterial infection in the throat can give us 'bad breath' (an emotive issue in itself), but our feelings about that are on a very different level to those which are brought up by the slightly smelly discharge associated with some types of vaginal bacterial infection. This obviously has a rather disastrous effect on our sexual feelings, and the fear of being 'smelly' can last a lot longer than the infection.

As we have seen, thrush is not an infection as such, but a proliferation of the yeast (which lives naturally in the vagina) which is brought about by a change in the environment of the vagina from acid to alkaline. So the treatment is aimed at re-establishing the normal acidity in order to maintain a balance. I would also include in the treatment some form of symptomatic relief – the concept of symptomatic relief is practically heresy within alternative medicine, but being driven nuts with itching is not very conductive to 'whole health'. Unlike what we are led to believe, there is nothing 'morally wrong' with wanting symptomatic relief. In fact, having relief from symptoms is more likely to make us open to the kind of change in lifestyle that may be appropriate if we want a long-term 'cure'.

The best way to change the environment of the vagina is to eat *live* yoghurt. This will internally acidify the blood stream, and therefore subsequently the walls of the vagina. It is really important that the yoghurt be live; this is determined by whether the milk has been pasteurised before or after (if at all) the addition of the culture. Yoghurt which has simply lactobacillus or acidophillus for example on the list of ingredients is not necessarily live. This important distinction is one of the reasons why women who have tried yoghurt in the past are disillusioned because it only works for a bit, if at all – yoghurt which does not say *live* on the pot has only a very limited use (apart from tasting nice!)

So, eating live yoghurt every day, and several times a day in the middle of a bout of thrush, is the main crux of treatment. Symptomatic relief can be had from soaking menstrual sponges (small sponges obtainable from Boots or other chemists) in dilute cider vinegar, then putting it inside your vagina. It may feel a bit hot at first, but will cool off, and the relieving effect lasts for anything up to several hours. Putting cider vinegar in the bath is also helpful, particularly for a bout of thrush which is located mainly on the outside of the vagina or the vulva. Another way to apply cider vinegar is via a douche, which for some unknown and presumably culturally idiosyncratic reason, is really difficult to get hold of in Britain. What you can do though, is to get a 'disposable douche' from a posh chemist, chuck out the perfumed chemicals they have in them (they are an expensive version of vaginal deodorants), then refill them with a 50–50 solution of cider vinegar and water. Then lie in the bath, insert the tube into your vagina, then gently squeeze the solution into your vagina.

If you do this every day for three or four days, then alternate days, then gradually phase out the douche applications over a period of a couple of weeks, this will also help to maintain a long-term alteration of the environment of the vagina. It is important not to douche for a day or so either side of your period, because the os is more open around this time, and there's a risk that you may squirt a bit of the solution up into your uterus.

A change of diet will not only be generally helpful, but may also be a way of altering blood levels of acidity. Vitamin B foods are particularly important, and can be found in whole grains, brown rice, green vegetables, liver, sunflower seeds, yoghurt. Certain foods are known to precipitate thrush occasionally; commonly cheese, mushrooms, bread and other products made with yeast, and yeast extracts, e.g. marmite. Alcohol can also be an important trigger factor because it's high in sugar, and also because it destroys the Vitamin B in your body. Any food or drink high in sugar will increase the glycogen cells in the vaginal walls.

If you think there's any possibility that you also have an infection along with the thrush, then putting a clove of garlic inside your vagina will act as a very effective local antiseptic. You can change this every four or five hours; it doesn't matter if you leave it in for a bit longer than this, but it ceases to be so effective. If you have difficulty getting it out again, then tie some dental floss around it so you can pull it out like a tampon. But whatever else, don't worry that it'll get lost – there's nowhere else for it to go.

PART II

VAGINAL INFECTIONS, HERPES, VAGINAL WARTS, AND BARTHOLIN'S CYSTS

One of the most common vaginal infections is trichomonas, commonly referred to as 'trich'. Trich is caused by an organism that does not normally inhabit the vagina. It is possible not to have any symptoms, and there is some evidence to suggest that emotional stress and generally being run-down may precipitate a flare-up, persistence, or recurrence of symptoms. The symptoms of trich are likely to be more severe just before or just after your period because the vagina is more alkaline then, and trich thrives in an alkaline environment. Symptoms will usually include a vaginal discharge which will smell bad, and is usually yellowish/greenish colour. The entrance to the vagina may be red and sore due to irritation from the discharge and this soreness may extend to the whole vulval

23

area. Trich can lead to serious complications such as pelvic inflammatory disease if the trich migrates up the vagina to the uterus and Fallopian tubes, so it is important that the treatment is carried out effectively. Trich is becoming less and less responsive to allopathic (western) treatment with antibiotics, but whether you choose alternative or western treatment, it is important to do it well and finish the prescribed treatment until you are sure your vagina is healthy again.

Since trich is a protozoal infection, the mainstay of the treatment is directed towards getting rid of the infection, as well as balancing the acid/alkaline environment of the vagina. Garlic is a really effective treatment used in the form of garlic pessaries. Peel a clove of garlic, make a few little nicks in it to release the oils, and put it inside the vagina. Change the clove every four or five hours, but as I explained in Part I, it doesn't matter if you leave it in longer but it is gradually less effective. Using garlic locally in this way will often increase mucous discharge because its action increases the sloughing off of dead cells in the vagina. Repeat this treatment over several days, and phase out the frequency over a period of a couple of weeks – it is not possible to be more precise because a lot will depend on the general health of the woman, the strength of the trich, how long the infection has been there, etc. Enough exercise, sleep, and a generally good diet will all help your body to build up resistance to infection. Herbal vaginal douches are also very effective, preferably in conjunction with other methods – I usually recommend Golden Seal in a solution of one teaspoon per pint of boiling water, simmer for 15 minutes, strain it, and then dilute the solution 50:50 with water. (See Part I for detailed information about douches.) Use about half a pint of this solution in a douche every day for about five days, then leave it for a few days, then douche again for another few days. It's good to keep on having breaks, then re-douche if necessary. The breaks are important in order that the vagina has a chance to settle down and re-establish its balance. Personally I think that Golden Seal is the most effective herbal antiseptic/anti-infective, but there are any amount to choose from if you look up a good herb book.

The other common vaginal infections which are bacterial are gardenerella and haemophillus – this is an infection of the secretions of the vagina (as opposed to the vaginal walls in the other conditions I have talked about). Gardenerella is a natural inhabitant of the vagina, and again is only a problem if the environment of the vagina changes. Therefore the treatment will be as for the other conditions (i.e. acidify the vaginal environment), and again with emphasis on the garlic because it is a bacterial condition, and the herbal douche to flush out the bacteria.

To sum up: if you understand the cause of the problem, and the physiological process, then it is easy to know which treatment may be most effective, and which aspect to emphasise. If you are in any doubt, then go and have a test to ascertain whether it is thrush, a bacterial infection, or both, and then go ahead and try the treatment!

I am not going to cover sexually transmitted disease in this article; STDs are one of the few areas of allopathic treatment where I feel they do better than us! The nature of these infections is such that the treatment needs to be quick and effective – a course of heavy antibiotics frequently will be for these conditions. You can then treat the possibly resulting thrush by taking large amounts of *live* yoghurt during and after a course of antibiotics, to ward off an attack.

Herpes

The naturopathic treatment for this condition is mainly dietetic and if it is followed within a general context of a good diet with plenty of fresh fruit and vegetables, whole grains, etc., then it is surprisingly effective. This is obviously good news for a condition for which there is effectively 'no cure' at the moment. Naturopathic treatment is not a cure either, but it can give virtually 100% remission. Unfortunately it is also one of the few conditions where it is vital that you follow the recommendations 100%. One of the feelings that commonly goes along with herpes is that of powerlessness, understandably, since there is no treatment. Many women who have followed the diet and found it effective report that it is worth it to be so strict not only for the relief from physical symptoms but also because it gives them a strength and a sense of their own power that they do *not* have to become victims to their own herpes.

Given the kind of approach which has been taken by the media, it is not surprising that there is an intense social fear and disgust of herpes sufferers which has only diminished because the focus (and homophobia) is concentrated on AIDS at present. The hysteria around herpes has currently died down and there is serious research to find a 'cure' – unfortunately, the kind of desperation experienced by herpes sufferers, partially as a direct result of media exposure, means that allopathic medical research has a captive audience of potential human guinea pigs on which to experiment.

'Stress' is often a component in the precipitation of a herpes attack, and an integral part of the treatment is the treatment and 'management' of stress. As part of a generally good diet, there needs to be a large amount of Vitamin B foods, such as whole grains, green veg, liver, yoghurt, sunflower seeds and possibly with the use of supplementation as well, a good quality B complex. Some kind of relaxation or meditation, or simply finding better ways of dealing with particularly stressful aspects of your life, may be helpful. I say this within a political context which recognises that there are aspects of 'therapy' which can only be palliative to what are obviously intolerable conditions in our lives. But the point is that frequently we are not in a position to change our lifestyles immediately, and something which can give a sense of your own strength and ability to handle difficult situations can have a revolutionary potential in

25

itself. The dietary aspect of the treatment of herpes is centred around two of the 'amino-acids' – arginine and lysine. Protein foods – milk, fish, cheese, eggs, pulses – are made up of 'amino-acids', and certain foods have higher levels of some amino-acids than others.

The theory, loosely, is that under laboratory conditions, the herpes virus grows well in the test tube if it is supplied with arginine, and lysine inhibits the growth. So it has been suggested, and it is certainly true in practice, that a diet high in lysine and low in arginine can help prevent an outbreak of herpes.

I have reproduced a diet sheet giving lists of food high in arginine and lysine. It is important to remember that it is not that these arginine foods are innately 'bad', in fact they are mostly nutritious foods which are high in Vitamin E. The point is, that if they are high in arginine they are therefore a possible trigger in an outbreak of herpes. It is the experience of the many women that I have treated for herpes that the use of supplementation (i.e. taking lysine supplements) is not as effective as following the diet strictly. I don't say this just because I'm generally anti-supplements, but out of concern that the most effective method of treatment is presented.

High lysine foods (foods to eat)				High arginine foods (foods to avoid)	
mg lysine excess	food		portion	food	lysine deficiency
+ 930	fresh fish	4oz	1/2cu	Hazelnuts	−2250
+ 880	shark	4oz	1/2cu	brazilnuts	−2110
+810	canned fish	4oz	1/2cu	peanuts	−2060
+740	chicken	4oz	1/2cu	walnuts	−810
+720	beef	4oz	1/2cu	almonds	−710
+520	goat's milk	1cu	1/2cu	cocoa powder	−650
+420	cow's milk	1cu	2tb	peanut butter	−510
+420	lamb	4oz	1/2cu	sesame seeds	−450
+410	mung beans, cooked	1/2cu	1/2cu	cashews	−420
+380	pork	4oz	1/2cu	carob powder	−310
+280	cheese, all types	1oz	1/2cu	coconut	−290
+270	beans, cooked	2cu	1/2cu	pistachio nuts	−240
+240	lima beans	1/2cu	1/2cu	buckwheat flour	−230
+220	cottage cheese, dry	1/2cu	1/2cu	chick peas	−210
+210	mung bean sprouts	1/2cu	1/2cu	brown rice	−190
+190	yeast, brewer's	1tb	1/2cu	pecans	−180
+170	crustaceans	4oz	4sl	whole wheat bread	−160
+130	soybeans, cooked	1/2cu	1/2cu	oatmeal, cooked	−130
+120	egg	1	1/2cu	raisins	−130
+100	human milk	1cu	1/2cu	sunflower seeds	−120

To summarise: get enough sleep, plenty of exercise and fresh air, a good diet, and ensure that at each meal you have much more lysine than arginine foods.

Vaginal Warts

Vaginal warts or vulval warts are on the increase, as are some of the other venereal diseases. They tend to be of concern partially because they are very likely to be transmitted, and also because there is *some* evidence to link them with an increased likelihood of developing cancer of the cervix at a later date. Vaginal warts occur more frequently in women who have one of the other sexually transmitted diseases or one of the common vaginal infections, or who use the pill or who are pregnant. As with some of the other conditions I have talked about, a damp moist environment provides ideal growing conditions for genital warts. Although sometimes warts will disappear spontaneously, it is generally a good idea to try to get rid of them as quickly as possible. Warts are notoriously difficult to treat, whether by alternative or western methods, and again, as for infections like trichomonas, it is really important that, whichever method you choose, you follow the treatment correctly.

The 'alternative' treatment for warts includes generally following a good diet in order to build up your resistance, and at the same time to use some of the blood-cleansing herbs like Cleavers, and anti-infectives like Echinacea. The herbal remedy specifically to be used locally on the warts is tincture of thuja which is fairly easily obtainable from most herbalists; tincture of colchicum is in theory very useful since it inhibits cellular division – I say 'in theory' because it is practically impossible to obtain in this country because it is extremely toxic if taken orally.

Bartholin's Cysts/Bartholinitis

The Bartholin's glands lie just inside the entrance to the vagina, and secrete a fluid that keeps the vagina moist. In bartholinitis the skin around the opening of the gland may be red and swollen, and there may be pus mixed with the glandular secretions. The opening to the gland may become gradually closed up and a collection of pus may form (abscess). As the infection progresses, the whole area around the gland may become involved and is acutely uncomfortable. After the infection is over, the duct of the gland may be partially or totally obstructed by scarring – this means that the secretions can't be released, and one or two Bartholin's cysts full of these secretions may develop.

Alternative treatment for conditions affecting the Bartholin's glands will be either anti-infective if there is an abscess, or geared towards stimulating glandular activity for a cyst. In either case, alternate hot and cold compresses applied locally may be helpful both as pain relief and as a glandular stimulant. They can be applied with a flannel or small towel; the heat will dilate the capillaries on the surface of the skin which will therefore bring blood to the area, and the cold will constrict the capillaries which will encourage the drainage from the area. Alternate the hot and the cold, keeping the hot wet flannel on for about half a minute, and the cold one on for a few seconds – repeat about three times each, several times a day.

Again a good diet is always helpful to facilitate herbal treatment, and in the case of an abscess, I would recommend a short fast in order to speed up the elimination of the infective bacteria. Herbal treatment will include the use of all the usual anti-infectives such as garlic, echinacea, cleavers, dandelion, burdock etc. The treatment for blocked glands is fairly limited, but a strong solution of thyme applied locally may be useful, or a few drops of lemon juice on to the cyst may also be effective – both of these should be done for several weeks in conjunction with the hot and cold.

If you decide to try any of the treatments that I have outlined in the two parts of this article, remember that it is really important that you carry them out rigorously. It is also worth bearing in mind that everyone is individually different, and what may be good for one woman is not necessarily the best treatment for you. In these two articles I have tried to describe the treatments that are usually the most helpful, but obviously it is impossible to do more than generalise.

Pelvic inflammatory disease
Jessica Pickard and Kay Canberry
SR 127 December 1982

KAY'S STORY

When I was first knocked flat by an infected fallopian tube (salpingitis) I turned to the feminist health book *Our Bodies Ourselves* looking for remedies.

I was horrified. In the case study quoted, the woman had had salpingitis or pelvic inflammatory disease (PID) for ten months, and even after an operation was still not well.

I gulped down more antibiotics and retreated to bed, certain my problems wouldn't go on as long as that poor woman's had. After all, the casualty officer at the hospital had told me I would be OK in a few days.

That was nearly four years ago. My naivety and ignorance have since been thoroughly dispelled.

Pelvic inflammatory disease is the general name given to a group of related infections of the female reproductive organs. Usually the fallopian tubes are involved (salpingitis means inflammation of the fallopian tubes) – but often ovaries and uterus are affected too.[1]

PID can be caused by a number of different micro-organisms which manage to make their way past the vagina's and uterus's natural defence system to establish themselves in a fallopian tube and multiply rapidly. The cause is often a mystery; use of an IUD is sometimes blamed, sometimes a botched abortion is the obvious cause. Another theory is that bacteria from the anus find their way into the vagina and move upwards.

There are a number of bacteria that can cause infection, and it's suspected that viruses may be guilty as a cause; therefore antibiotics would be largely ineffective. Only recently chlamydia has been identified as a possible cause. As it is, for a great many women the disease proves distressingly resistant to antibiotics and drags on for years, flaring up sporadically, causing constant pain and draining the sufferer's vitality. All that doctors seem to be able to offer the chronic PID victim is surgery to remove progressively diseased tissue. Sometimes a tube removed will clear up the infection – but for some women even a complete hysterectomy won't wipe out the symptoms.

PID is serious business. It can mean permanently damaged fallopian tubes and infertility; and it can wreck the life of the sufferer.

PID is on the increase. A recent estimate said that in London PID may account for some 20% of gynae outpatients' attendances.[2] It seems likely that pelvic infections are increasing as women's sexual activity increases but many sufferers have had only one or a few sexual partners. It also seems likely that a heterosexually active woman is more likely to contract PID than a lesbian, but any object which enters the vagina (tampax, fingers, whatever) can introduce infection.

And yet, despite its potentially disastrous consequences, this disease is largely hidden from view. Most sufferers will never have heard of PID before they fall victim to it, and they'll soon discover that most doctors are pretty vague about it too.

This means that the psychological aspects of the disease can be devastating. For the chronic PID victim life is a permanent battle against pain and fatigue. At the same time she is likely to feel guilt as she tries the patience of friends, family, employers and lovers. Permanently low on energy, often in pain, her social, sexual and work life become devalued. Add to this both the repeated disappointments when successive 'remedies' fail, and the physiological effects of long courses of antibiotics and/or surgery.

All this is made worse by encounters with the medical profession. It should be said that some gynaecologists are open, sympathetic and honest about their inability to cure PID. But by far the most common experience reported by women with PID is a sceptical junior doctor trying to prescribe tranquillisers, or experienced senior gynaecologists patronisingly reassuring them that the next operation will surely do the trick. Many a demoralised woman has dragged herself out of a gynaecologist's clinic, almost beginning to share the doctor's conviction that she's imagining her pain (this of course applies to women with other gynae problems too).

As an added twist, many women report their doctor's obvious exasperation as they trail back yet again to the clinic, having failed to do him (usually) the honour of letting him cure them. That a debilitated woman should be made to feel this sort of guilt is not surprising – though no less deplorable when you consider that the standard postgraduate gynae textbooks tell future consultants that 'management of the chronic pelvic woman represents one of the most trying and all too often unrewarding problems for the gynaecologist'.[3] Even where the texts make worthy attempts to encourage doctors to take their PID patients seriously, they add remarks like, 'patients with this condition are the cross that every gynaecologist has to bear'.[4]

Small wonder then that women with chronic PID can become demoralised to the point of despair, feeling helpless, hopeless and isolated.

That is why Jessica and I want to contact as many sufferers as possible, to pool information and give mutual support. We've both had PID badly for nearly four years. We've been through the antibiotics, the operations and the demoralisation, and now we are faced with the hysterectomy option – an agonising decision for young childless women, particularly when there's no guarantee of complete cure. But having talked to other women who have had startlingly similar experiences, we have stopped feeling weak and isolated.

We have not managed to come up with wonder cures – although some women have been helped by homeopathy and acupuncture and we would like to know more about diet and herbal treatments. But mutual support has helped us to cope both with the limitations that chronic PID imposes on our lives and with doctors who treat us like problem children.

We now need to use knowledge and solidarity to translate our self-destructive guilt into anger at a medical world that trivialises our health problems. If we make enough noise perhaps they'll stop fobbing us off with false reassurances and get down to some much needed research to find a cure for this neglected disease.

And if *we* pool our own experiences perhaps we'll find that we have as much to teach the medical profession about PID – if they'll listen – as they have to offer us.

NOTES

1 *Our Bodies Ourselves*, Phillips and Rakusen eds, Penguin, 1978.
2 *Gynaecological Therapeutics*, D. F. Hawkins ed., Bailliere Tindall, 1981.
3 *Integrated Obstetrics and Gynaecology for Postgraduates*, Sir John Dewhurst ed., Blackwell, 1981.
4 See (1).

Living with herpes
Sue Blanks and Annie
SR 101 December 1980

Genital herpes (Herpes Simplex Virus Type 2, or HSV-2) is a sexually transmitted disease which affects women and men. While the more commonly known variety (HSV-1, or 'cold sores') affects the mouth and lips, HSV-2 affects the genitals – but there is about a 10% crossover. Women get it on the clitoris, labia, anus, cervix, and occasionally in the vagina. Some people also get it elsewhere (for instance, the buttocks and thighs). It is extremely contagious and during the past decade has reached epidemic proportions.

Usually the affected area itches and tingles, and sometimes nerve endings ache or are painful anywhere on the body. Then sores appear (blister-like eruptions). These can be *very* painful; they burst and weep and may bleed. They can last from about four days to over two weeks. While the sores are there, herpes is extremely contagious. It is not only easily passed on to a partner's genitals, but can be transmitted to the mouth and eyes. The symptoms come and go – some people only ever have one attack, while others have frequent occurrences (one of us has only had 20 days free of it in the past four months). And while the symptoms are present, there is little that can be done, either to soothe pain or clear up the sores. You just have to wait for them to go away.

There is a strong suggestion of high risk of cervical cancer in women who have had herpes, especially HSV-2 of the cervix. They are recommended to have six-monthly smear tests for life.

A woman who has or has had herpes is three times more likely to miscarry than normal. A child who is delivered vaginally while the mother has an active attack of HSV-2 is likely to catch the virus through its eyes, skin or mouth. Two-thirds of babies infected this way die, and most who survive suffer severe damage to their brain or eyes. Pregnant women who have ever had herpes should inform their midwife.

1 ... 'BEING A HERPES SUFFERER IS LIKE A LIFETIME OCCUPATION.'

I have been a herpes sufferer for seven years. It's only during the past year that I've had it really badly – my worst bout lasted for over *six weeks*.

When I have an attack of herpes, I have a sense of disgust about my body. I feel revolted. I don't want to touch myself, look at myself, think of those gaping sores. I feel tainted, contaminated, like one big sore – it's hard to think of myself in terms other than 'herpes' and all that this means.

If I am in a relationship, I fear passing on the disease. Although I am scrupulous about not letting my lover touch my genitals ('Knickers on' is the name of the game – one lover remarked that he couldn't picture me naked!), I get tense even if I am touched anywhere *near* the diseased area. I freeze and push away what may be a loving hand; I end up withdrawing from any physical pleasure, and this is further aggravated by resenting giving pleasure when not receiving it (not your lover's fault, but still . . .). The alternatives are: give but don't receive, or don't give at all – no sexual contact. Some choice. It's bad enough when you have an understanding, loving partner but really difficult to cope with when you want to go to bed with someone for the first time. Giving but not receiving is really only possible in a loving relationship or a business one – and not many new partners fit either description!

When I have a series of herpes attacks, I feel extremely depressed by the thought of having a seemingly never-ending series of illness. I feel hopeless, thinking 'When will I get better? Will I *ever* get better?' When I'm feeling really down, I can't imagine recovering and leading a normal life. Being a herpes sufferer seems like a lifetime occupation, and the prospects seem daunting – eternal celibacy? self-hatred? (it's hard to love a body with herpes). There just seems no end; I have been driven to wondering quite seriously whether it was worth continuing living.

Even when I'm fortunate enough not to have an attack of herpes, I still carry with me the knowledge of having an incurable disease and the ensuing feelings of hopelessness. (Apart from the active sores, there's the link with cancer and the problems with pregnancy). I feel bound to tell a new partner of my affliction. It is then his choice whether he wants – is prepared – to have a sexual relationship with me. Although I consider it necessary to be totally honest about the disease and its implications, all the time I fear a reaction of disgust and rejection, which however understandable, would destroy me. So I tend to mention it fairly early on in an encounter, which allows a potential partner the chance to avoid getting sexually involved. It's all a very conscious form of protecting myself from embarrassment and hurt.

In a long-standing relationship, the problems are still present. There is the need for complete trust by a partner to believe me when I say I'm clear. To be worthy of this trust, it's necessary to do frequent self-examinations (including internal examination with a speculum to check the cervix) which means that even when 'clear', herpes must never be far from my mind. I am not allowed to forget it.

After an attack, especially a long bout, it's an enormous relief to be able to resume a full sexual relationship, but this isn't without its problems. There is often 'performance anxiety': fears of failure and lack of satisfaction due to built-up hopes and frustrations during the abstinence. The sex life of a herpes sufferer is generally disrupted – a bout of herpes is followed by a resumption of sexual activity with its initial anxiety and problems, then just as the two of you are getting used to one another again, you get another attack. Vicious circle.

And even when I'm clear, I'm permanently afraid of getting it again. It's always on my mind.

2 . . . 'SO I'M ALSO ASKING HER TO TAKE THE RISK IN MAKING LOVE WITH ME.'

I'd been working very hard and remember coming home absolutely shattered. I had a temperature of 101 and felt like I was getting flu. I'd half-noticed a sort of itchiness on my fanny, and thought it was thrush. A couple of days later it turned out I had herpes. Herpes – I didn't know the first thing about it except it was making me feel terrible. For the first two weeks I had to wear a long skirt and no knickers. I could hardly walk, and pissing was agony. No one suggested anything as a cure or relief except salt baths. Then I began to read about it and the sum total of that was to freak me out completely.

At the time I was having several different relationships with men – some were fairly casual, others were more regular and closer. Soon after catching herpes, all gradually stopped except one. I still hadn't really absorbed what I'd read, and so screwed occasionally even when I had herpes . . . I really regret that now. That relationship ended summer before last, and since then I've been coming to terms with my depression at having the 'lergy'. Over a period of time I also stopped sleeping with men. It's not exaggerating to say that there were a couple of times when, faced with the prospect of eternal celibacy, I thought of doing myself in. I've worked through that now to a certain extent, and as well as becoming a lesbian, recently I've learnt to cope with the physical requirements necessary to prevent an attack. I remember to eat well, take my vitamins, take time off to do things I enjoy, and so on.

But the main theme still going round in my head is this: picture yourself meeting someone you like – you get on well, you're having a good time. Maybe you want to sleep with this person. Pre-herpes, that was great. (Aside from the usual zillion hang-ups). Now the scene is this: mmmmmm, she's really nice, shit, when do I tell her I've got herpes. (In fact I would never sleep with someone now when I've got an attack, or without telling them first). Do I say to myself, 'You can get so much out of being friends, don't tell her', but put off any expectations of hers about sleeping with me?

Usually what happens is I get pissed out of my box. That way I can say it without 'caring' too much about the consequences – rejection. I can understand the fear of catching something. Most people don't even know what herpes is, or what the implications of having it are. So what can I expect? What would I expect? Gradually I've come to realise that I can't expect anyone to jump into bed with a herpes sufferer. It's my responsibility to tell any prospective partners. It's also a turn-off, I know that. I *do* expect friendship, certainly, and I need warmth, love and sensual

33

closeness as much as anyone else. I often think that my most idealistic expectation is of meeting someone who understands – because if I sleep with someone I am in fact asking them to put a lot of trust in me, and in how well I know my own body; trusting me when I say 'I'm clear, it's OK, you won't get it'. But although I do the very best I can, (and that is a hell of a lot), I can't be 100% certain that I'm not infectious, so I'm also asking her to take the risk in making love with me. As if there weren't enough problems in bed already!

Sit and think about what this would be like for you in your relationships. Can you *feel* what I'm talking about? No wonder so many women just don't want to know about their herpes.

So coming to terms with a total dive-down in my sexual identity/activity was (is?) definitely the hardest thing. One more word about what I expect: *honesty*. Given that I'm having to reveal something I'm incredibly sensitive about, I expect a woman I meet and like and desire to be honest with me about how they feel. If they feel repulsed by the herpes it is essential that they say it. Their reaction I can cope with. Otherwise the reason for their rejection is unclear. I'm going to feel rejection as a person, as who I am, rather than someone nice who has something pretty nasty. The 'nastiness' of the herpes I can and do cope with. The unclear rejection I *can't*. It's devastating.

Think about it. That's what I see as the other person's responsibility. Lack of explanation can make me feel like a leprous creep. I'm in the middle now of having to say this to someone and it's not easy to say, 'It's OK – I'm sad of course, but we won't make love if you don't want to.' I *don't* want to ever end up like I have to go out and look for other lonely herpes sufferers.

FORMING GROUPS

When we first met, we felt incredibly relieved to be able to talk about the things we'd never been able to say to anyone, sharing our experiences of having to cope with herpes. Sharing our experiences has made us a lot stronger.

Having herpes forces you to re-examine your feelings about your body and your sexuality. You have to think about what sexual activity means to you and the part it plays in your life. For a lesbian it also means having to counter the assumption that it's only passed on heterosexually.

We want to spread information to women about herpes. Most people don't know anything about it, including the medical profession. It's very difficult to find out anything for yourself, either from books or from doctors and clinics. The medical establishment's line seems to be: 'No cure, therefore don't give too much information (we don't want to freak our patients out, do we)'. We think it's essential for herpes sufferers to be fully informed – as women, we don't want to be 'protected' from the truth, but we *do* want support. We want to hassle doctors/clinics to provide more information and facilities as a matter of course (for instance routine six-monthly smear tests), and the drug companies to include HSV-2 in their research into virus cures.

Womb loss
Kath Cape with Sheffield Women's Health Group and Sheffield Radical Nurses
SR 112 August 1981

More and more women today are having to go into hospital to have their wombs removed. It has been estimated that in England and Wales, by the age of 75, one in five women has had a hysterectomy.[1] Yet despite the frequency with which the operation is performed there are many questions left unanswered. Why do women have to have a hysterectomy? Are there alternatives? How will a woman feel afterwards?

There are various types of hysterectomies. Firstly there is *subtotal hysterectomy* when the body of the womb is removed, but the opening of the womb (the cervix) is retained. This operation is less frequent than is *total hysterectomy* in which the whole uterus is removed. This operation can be performed vaginally by pulling the womb down through the vagina, or more commonly by cutting open the abdomen and lifting out the womb. An abdominal hysterectomy can be carried out by a vertical or a horizontal incision. The vertical incision usually heals more rapidly as it takes less strain when you cough or walk. However, it is rarely done because of the attitude that an obvious scar spoils a woman's appearance and a discreet 'bikini' scar is more 'aesthetically pleasing'. Finally there is *total hysterectomy* combined with *bilateral salpingo oophorectomy*, when not only the womb, but also the ovaries, the fallopian tubes and the upper part of the vagina are removed.

All of these operations, and particularly the last, are major, with all the risks that involves, such as haemorrhage, infection and – particularly with hysterectomy – subsequent problems with urinating because of the closeness of the womb and the bladder. Even if no complications develop a woman can be in hospital for any time up to a month and can be left feeling physically very drained.

In addition, if the ovaries are removed a woman who before the operation still had her periods will immediately go into the menopause. Yet doctors often fail to explain to their female patients how major an operation a hysterectomy is. In fact, one doctor assured a woman that 'there is no difference in removing your womb and/or ovaries than there is in removing your appendix'!

After a hysterectomy women sometimes feel not only physically weak but also emotionally drained. This is partly due to the nature of the operation and hormonal changes, but also it must have something to do

35

with many women's sense of loss and isolation which so few of the medical profession are prepared to deal with. One gynaecologist estimated that between 36% and 55% of women who have hysterectomies suffer from depression after the operation. A woman who wrote to us about her experience declared that 'when I came out of hospital I felt very weak and absolutely awful for three months . . . I only really started to feel better *three years later.*' Another woman said that the five weeks after the operation were *hell.* 'I was physically weak and mentally broken.'

However, for other women hysterectomy can provide an immeasurable relief from crippling health problems such as excessive bleeding or excruciating pain. For these women, after the first few months of recuperation, the hysterectomy can give a new lease of life. One woman who talked to us explained; 'It took longer to recuperate than I was told, but after three months I was doing things that I could never do before and I suppose at about six months there were no bars to what I could do. I was astonished by the flowing back of full health. For many women hysterectomy's a boon, it's literally a lifesaver.'

The effect that a hysterectomy has on a woman's sexuality may depend on how ill she was prior to her operation. During orgasm, the uterus contracts and studies suggest that more intense orgasms are sometimes associated with stronger contractions. So, for some women after a hysterectomy orgasm may not reach the same physiological intensity as before. If the ovaries are also removed there may be a reduction in vaginal lubrication resulting in painful intercourse and/or delayed sexual response. Some women find these changes distressing and feel there is a marked decrease in their level of sexual pleasure. For other women though, these changes are totally insignificant as compared to the relief the hysterectomy brings. If a woman has a severe pelvic infection or a heavy, tender uterus, orgasms will be painful and the removal of the womb will increase the possibility for sexual pleasure. One woman said, 'I enjoy my sexuality in a way that I've been deprived of doing for five odd years.'

One reason why a hysterectomy might be performed is for treatment of fibroids. Fibroids are hard, spherical tumours growing in the womb which are *not* cancerous, and which can vary greatly in size and in numbers in the uterus. Why they develop is not known. Very often they exist without causing any problems, but sometimes they enlarge the cavity of the uterus so much that excessive and painful bleeding occurs during menstruation and pressure is put on the bladder making you feel like urinating all the time. Sometimes, too, the fibroids grow so large that they block the menstrual flow and the blood is trapped internally, creating painful periods with very little blood loss. However if fibroids are not causing any problems there is no need to have *any* form of treatment, let alone a hysterectomy.

If fibroids are causing an increased menstrual flow which is not terribly troublesome, they can be treated conservatively by a diet rich in iron, supplemented by iron tablets, to safeguard against developing anaemia. In these cases regular blood tests should be carried out to ensure that a woman is not becoming anaemic. If, as a result of fibroids, a woman is bleeding heavily and is in excessive pain, surgery may improve her life. However, a *myomectomy* rather than a hysterectomy can sometimes be performed. This is when the fibroids are cut away from the wall of the womb but the womb itself is preserved. However, myomectomy is not usually performed or even discussed as an alternative. When doctors take a woman's complaints of bleeding or pain seriously they tend to follow the most common surgical option for fibroids – hysterectomy. On the other hand, they are just as likely to dismiss a woman's complaints as trivial, a sign of neurosis, and do nothing until she literally collapses and ends up with a hysterectomy!

Endometriosis is a condition whereby the endometrium lining the uterus is also present in other areas of the abdominal cavity, principally on the ovaries. There it undergoes menstrual changes just as the lining in the womb does, in response to hormonal stimulation. But, as menstrual blood cannot escape from the ovaries, it is retained and can form blood cysts. Why endometriosis occurs is not entirely clear. The major symptoms are painful menstruation and painful intercourse.

Endometriosis can be treated by hormone therapy. If this has no effect surgery is usually employed. However, a hysterectomy may not be necessary, particularly if the endometriosis is localised. Then all that need be done is to remove the cysts. However, surgeons often pressurise women, especially older women to have hysterectomies in these situations. Many gynaecological text books boldly advocate hysterectomy for women past childbearing age. For example, 'Hysterectomy should be employed for endometriosis in patients aged over forty.'[2]

Hysterectomy is often performed for prolapse of the womb. This happens because of a weakening of the muscles of the pelvic floor (the area around the vaginal opening), or a weakening of the muscles and ligaments which hold the womb in position, often as a result of obstetrical intervention in childbirth. A prolapse can be prevented by good care during pregnancy and childbirth and by achieving good muscle tone through exercising the same muscles used to stop the flow of urine. When a prolapse does occur symptoms are a feeling of heaviness and pressure when bearing down. Sometimes the uterus can actually be seen protruding below the vagina. It is unnecessary to perform a hysterectomy for this condition as it's always possible simply to repair the prolapse by strengthening the ligaments that hold the womb in place. Again this abuse of hysterectomy reveals doctors' disregard for women's bodies.

It should be stressed that the incidence of cancer affecting the womb is fairly low. In 1970 one woman in every 2,250 was diagnosed as suffering from either cervical, uterine, or ovarian cancer, while approximately one woman in every 250 had a hysterectomy. Only a small percentage of hysterectomies are carried out because of cancer. As women, it's important for us to realise this, because often our first reaction when we're advised to have a hysterectomy is that it must be cancer. One woman who talked to us told how she was so scared of being told that she had cancer that she never asked why she needed a hysterecomy until after she'd had the operation.

Is hysterectomy the only form of treatment for cancer affecting the womb? In the case of uterine cancer it may be, but in the case of cervical cancer a variety of tests and measures should be carried out as rapidly as possible after abnormal, cancerous type cells are detected in the cervix by a smear test, to see how far the cancer has spread before it is decided a hysterectomy is necessary. These tests and measures include examination by a colposcope and the use of a punch biopsy. After these investigations, if the cervix's cells still continue to be growing in a severely abnormal fashion, a cone biopsy can be performed which, if the cells are *not* invasive, may be all that is necessary, although smear tests should be repeated regularly to keep a check on things. If the cells are invasive a hysterectomy may be necessary.

Those are some of the most common reasons that surgeons give for performing hysterectomies. But there are a host of other reasons why a physician may decide upon a hysterectomy. Sometimes it is used as a form of sterilisation. It is also advocated for what the medical profession term 'neurosis'. One woman told us that her doctor advised a hysterectomy partly because her womb was prolapsed, but also because he thought it might 'cure' her 'nervous problems', and to stop her being so 'obsessed' with her 'ailments'. Dr James Simmons, executive Vice President of the American Medical Association, told a congressional hearing in 1977 that 'anxiety relief *justifies* a hysterectomy for a woman with an extreme fear of cervical cancer.'[3] Yet major surgery can never be justified as a 'cure' for depression. It is merely a convenient way a doctor can rid himself of the responsibility of trying to find out the fundamental reason why a woman may be depressed. Although many of these reasons go beyond the power of the doctor to solve, this does not excuse him or her from considering them.

Hysterectomy is a major operation which can leave women feeling not only physically weak but also emotionally shattered. It is often performed without enough good medical reasons as a quick, radical solution to a variety of gynaecological problems. This is particularly true if the woman is older and considered 'past it', as no longer serving a useful purpose as the 'bearer and rearer' of a future generation.

In some situations it is indeed the only solution to a woman's medical problems and can afford great relief. Yet this is often because doctors for months or even years previous to surgery have failed to take a woman's complaints seriously and thus have allowed both her and her womb to deteriorate to such an extent that major surgery becomes a lifesaver.

What is abundantly clear is that doctors, in keeping with their general disregard for women's health, particularly when treating gynaecological problems, consistently fail to take a woman's needs and feelings seriously, fail to listen to what she has to say, and fail to consider in conjunction with her, the best form of treatment. When we have any health problem we want to be able to make a fully informed decision about what sort of treatment we should have, but this information is precisely what we lack. So we ourselves need to collect it by talking to other women and by demanding it from doctors. When doctors suggest to us that we should have a hysterectomy we should be ready to challenge them. We have to ask why they want to do a hysterectomy and why they aren't trying alternative forms of treatment for whatever problem we have.

We need to talk to other women who've had hysterectomies to balance out if what we are suffering now is worse than what we would suffer if we have a hysterectomy. If it seems that removal of the womb is the best thing for us, we must be sure that they are not going to remove the ovaries too, 'just in case'. It's difficult to challenge the attitudes of the medical profession but we have to try, for the sake of our health and well-being.

NOTES

1 Oliver Gillie, *The Sunday Times*, 8 December 1974.
2 *A Summary of Gynaecology* by C. Burnett, 1974, p. 30. Faber & Faber.
3 Quoted in the *Boston Globe*, 10 May 1977.

MARGARET
Interviewed by Sue O'Sullivan

I don't think they want to give you a lot of information, it depends on whether you ask a lot of questions. I asked questions but then some women might not and anyway doctors only tell you more or less what they want to tell. They never said anything about how I might feel emotionally after the hysterectomy and they didn't agree about how long it would take to recover.

I had cysts on my ovaries but I didn't lose them in the operation. You know, it's not the same – you feel there's something missing. And for me it seemed as if I didn't have so much control on the muscles of the bowel.

Also it takes time to adjust because you don't seem to have the same feelings inside. You definitely feel different. Some people think you're silly because they can't see anything's missing, like you could an arm or a leg, but you *know* it's missing.

I think for so many working women their life is their family. Then suddenly you're not able to have a child and it's a shock. Having a job isn't the same as having a career – maybe women with careers don't put so much importance on their family.

The women who seemed most depressed in the hospital were women in their fifties and maybe they were of the generation who couldn't talk about such things. It may have been a shock to them to have these young doctors coming round and asking them questions about their wombs and vaginas.

VAL
Interviewed by Sue O'Sullivan

I knew I had fibroids for a long time. I had a helpful GP but her attitude to my heavy bleeding and feeling ill was 'how old are you anyway? Well, go to the hospital, see a consultant and you'll probably have a hysterectomy.' I asked why – what if I wanted children? I'd never seriously considered having children but it annoyed me that to her I had no 'need' for a uterus because I was a lesbian and in my mid-30s. Anyway she said 'nonsense – in your situation! It would be irresponsible!'

Everything got worse – I had to arrange my life and work around these awful periods and pre-menstrual tension. One day I felt really breathless and ill and went to a friend who's a doctor. He examined me and said I had to go to hospital right away – my womb was the size of a 28-week pregnancy. I saw a consultant who asked me about husbands and stuff like that . . . I sat there and looked at her and felt little and lumpy. I finally said, 'well, hmm, I have relationships with women.'

Although I felt terribly patronised by the consultant I also felt intimidated. I asked about an alternative to hysterectomy which I knew about called myomectomy. She agreed it existed but said it was terribly complicated and created a lot of blood and if anything went wrong they'd have to take out the uterus anyway. It took two weeks for me to decide and I went back and said yes.

During all this and when I was in the hospital *nobody* said anything about sex. I knew you could get depressed but I felt if you were pretty confident about who you were you could take the view that the hysterectomy was taking away a useless organ. But really it now seems to me from my own experience and talking to other women that the emotional after-effects of hysterectomy get to all different types of women across the board regardless of class, education and so on.

I think the sex thing has had a huge effect on my depression. I don't know . . . it could be hormonal or it could be suggestion, but I know it's not just those. Now, I'm as much into sex as I ever was. And I feel amost completely uninhibited but the thing that happens is – all this excitement – I work up to the orgasm and it's not the great thundering thing it used to be. And I know my own and women's bodies well. I find myself thinking, am I going to have a good orgasm! And I don't, or it dribbles off. Most times orgasm is no harder or easier than before the operation but its intensity has definitely diminished.

It would be difficult to tell women that this may happen to them if they have a hysterectomy. What *should* be happening is the possibility for talking about sex and sexuality beforehand if a woman wants to have that talk. There's a real need for the medical profession to understand sex and sexuality. After all, sex does not, in these days, equal missionary position intercourse. Most people have different kinds of sex whether they're lesbian, gay or heterosexual. Maybe we don't all swing from chandeliers but many people enjoy cunnilingus.

I do feel better phsyically now . . . and if I took care of myself properly I'd be even better. Not having periods is a blessed relief! It's amazing how fast you forget. I find myself forgetting the feeling. But if I'd known before what I know now I'd have pushed for the myomectomy. It's easy to say that now and I'll never know whether I would have believed it if people told me my sexuality would change . . . Still . . . if I had known I would have tried to keep my uterus.

Womb loss – a friend described it as a loss. I have a sadness inside me at the loss of my orgasms as they used to be too. Maybe I should have had my uterus brought to me and then buried it in my garden. Had a ritual about losing it. I did think about all the countries where people bury the placenta after child-birth. We have very basic feelings about these things and maybe it would have helped if I'd had a ritual to help me mourn the loss of my uterus. You know, every once in a while it crosses my mind that I'm not 'as other women' – and it's extraordinary to me that I should have this feeling . . . after all I've never had it about other aspects of my life.

LEE
Interviewed by Kath Cape and Sally Leahy

The reasons why I had to have a hysterectomy started with having a sterilisation. My sterilisation was one of the 4% that go wrong and I wound up getting peritonitis and pelvic inflammatory disease and then a whole string of symptoms which went on for five years – very, very painful periods, no bleeding, unexplained swellings. Well, really I had two entire sets of clothing, one which I'd wear from when I was pregnant and one which I'd wear when I was okay. My GP just laughed at me. He said I had wind. Then he sent me on a round of general physicians and I had barium enemas, barium meals, changes in diet and I kept on reminding him, each time, that I had really painful periods and I didn't bleed hardly, but he said 'you haven't got fibroids'. When I went to the gynae consultant he said 'you haven't got fibroids,' but I did have *fibroids*. Yet because I didn't fit into the stereotype they dismissed my other symptoms. They just won't learn that people are different. Anyway, I got iller and iller and had more and more pain and I could do less and less. So finally for the hundredth time I went down to the GP at a point at which I couldn't even walk any more and then he sent me straight off to the hospital. I knew then that they would have to open me up and I knew I couldn't go on unless they did!

Well, for me the hysterectomy was a life saver – the relief on recovering my health was immense. I'd forgotten what it was like to cross the road and dart between the traffic. My daughter had forgotten what I was like when I wasn't tired and weak and irritable. Of course, I didn't feel great straight away! At first nothing was right . . . when you pee it's agonising and you can't shit and unfortunately that goes on for weeks and weeks and there's the depression. You grieve for the loss of an organ that matters to you, that you've experienced as part of you and which has in some way defined your femininity. The fact that you bleed every month – all those sorts of things. But then after three months I was doing things that I could never do before and then after, oh, six months or a year I was biking 20 miles, I was dancing for hours at a time and at last I could enjoy sex again.

Throughout the years it was a constant struggle with the doctors. They wouldn't listen to what I was saying, they wouldn't give me any information and that was the same with all the women on the ward I was on. I mean, there were women on the ward who thought they'd be coming in for a D and C and woke up without a womb and didn't find out for days. I had a real battle to keep my ovaries. I said if you take my ovaries out you'll have to bring them to me in a jar and *prove* there was something wrong with them. They never take into account your own needs and feelings. For one woman it might be important to have her periods however painful and discomforting they are. They might be so essential to her sense of herself that she doesn't find excessive bleeding intolerable. So, okay, in her case let something be worked out so she doesn't weaken too much. But for another woman the bleeding is intolerable and yet the doctor does nothing, just lets her bleed and bleed until she collapses.

Cervical Cancer – the politics of prevention
Lisa Saffron
SR 129 April 1983

The thought of millions of pounds wasted on the South Atlantic escapade while the NHS is cut back makes most health activists sick. It is obvious that health care workers deserve better pay and that important services are cut for lack of money. What is not always obvious is the best way to improve our health. An example is the prevention of cervical cancer. Prevention can really mean two different but complementary approaches – taking steps so the disease doesn't appear and detecting it at an early treatable stage.

Medical prevention is early detection by cervical smear screening.

However, the steps needed to prevent women getting cervical cancer in the first place are outside the realm of the medical profession. This primary prevention can only come out of an understanding of the social causes of disease. As feminists involved in women's health, we can campaign for NHS resources to be used for early detection. We must also publicise the class nature of cervical cancer. We need to counter the victim blaming approach of the medical profession with a more realistic analysis of the social causes of ill health.

Cervical cancer starts in the cervix. Healthy organs and tissues are made of millions of cells whose growth and metabolism are governed by strict controls. We are constantly replacing our cells – as old ones die, new ones are formed. Cancer cells are not susceptible to these control mechanisms. They can grow and multiply rapidly, finally invading the surrounding healthy tissue. If these malignant cells get into the blood or lymph system, they will spread to other parts of the body.

Before cervical cancer ever develops, there are signs that can only be detected by cervical smears. A woman would only know of her potential illness by a positive smear called Class III (see box). This stage can last as long as ten to 20 years causing her no trouble. The next stage, called carcinoma-in-situ or Class IV, may also cause her no symptoms and may last for five to ten years. As the cancer grows, it may cause bleeding between periods, after penetrative sex, or after the menopause. The final stages are invasive cancer, when the cancer cells invade inner layers of tissue and finally spread to the rest of the body through the lymph and blood system. It is only when it reaches this stage that it becomes fatal.

Result	What it means	Other names
Class I	Normal	Negative
Class II	Unusual but not pre-cancerous. May be infection or irritation	Negative
Class III	Abnormal cells which may be pre-cancerous. Suspicious.	Dysplasia CIN 1. CIN 11
Class IV	Cancer cells in a localised, distinct area divided off from surrounding tissue.	Carcinoma in situ CIN III
Class V	Cancer that has spread	Invasive cancer

Cervical smears (the same as pap smears). What the results mean.

Cervical cancer does not strike all women equally. It is a disease of poverty, of old women, and of women who are or have been heterosexually active. In 1980, 2068 women died of cervical cancer in Britain. Of those women, 60% (1,233) were between ages 40 and 69. Only 196 were younger than 39.

Worldwide, cervical cancer is the most common of the cancers specific to women. It is less common in industrialised western countries than in Third World countries though the rates vary from country to country. In Britain it leads to relatively few deaths. Women are much more likely to die of breast cancer, lung cancer, cancer of the large intestine and rectum, stomach cancer, heart disease and strokes. But within Britain, it is the poorer women who are dying of cervical cancer. Using statistics and categories from the Registrar General (for what they are worth), women in Social Class V (unskilled workers) have four times the death rate of women in Social Class 1 (professionals).

As with most illnesses, it is the working classes who suffer more. Poor housing, filthy jobs, lack of good food, stress, unemployment and a polluted environment inevitably take their toll. In Britain statistics are collected by social class but not by race so it is hard to figure out how Black women fare. In the USA, Black women have about twice the death rate from cervical cancer than white women.

It should be obvious that we live in a society which makes us sick and those oppressed most are going to be the sickest. But this reality is generally ignored by the medical profession who have discovered something they think far more exciting – the link between cervical cancer and sex. The terms sexual activity, promiscuity, marital stability, coitus at an early age and prostitution are all bandied about in medical journals as defining the type of woman most likely to get cervical cancer. Most of these terms are ambiguous and rarely clearly explained. We don't know how many sexual partners a woman must have before she is labelled promiscuous nor even what sexual activity really means. We suppose they mean penis-in-the-vagina intercourse, but is is never stated. This is very confusing to women who are sexually active with other women, by themselves or with non-penetration sex. The clearest statement that can be made is that celibacy does seem to protect. As early as 1842, it was observed that nuns don't develop cervical cancer.

This may also be true for lesbians, even those who become lesbian after heterosexual relationships. But I don't know of any studies which have asked this question. Perhaps the results would be too embarrassing to

Certain groups of women don't get it, or at least - not as often as the rest of us....

FIGURE 5 Some women tend not to get cervical cancer *Viv Quillin* (*SR 129* April 1983)

publicise. Imagine a Health Education leaflet based on the latest research findings:

ARE YOU PROTECTED AGAINST CERVICAL CANCER?
No need to join a nunnery!
Be a lesbian!
Recent studies conclusively prove etc. etc. . . . .

In the meantime, the focus on sexual activity has lent itself well to victim blaming and moralistic warnings. Even 'ordinary married women leading virtuous married lives still incur some degree of unavoidable risk', according to one medical journal. It seems we can't win.

A double standard of morality is seen in nearly all the writings on cervical cancer. Very few studies have asked about the men's sexual behaviour. One that did found that women whose husbands had 15 or more sexual partners outside marriage were almost eight times more likely to get cervical cancer, even though the women themselves were monogamous. The interesting thing about the study is the tact with which the men were interviewed. To avoid arousing feelings of responsibility or guilt, the men were not told that the interview had anything to do with their wives' illness.

Women, of course, are not treated with such delicacy. An anonymous woman wrote in the *Guardian* (7 June 1982) of the outcome of a positive smear test she had: 'I was told by the gynaecologist at the time that nuns didn't get it, it was a result of my promiscuity and a cone biopsy (surgery to remove a cone shaped piece of the cervix) would have to be performed. . . . What were the chances of it recurring, I asked? Almost nil, providing I behaved myself and didn't sleep with my boyfriend, I was told. Needless to say it was some time before I felt like doing so! I crept from the surgery feeling guilty and unclean. . . . I wondered what constituted promiscuity and one gloomy evening I dared to count the number of boyfriends I had slept with. From the age of 19 to 28, the years I had been sexually active, the grand total came to six – less than one a year. So did I deserve my punishment? It certainly felt like punishment at the time.'

The medical approach is to detect pre-cancerous stages by the cervical smear. If the test is positive, they treat the cervix so that cancer never develops. Healthy women must be screened since these early stages cause no symptoms. The argument is that cervical cancer can be prevented by making sure that all women get regular cervical smears throughout their lives and treatment if these show up positive.

The approach is not without problems. Even if we accept the value of screening, there are reasons why the women most at risk of cervical cancer do not get cervical smears. More fundamental is the tendency for over-treatment as a result of positive smears and the effect this has on women's health.

In Britain GPs are paid to give cervical smears to women over the age of 35 and to women who have had three or more children. Despite this policy, many women are not being screened and they tend to be the ones most likely to get cervical cancer. It is relatively easy to screen young heterosexually involved women if they come to antenatal or family planning clinics. But without a direct policy to screen older, working class women, it won't happen by itself. Health service administrators have wondered why 'these women do not present themselves for screening' without asking the more relevant question – what it is about the health services which puts women off.

GPs in working class areas have longer waiting lists, longer waiting times, more difficulties making appointments, longer journeys to the practice and few interpreters for those who don't speak English. The GP's attitude to older women is even more dismissive than to women in general. GPs too often consider middle aged women neurotic and in turn many women are very conscious of the demands they make on the GP's already burdened time.

Although a cervical smear is a simple test to do, compared to other medical procedures, it does involve putting a speculum into the vagina. This invasion into an intimate part of the body is not relished by women. As there is an atmosphere of contempt for women's bodies and impatience with their 'trivial' complaints, doctors are less than enthusiastic about initiating speculum exams.

We still live in a society where women are so oppressed that they feel they have no value in themselves. Many middle aged women think of themselves as less important than their husbands or children and do not go for a cervical smear to protect themselves in their own right. This attitude will only be changed as the general struggle against women's oppression grows stronger. It is not even clear that the propaganda on the value of cervical smears is as widespread as it could be.

These are some of the reasons why cervical smear screening programmes are not entirely successful. It is possible to imagine that these problems could be overcome by a socialist government committed to the NHS along with a strong feminist movement. But there is still another, deeper dilemma about cervical smears. Not enough is known about the natural course of cervical cancer to predict which changes in the cervix are really pre-cancerous and which would heal by themselves. The outcome is the danger of over-treatment.

The stages of cervical cancer detected by the cervical smears are part of a continuum and the common understanding of the illness is that it progresses through the early, symptom-free stages to invasive cancer. However, that does not mean that the progression is always inevitable or even irreversible. It is common for women to have abnormal cervical smears, especially Class III, which return to normal if left alone. To treat them as early stages of cervical cancer and claim that vast numbers of women are being cured of a fatal illness is entirely misleading.

Some of these women would have gone on to develop cervical cancer but the majority would not. It is very difficult to find out how many would have (let alone which ones) but there have been studies which suggest that only 10% to 40% of women with Class III and IV cervical smears will get invasive cancer. In one study in Denmark, 40% of the women with carcinoma in situ (Class IV) who had no treatment developed cervical cancer. Some cancers may grow very fast within a year, almost bypassing the early stages, and it is these which probably have the worst outcome. It seems there is a continuum but even without treatment, it may stop at any stage, go back to normal, or proceed at different rates.

The acceptance of the continuum means that it becomes logical to treat not only carcinoma in situ but the earliest stages of Class III. The medical response to a positive smear is usually some form of destruction to a small area of the cervix. There is a range of procedures available from which doctors choose according to their own inclinations. Although none are considered major operations, all have a cost to the woman. If a general anaesthetic is given, that carries its own risks. Cone biopsy may occasionally lead to haemorrhage, infection or damage to the cervix causing future miscarriage or painful periods. New techniques such as laser treatment appear to cause less physical trauma and quicker healing. But all destroy a part of the cervix and the psychological as well as the physical cost of this invasion must be justified.

It is the nature of western medicine to start with the most drastic measure, to use a sledgehammer to crack a nut. Coupled with contempt for women's bodies, our reproductive organs don't stand a chance. The unspoken rule of thumb seems to be that there is no cervix so healthy that it isn't better treated and no testis so diseased it isn't best left intact. Men's reproductive organs simply do not get the kind of attention that women's do. Their importance is recognised by a predominantly male medical profession.

Are there not any gentler ways to make a positive cervical smear go back to normal?

One possibility has come from research on the use of the sheath. It is well established that whatever causes or starts the cancer must come from the man's penis. It may be a virus and many people think there is good evidence that herpes is involved. Or it may be an irritating chemical. (It is quite likely that there is more than one cause.) The use of a mechanical barrier like the sheath should stop further contact.

This was the reasoning behind some American research about the effect of the sheath. Women with positive cervical smears including many with carcinoma in situ were divided into three groups. All were told to use the sheath. Two out of the three groups were also given other treatment. While using the sheaths, none of the women had any progression of the disease. Even more remarkable was that all the women (except for three) completely returned to normal, even the group who only had the sheath as treatment.

FIGURE 6 Don't put that thing in me *Viv Quillin* (*SR 129* April 1983)

This study is a good example of doctors' attitudes to women's role. Women past childbearing age were given hysterectomies rather than the sheath treatment. Only in a male-dominated society could doctors have such disregard for a woman's physical integrity.

If the thinking behind the study is correct, then it seems likely that a sheath would be as effective in preventing cervical cancer as in treating early stages. In fact it should protect the cervix from coming in contact with the irritating chemical or virus in the first place. It is known that sheaths are good protection against VD. So why not against cervical cancer?

Diaphragms have in common with sheaths the fact that both act as a barrier to sperm and to sexually transmitted diseases. In one study in Oxford women who used diaphragms had much less cervical cancer and Class III cervical smears than women who used the pill or the coil. After taking many other factors into consideration, it appeared that the risk in diaphragm users was only one quarter that in women using other birth control methods. In contrast, the pill may actually encourage Class III cervical smears to progress to carcinoma in situ. However, the pill's role in cervical cancer is not clear. Some claim that the increased risk of the disease connected with pill use is not statistically significant.

Although none of these studies prove anything conclusively, they do lead us to think along certain lines. It may be that barrier methods of contraception (sheaths, diaphragms, cervical caps) are more effective in preventing cervical cancer than yearly cervical smears. Yet they are scorned as an effective method of birth control by the majority of the medical profession and by many women. Partly this is due to lack of information about their use and effectiveness and partly to lack of interest in a method which requires that women themselves be in control. If there were a will to encourage barrier methods they would be offered as a first choice of contraception and more research might be done to eliminate the need for spermicide.

While encouraging women to come for cervical smears to prevent cervical cancer, the medical profession actively encourages them to use the pill, a method which may even promote the disease, and discourages them from barrier methods which protect against it. The irony seems to be lost on those who work in mainstream preventive medicine.

Even if all heterosexual couples were using diaphragms or sheaths, it would still be better to prevent the man's penis from becoming contaminated with whatever causes the cancer in the first place.

The occupations husbands have that put women at greater risk from cervical cancer are: the armed forces, miners and quarrymen, farm labourers, fishermen, barge and boatmen, furnacemen, forge, foundry and rolling mill workers. When these facts are examined at all, they are generally attributed to the men's promiscuity when away from home.

However, this explanation falls flat when it is seen that the wives of commercial travellers who are away from home often don't suffer any more from cervical cancer than other women in their class. It is difficult to understand what common chemicals these workers might come in contact with and there may not be one but many.

Most of the information about husbands' occupations is based on very scanty statistics. It isn't possible to conclude anything concrete. However it could lead to a more productive approach to prevention which hasn't been achieved by the obsession with sexual activity.

There is much more to the cervical cancer story than can come out in one article. The main points I want to raise are that although cervical smears can detect early stages, many of these would not progress to cancer if left alone. Secondly, there may be less drastic ways to deal with them. Even so, the cervical smear screening programmes are not accessible to the women most likely to get cervical cancer.

Cervical smears are meant to *detect* early stages but they don't *prevent* exposure to the cause of the cancer. Sheaths and caps act as barriers to viruses and chemicals and do protect against cervical cancer. True prevention may only come from greater attention paid to the hazards at the workplaces of men and of women.

Cervical Cancer – doctors hide the truth
Jean Robinson
SR 154 May 1985

Oxfordshire really hit the headlines on the cervix cancer story. Fleet Street reporters virtually camped on our doorsteps. But what they wanted was the name of the dead woman – not what we see as the real story.

The Community Health Council was contacted last year by a woman who had already had major surgery and chemotherapy and knew she was probably dying of cancer of the cervix. When she was found to have invasive cancer, a check on the smear taken a few years before showed it was abnormal – but she said she had never been told this.

When I spoke to her on the telephone I learned that she had been questioned in hospital about the number of sexual partners she had had. She was not asked how long she had been using the pill. Yet she had been on it for years, and it was still prescribed after her abnormal smear. From a minor, pre-cancerous, cervix abnormality she had developed rampant cancer all over her body in a few years. This is very unusual – or at least it used to be unusual – in a young, healthy, middle class woman. The normal progress of the disease is thought to take 10–20 years. A second woman, who fortunately did not become seriously ill, was picked up on a reminder from the laboratory, after no action had been taken on the initial report to her GP. Then we had a third case – a woman under 30, again a long term pill user, where there had apparently been no follow-up of an abnormal smear found at a hospital check during her pregnancy. She already had invasive cancer at her second check a few years later, but after major surgery and radiotherapy is doing well. The CHC was not prepared to see any more women die. Oxford has a better standard of medical care than most areas. If cases can slip through the net here, then more will be happening elsewhere. A report of similar cases had appeared in the *British Medical Journal* last year from Nottingham, but it had been missed by the press.

I was the CHC's representative on the health authority's working party on cervical cytology. As soon as we knew of the first case I was pressing for women to be sent information direct from the laboratory if they had an abnormal smear, so that if the GP forgot, or the letter was misfiled, or the woman moved, at least the information had a chance of reaching her. There was no need for the letter to be an alarming one. It could explain quite truthfully that some smears need to be done again because there are not enough of the right kind of cells in them, or there may be an infection which can easily be treated. But the woman did have the right to know what the smear showed and what it meant. The GP could be sent results a day or two beforehand, so that the doctor would already be able to answer any questions she had.

The issue so far as I am concerned is women's right to know what is happening to their own bodies. A woman who knows she has mild or moderate dysplasia may choose to come off the pill, get her partner to use a sheath (most women recovered without treatment in a large American study when a sheath was used), make sure she has adequate folic acid in her diet (the pill lowers folic acid levels and cervix abnormalities can be cured with vitamins when this is the cause) and also check whether her partner is sleeping around. She should, of course, know that every additional sexual partner she has is going to add to her risk.

If her partner works with dust, metals, machine oils, chemicals, tar, diesel fumes or meat, it may be particularly important to use barrier contraceptives and check his standard of genital hygiene – including making sure he does not use talc on his genital area. *Never* have sex – oral or vaginal – with a man who has genital warts.

The Oxford story has now been turned into a discussion of computer-ised facilities and a national recall scheme. The Labour health spokesman, Frank Dobson, has even demanded that women should be sent a letter asking them to go for screening, sent a second letter if they do not go, and finally 'a health visitor should be sent to their home'. The health police with a vengeance. Neither the ethics, the efficacy, nor the adverse effects of screening have been adequately discussed by women's organis-ations. Of course we need better organised screening and more money for health care. But isn't it time for women to ask why the medical profession advocated a policy of screening but denied women information that would allow them to choose primary prevention? Why did the infor-mation that women's promiscuity 'caused' cervix cancer get through to the public whereas the risks of male promiscuity, the textile industry for women workers, men's dusty jobs or the pill did not? More young women are dying of cervix cancer now – in spite of screening – than died 35 years ago before it existed. Many more are losing their uterus before they have had a child. Women's groups respond by saying that screening should be more frequent – not realising that it is the pill that is blowing cancer up fast.

The fact is the cervix cancer screening programme has been based on a view of women as passive patients. To be urged to come for smears, rebuked as irresponsible if they do not, scolded like naughty children if they have the disease that screening was meant to detect, then sent home to go on living with the same promiscuous man or go on taking the pill. A view of women as active controllers of their own bodies would suggest a different policy and would go for primary prevention (including telling men that they can give women cancer, and making GPs provide the sheath free – which at present they refuse to do) backed by screening of a kind women want. It would be a whole lot cheaper for the NHS and save more lives.

Of course Fleet Street doesn't want to know any of this. They just called me again. 'Just give us the name of the woman who's been seriously ill. That's the human story our readers want. . . .'

Let it flow – what tampons do to your vagina
Lisa Saffron
SR 16 May 1981

Since toxic shock syndrome (or TSS) hit the headlines, the choice of what menstrual product to use has suddenly become a major health issue.

After 29 deaths and more than 300 seriously ill, many women are now too frightened to use tampons. But is TSS a good enough reason to reject tampons? How can we make rational decisions? As always, there isn't enough information. We can react to the lack of knowledge in the way most doctors and tampon companies have, by saying there's no evidence of danger. Or we can react by saying there is not enough evidence of safety.

Feminists have been trying for years to find out what's in tampons and what they do to us. 'For nearly 50 years tampon manufacturers have been promising women freedom and security. But at the same time they have been denying women an equally essential right: the right to be informed. Without information, women are neither free nor secure.'[1] The trouble is that it's not always easy to evaluate the little bit of information that is available. We inevitably end up taking risks without being able to fully appreciate the consequences.

Tampons, first marketed in the 1930s, were made of simple cotton with cardboard applicators. Although natural in some contexts, cotton is a foreign body to the vagina. Still, it's hard to think of it in the same league as superabsorbent carboxymethyl-cellulose, polyacrylate fibres and polyester foam found in some modern tampons. Perhaps there were cases of fatal and unusual illnesses that no one thought to associate with cotton tampons. Or maybe it's no accident that TSS appeared soon after the introduction of superabsorbent tampons.

In 1979, Proctor & Gamble were the first to introduce their superabsorber, 'Rely', in the USA. A year later, Rely was withdrawn from the market after having reliably increased the risk of TSS. Tampax, Playtex and Kimberly-Clark were soon ready to capitalise on the same market. When questioned by Judy Norsigian of the Boston Women's Health Book Collective, the firms were coy and blandly reassuring about their products. Tampax would not 'provide for proprietary reasons, the precise formulation but . . . certain substances are used to increase the absorbency of the rayon. Our investigations indicate those ingredients are harmless.' Kimberly-Clark divulged that their tampons include 'partially solubilised cellulosic materials used to increase the absorption capacity. All of these components are essentially inert from the biological standpoint.' Presumably by inert they mean that these components have no effect on the tissues of the vagina.

But they can't be totally inert or they wouldn't be doing their job. Tampons are meant to absorb fluid. A super-absorbent tampon soaks up 17 times its own weight in fluid, about one ounce or more. We lose anywhere from one to five ounces in irregular spurts over a period of days. The tampon doesn't distinguish between menstrual blood and normal secretions of the vaginal wall. What effect does this have on the vagina? Kimberly-Clark sponsored an investigation by two Wisconsin researchers to find out,[2] though they didn't wait for the results before they put Kotex Security tampons on the market.

The Wisconsin researchers looked at the microscopic effects on the vagina of both regular and superabsorbent tampons of three unnamed leading brands. After wearing the tampons from one to five hours *between* menstrual periods, varying degrees of dryness could be seen through the microscope but not by the naked eye. Dry patches and areas where the surface layer of cells peeled off in sheets were the most common changes seen. Where the cells peeled off into the deeper zones of the vaginal wall, it was called a micro-ulceration. Both the regular and the superabsorbent tampons left very few women with normal moist vaginas. Nevertheless it was the supers which caused significantly more micro-ulcerations.

Who wears tampons between their periods anyway? Evidently some women do, since large but painless ulcers were reported in 14 women who had been wearing tampons continuously for weeks and even months, because of break-through bleeding or heavy vaginal secretions.[3] One woman had a three-square-centimetre inflamed ulcer containing fibres, presumably from the surface of the tampon. She had been using Tampax daily for six months. All these women changed their tampons often. The ulcers healed as soon as the women stopped using them.

The same Wisconsin researchers then set out to discover what changes tampons caused when worn *during* the menstrual period. Again most women suffered some degree of drying regardless of brand or whether the tampon was regular or superabsorbent. The supers tended to go all the way and produce micro-ulcerations more commonly than did the regulars. All healed quickly when women stopped using tampons.

Has anyone done studies on the microscopically visible effects of diaphragms, penises, condoms, spermicides, sea sponges, or anything else which goes into the vagina? The wall of the vagina does have remarkable properties of regeneration. The surface cells are constantly being replaced. Deeper layers are renewed about every two and a half days. Is the wear and tear from tampons more worrying than from any of the other intruders into the vagina?

It seems we can safely conclude that continuous use of tampons (for weeks or months) is definitely unwise and superabsorbent ones are more potentially dangerous than regular ones. What's interesting is that Kimberly-Clark did nothing with these findings after sponsoring the research. Kotex Stick and Kotex Security are still as big as ever on the American market.

Since even regular tampons are not inert from any biological standpoint, the advent of TSS should not have been such a shock. In November 1980 the *British Medical Journal* described the 20-day ordeal of a previously healthy 16-year-old woman suffering from TSS. After two days of high fever, vomiting and drowsiness, she was admitted to hospital in Leeds. On the day of admission she developed diarrhoea, a sunburn-like rash all over her body and went into shock. She was treated for shock and slowly improved. Ten days later the skin peeled off her hands and trunk and her lungs filled up with two and a half litres of fluid. The bacteria

Staphylococcus aureus was grown from a swab taken from her vagina. Luckily she survived the infection.

Her doctors were observant enough to notice that she was menstruating and was wearing a Tampax regular tampon, a fact which could easily have been considered unimportant. This all happened in February 1980. The full significance became apparent to her doctors only when studies reported by the USA Center for Disease Control (CDC) in June suggested that TSS is associated with tampon use and bacterial infection by *Staph. aureus*. This, then, was the first reported British case of an extremely rare disease which, since 1975, had affected more than 300 Americans, killing 29.

The great majority of victims were menstruating women under 30, a small percentage were men and non-menstruating women. Earliest estimates of the number affected were three in every 100,000 women of menstrual age per year. This is probably on the low side because not all women of menstrual age are actually menstruating and because there are more cases than are recognised and reported. At the moment an illness counts as TSS if it meets the strict criteria laid down by James Todd of Denver, who first described it in 1978.[4] The symptoms suffered by the Leeds victim would fall into this category. But very few illnesses affect everyone the same way. It is likely that Todd's criteria apply only to cases at the severe end of the range and that some cases of 'flu during a period are actually mild versions of TSS. This would raise the estimates but still leave it as a rare illness – about the same order of magnitude as dying from thrombosis due to the pill.

In the USA especially, TSS is the subject of intense publicity despite its rarity. This is because it almost exclusively strikes healthy young women, is severe, and has a high death rate – 10 of the cases reported so far have resulted in death. Its notoriety has meant that it has been energetically investigated. As of March 1981, what have these searches revealed?

First of all, is it a new illness or have people only recently begun to recognise and report it? TSS is too dramatic to have been missed. Symptoms were reported as early as 1927. Between then and 1979, 20 cases were described. If there had been more, there is no doubt they would have reached the medical journals. Since January 1980, 299 cases came to CDC's attention. Why has it appeared now? Part of the answer may lie with the bacteria, *Staphylococcus aureus*. It might be a strain which has recently become more virulent or more able to grow in the vagina. As with influenza, different strains of *Staph. aureus* are more common at different times.

More clear-cut is that the introduction of Rely tampons coincides with the increase in TSS. In one study by CDC,[5] 71% of a group of women who had had TSS had used Rely tampons. If 71% of any group of menstruating women had used Rely tampons, then no one could blame Rely. But in fact, only 26% of a control group of women had used Rely. The control group was made up of women friends of TSS victims who lived in the same area and were roughly the same age. So a major difference between women who had TSS and women who did not was the use of Rely tampons.

However, Rely is not the only brand used by women who have had TSS. All brands, including Tampax, Kotex, Playtex and Lil-lets, have been involved. At this time, there is not enough information to say that the superabsorbent tampons are riskier than regular ones, though it does seem likely.

How do tampons increase the risk of TSS? The tampons themselves are *not* contaminated with *Staph. aureus*. The bacteria are either already in the vagina or may be pushed in with the tampon from the skin outside. About 10% of women normally have *Staph. aureus* in the vagina while they are menstruating,[6] just as it is commonly found in the nose, armpits and skin all the time.

Obviously the mere presence of disease-causing bacteria is not enough to lead to disease. Blood is a perfect growth medium for bacteria. The environment created in the vagina by the warm blood-soaked tampon, especially the superabsorbent ones, may be ideal for the particular virulent strain of *Staph. aureus* to grow and produce a poison. Another possibility is that the tampons cause micro-ulcerations through which the poison seeps into the bloodstream. (The tampon applicator may scrape the vaginal wall and thus play a part. But not all the brands involved had applicators.) In most of the cases so far, *Staph. aureus* was grown from swabs taken from the vagina but not from samples of the bloodstream. In other words, the bacterial infection remains in the vagina while the poison causes symptoms affecting the whole body. The identity and exact role of the poison is still unknown.

Suitable conditions for *Staph. aureus* can occur, but less frequently, in men and in women at times other than menstruation. A London medical student recognised the mystery illness she had had three times in 1978 as TSS. Once she was menstruating and wearing Lil-lets Super Plus. The other two times were right after using a diaphragm for contraception.[7]

The only clear advice is that we can *almost* entirely reduce our risk of TSS by not using tampons. Since Rely was never sold in Britain, we can't single out any one brand on the market as being riskier than any other, as far as TSS goes. If we do use tampons, there is no evidence that frequent changing reduces chances of infection. In one CDC study,[8] more TSS victims than women in the control groups had used tampons continuously throughout their periods. However, just the opposite was found in another CDC study.[9] It seems likely that the harm tampons do could occur during insertion or while they're still dry and *not* mainly after they've been in too long. There is also not enough evidence to say that limited use, just during the day or just during the heaviest days, for instance, will reduce the risk.

Women with high fever and vomiting or diarrhoea during their period should remove the tampon and see a doctor. Antibiotics are no use in treating the illness but may be helpful in preventing recurrences, which are common. Tampons should not be used until the *Staph. aureus* is cleared from the vagina of these women.

Many women will choose to continue using tampons even after becoming aware of the risk. At least there is a need. But there is no need for perfumed tampons. Odour can only offend the nose if it wafts through the air and tickles the nostril hairs. Trapped in the tampon within the vagina, menstrual blood has no chance to come in contact with air. We won't even be able to smell the perfume. When this point was put to Playtex, Anne Clark of their Family Products Division in Surrey returned this gem of a non-answer:

To claim that deodorant tampons are unnecessary is open to dispute. Non-deodorant tampons attempt to control such biological odour by containing the menstrual fluid within the vagina, and are effective only to a limited degree, even if properly placed. Clinical studies conducted by an independent laboratory demonstrate that Playtex Deodorant Tampons substantially reduce menstrual odour as compared with non-deodorant tampons.[9]

I have visions of white-coated laboratory staff moving from woman to woman with their notebooks, recording the results of a sniff between the legs. But maybe the odour was not assessed under such realistic conditions.

The concern is not only that women are conned into using unnecessary products. If even cotton and rayon are not innocuous in the vagina, what possible effect can a perfume have? The vagina and vulva are very sensitive to chemical attack. Irritation of the mucous membranes, inflammation, swelling and itching are typical reactions. Playtex try to cover themselves by printing a 'caution statement' on the tampon package. This is done, Anne Clark says 'so the small group of women who may be hyper-sensitive to perfumed products will avoid *improperly* attributing ailments to the deodorant factor.' Playtex deodorant tampons are among those causing TSS but Playtex are no more to blame than any other brand. The two issues have been confused in many press reports, leading quite a few women to believe that the Playtex deodorant tampons are the main cause of TSS.

Deodorant tampons manage to slip through the various regulations designed to protect the consumer in Britain. They do not come under the Cosmetic Products Regulations 1978 because cosmetics apply only to external use. The Medicines Act also doesn't cover tampons so the DHSS is not interested.

Luckily women themselves are campaigning against the product. In response to concern from the readers of *Woman*, *Woman's Own* and *Honey*, the International Publishing Corporation has banned the advertising of

FIGURE 7 Getting rid of shh-you-know-what *Viv Quillin* (*SR 106* May 1981)

deodorant tampons. After pressure from women's groups, Woolworth's in Colchester stopped buying from Playtex, to name successes.

Long before TSS, women had experimented with alternatives to tampons. Diaphragms to collect the blood, rather than absorb it, work for some women and have the advantage of being reusable and free (from the FPA). Natural sea sponges are even more popular. Testimonials from satisfied sponge users stress the comfort (less drying than tampons), the cost (about 75p for a sponge lasting many cycles), the ecological benefits (*if* carefully harvested, they're renewable) and the freedom from having to rely on profit-making multinationals.

But evidence that tampons may be hazardous does not make sea sponges safe. There was one case of TSS in a woman who had been using a sponge, but it is not known whether she was also using tampons. Still, it is not hard to imagine how sponges might create the right conditions for *Staph. aureus* to grow and produce the TSS poison.

Sea sponges may be natural (especially in the sea), but that does not necessarily mean they are either pure or harmless to the vagina. A sponge is the fibrous skeleton of an animal, fished mainly from the Mediterranean and the Gulf of Mexico. When sponges were analysed by the University of Iowa Hygienic Laboratory, traces of chemical pollutants which could have come from oil spills in the ocean were found along with sand, bacteria and fungi. Because of the complex internal structure of the sponge, simple rinsing was not enough to cleanse it of deeply embedded sand. They found that the sponge surface crumbles when rubbed lightly.

What is the significance of these findings? Sand and sponge crumbs could conceivably irritate the vagina. Although the bacteria and fungi found are not normally disease-causing ones, they might be able to exploit a new situation like the vagina and cause an infection. Other more hazardous organisms might appear in the future or after contamination during use. The potential hazards of the chemical pollutants is completely unknown but not, therefore, non-existent.

The Emma Goldman Clinic for Women in Iowa has discontinued the sale of sponges until more is known about the possible health hazards. They stated that 'while the staff supports studies such as that conducted by the University Hygienic Laboratory, we find it alarming that tampons have been in use for decades on a large scale and have generated consider-able profit for large corporations without having been similarly tested.' Ironically, tampons will get away with nothing more than a warning on the package while the Food and Drug Administration in the USA is actually trying to halt the distribution of sponges. Sponges have never been approved for use as a menstrual absorbent, so any seller or advertiser is liable to prosecution in the USA.

As with birth control methods, there may be no ideal solution, only a choice between unknown risks. So far there have been no reported cases of TSS in sanitary pad users. Some brands are now made of the same superabsorbent materials found in tampons and some are deodorised. Once again there's no reason to assume something is safe or will continue to be safe just because we don't know for sure it's dangerous.

Perhaps TSS is the Goddess's punishment for making menstruation too hidden, perpetuating the taboo that women's blood is a periodic pollution and a source of shame. For myself I don't use tampons because they make me feel out of touch with my body, as if I'm trying to deny the fact of my bleeding. I feel too much pleasure in the sight and smell and touch of my blood to give up my sponge and my pads, despite their imperfections. I find I choose any method which lets me feel good about menstruation. For me, that's a more powerful basis for my personal decision-making than fear of rare health hazards.

With such a low risk of getting TSS, it's very unlikely that I as an individual will be unlucky enough to be another victim. But some women will be. We have a responsibility to make women's health our collective concern. Tampons are not strictly regulated in Britain nor are they adequately tested for their effects on health. The companies have no obligation to inform us of what they're putting in their products. Let's keep a wary eye on anything coming our way, especially when profit is the motive for their manufacture. The self-interest of tampon companies hardly coincides with ours.

NOTES

1 'The truth about tampons' Nancy Friedman, 20 October, *New West* 1980, p. 33.
2 Edward Friedrich and Kenneth Siegesmund, 'Tampon-associated vaginal ulcerations', *Obstetrics and Gynecology*, February 1980, p. 149.
3 Steven Jumerson and John Becker, 'Vaginal ulcers associated with tampon usage', *Obstetrics and Gynecology*, July 1980, p. 97.
4 James Todd and Mark Fishaut, 'Toxic shock syndrome associated with phage group 1 staphylococci', *The Lancet*, 25 November 1978, p. 1116.
5 Follow-up on TSS in Center for Disease Control's Morbidity and Mortality *Weekly Report*, 19 September 1980.
6 Kathryn Shands and others, 'Toxic shock syndrome in menstruating women', *The New England Journal of Medicine*, 18 December 1980, p. 1436.
7 'Toxic-shock and tampons' by a medical student, *British Medical Journal*, 22 November 1980, p. 1426.
8 'Tampons: abundant advice may outrun the evidence' *Medical World News*, 19 November 1980, p. 9.

PMT
Sue O'Sullivan
SR 116 March 1982

The recent flurry of media interest in pre-menstrual tension (PMT), after it was successfully used in court to explain and excuse serious crimes, has died out as fast as it originally appeared. It might be argued that any public discussion of the menstrual cycle was a good thing, given the shame, secrecy and ignorance which still surround the subject. Certainly women who suffer badly from PMT will welcome, on some levels, a validation of their condition – too often seen simply as a psychological problem or just as women's lot . . . 'grin and bear it, dear'.

Unfortunately, but not surprisingly, the court findings, and the research and arguments they were based on are too easily used against women even as they were used for women to get them off criminal charges. What will linger much more as 'general knowledge' are half-truths about the menstrual cycle which will maintain and fuel biologically determined views of women's instability and inability to act responsibly in the world – views which blame PMT for women's 'uncharacteristic' behaviour in the family at 'certain times' of the month. 'In the premenstrual phase women may be irritable, angry and emotionally labile. During the postmenstrual phase, however, they float through life, wafted along on a tide of hormones, euphoric, placid and tolerant, womanly in every way and easy to live with.'[1]

Katharina Dalton's (whose findings and views on PMT were used in the court cases) husband put it 'nicely' in the foreword to her book *The Menstrual Cycle*: 'These findings [show] the extent to which the cyclical changes in the levels of a woman's hormones are responsible for her unpredictable changes of personality.' And further, 'Every woman is at the mercy of the constantly recurring ebb and flow of her hormones.'

Dr Dalton is now the popularly accepted 'expert' on PMT. Her views are reproduced as gospel in women's magazines, newspapers, and increasingly in the literature of organisations such as the Royal Society for the Prevention of Accidents, whose latest leaflets on the dangers of PMT all feature a fractured women's symbol. They are reflected in the material of the medically and establishment oriented Women's Health Concern (a charity among whose supporters are drug companies) which describes itself as being known as 'the national sorting house for women's health problems'.

Dalton locates the primary cause of PMT in hormonal imbalance and recommends treatment with progesterone. But there are questions and criticisms about Dalton's research and her treatment. As feminists we have to come to grips with a contradictory situation: Dalton, a woman doctor, pays attention to women's menstrual cycles. She says it is a 'real' condition – not a neurotic one. She has set up a clinic to help women suffering from PMT. It's obviously her life's work *but* . . . her most widely adopted point about PMT is that during their premenstrual period women commit irrational, nasty, evil, criminal, accidental acts. She uses her statistics to prove that women batter babies, commit suicide and crimes, disrupt their home life, and miss work more during this time.

There are a number of points it's useful to make in any discussion of PMT. One of them is to do with the politics of scientific and statistical evidence. There is nothing neutral about science. Facts depend on the questions asked, how they are posed in relationship to other things, and what the researcher expects to find. All the recent scaremongering about increases in female suicides, accidents, crimes of violence and depression, hardly ever makes the point that men commit suicide more than women, commit more crimes of violence, and are involved in more fatal accidents than women. And some of the media's descriptions of how women behave in the family when suffering from PMT read like cries of anger at impossible relationships with men, children and frustration with the drudgeries of housework, rather than 'irrational' behaviour.

Our premenstrual increase in emotional and behavioural determinants doesn't come anywhere near the violent havoc men cause in the world. The argument that women can't be trusted in positions of power and responsibility becomes ludicrous when one looks at the state of a male-dominated world now. And nowhere do we read that women should not be allowed to partake in the responsible work of having and raising babies and small children because of PMT.

Strangely absent from any arguments about PMT is any recognition that men are subject to cyclical patterns of hormones which affect their emotions and responses and which are apparently less predictable than our patterns. Although this is generally recognised among researchers, it

FIGURE 8 Is PMT a threat to marriage? *Fanny Tribble* (*SR 116* March 1982)

is ignored by men themselves; most would hotly deny that they had cycles.

Dr Anthony Clare, a critic of Katharina Dalton and the school of hormone imbalances, raises doubts about her treatment: 'One of the few double-blind studies of progesterone in premenstrual depression failed to establish its superiority over placebo [dummy], while an American study claimed to show an improvement using doses of progesterone of between 1 to 5 mg. doses so small that they must be considered homeopathic.'[2] And in a letter to *The Times* late last year he said, 'No consistent biochemical or hormonal abnormality has been discovered. There is considerable controversy over the likely cause and most appropriate treatment. Some even doubt the existence of the condition.'

Feminist and other critics state quite frankly (and have done for the last ten years or more) that far too little is known by anyone about the female hormonal system to draw anything more than hit or miss conclusions about what causes PMT, what PMT causes, or about treatment with hormones. And there are serious questions about the political conclusions which are drawn from Dalton's work and treatment. Conclusions which *fail* to see women as social beings in an exploitative, sexist and male-dominated society, or see women as ultimately determined by their biology . . . their 'raging' hormones . . . which need to be controlled and stabilised.

All research does indicate that retention of fluid is one of the main problems women have premenstrually. As long ago as the mid-1950s I was told to avoid salty foods and reduce fluid intake before my periods as a way of lessening period pains. Now some people believe this may help PMT too. Other self-help suggestions include taking vitamin B6 (pyridoxine), especially in the week before a period is due; calcium (always in conjunction with magnesium) and Vitamin D. Another possibility is food rich in potassium. Certain herbal teas are considered useful and exercise, particularly yoga, seems to help some women. All this may be difficult for many women to put into practice, but it would be worth attempting – perhaps a little at a time.

Unless we look at the whole of our life – the way in which mind, body and society interact – we can find ourselves lulled into a mainly doctor-orientated, drug-centred view of health. As long ago as 1946, an American researcher into PMT said that the most common causes of its symptoms were nutritional deficiencies or poisoning from toxic substances in work environments. He was against giving hormone treatment, being sure that hormone-like drugs worsened the underlying cause, because they 'actually increase the body's nutritional requirements and strain the organs of the body which filter out poisons'.[3]

We know that PMT is real, that many women are affected in varying degrees, and that whether it is physiological *or* psychological *or* an interaction of both, it exists as a problem and must be taken seriously. The causes of PMT are probably many and varied – it is *not* a disease. But why shouldn't we take the *positive* things about our menstrual cycle seriously as well? What if we were allowed to fully develop the positive aspects of experiencing a flux and flow of ups and downs – to be more in touch with our cycle and the changes it brings? To rid ourselves of shame or disgust about our menstrual blood? An American feminist book on menstruation says, 'To reject and eliminate the body processes, to let our moods be dampened through progesterone or estrogen or testosterone, is in part to agree with those who hold that womanhood is an inferior state of being.'[4]

NOTES

1 *Pulse*, 29 November 1980.
2 *Modern Medicine*, January 1979.
3 Morton Biskind, quoted in *How to Stay Out of the Gynecologist's Office*, Federation of Feminist Women's Health Centers, 1981.
4 *The Curse – A Cultural History of Menstruation*, Janice Delaney, Mary Jane Lupton and Emily Toth, Mentor Books, 1974.

Menopause – growing old in a man's world
Jean Shapiro
SR 127 February 1983

'It's your age . . .' How many of us have been fobbed off with this 'explanation' of one of a number of apparently unrelated problems that may occur in the middle years? How many have been misdiagnosed because 'menopause' is a convenient let-out lable, just as 'hysteria' is the tag put on to the younger woman with symptoms that don't interest her doctor? But it's not only doctors who dismiss the older woman. In a society that places such a premium on the stereotype of the sexually attractive woman – slim, youthful body, smooth, unlined skin, the ability to bear children and look after them with uncomplaining energy and zeal – we're all infected to some extent by ageist attitudes. No wonder that the loss of these powerfully reinforced images, a loss clearly marked by the menopause, is dreaded by so many women and found unaccept- able by almost all. No wonder that we ourselves fall for the idea that any physical or emotional ill we may suffer is attributable to 'the change'. The sexist propaganda that dismisses women as either 'premenstrual' or 'menopausal' is insidious.

What is the menopause? To start with, the word is a misnomer, because periods (menses) seldom suddenly pause or stop. The *climacteric* is the accepted word for the whole process that usually begins between 45 and 50, but sometimes earlier and occasionally later. At this age the amount of hormonal stimulation produced by the pituitary gland to the ovaries and uterus begins to diminish. Oestrogen and progesterone are the hormones responsible for triggering off the monthly shedding of the lining of the womb. These hormones are mainly – but not solely – prod- uced by the ovaries. Since our mid-twenties there's been a slow falling- off of oestrogen from the ovaries: at the menopause, steady production is replaced by a stop-start pattern, and there's a general reorganisation of the whole endocrine system. Other glands – particularly the adrenals – compensate for the less productive ovaries, and thus it's incorrect to assume that the loss of ovary function (or the loss of ovaries through surgery) means total withdrawal of oestrogen. The body may take some time to adjust to the lower levels of the hormone produced by other glands (and this process is abrupt following surgery), but when it has adjusted – which may take about five years – the menopause and its unpleasant side-effects will be over.

Research in Britain and elsewhere seems to show that there are three major symptoms directly attributable to the menopause – apart from the irregularity, scantiness or flooding and ultimate cessation of periods, of course. These are hot flushes, vaginal dryness and osteoporosis (porous and fragile bones). Other symptoms complained of by women in the menopause – headaches, weepiness and depression, irritability, 'vague- ness', anxiety, insomnia, fatigue, lack of sexual feelings – are conditions which are just as real and which can be even more worrying. But it's being suggested now that these problems are much more likely to stem from difficulties and imbalances in the sufferer's daily life, or are reactions, both physical and emotional, to ageing itself rather than to the menopause alone.

It's interesting that the women whose views on the menopause we quote bear this out. Women who have suffered more than the 'normal' symptoms say they were under stress or had suffered a bereavement coinciding with the menopause. To someone suffering from the traditional and severe menopausal troubles these conclusions may seem insensitive and over-simplistic. But it's difficult to disentangle the various strands of cause and effect. Do you have good menopause because you're basically happy, or are you happy because your menopause is easy? Is the meno-pause the cause of your depression, or do you have major menopausal difficulties because your life is unsatisfactory and depressing?

Whatever the answers, we're talking about something that's all too painfully real to very many women. But if we accept that the menopause is a stage of life that has to be lived through as positively as possible, we have to consider ways of making the transition easier. Is hormone replacement therapy (HRT) the answer?

Before discussing the situations in which HRT is of apparently clear benefit, it's as well to look at its history and to see why there have been so many doubts about its long-term effects.

In the early days of HRT it was peddled (and that's the right word) as a cure-all elixir of life after 50 that would keep women 'feminine forever'.

But experience soon showed that the hormone pill or implant didn't erase wrinkles, let alone restore youthful figures and lift depression. It *could* treat effectively the three common physical symptoms (hot flushes, dry vagina and osteoporosis, with shortening of stature), and that was just about all.

And this was at a price. By the early 1970s, millions of American and thousands of British women had been taking oestrogen – synthetic or 'natural' – for some time, in many cases intending to do so for the rest of their lives, as the drug companies were suggesting. But then it was found that an uncomfortably large number of these women were developing endometrial cancer. Not surprisingly, publicity about this caused a big drop in oestrogen therapy, and the companies and researchers had to think again. The answer, as they saw it, was combining oestrogen and progestogen therapy. Progestogen, which actually protects the endometrium (lining of the uterus) would be taken along with oestrogen for the last 10 to 13 days of the month.

In Britain this form of HRT became more widespread earlier than it did in the US, where much of the disquiet about hormone replacement still relates to oestrogen rather than combined hormone therapy. British doctors have always been more cautious (some enthusiasts for HRT say more conservative and obstructive). But there is now a sizeable question mark over the use of progestogen as well.

Although the balance of the hormones may be different just because it's generally recommended that progestogen be taken for about 13 days of the month, this form of HRT is very similar to the 'combined' contraceptive pill, and this, as everyone knows is under a certain amount of suspicion, especially for women over 35. Progestogen has been linked with adverse changes in blood cholesterol levels (possibly increasing the risk of heart attacks) as well as a higher incidence of high blood pressure and thrombosis. Whether or not there is any link between breast cancer and HRT is unclear.

Women having HRT in whatever form should be carefully and regularly monitored for all side effects, and the dose adjusted to the lowest possible level compatible with improvement of the condition being treated, and many researchers believe that the treatment should be short overall. The therapy, in any case, is not suitable for women with high blood pressure, migraine, heart disease, diabetes or a history of thrombosis or liver problems. Once a woman is aware of the possible disadvantages of HRT, she is better able to decide *for herself* whether any risk is counterbalanced in her own case by the benefits she may derive. She may conclude that self-help measures, or some other treatment, are worth a try.

Most prominent among the physical symptoms of the menopause are hot flushes. Not all women have them, but those who do experience them as a sudden feeling of heat all over the body, quite unrelated to the external temperature, with profuse sweating and flushing on face, neck and sometimes elsewhere on the body. These sensations aren't only disconcerting and inconvenient. Many women find them socially highly embarrassing – they don't want to tell the world they're in the menopause. Fortunately the flushes last only a few minutes at the most; they may not happen more than a few times; and at worst the problem is usually over in about two years.

In most cases HRT can banish hot flushes for as long as it is taken. The alternative seems to be acceptance of the problem, realising that it is often much less apparent to other people than the woman believes. The very profuse night sweats that can accompany hot flushes can be anticipated by having a change of bed-linen handy, thus minimising the period of broken sleep; and talcum powder and cooling, refreshing sprays can be a comfort.

HRT can also make a dramatic difference to the woman with the second major problem – vaginal dryness or 'atrophy' as the medical textbooks repellingly call it. Dryness not only makes heterosexual intercourse difficult and painful but can also affect lesbian vaginal sex. The thinning of the skin in the genital area can lead to proneness to vaginal and urinary infections. Women who prefer local HRT treatment to taking pills by mouth can use oestrogen cream with the same effect – an increase in lubrication. But since the hormone is very well absorbed in the vagina, it is unfortunately not without the same side effects as HRT taken orally.

Women with the problem of vaginal dryness do have alternatives, however. Lubrication is often maintained and improved by regular sexual activity, whether with a partner or by masturbation; in many cases this is made easier by the use of KY jelly, a safe lubricant obtainable from any pharmacy.

Successful treatment of the third common physical symptom of meno-pause – osteoporosis – is also a widely publicised claim for HRT. Recent research, however, while accepting that hormones can be effective in preventing porous and fragile bones during treatment, tends to show that this does not apply in the long run – and we've seen that there are very good reasons for not prolonging HRT for more than a few months or two years at the most. And when we also know that osteoporosis is not an inevitable consequence of the menopause (it's been suggested that slightly built women, particularly those poorly nourished earlier in their lives, are more likely victims than Black women, and white women with large frames who are slightly overweight by current standards), it seems even more pointless to administer a doubtful remedy 'just in case'. Better nutrition earlier in life, particularly for lactating women, is a preventative measure, since bone loss can begin by about 30. But older women can increase their Vitamin D and C intake, make sure their calcium intake is adequate, and above all take plenty of exercise. This doesn't have to be violent to have a beneficial effect on the bones, which, like other parts of the body, need use to remain healthy.

Some research shows that if the vitamins and calcium are accompanied by fluoride (the exact quantities tailored to the individual woman) this therapy is just as effective in the long term as HRT is in the short term in maintaining the strength of the bones. It's being used successfully in one centre in New York and is the sort of treatment we might see in menopause clinics in the future.

It's now generally accepted that HRT can do nothing directly to help the woman who is emotionally disturbed, depressed, lacks sexual feelings, or believes she is suffering from other psychological effects of the meno-pause. Of course anything that improves a distressing physical condition must affect mood, and something like relief from night sweats can also improve well-being, if only because the debilitating result of insomnia can spill over into the whole of a woman's life. But in the long run a woman suffering from the emotional disturbances so commonly attributed to the menopause may get more help from examining her family set-up, her relationships, and the pressures put upon her as a woman in a sexist and ageist society. And if that help is sought through discussion and support from other women – as is happening in some older women's groups in Britain now, following the lead of American sisters – the whole process of menopause can take on a very different character.

This sort of group can begin to consider the extent to which they've been pushed into expecting and adopting the stereotype of the unbalanced, depressed, ailing, inferior human being who's ill all the time (and therefore useless); the one who's taken over from the unbalanced, depressed person with PMT who was ill (and useless) only part of the time. They can also consider and learn about the extent to which physical, biochemical changes are affecting them, independently of the pressures and propaganda of a sexist society.

Such women are changed by their experiences in the group. For them the menopause is no longer something threatening, or shaming, or a loss of purpose in life. They can welcome the new freedoms, try new ways of looking at the world, see themselves at last as important, as individuals. For them this is a real 'change of life'.

MENOPAUSE EXPERIENCE – BY WOMEN FROM THE OLDER FEMINIST NETWORK

In common with many women, my menopause coincided with the death of my mother and the emergent adolescence/adulthood of the children I have parented. Both partings were painful and the loss of my mother a particularly protracted agony. The emotional and mental confusion at these events was hard at times to disentangle from the effects of my body's journey from pre- to post-menopause.

My confidence during this long (four/five-year) period was almost totally undermined. I was plagued with a sense of unworthiness. I felt a fraud at work and a burden at home, foolish and friendless. The concern, support and love offered by those around me I construed as pity. My use of alcohol as a helpful prop to cover awkwardness and ease difficult times turned into a guilty habit and a fear of dependency. There seemed no way through my ever deepening depression and I lived with a sense of despair.

This mental, emotional and even moral turmoil went alongside many acute and painful physical symptoms starting with severe and protracted heavy bleeding, acute pains in the limbs, headaches, water retention and swellings of the hands, feet and face. Needless to say, my sexual confidence suffered badly.

But I was fortunate – throughout this time I had the constant support and care of my lover – a woman. Retrospectively I feel lucky that being a lesbian, my partner was able to identify and sympathise with my condition. I know that many heterosexual women at menopause suffer from the painful sexual attentions of their men or sexual rejection. Neither happened in my case and the certainty that I was still a whole person, friend and lover to my partner was a real life-line.

Most women of my age, 50, have unluckily missed the sisterly support of the women's movement. The experience of the menopause has been privatised. The guilt and confusion at the grip this condition has had on this period of their lives is confirmed by the medical profession's indifference and ignorance. I certainly failed to find any medical help or advice. The assertion frequently made by doctors, and by women too, even in books purporting to be about the menopause, that looking after oneself, keeping fit, slim and active will adequately see one through this time doesn't help. In my case such advice only created more guilt and self-doubt. My only therapy was that my lover and many of the circle of women I knew through her loyally supported and helped me by hanging on to me even when I was hell bent to escape to isolation and hopeless self-absorption.

All in all my menopause was an awkward, painful, disconcerting and miserable affair – but I've gained much from it. I have been forced to reconsider myself – in every sense. Brought face to face with my failings, I've had to search to find my qualities, losing my youthful body I had to learn to love my ageing body in which I genuinely began to feel a new ease.

Looking back too I now see that in spite of everything it was a highly productive time. I maintained an efficient, even creative, hold over my work, published a book, exhibited many drawings and created a garden out of a wilderness – quite a nice metaphor for what I feel the menopause has meant to me.

I'm 52 and in the menopause. My symptoms include minor flushes lasting from a few seconds to one minute – not troublesome. On the first day of my period I suffer extreme cramps like those I had in my teens, and heavy bleeding, leaving me totally exhausted. Sometimes my breasts are so sore I can't touch them. I seem to be getting more irritable, less patient. I also get constipation at regular times of the month, and I suffer from dry skin.

Although I've been working harder than ever before, I haven't burnt up the calories as I did, and my flesh has lost elasticity. I now do daily exercises and watch my diet.

Very sad is the fact that I have lost all sexual need. Since I have always enjoyed very good sexual relationships, I hope this is only temporary.

But at this time I've been through an extreme emotional experience, so it's difficult to separate minor symptoms like boils and mouth ulcers, sore throats and minor memory lapses from the major change.

Despite everything the menopause is not frightening and I've had a lot of help from *Menopause: A Positive Approach*. I haven't consulted a doctor – whatever my complaint I'd only get Valium or its equivalent.

Despite nursing training, my knowledge about the menopause was hazy. I had absorbed society's attitudes entirely negatively. I had thought of the menopause as the beginning of an unattractive old age. My notions were entirely false. There were no sudden visible signs of ageing, skin and colour remained good and a look in the mirror didn't cause alarm. All right, I did put on some weight.

My GP didn't give a straightforward answer to my questions about contraception, but my husband was willing to use sheaths until we could be sure of safety – that lasted about four years. There wasn't much help in published material – just glowing accounts, written in the 1970s on HRT, in great demand by the middle class. I put it out of my mind.

But suddenly I was struck with back trouble, and I began to wonder why so many older women get arthritis. Was it connected with the menopause? I had read somewhere about a problem with calcium absorption. Still I couldn't get answers from my doctor, and the back trouble cleared up. At work my hot flushes embarrassed me. If I'd been more 'liberated' then I might have talked about the menopause.

Everyone associated depression and menopause. Yes, I was depressed at times, but there were other reasons. Life goes on, perhaps better in some ways. I can do things I haven't had time for until now. I've accepted that I'm regarded as old – and I don't care. But I do wish there was more information about the menopause, more research by women and for women. And women should get together and discuss our fears, worries and experiences.

It started about four years ago, when I was 50. I'd go six weeks without a period, then have two floods in a fortnight. The heavy ones were very debilitating.

I went to my woman GP and she put me on Duphaston (synthetic progesterone) to take for three weeks and then a week off. I took it for about three months – it did the trick and regularised the periods.

But within a year I started getting very bad headaches – the sort that don't disappear with a couple of Paracetamols. I was having a very distressing time emotionally – my father and a love affair were both dying (I don't mean my lover was dying, just the affair) and I became very depressed. It was like a heavy, suffocating cowl over me. I don't remember any other physical symptoms – certainly no hot flushes. But I found myself looking longingly at the wheels of buses, wondering what it would be like underneath them.

That's not me at all, so back I went to my doctor, who put me on to HRT. She explained to me that there had been a lot of prejudice against it on the grounds that it might be carcinogenic, but by taking oestrogen and progesterone together, with a week off to shed the lining of the womb, it would be safe. And I wouldn't 'dry up' or get brittle bones and I would have a yearly cytology screening and regular blood-pressure checks. So I started on Cyclo-Progynova and it changed (saved?) my life. I get no side-effects at all. At the Older Feminists' meeting there seemed to be an incredible amount of fear and prejudice about HRT. This is *my* experience – I've been taking it for more than two years and haven't regretted it for a second. You women who light up your twentieth cigarette of the day and tell me *I'll* get cancer – give up the fags and improve your life with HRT!

CHAPTER 2

IN AND AGAINST
THE SYSTEM

External forces determine women's lives at every point. And yet we are continuously enjoined to take our own health in hand, as if health were primarily an individual's responsibility. While it is true that we need not be passive victims of society's injustices, it is as true that the material reality of the institutions, social relations and ideology of our society are determining and defining factors in each individual's life. To the extent that we are all part of our society, no matter how rebelliously, it is not surprising that as feminists we recreate some of what we despise. To the extent that as feminists we are against the system, and act to change it, we become active agents for new ways of living and organising. Agents of hope.

This chapter, then, is about women coming up against and struggling within various structures and systems in our society. The most obvious, in a book about health, is the National Health Service, and the way in which the medical profession operates in relation to women. But it is also about how other structures, not directly concerned with health create and perpetuate ill-health. These include the prison system, racist immigration policies, the effects of waged work, and cutbacks in the health service. It also takes into account the heterosexism which underpins the unhealthy sexism of our society.

But within less formalised or powerful structures there are also barriers and oppressions which women come up against in their move towards living fully and at ease. Feminist alternative structures, that is, the way in which we organise *ourselves*, have not been as ideal as they were meant to be. Women with disabilities have consistently criticised the way in which they have been excluded from participating in feminist meetings, projects, jobs and social events by the inaccessibility of venue. They have also pointed out that the way in which many feminist events are organised – noisy, often smoky, and with bad seating – is not exactly conducive to *anyone's* good health.

In *Spare Rib* women initially wrote about their own experiences, and then went on to develop a critique of a system which was seen as white, male, and drug and technology orientated. The medical system was increasingly recognised as one of the mainstays of women's oppression – operating on both an ideological level and a hard daily one. Who pronounced on women's 'raging' hormones, their 'natural' role as mothers, their responsibility to create and maintain healthy families? Who experimented on women with dangerous birth control methods, and suggested *more* tranquillizers as the 'solution' to women's unhappiness and exploitation?

Yet the NHS had been created in the immediate post-war years as one of the most popular aspects of the welfare state; one which is now facing vicious cutbacks. Feminists have been active and forceful in campaigns to save hospitals such as the Elizabeth Garrett Anderson in London. Feminists have also supported and been involved in the trade union struggles of nurses, porters and other ancillary workers within the NHS.

All this has thrown up contradictions, not least the irony of trying to *save* 'the system' we have at the same time been criticising. Could the NHS be changed from within, supported by pressure from without? Could the racist nature of it be challenged in a meaningful way, despite the fact that it is an integral part of a wider racist, sexist and heterosexist society? And was there any real alternative for the majority of people who worked in and used the NHS? In *Spare Rib* these questions were at the heart of many articles, and remain there today.

Although *Spare Rib* has generally stood against any moralistic notion of a hierarchy of oppression in regard to class, race, sexuality and age, it has favoured articles which reveal the reality of different women's lives and relationships in this society. A number of articles have put forward a strong and angry indictment of institutionalised and individual racism in British society, and explored how Black women are treated by the NHS, both as workers and as patients.

Often in *Spare Rib* it was through issues of health that the sexist, racist and class-divided nature of other institutions and structures was exposed. Whether the articles were about women's health in prison (their very lives), or restrictive immigration laws, or the factory or typing pool, or asbestos used to build homes, they used issues concerning health to reveal larger patterns.

'In and Against the System' attempts to convey the possibilities and tensions which feminists face politically as they live within a society which they passionately wish to change. It suggests that our awareness is sometimes jagged and incomplete, and our tactics occasionally at war. It says that some of us have a long way to go if we are to present a truly liberating politics of health. But it also suggests that working with these tensions and contradictions can yield the richest harvest.

Vision and reality – beyond defence of the NHS
An interview with Jeannette Mitchell and Sally Goldsmith by Sue O'Sullivan
SR 95 June 1981

Thinking about health and society is a way in which fragments of experience can begin to mesh together and make sense. We all know that women use the National Health Service more than men. Although feminists have always made demands on and worked within the NHS there's been argument in the women's movement about the best ways to get what women need and to make profound changes. Some women have opposed having anything to do with a male-dominated, hierarchical NHS. Others criticise the politics of asking for handouts or reforms from a state institution.

Now faced with an economic crisis and a reactionary Conservative government hell bent on dismantling the NHS, many women are reviewing the old dilemma. Avoiding the NHS, using self-help and alternatives is fine when it's done through informed choice. But many people don't have other options and there are occasions when anyone might need NHS resources. This recognition does not have to mean a retreat into defending something rotten.

Community Health Councils were set up in the 1974 reorganisation of the NHS to represent the 'interests' of the public. There are over 200 in the country but one survey found that only a small minority of the population knew they existed, let alone what they did. Although they are part of the NHS, their power is limited and their role unclear – they're often referred to as 'toothless watchdogs'.

Jeannette and Sally do believe there is a positive role for their CHC but only if it is stretched to the limit and beyond. Unlike some CHC workers, the women at Brent don't want to be in continual negotiation with the NHS. Their work is directed outward, helping to build up a network of active local groups concerned with Brent's health, who will put pressure on the NHS themselves. They are trying to combine a critique of the quality of the NHS with a battle to keep and extend its facilities. Their feminism and socialism are part of everything they do.

We want to help people define their health needs. We see ourselves as a resource to community groups, offering our facilities and information, making connections. For instance, we know who the feminists are who would speak on birth control at an abortion meeting. We know which pensioner would be useful to which trade union group; it's nothing fantastic but it's useful work and a start.

It's easier to work in small groups at a local level; easier to try out new forms of organisation and action. But we do want to communicate our experiences nationally. We want to argue for doing things entirely differently than in traditional campaigns and in particular campaigns against cuts in public spending. It's building up our experience and strength here in Brent which gives us a 'voice' anywhere else.

We try to incorporate into what we're fighting *for* an idea of something better – an idea of what people actually feel they need. In order to fight people have to believe there's a possiblity of winning. Discussions with local people about the things *they* want made our recent campaign around Willesden General Hospital much more than a defensive manoeuvre. Instead of getting stuck in fighting the closure we developed a big campaign to make it a community hospital. Willesden was popular already but we felt it was essential to incorporate into the fight some sort of innovative and perhaps rather utopian ideas. The pensioners talked about what health care facilities they actually needed and the women's centre developed ideas about a Well Women's Clinic. It became *their* hospital, not the authority's. Somehow you have to incorporate a vision into the fight; otherwise it's very difficult to keep people with you.

You have to admit that people do find our present hospitals oppressive, yet we must still prevent closures. One woman said, 'How can I get women to come out on a demonstration against cuts in the NHS when I know and they know that doctors are going to go on acting the same old way?'

It's only when you're seen to be struggling for something different that you generate support and enthusiasm. Fewer people are coming out against the cuts now than did in 1974 under the Tories. The mass of people have never felt the hospitals were theirs to defend.

We played around with the idea of a hospital until our conception of the meaning of a health care unit started to change. We imagined a hospital not simply treating people as they come in but acting as a resource for people fighting against what's making them ill – a mind blowing idea because it makes a connection which is never made. By not focusing on *what* makes people ill the health service obscures the causes of ill-health in our society.

Feminists have started to reveal the social reasons why women get ill but we need to extend this process. The most obvious example of the social production of ill-health around here is the number of women going balmy having to look after the kids all on their own – there aren't enough nurseries or other childcare facilities, the housing is bad, there's dampness, not enough money. There's a high level of lead around the North Circular Road. There are places of work like Futters, a local factory where Asian and Black women work for low wages in unhealthy conditions. They're coming out in rashes all up their arms; they have problems from breathing in dust.

We were approached by people organising a strike there and we found a doctor who would talk to the women and write an account of the way she thought their working conditions could be a reason for their ill-health. Two Indian women came to the CHC; one of the women took out her bag and emptied it to show us bits of the components from the machines in the factory and she explained how and what exactly she had to do. She had to touch all this oil with metal filings in it. She showed us the rash on her arms. The feminist doctor wrote it all up in a pamphlet called *Black Struggles in Brent*.

If you look at Futters (or Grunwicks, where a mainly immigrant women work force were on strike in 1976–78), the health issue is there. Pregnant women not being allowed to go to the toilet. Blatantly unhealthy conditions. Low wages lead to low health. But the labour movement almost never sees the health aspect; for them it's just called 'wages and conditions'.

In many ways health can be a more concrete way to talk about change than wages because wages don't necessarily question or challenge the basis of the way we live. As feminists we've always had reservations about focusing primarily on wages. We're aware that living standards are related to *how* you live, not just the amount of money coming in. It's not that wage struggles aren't important but that there's so much more to understand. Sometimes the question of wages masks all the other things involved.

People fight shy of contradictions. But things are often tricky and sometimes that very trickiness – sussing it out – can lead to the most fertile ways of struggle. You have to examine contradictions and work your way through them. For example, we don't want old or mentally handicapped people institutionalised. But if they're not in institutions who takes care of them? What's referred to as 'the community' by the planners often turns out to be individual women who are left shouldering the burden. And yet it shouldn't be a question of either individual women 'caring' or of institutionalisation. The women's movement has talked about different ways of living but people are still pretty scared of anything except the nuclear family, and the other side to the 'sanctity' of the nuclear family is usually a state institution.

We're short of beds for the elderly in Brent and we have a small geriatric hospital which is going to be closed soon. It's a dreadful place – people just sit around. They don't get a bedpan, nurses are short-tempered, people can't get privacy. But on the other hand, there are many old people in Brent who need a hospital bed. So, do we defend a hospital which nobody likes, and if we do will the community give us any support?

We've got really militant active pensioners in Brent. Some of them came on the women's health course. They turn out for local demonstrations; in turn the women's centre is supportive and turns out for them. We see that the way the elderly are treated has a lot of similarity to the way women are treated. Fifty pensioners were at our last meeting. People may not always attend a political meeting but they will come to find out about their own bodies and how to deal with the health services.

We decided to take a broad look at services for the elderly, including primary care. We looked at social factors; you can't talk about health for the elderly without talking about pensions. Now we're writing a report with the pensioners. We're going on the offensive. The report will say what pensioners feel about the health service and what they would like to see. For instance they don't want hospitals for geriatrics only. They want Well Pensioner Clinics in the community, with general information about problems which concern them such as eyesight, arthritis, blood pressure, nutrition and bladder trouble.

The document will be demanding things that in the immediate future may not be possible but it will be a document of principle. We'll circulate it to pensioner groups and trade unions and others for support and to find out what specific demands make sense to all the groups – if they find something to fight for together. The trade union wants to fight the closure and we have to involve them in order to push them beyond the defence of jobs into a fight for something better. Arguing out the contradictions and finding mutually acceptable tactics for all the different groups is important and difficult.

Our fantasy is that between the trade unions, the women from the health course, the pensioners, people who've been involved in the community hospital struggle and all the groups which supported it (about 50 including the Methodist Church and the tenants' associations), we have a growing connection. Our fantasy is to create and crystallise a movement of all those people which could give expression to their feelings of resistance.

Questions of health so often go back to the way we live. The government would like us to think it's all about the way individuals choose healthy or unhealthy life styles, but of course that's only a part of a much larger situation in which individual choices are often impossible. If you think about health in a political and collective way it leads quickly to seeing how the whole society has to change. You start thinking about what to do about a particular health issue and suddenly see that there's a lot more that has to be done. We've heard so often that change is the unknown – better stick with what you want, but around health you can sometimes see so well that change could be exciting and not frightening.

The Tories have decided to restore 'profitability'. Tory philosophy isn't interested in any of the long-term effects of the cuts. They're lowering our expectations. 'What right have I to expect a bus to arrive at the bus stop in the morning?' 'What right have I to expect hospitals to meet my needs or my kids' needs?' Women are being stoic about all this. Women have always been the ones who have to manage somehow – but at what cost?

People involved in campaigns against government policy are often looking at cuts in the manner of the 'Cuts Can Kill' slogan. Has anybody died because of the cuts? Have you got any horror stories about the cuts? But what the cuts really mean is a strain and a burden. More work and more worry all the time. It's taking the crisis into individual families' lives, individual women's lives and it's often a very private crisis.

In the end we have to go beyond hospital closures and health cuts and face the fact that it's the whole bloody lot, the whole structure of our society, economy, institutions, male power, everything that has to be changed. We don't want more of the same because our oppression is embodied in the content of these services and the way they're organised. We need the resources but not the power relations. Even in a society which is neither capitalist nor sexist we'll get ill sometimes and we'll take risks sometimes but we'll be making decisions and taking control of our lives. If we take health in the widest way possible, then aa society without oppression is a society with good health. All you can ask of any society is good health isn't it?

Jeannette Mitchell died on 15 October 1986 at the age of 33. In accordance with her wishes, a trust fund is being set up which will give small awards to people with plans for the imaginative and visionary political schemes that Jeannette might have approved of – not only to do with health. The token fee for this article will go to the fund. For more details contact Sally Goldsmith, 37 Melrose Road, Sheffield S3 9DN.

The racist and sexist delivery of the NHS – the experience of Black women
Protasia Torkington
SR 138 January 1984

The oppression of Black women as consumers of the National Health Service cannot be fully understood without the recognition of the basis on which the service is delivered. The National Health Service does not operate in a vacuum but rather within a society whose values and norms it reflects and reinforces. In a capitalist society such as Britain where racial and sexual discrimination exists and is essential to the system, it is to be expected that the delivery of the service will be biased against the working class, women and Black people. In such a situation many Black women will inevitably experience the yoke of triple oppression arising from classism, sexism and racism.

For many women, apart from the class bias, the NHS operates in a sexist way. Women are frequently treated in the most demeaning and dehumanising manner by the medical professionals who often view women's complaints as either trivial or neurotic. This can justify an unsympathetic reaction to menopause problems or the irresponsible prescription of tranquillisers, to name but two examples. Women who have been through ante-natal and labour care know only too well the stress they experienced when subjected to depersonalising and dehumanising care. It is not surprising that such 'care' for many women becomes the *source* of complications – for example, high blood pressure in pregnancy.

My knowledge of the National Health Service is in part based on my own experience as a Black woman and a consumer of the service and in part on my own research work which focuses on the experience of Black people in the National Health Service.

Racism in the health service operates at various levels. In many cases it is covert, but quite often health workers in hospitals, health centres, clinics and surgeries express overt racist attitudes. In saying this I am fully aware that the response of many white people, including the 'liberals' who appear to be genuinely concerned about the welfare of Black people, is a demand for proof that racism does exist. If the kind of proof expected is not forthcoming, the whole question is dismissed with the usual cliches of 'chip on the shoulder' or 'Black people are extra-sensitive'. This response remains prevalent despite the fact that everyone knows the difficulty of coming up with either a written or verbal evidence to prove that discrimination has taken place. This is so because it is very rare in

77

any social context for a Black person to be told that she is treated in a particular way because of the colour of her skin. Because of this, even when discrimination is widespread the victims are rarely in a position to have categorical evidence of the particular cases where it has occurred. *But then for Black people there is no need for this kind of evidence to prove that they are victims of racism.*

For many Black people proof does not only lie in the spoken or written word. Before even a word is spoken the non-verbal communication of eye-contact or eye-contact avoidance, facial expression and body posture have already said something about the attitude of the white person they meet. Even the same word said to other patients may be said to a Black person in quite a different way, conveying different emotional expression, e.g. dislike, impatience, aggression, disgust, etc. Everyone is familiar with the feeling one gets when faced with a hostile or an unfriendly person, and it is precisely that feeling which leads to statements such as 'so and so does not like me'. Quite often such a statement is accepted as true without any concrete proof supporting it. And yet in the field of racism reliance on 'feelings' in defining the existence of discrimination is often questioned.

In the case of Black women, however, the extent of racism and the degree of tension to which it gives rise is not only based on 'feelings' about the racist attitudes of some health workers. In the course of my research I have come across many instances which suggest ill-treatment of Black women in the National Health Service.

For example, a Muslim woman was left in a hospital for two days without food. The ward staff knew she was not eating hospital food but assumed that relatives were bringing her own religiously acceptable food. But nobody actually checked if this was the case. As it happened, her husband was at sea and she had no visitors for those two days in hospital, and nobody told her that she could ask for Muslim food.

In another instance a pregnant woman who was diabetic was admitted for stabilisation with insulin. But she did not like hospital food and therefore requested her husband to bring her food from home. The nursing staff, however, would not let her eat her own food because it was not 'a diabetic diet', but they continued giving her insulin. For two days she lived on crackers and bread and when the dietician was informed it took her three days to find an interpreter which in all meant five days without proper food. All it needed was to substitute hospital food with the food that the patient preferred to eat. In any case the very process of stabilisation should be based on the food that the patient is given to live on after leaving the hospital.

In the above examples the temptation is to explain the experience of these women as arising from cultural differences in food and in language. What must be stressed here is that cultural differences in themselves are not the real problem. The problem arises when white culture is imposed on other groups, and the groups' own cultures are treated as deviant or even bizarre. It is the response by those in power to the difference in culture that is crucial in the experience of some Black women. It would be misleading, however, to see even this racist response to cultural differences as determining the overall experience of Black women in the National Health Service. Many Black women are British-born and their experiences cannot be explained in terms of cultural differences.

On one occasion, for example, a Black in-patient woman asked for painkillers and the staff nurse in charge of the ward ignored her the whole day. Whenever she reminded the staff nurse of the request the staff nurse became very hostile and informed the patient that she knew best when and to whom to give painkillers. There are also many reports of Black women providing their own sanitary towels because if they ask for them in hospitals on many occasions they are ignored or humiliated by the nursing staff.

Clinics and health centres are other areas in which Black women come up against overt racism. One professional Black woman told of how she was left from 12.30 pm to 5.30 pm in a clinic where consultation with the doctor is in the order of arrival. The sister in charge of the clinic pushed her notes to the bottom of the pile. Patients who came long after her were called in to see the doctor. In fact the nursing staff went off duty and it was only when the doctor came out to go off as well that he noticed her and only then was she examined.

In a health centre where consultation is by appointment many Black women find that they wait for hours to be seen by the doctor, and when they do, it is usually not their own doctor but the one the receptionist has decided they should see. Some women decide in the end to leave:

'I had an appointment but I waited for four hours. My baby was quite ill and it is not fun sitting with an ill baby all those hours in the clinic. At the end I just told the receptionist I am going home and the doctor can come home and see the baby. But for those four hours I noticed how badly that receptionist treated Black women. She was really nasty especially to the women who spoke little English. She spoke to them as if they were half-witted children.'

These are just a few of the many examples of what happens to Black women in the National Health Service. There is no doubt room to argue that such experiences arise from factors other than racism. However, reports from Black nurses who not only witness the general treatment of Black patients but also hear what their white colleagues say about Black people generally tends to narrow the scope of this argument.

In London, for example, one nurse told the *Black Workers and Patients Group* about the most appalling treatment a Black man with a stroke received at a hospital. The day nurses left him dirty in a wet bed and relatives cleaned and changed his bed at visiting times. When the Black nurse who worked nights came in and saw the relatives changing the patient and heard what they had to say she asked her white colleague why the man was left in this state, she replied:

'These Blacks are always complaining. They think we are here for them alone. What's more these Blacks stink – their skin goes funny and flaky. It is like fish skin.'

But in fact, as this Black nurse observed, the young student nurse was not the only one with such racist attitudes:

' . . . as the report was given I became acutely aware of how the Black patients were regarded by the nursing staff. The white staff nurse, who was giving the report to us night staff made racist remarks about all four patients in the ward, such as "they are stupid", or "you cannot explain anything to them about their condition because they wouldn't be able to understand". This staff nurse also remarked that if Mr X did not have his curry he got depressed – "He must think this is Calcutta".'

The few examples of the experience of Black women are not isolated instances. My research has revealed many such incidents. It is true that the actual discriminatory acts are committed by individual health workers, but the crucial point to remember here is that it is the system which enables them to behave in a racist, sexist manner. They hold all the power and patients have none, a situation more reprehensive because the ideology within the health service sets health workers as servants of the patients.

The powerlessness of patients which is discernible in their dealings with all health workers is not only confined to the scope of Black women. There is for all patients a barrier between them and the providers of the service. This barrier is maintained and reinforced by constantly pushing patients into a child-like role, passive, dependent, to be seen and worked upon but not heard or consulted. Any attempt on the part of the patient to regain her individuality and adulthood by participating in decision-making which affects her body and welfare is mercilessly put down. At one level therefore the experience of Black women has to be seen in this wider context of the relationship that exists between providers and consumers of the service.

It is often easy to see what is wrong with the system. What I have found to be the most difficult task is to come up with constructive criticism. In the case of Black women, for example, what can be done to change their negative experiences in the National Health Service? The obvious answer is change the system which enables the health workers to have all the power and the patients to have none. But also this is easier said than done. That is not to say that changing the wider system should not be the ultimate objective of all action taken. But this is long-term; in the meantime we Black women are faced with the appalling oppressive experiences, more so than our white counterparts because of the added dimension of racism. In my view there is an obvious need for short-term strategies provided they do not exclude long term strategies. The need to have something done about the racist delivery in the health service seems to have been in the minds of some of those who control resources. The answer for them appears to lie in project work.

In the last five years projects aimed at dealing with racial issues have mushroomed nationally. Many of these projects appear to have as their base a belief that the problem lies in the need for health workers to have more information about Black people, in particular their cultural habits. Some of them accept now that it is not just cultural differences but also that a fair amount of racism is involved, hence the incorporation of racism awareness in their training courses. The crucial point which such an approach misses however, is that health workers are not just sometimes ignorant, but that they are also a very powerful group which wants to keep control in its interaction with the consumers of the service.

Training courses therefore, including racism awareness, are not going to change this unequal distribution of power between the professionals and the patients. Apart from the power conferred on them by the capitalist, racist, sexist structure, professionals oppress consumers through their control of knowledge. It is for this reason that I believe what has a chance of bringing about significant changes, albeit in short terms, is the ability of consumers to challenge, not after the event but as it happens, the behaviour of health workers in hospitals, surgeries, health centres and clinics. This they can do effectively if they have enough information not only about the services they are getting but also about how such services should be delivered and what to do as a group or individuals if they are not satisfied with the services or the way they are delivered.

Even more important is the need for women to have some knowledge about how their bodies work and what can go wrong, and how and to what extent medical intervention can be of help. What I am saying is that if such projects are really concerned with the negative experience of Black women then some of their responses should go towards giving Black women ammunition with which to fight back when faced with an incompetent, racist, sexist health worker. It is only then, when the client group begins to fight back, that the health workers will be forced to put into practice theories of attitude change and racism awareness from the training courses. Until that happens such projects will remain games, but dangerous games because at an ideological level, now armed with greater knowledge about 'cultures of blacks', those in power can comfortably blame Black people when problems remain unsolved.

Although the focus here has been on the experience of Black women, the discussion, I hope, has brought to the foreground the whole question of control and dehumanisation which faces all women in a capitalist and sexist society. It is this society, riddled and sustained by class, race and sex inequalities, which is essential to the production of ill-health. If nothing else, our common experience as women who experience and recognise these inequalities should serve as a platform from which women of all races, creeds and classes will not only share and articulate their experiences but will also fight for their rights within the National Health Service. *White women who do not see the oppression of Black women as their concern must remember that as long as some women are oppressed no woman will be free.*

. . . the causes of illness

The formulation of health policies and the delivery of services at operational level is directed and controlled by male, middle class professionals who have little concern or understanding of working class health needs. The vast number of women health workers, many of whom are of working class origin, make no difference in this pattern. As nurses, their role within the existing system is that of servants, carrying out the orders and wishes of the male, medically dominated health service. This domination is reflected in the way resources are distributed. The bulk of the expenditure of the National Health Service is in the hospital sector, particularly the 'cream' of London teaching hospitals.

The direction of expenditure in these centres is determined by the personal and class interests of those professionals who have fought to the top of the hospital hierarchy. For them an 'interesting' pathology is often more attractive than preventative or social medicine which in the long run would serve the interest of the whole population, particularly those whose health is so negatively affected by economic and social factors. The reality of this link between socio-economic factors and ill health is neutralised by the narrow definition of health employed by most of the medical profession which effectively obscures the economic and social causes of illness. This blinkered conception is influenced by the dominant medical ideology which conceived medical care as a hospital-centred, highly technological provision to be dispensed on an individual basis.

Blaming Black women – rickets and racism
Protasia Torkington
SR 139 February 1984

Rickets is an old disease caused by vitamin D deficiency which in the past crippled many white working class children. In 1920 it was discovered that rickets is caused by lack of vitamin D which the body absorbs from the sun and from food. At the beginning of the Second World War a national campaign was launched to fight the disease. The aim was to fortify such foods as dried milk, cereals and margarine with the vitamin. In addition parents were encouraged to give their children Cod Liver Oil and other vitamin D supplements. The decision to fortify food came as a response to the realisation that reliance on parents to continue giving their children vitamin supplements throughout the pre-school years was not going to be the most effective way of combating the disease.

In 1959 rickets re-emerged, making its first appearance among the children of deprived families in Glasgow, including the Asians who had settled there. A study done in this area showed that infantile rickets, which affects children from six months to three years, occurred in all groups including white children. Children however are not the only victims. It is now known that the adult form of the disease – osteomalacia – affects Asian women, particularly pregnant women, lactating mothers and the elderly. Like infantile rickets, osteomalacia among the elderly affects all groups including the white elderly. This information, however, was ignored by the DHSS in its campaign against rickets which was launched in 1981. The Asian community was singled out.

The problem was located in Asian culture. It was argued that Asian women do not absorb enough vitamin D from the sun because they wear all-embracing saris. In addition the Asian diet was seen as inadequate because, it was pointed out, it contains little vitamin D. The emphasis of the campaign was therefore on encouraging Asian women to expose themselves to sunlight, on changes in diet and on the use of vitamin D supplements. The use of vitamin D supplements which was found inadequate in controlling the disease during the war is now being put forward as an effective method of dealing with the problem. Not only is the government adopting a double standard, but in doing so it is also saying, in effect, that Black women and their children suffer from rickets because of Black women's ignorance. However as Brent Community Health Council has rightly argued, 'white mothers are no better informed than Asian ones about the need for vitamin D in the diet. Yet all the publicity about the inadequacy of Asian diets creates the impression that Asian mothers do not know how to feed their children properly.'

A year after the campaign was launched, the number of those affected by the disease increased from the expected 10 cases per 1,000 to 17 cases per 1,000. So how realistic and effective were the recommendations for the elimination of rickets? Let us have a closer look at them.

Many studies have shown that the great bulk of vitamin D is obtained from the sun. One study confirmed that where there is intense sunlight to which people are exposed for long periods the contribution from the sun can be as high as 80%. But given the nature of the British climate, there is not a great deal of sunlight available. Whatever is available is weak and in any case experts tell us that maximum benefit can only be gained by sunbathing in a bikini. Apart from religious and social considerations which may prevent Asian women from sunbathing in bikinis, there are other practical problems which the DHSS seems to have overlooked. Sunbathing in a bikini assumes the privacy of a back garden, a privilege not enjoyed by many Black people. Many Black people live in poor, crowded, inner city areas with few nearby parks. With racist attacks on the increase not many Asian women will be keen to go out on their own, and even indoors there is a tendency to keep curtains drawn to avoid racist harassment. In any case, as many Asian women go out to work during the day, it would be impossible for them to get out in the sun during the week.

If the all-embracing sari is responsible for the rickets in women, how is the disease accounted for in adolescents who do not wear saris and are exposed to the same amount of sunlight as their white counterparts? Difference in skin pigmentation cannot explain why Asian schoolchildren suffer from rickets. Studies have shown that skin pigmentation is not a major influence in the vitamin D factor. But even if it were children from Africa and the Caribbean, some of whom have darker pigmentation than Asian children, should experience the same problem, and they don't – not to the same extent.

To encourage Asian women to violate their religious values by exposing themselves to the sun is therefore unrealistic not only in terms of the amount of vitamin D that could be obtained from British sunlight but also in terms of the constraints imposed by the social, economic and racist structure of British society. I am not, however, arguing here for cultural relativism. In other words, I am not saying that the Asian culture which encourages women to stay indoors is good for 'them' because it is 'their' culture. On the contrary, I firmly believe that any culture which restricts the movement of a particular group of people is oppressive to that group. But that is a totally different issue to be taken up by Asian feminists and not by the DHSS in its role as the provider of the health service.

In the rickets campaign it was strongly argued that the vegetarian Asian diet lacks vitamin D. Asians were therefore advised to change their food eating habits and adopt an English diet. But such an argument assumes the homogeneity of the Asian people and ignores variations in dietary habits. Although some Asians exclude meat in their diet, very few, mainly Hindu women, abstain from eating fish and eggs. But this in any case would make little difference since fish and eggs as single items have little vitamin D in them. This brings us to the important question of how much vitamin D English people get from their diet.

The average person living on an English diet gets 1% vitamin D from meat, 18% from eggs, 14% from fish, 15% from dairy products and 6% from cereals. The single largest contributor of vitamin D is margarine with 40%. Since 1940 there has been statutory fortification of domestic margarine with vitamin D and the majority of the British public has been ingesting vitamin D without even being aware of doing so. And yet the emphasis on 'educating' Asians gives the impression that white women are better informed about the sources and need of vitamin D in the diet.

The English diet is not rich in vitamin D – it is high on proteins, sugars, fats and refined starch. These ingredients, it is now suggested, are responsible for western diseases such as cancer, diabetes, coronary and other heart diseases. The DHSS in its own pamphlet, *Eating for Health*, exhorts the British public to eat less meat, eggs, fats, sugar and refined starches and increase the intake of fresh fruit, fibres, pulses, etc. This will bring an English diet closer to the present Asian diet and as the *British Medical Journal* pointed out, to ask Asians to adopt a traditional British diet is like asking them to jump from 'a frying pan into the fire'.

What is not explicitly stated in the rickets campaign is the fact that a British diet relies on margarine for its high content of vitamin D. Asians, some of them, prefer butter to margarine. The Asian community has repeatedly asked the government to fortify food that is consumed by Asians, for example chappati flour, milk and butter. The government has refused to do so. The fortification of chappati flour was rejected on the grounds that it would lead to toxicity for those who do not need extra vitamin D among the Asian community. The question of toxicity was not, however, raised when margarine was fortified. Milk and butter were rejected on the same grounds with the additional problem of food adulteration to which the British public might object. But in fact the British public is constantly consuming adulterated foods. Many products in supermarkets are advertised as vitamin-enriched. There is no systematic monitoring of the amount of vitamin D people consume in these products – a surprising attitude in a government which is apparently so concerned with vitamin D poisoning.

All the publicity about the Asian diet and their culture has done little more than blame the victims who suffer because of the DHSS's refusal to fortify foods consumed by the Asian communities.

There is also a reluctance on the part of the DHSS to accept the extent of rickets in the population. It is now well known that osteomalacia, the adult form of the disease, is common among the elderly of all races. There are also studies which suggest that although white teenagers are not showing visible signs and symptoms of rickets, they are nevertheless at risk. It seems to me that sooner or later the government will have to face the one crucial question: is rickets merely an easily identifiable forerunner in the range of deficiency diseases which will in the near future affect *all* those in the low socio-economic bracket irrespective of colour or race?

In this article Protasia Torkington has drawn on the Rickets Report *by Helena Sheiham and Alison Quick, published by Haringey Community Health Council in 1982. This contains a full debate on rickets.*

Letter from Zoë Fairbairns
SR 24 June 1974

Advertisers please read this
Dear Sisters,
I don't know why you published sexist advertisements in *Spare Rib 22*. If it was out of financial necessity, then those of us who object to them will

have to face the fact that either we have sexist ads or we have no *Spare Rib*. But if you didn't see them as sexist and insulting to women, I would like to explain why I felt insulted by them.

Firstly, the Health Education Council's 'Is it fair to force your baby to smoke cigarettes?' Why is this important message, which can only be directed to women, being sold in the time honoured male-oriented way of publishing a picture of a naked woman? Very few women are going to identify with this model. For a start, she's standing in a position in which no one will ever see herself, secondly how many women look that

FIGURE 9 Health Education Council *Advertisement* (*SR* 22 April 1974)

slim and beautiful, are that well-coiffed and made-up during pregnancy, thirdly, how many of us, pregnant or not, *smoke in the nude*? The ad is totally misjudged in its appeal, and strikes me as yet another example of admen taking any opportunity to photograph a nude woman.

But my most serious objection is to the back page ad, again the Health Education Council, this time asking 'How can another woman make you pregnant?' (Answer: by talking to you and giving you bad advice.)

Of course some women get pregnant as a result of bad contraceptive

FIGURE 10 Health Education Council *Advertisement* (*SR* 22 April 1974)

advice, and some of that advice comes from other women. But the most famous lies about contraception: 'Don't worry, I'm sterile' were not invented by women.

The ad also draws a false distinction between, on the one hand, *women* (unreliable sources of advice on contraception) and, on the other, *your doctor or family planning clinic* (reliable). The implication is that Family Planning doctors are male; this will put some women off right away, while it will imply to others that women doctors are less reliable than men.

At a time when women's self-help health groups are growing, and when the women's movement is breaking down distrust between women, I was really sad to see this ad in *Spare Rib*. Incorrect information is a problem, but I think the person who designed this ad got carried away with a snappy slogan; men spread inaccurate information too.

Sickle cell anaemia – women speak out
Dorothea Smart
SR 126 January 1983

WHAT IS SICKLE CELL ANAEMIA?

Sickle cell anaemia is an inherited blood disorder which is regarded as a 'Black' disease, and affects approximately one in 400 of the Afro-Caribbean population, and also people originating from Asia, the Middle East, and the Mediterranean. In the last few years more attention has focused on sickle cell, an illness which is more common than haemophilia or cystic fibrosis. This has highlighted inadequate information, services and treatment.

The illness is inherited from both parents who are usually 'silent', healthy, carriers of a 'trait'. 'Haemoglobin' is the component of red blood cells which carries oxygen to all parts of the body. To inherit sickle cell anaemia, the haemoglobin passed on to the child is 'sickle' haemoglobin, so-called because these cells can change from normal shape to a half-moon/sickle shape. If *both* parents are carriers of sickle cell 'trait' there is a one in four chance that each child could be born with sickle cell anaemia, which is the *illness*. Sickle cell 'trait' occurs when a child inherits the usual haemoglobin from *one* parent and sickle haemoglobin from the *other*. In this case it is not an illness, and *never* changes to sickle cell anaemia, the illness. In fact it offers some protection against a serious form of malaria. The 'trait' is found in one in ten Black births.

Although sickle cell anaemia is present at birth, symptoms do not occur until six months of age, or later. Pain, anaemia and infections are the major problems that may occur in a child with sickle cell anaemia. The main problem is caused by the 'sickling' of the red blood cells. In assuming the 'sickle' shape they also become rigid and can jam up small blood vessels, stopping the flow of blood, causing mild to extreme pain. 'Sickling' occurs when there is less oxygen in the blood, or if the blood becomes too thick due to less water in the body. Therefore 'crises' can occur with dehydration, under anaesthetics, at high altitudes, following strenuous exercise, with stress, and during and after pregnancy. However, often the reason is unknown.

Although there is no cure, problems and complications can be reduced by access to specialist medical care. Common forms of treatment may include drugs for pain relief, antibiotics to prevent or treat infection, folic acid tablets to help produce healthy red cells, and plenty of fluids. Blood transfusions may also be given.

Sickle cell anaemia is a serious illness and can cause early death. However many individuals survive into middle age.

INTERVIEW WITH J, A SICKLE CELL PATIENT

J: I've known I've had sickle cell anaemia since I was 8. I'm now 25. I've suffered with 'crises' for the last four years. They've steadily been getting worse, and with it the disbelief of the profession of my pain. Because you're Black and you're in pain, you come up against a brick wall; they just think, 'This is trouble.' They're reluctant to do much about it.

D: Do you think that if white people suffered, the profession would know more about it?

J: Yeah! that's true if white people got it as well it'd be taken a lot more seriously. If more care was taken then people wouldn't suffer, people may not even have died! Sickle cell [anaemia] is something that can kill! The haemotologists [who treat sickle cell disease] know what they're about, know what they want done with their patients. But, they come up against the sister, registrars and housemen, who are in charge of you on the ward. They write up your chart and see you every day. If you've got a complaint or a question they're the ones you see first. Haemotologists? They 'might' see you every day, but they haven't got as much say, they can only give advice. It's only because I stuck up for myself, causing them trouble, worrying my haemotologist, that they all made decisions together.

D: I think the trouble started with you, over your high doses of pethidine [A painkiller used by the medical profession which can be addictive]?

J: My brother has sickle cell [anaemia], he's been on higher doses! There is this stigma about pethidine, they think I'm going to get hooked every time I go in there! Surely after all the times I've been in there, they should know how much dosage I've had, how much I can take, know that when I'm better I don't want it anymore! They thought that a certain amount of pethidine should cure it, but what it 'should' do and what it actually did was two different things. They don't know the extent of 'sickle' pain.

89

D: So they just assume you're lying?

J: Yeah! I said to a senior staff nurse, 'They're never going to believe me.' After the blood transfusions, injections, and everything else, I was still in a load of pain. They just couldn't understand it! In the end they started giving pethidine to me through the vein, because they realised the injection wasn't getting to me any more! So they contradict themselves.

D: Do you think if you were a Black man things would have been different?

J: I met a man in hospital, we were on the same ward for a couple of days. He appears to have had no trouble. My brother goes to a different hospital admittedly, but their attitude is completely different, they take him a lot more seriously. They know that when he's in pain, when he asks for an injection, asks for help, he needs it! More often than not it's, 'Do you need . . .?', 'Are you in pain. . .?' Whereas I had to demand, and maybe two hours later I'd get it. By then I was in double the pain – so that's what they call being 'hysterical'!? Being left in pain!

D: You couldn't win either way, if you kept quiet you weren't in pain anyway!

J: Right! And when I said something I was being 'hysterical'.

D: When you came on my ward, one of the senior nurses said you were 'trouble' when she'd nursed you before. So they all formed this idea of you being a 'problem'.

J: On that ward I reported one staff nurse. After that the sister 'advised' me to ask for a transfer. She knew that if I reported her again, she'd be out. She didn't want that, so she was telling me 'You can get lost', her nurses were more important than her patients!

D: Exactly the same thing followed you up to the other ward?

J: Yeah! I thought I was going to get a fresh chance. But no matter how they change the nurses around, your records are always there, so you're gonna have the same problems. I can't go on to either of the two wards I've been on and feel sick and have them believe it. I've never had any trouble on the other ward, but I know it followed me, just because of one nurse. A Black student nurse told me a lot of the nurses were scared of me; they didn't want anything to do with me. Anything that had to be done for me they looked to her to do it. One night I had an enema and a staff nurse came in and saw me dripping wet with sweat. I just didn't know what to do! I was on the verge of passing out. I tried to hold her hand, she didn't want to hold my hand. This was so clear to me. She just left me there! Two juniors found me, one of them was the Black nurse. I went through a lot with her, she treated me differently; it shouldn't have made any difference, they were all nurses.

Sometimes I knew my water was coming from an ordinary tap instead of the drinking tap, so we'd spill it behind the curtains so she could refill it. Things like that we had to do for me to survive on the ward. I had to fight. A lot of the time I nearly gave up. After four or five weeks it's no joke any more! I got to the stage where I didn't care what they thought, trouble or no trouble. Being polite was getting me nowhere, so I'd rather drive them mad and get me somewhere!

INTERVIEW WITH ELIZABETH ANIONWU

E: You asked me if there were any difference between the incidence of sickle cell disease amongst men and women. It's equally distributed. What is interesting is that studies in the United States, and my own experience in this country, seem to show that women cope more with illness. They don't seem to be admitted as frequently. Amongst our group, offhand, I can think of more women who are working, studying and bringing up families, despite the illness, and appear fairly well 'adjusted' to the fact they have a chronic illness. Whereas men don't appear to have adjusted so well. This does affect the nursing care they get. It is the men who are having much more difficulty, classified as 'problem' patients. Your interview with J doesn't accord with this though.

D: Could you say something about pethidine, as this is where her trouble began.

E: In talking about pethidine we have to talk about pain as the main problem in this illness. The pain is commonly experienced in the long bones of the body, but also the abdomen, chest and back are frequently affected. The major problem is the professionals! I don't think they understand why there should be pain – what type of pain. Pain is a very difficult thing to judge and yet when I give lectures to student nurses about it, I ask them would they accept that a person having a heart attack has pain? Oh, and there's total acceptance; everybody's sympathetic.

But when it comes to sickle cell disease, there's no doubt in my mind that nurses do not believe the patient is in pain! Also there is an incredible amount of fear amongst health workers that they are going to make drug addicts out of patients if they give them pethidine as frequently as the specialists, who are geared up to sickle cell, would like. A Black student nurse told me of a patient who had been given water by injection, based on the assumption that this patient really didn't have the pain and was just playing up! This is a frightening indictment on nursing and on the care of Black patients, because underlying all this is, firstly, the ignorance of the profession about sickle cell which affects Black people. Secondly, although there is quite a lot of literature in the medical press now, how come we still find this degree of ignorance? Overriding this are attitudes towards Black people as a whole which all tumble up in the care of sickle cell disease. What nurses and doctors have got to accept is that the pain involved can be very severe. Most patients, if you take the trouble to ask them, are frightened of the battle of words and thoughts between the patient and the medical staff that is going to take place once they are admitted. That battle is about whether people believe them.

According to some nurses you get the 'clock-watching' syndrome, when a patient is prescribed pain relief four-hourly, and the patients find that they're needed that frequently, or even *more* frequently. Some specialists will prescribe drugs 'PRN' (whenever they're required). This causes eyebrows to be raised because of fear of drug addiction. But once the patient trusts that the staff believe she has pain, our experience is that less drugs are prescribed during the hospital admission.

Patients with this illness are in and out of hospital. They know the situation on the ward, that a student nurse may not be the best person to approach, but they also know that possibly the only way they can get any relief is by being a 'problem' patient, making very loud, aggressive demands on the nursing staff. They don't come in acting like this! It's the constant experience of not being believed.

I, and a lot of medical staff involved with sickle cell disease, are deeply concerned about this, because pain is pain and why should the profession have this position of power and control in relieving such a distressing symptom!

Dorothea Smartt, ex student nurse, Black feminist and Sami, active in London.

The immigration officials just laughed: atrocity at Heathrow
Amrit Wilson
SR 55 February 1977

The only Black people now admitted to Britain are dependants of people long settled here, and these dependants are mainly wives and children. It is against them that the British government's range of immigration procedures is currently aimed.

To come to Britain as a wife, an Asian woman must first get an entry certificate from a British High Commission in India, Pakistan or Bangladesh. This involves an interview for which she must wait on average two years. At the interview she must prove that she is the wife of the man she intends to join.

For this women have been forced to have sexual examinations, to give details through male interpreters of what happened on their wedding nights, and to explain why they want to join their husbands in Britain. Their statements are rarely given the slightest importance unless they can be used to catch them out.

The proportion of women wrongly rejected when they do finally get an interview is shown by a Runnymede Trust study – of 57 cases of entry certificate rejections examined, 55 were of those who had right of entry.

In Britain the same sort of brutality is being repeated behind the locked doors of the immigration detention centres. Zahira Galiara's story illustrates this. She is 18, a Muslim and comes from Bardoli, a village not far from Bombay. Her husband Aszal, whom she had known at school, is 21 and has lived in Britain for the last five years. They got married last January and on 20 October flew to Britain, reaching Heathrow at 1p.m.

They were held up by immigration officers. Aszal had all the documents required of a returning resident; he was questioned and made to wait for four hours, then told he could go. Zahira, who had her marriage certificate, had as a spouse a right to enter Britain. But because she didn't have an entry certificate from the British High Commision in Bombay, immigration officers would not let her in.

Although in an advanced state of pregnancy, she was questioned and made to wait for the next 12 hours without food or water. At one at night she was told she must go to a detention centre. Aszal was forbidden to accompany her because 'at this place men are not allowed'. 'Tomorrow morning,' they told her, 'you will be put on a plane back to Bombay.'

Zahira was taken to Harmondsworth detention centre (a building where on average 30 to 40 men, women and children are held, some for days, others for months, while the Home Office decides whether they are to be let in or sent back). 'I was taken to a room,' Zahira told me, 'which I had to share with three others, two Indian women and one black man. I just lay there completely exhausted. I could not sleep. That night I started having labour pains.'

In the morning she was taken to Queen's Building detention centre at Heathrow where Aszal was waiting for her. They asked to see a doctor. About 11 a.m. Zahira said she was taken to another part of the building where she was superficially examined. Though she speaks no English, Aszal was not allowed to accompany her. The doctor's opinion was that she was fit to travel; she would be put on a plane at 3.30.

'When she came back from the doctor,' Aszal says, 'she was crying in pain, but the immigration officials and Securicor men (who guard all detention centres) just laughed and said she was pretending because she didn't want to be sent back.'

Even when Zahira was screaming in pain they refused to call a doctor. Aszal, who tried to call an ambulance from a public phone box, was stopped by a Securicor guard. Only when the baby's head began to emerge was a doctor sent for. 'By the time he arrived,' says Aszal, 'the baby was half out, the only people to help were myself and an Indian cleaning woman.'

Zahira and her baby, a girl, were eventually taken to Ashford hospital. But the baby was premature and according to the hospital born with severe abnormalities. It died soon after. Zahira was given permission to stay on in Britain.

The Galiaras are now considering legal action against the Home Office. Racist immigration procedures are implemented by immigration officials, some of whom have been shown to be members and supporters of the National Front, but the Home Office is responsible for their actions.

On 20 November there was a demonstration outside Queens Building detention centre protesting against the treatment Zahira received. As a letter in *SR 54* pointed out, it would have been good to see more women's groups there. Interestingly, the Minister with Special Responsibility for Immigration (and the sexist immigration law) is Shirley Summerskill, who represented Britain at the United Nations Status of Women Commission.

FIGURE 11 Sitting in at Heathrow Airport in protest against 'virginity tests' on Black immigrant women *Angela Phillips* (*SR 83* May 1979)

Immigration tests in Britain and India
SR 81 March 1979

The uproar over the harassment and humiliation of Black immigrants may be dying down in the press, but Black people's organisations are determined to keep the protests going.

The Asian women's group AWAZ (which means 'voice' in Hindi) organised a demonstration at Heathrow airport on 10 February, calling for a public inquiry into the workings of the immigration service.

It is not just a question of winning concessions – getting virginity tests or X-ray tests banned – though these would be important steps. The demonstration also demanded that the ministers and immigration officers responsible be made accountable for their actions, and asked whether the

FIGURE 12 Indian women protest in Delhi *Subhadra Butalia*
(*SR 81* March 1979)

Labour government condoned the present police state situation where people have to show their passports to get medical treatment, to claim welfare benefits, even to send their children to school.

As a result of pressure, Merlyn Rees now claims he has put a stop to virginity tests, both here and in the Indian sub-continent (though since he says he never knew they were happening, it's strange that he thinks he can control them now). On 10 February, Foreign Office Minister Evan Luard said such tests were not carried out on women at British posts overseas. However, he did admit 'two possible exceptions to this' and assured the Commons that it would never happen again.

But on 21 February, External Affairs Minister Atal Bihari Vajpayee told the Indian Parliament that there had been at least 34 cases of virginity testing at the British High Commission there. Angry Indian MPs called this 'rape' and 'criminal assault', and David Stephen, political advisor to the Foreign Secretary, scurried off to India and Bangladesh to try to patch up relations.

The other big embarrassment has been X-ray testing, exposed in the *Guardian*. Would-be immigrants are being subjected to X-rays, supposedly to prove – by bone age estimates – whether they're telling the truth about their age and identity. Since the 1971 Immigration Act, only the dependants of Black immigrants already here are allowed to come to

Britain to stay. Before admission they have to get entry certificates issued at the British High Commission in the country they are coming from. Trying to get these certificates is an ordeal that can take years.

Entry certificate officers go to great lengths to 'prove' that children are too old to have the right of entry as dependants. And to prove she is the person she claims to be, married to the man she claims to be married to, a wife may have to face many personal and sexual questions, as well as being subjected to medical examinations. One case documented was of a pregnant woman whose skull was X-rayed. The doctor concerned claimed he could accurately assess age by seeing how far the sutures of the skull had closed up – a highly disputable claim. And DHSS regulations forbid the use of X-rays on pregnant women except in extreme emergencies, because of the danger to the foetus. With the risk of radiation, X-rays should be used only when medically essential. In these cases there is no excuse.

The government now claims to have stopped X-ray tests on pregnant women in the Indian sub-continent. But what about non-pregnant women and children? And what about tests still being carried out here?

Another issue that came up was that of immigrants from 'certain countries' being given chest X-rays to see if they are carrying a contagious disease. The tests are done by clerks not registered as radiographers. A *Guardian* article quoted the clerks' union NALGO as saying that if the clerks stopped giving X-rays they would lose additional money and job interest! They threatened industrial action if more radiographers were taken on.

The next day NALGO, in an official statement, said their members were not involved in the gynaecological tests, which the union deplores. They also say the clerks are sufficiently qualified, as they've been doing X-rays for 12 years – but nowhere elsein the NHS are people not registered as radiographers allowed to do X-rays. It's no coincidence that it's in the immigration service that standards are lowest.

Four groups who supported the demonstration at Heathrow – AWAZ, the Black Socialists Alliance, the Indian Workers' Association (GB) and the Brixton Black Women's Group – have since formed a 'committee against racist immigration procedures and police harassment'. They are planning a major demonstration for 8 April, organised entirely by Black women. The women feel this autonomy is important, though they want the support of Black men and of white people, 'so long as they're prepared to take a lead from Blacks'. There were disappointingly few white feminists on the last demonstration, so this is an opportunity to show support.

Subhadra Butalia reports from New Delhi:
A wave of indignation swept the country as the Indian press flashed the news of vaginal examination of a woman seeking immigration to the UK. Leading newspapers condemned the practice as obnoxious and 'yet

another shocking evidence of the racial discrimination practised in the UK against coloured people'.

Women's organisations in Delhi, Madras, Bombay, Pune and other parts of the country held emergency meetings and assailed the British immigration policy which commits assault on the female body. They demanded immediate withdrawal of this hateful practice and an apology from the British government.

In Delhi, more than 300 teachers and students of Delhi University and Jawahar Lal University stormed the British High Commission building. They flourished placards which said, 'Castrate Heathrow Rapists', 'We'll Fight You On Our Land', 'Down With British Racism'. They compelled High Commission officials to come out and receive the memoranda, which condemned the increasing wave of racism in Britain and demanded better conditions of work and living for their countrypeople settled there.

While Britain's smug indifference continues to agitate Indians, activists have been putting forth proposals to fight this evil in their land and ours. One definite proposal is the formation of liaison committess to be posted at all entry points in Britain. They should have the power to assist the immigration machinery and also to look into and sort out the problems of immigrants. The other is a retaliatory measure coming from militant groups which says that the government of India should impose the same controls on Britons entering India. What they do to our people there, we should do to theirs here. What has Britain to say to that?

Women are dying in prison
Chris Tchaikovsky (Women in Prison)
SR 135 October 1983

It is nine years since the word went around D Wing . . . 'Pat Cummings?who?/burned to death/last night/in her cell/in the Obs/Christ/screws bent her bell back/couldn't hear her rings for help/wouldn't answer if they did/fucking bastards/the prison officer reckons she was a nutter/we're all nutters to them/right/what we going to do about it/can't let them get away with it. . . .'

Patricia Cummings burned to death in 1974 in Holloway Prison, the old Holloway that is. Today that Victorian building no longer exists. The new prison looks good. A council estate? A college? It blends neatly with the modern library next door. Things have moved on; it's clean, got a gym, a progressive drug unit, education, welfare departments, a new governor and women don't stay too long. Holloway is a short-timer or 'local' prison. So why are women gathering outside the prison every month and why are we lobbying the GLC and women MPs at Westminster to do something? Because, for all the glass and new bricks, NOTHING has changed . . . women in Holloway are still dying from mistreatment and neglect.

Julie Potter, dead. Died 1981 in Mount Vernon Burns Unit five weeks after a fire in her Holloway cell. Christine Scott, dead. Died 1982. Injuries sustained from throwing herself around her cell for *up to 24 hours*; final fatal blow from throwing herself from radiator to floor. An anonymous Belgian woman, dead. Died 1982. Heart failure/asthma attack. No asthma spray permitted in her cell in the 'hospital' wing. No medication given for her heart condition. Refused permission to contact her GP to confirm the need for medication. By the time they got to her, attended her with a spray, produced an empty oxygen bottle – she had died. Another death, 1981. A woman dying in a burning cell while two screws go off to ask the night officer what to do, without unlocking her door.

What the fuck is going on in the new Holloway? We know the officers have been issued with smoke hoods and there are procedures to follow before doors can be opened. We know the Home Ofice intend to issue flame-proof mattresses. The foam manufacturers say that they cannot be set alight, and *if they are*, give off non-toxic fumes. Who is kidding who? Women still earn so little in prison they split their matches (lighters are supposedly allowed but no one has any in Holloway). An adept splitter can get four lights from one match but slivers of the sulphur-tipped wood fly about. The observant might notice small burn holes in women's jumpers, skirts . . . bedding. Male prisoners make 'fishermen's lights' (tubular brass container, thick rope-like wick, flint, no flame) in their workrooms. Women do not have this facility. Death from burns, or death by sexism?

The Home Office is touchy and refuses point blank to discuss women prisoners; mother and baby units; Borstal girls who continue to mutilate themselves, unpicking the stitches after their cuts have been sewn together.

Prison stinks. The sanitary facilities at Durham prison are the same as those in the old Victorian Holloway. The women at Durham are subject to every screw-obstacle possible, because there are five high-security women in the prison. Security, lack of staff, the same excuses are trotted out for every 'right' denied, every 'privilege' lost. No prisoner wants to be transferred to Durham, or to Styal. But Cookham Wood, a model prison built for men but turned over to cope with extra women prisoners, has its own horrors. A hi-tec prison, with electronically opening – and closing – doors. A central control room, womanned by smiling prison officers. Concentration style 'open' fencing topped with barbed wire over civil-service-green supports . . . you can see the outside. Cookham hums like this typewriter I'm using, I wouldn't want to live with this hum around my bars for a week, let alone forever: the possibility facing one life at Cookham.

If we need an example of women's invisibility we need look no further than women in prison. Women prisoners are the least protected group in society. There are some 1,500 women serving sentences and over 3,000 moving through the prisons every year. They live in secret 'autonomous

FIGURE 13 Education authorities, church and doctors, all gagged by the Official Secrets Act *Illustration from a Women in Prison calendar* (*SR 135* October 1983)

states'. Our campaign is based around opening prisons up and freeing them from Home Office control. We believe women prisoners must have access to the National Health Service and to *call* the other outside social agencies. We are not alone in our belief, there are staff within the prison system who want to see changes as much as we do, but they are not allowed to say so. The Official Secrets Act keeps them all gagged, they are, primarily, civil servants and can say nothing which might 'embarrass' the Minister.

It is the Home Office we are after. Of course we are campaigning for women prisoners' rights, but without decontrolling prisons we can do very little. We refuse to accept that in 1983 every detail of the lives of over 3,000 girls, women and their babies and children should be subject to the complete control of one man and his secretariat.

When Patricia Cummings died in 1974, we shouted, barricaded, went on strike, formed the Prisoners' Action Group. They pulled us away from the Home Office inquirers, split us up, threatened women with loss of parole, took away our work, our smokes, our association, put us 'behind the door'. In the end we bought a bunch of flowers in remembrance, every woman that could gave 5p. They separated the flowers and placed them among others – theirs – in the prison chapel.

Nursing – behind the painted smile
Jane Salvage
SR 153 April 1985

In her book *The Politics of Nursing*, Jane Salvage takes apart the carefully nurtured myths, and draws a picture of a group of health workers under severe stress. Here she describes the images and reality of who nurses are.

The nurse in uniform is instantly recognisable, and even very small children draw pictures of Nurse in a white cap and apron. Uniforms themselves exert a kind of fascination and it's not surprising that the combination of uniformed women, high drama and illness and death should have made the nurse such a popular figure in the media.

Films, novels, newspapers, documentaries, soap operas, cartoons, recruitment advertising and even get well cards all bombard us with images of the nurse. And despite the variety of sources, and the many different kinds of nurses and nursing work, these images are remarkably consistent. They focus not on what the nurse does but on the way she is supposed to look – female, uniformed, young, white. She is seen not as a skilled worker who tries to do a difficult and complex job, but as a selfless ministering angel whose devotion to the doctor and whose tireless efficiency as his handmaiden enable him, the true professional, to do his job while she soothes the patient's fevered brow.

There are some exceptions, of course; moreover the image of the nurse could more accurately be described as a cluster of stereotypes, a complex series of interconnected images. All have one thing in common, though – the nurse is female.

Angels, battleaxes and sex symbols are the three groups into which most of the images fall. Angels appear so often that in Fleet Street the word is used synonymously with nurses. Innocent, unselfish, utterly dedicated to caring for the sick, they always put service before self; everyone agrees they have been exploited and should be protected, but no one suggests that they should take their destiny into their own hands. Their submissive nature can perhaps be traced back to one of nursing's roots, the religious orders which provided much of the early institutionalised care. Even the title 'sister' harks back to the convent, as do the chaste white uniforms and starched caps – some hospitals still provide caps which look very like nuns' veils.

Today, the vocational qualities vested in the angel figure are often emphasised to nursing students as their suggested professional goal. Dedication and service to others are put alongside patience, compliance, and a refusal to be ruffled or to show feelings of anger or hurt. The 'good nurse' does not complain but accepts with grace and composure everything thrown at her, and self-sacrifice is seen as a virtue – to the point where nurses are even heard to argue that raising wages would attract the wrong kind of people into nursing, and that low pay ensures getting 'the right kind of girl' who works not for money but for altruism.

The angel label is also an easy way for the public to show their gratitude for the work nurses do. Many patients are genuinely grateful and admiring: 'I wouldn't do your job for a million pounds.' Governments, too, use the same kind of language. Many nurses like this image of themselves, and fail to see that it has become a substitute for positive action to improve their pay and conditions. Moreover, the constant repetition of the praise is stale and ultimately devalues the virtues it is supposed to prize. If all nurses are angels simply because they are nurses, not because they do the job especially well, it's an empty compliment.

Another problem with the angels is that they tend, unless rescued by marriage, to age into battleaxes. The dedication which is depicted so charmingly in the soft young nurse turns into fanaticism in the middle-aged spinster, shown in the image of the fierce ward sister who insists on having the beds in a straight line and makes the junior nurses cry. Like the angel images, these dragons are a nurse version of a stereotype often applied to women in general – old maids who, failing to marry and have children as women 'should', turn sour and vent their frustrations in petty tyranny. These sisters and matrons are never shown organising the ward work or using their clinical skills; instead, they sweep through the ward while everyone stands to attention, like Hattie Jacques in *Carry On Doctor*, or become evil manipulators like Big Nurse in Kesey's *One Flew Over the Cuckoo's Nest*, who gets her revenge on men by terrorising her patients.

The angel and the dragon are old favourites, but in the last 20 years they have been joined by a third stereotype which has become the most popular of all – the nurse as sex symbol. Barbara Windsor in the *Carry On* films is perhaps the best known (and her sexy nurse is interchangeable with all the other dumb blonde characters she portrays), but there are many other examples of the feather-brained female who wears black stockings and whose main interest is flirting with the houseman. Newspapers love pin-ups of nurses in bikinis, captioned 'What the doctor ordered . . .', and the busty nurse is a favourite subject of seaside joke postcards, get well cards and even, one year, the trade union COHSE's Christmas card. Just a bit of fun? These images are the more acceptable end of a spectrum extending to pornographic films which have nurses as the focus of male erotic interest. *Naughty Night Nurses* and similarly titled films are often to be seen in the cinema clubs of Soho.

These images are all a distortion of reality. Not only do they fail to reflect the daily concerns and problems of the people who nurse, but they belittle nurses by describing them in stereotyped ways. They only tell part of the story, remaining silent about the fact that many nurses are male; that much nursing takes place outside hospital surgical wards and casualty departments; that many nurses are West Indian, Asian or Black British citizens; and that nursing is more than passing scalpels to the doctor, taking temperatures and wiping bottoms.

Most of all, the images sanitise nursing and deny the real hardship and stress of the work. Dealing with the physical and mental needs of numerous patients on a single shift, at a time when most wards are understaffed and the length of stay in hospital is going down, is physically and mentally shattering for the nurse. At the best of times it is a demanding job, and in current circumstances the nurse's ability to cope with those demands is eroded by her knowledge that she cannot do the job as well as she would like to. But what does she feel, confronted by the images of hospitals where the nurses have time to chat up doctors and run errands for them? Perhaps she comes to feel that it is somehow her fault if the job seems more like drudgery than romance.

The myths also give a false impression of what health care is all about. The stereotype nurse is likely to work in a hospital ward caring for surgical patients or others with diagnosed diseases from which they will soon recover, but the NHS actually deals with many other problems. Over half its beds are occupied by people with long-term problems caused by old age, mental or physical handicap or mental illness. In romantic novels and comedy films, however, doctors cure diseases, nurses clear up the mess and hold the patient's hand, the patient goes home well, and nurse and doctor celebrate by getting married.

In reality the doctor often does not know what the disease is, or may be unable to do more than alleviate the symptoms. Medicine can do nothing about the factors which cause so much illness today – such as bad housing, unbalanced diets, unsafe conditions at work, accidents, addictions or stress. Hospital stay for many people, like the 'revolving door' patients in psychiatric hospitals, does not produce cures, but only patches up the damage sufficiently to enable the ill person to go home – and face the same risks all over again.

Nurses are rarely shown working in the community, except for the occasional motherly district nurse on her bike. In fact about one nurse in ten works outside the hospital, doing such diverse jobs as supporting families with a mentally handicapped child, checking schoolchildren's eyesight, helping women look after their babies or counselling people with psychiatric problems. In hospital, the work is equally varied, and even on the surgical ward or theatre beloved by scriptwriters, its scope is enormous.

All this may seem obvious but it is important because it gives people a false picture of what nurses are like and what they do. People accustomed to seeing the nurse in the role of doctor's handmaiden will tend to treat them that way when they become patients, and they may not realise that good nursing care is as vital as medical expertise. They will look at the doctor, not the nurse, for advice and authoritative information, a reinforcement of the status quo which preserves the doctors' dominance of most forms of health care – possibly the biggest single obstacle to progress.

Nurses, too, are affected by the images. Many new recruits expect hospital life to resemble a *Dr Kildare* programme and the effort of readjusting their ideas to what they actually do find can be very painful. Even if they themselves manage to adjust and to develop a more realistic attitude to their work, they find that others refuse to accept it. If you are told enough times that you should act as surrogate mother, wife and mistress to both doctors and patients, you might end up believing it.

Some information is available on the numbers of men and women in nursing, but like many of the other figures, it is patchy. The General Nursing Council documented the gender of nurses between 1955 and 1971, and although the statutory bodies no longer do this, it is possible to draw some inferences from the GNC statistics. During those years, men made up between 4.3% and 6.4% of the successful candidates for the general part of the register. Overall, though, they now comprise around 10% of the nursing workforce, a proportion which appears to be dropping despite the growing numbers of men coming into the occupation.

The percentage of men in fact varies with grade, geographical region, and speciality. Generally speaking, the more senior the grade, the greater the proportion of men: they are much more likely to stay in the profession after qualifying, and they are promoted out of all proportion to their numbers. Thus there is only about one male to every 19 female nursing auxiliaries and assistants (1980 figures, England only); one male to every 10 female students; and one male to every five female registered nurses in all specialities. In senior jobs the figures are the most startling, with nearly half the top management and education posts occupied by men (though with enormous regional variations).

Further evidence of this male takeover (or, as has been suggested, this 'female giveaway') comes in the staffing of the statutory bodies, professional organisations and trade unions, and the membership of their councils and committees. The higher echelons of the trade unions have always been dominated by men, even in the public sector unions where women make up the bulk of the membership. The Confederation of Health Service Employees, traditionally, it is true, a stronghold of psychiatric nurses, had at the time of writing a male president, vice president, general secretary and deputy general secretary; only one woman holding one of six national full-time posts; no female regional full-time posts; no female regional secretaries; and only three women on its 28-strong executive council – yet around 78% of its members are women.

Nursing was one of the first occupations to look to overseas workers to boost labour shortages: the recruitment of 'aliens' as nurses began as early as 1941, and by 1949 – the year the NHS was founded – local

103

selection committees to recruit nurses and midwives had been set up in 16 British colonies. Unemployment and the deepening crisis of racism in the 1980s are creating new and adverse conditions for migrant workers as well as for indigenous Blacks, but they are still a vital part of the nursing workforce in many areas, especially in lower grades in the hierarchy and in unpopular specialities such as geriatrics and mental handicap.

Nurses who entered the UK on student visas to do their training are now being refused work permits if they decide they want to stay. Another trend is that Black recruits, wherever they were born, are encouraged to undertake training for enrolment rather then registration – even though they may have the necessary qualifications to enter the registration programme. This not only deprives them ultimately of the chance of promotion in UK hospitals, but may bar them from nursing work in their own countries. Hard evidence is lacking but Black nurses claim that channelling them into EN training is a covert form of racism.

Cherill Hicks, a journalist who carried out one of the very few investigations of racism and nursing, pinpoints the existence of two different worlds – a yawning gap between nurse managers' perception of race relations in the NHS, and the experience of Black nurses themselves. Anecdotal evidence suggests that Black nurses face repeated job rejection, difficulties in getting accepted for post-basic courses, and little hope of promotion. It all points to the existence of widespread institutional racism in the NHS. Despite strong statements from Black nurses themselves and the signs of deepening discrimination, the NHS and nursing in particular have made almost no effort to promote anti-racist policies and practices.

Things are not looking good for the poor old NHS. But how is the individual nurse faring amid all these problems? As part of the only group of people in direct contact with patients round the clock, she really is working at the sharp end, experiencing the effects of these policies and attempting to make good their deficiencies. What of her own personal survival?

Nurses are keeping the service going only at great personal cost. People going into a badly paid job like nursing and knowing they will work very hard on unsociable shifts may have low expectations, but even so there are many signs that nurses, traditionally uncomplaining and self-effacing people, are finding it hard to keep going. All the evidence suggests a great sea of unhappiness, or an iceberg whose tip appears in wastage rates or professional conduct committees but whose bulk is unseen and largely unheeded.

In many ways nurses are the victims of being part of a large labour force with a very high turnover. There are simply so many nurses, and so many of them changing jobs or ward placements so often, that they are treated as expendable, since for every one who drops out or disappears another always comes to take her place. It is hard to get across the message that the problem is a collective and not an individual one, although some individualised responses to tackling stress can be extremely helpful. The problems are experienced individually and pressure is felt by the individual nurse, rather than nurses as a group. Yet to achieve widespread success in fighting stress and indeed in preventing it, we must learn to think and act together. This does not mean smothering disagreement, but it does mean taking responsibility together, acknowledging the shortcomings of the system and trying to change it, being alive to each other's needs and ensuring that we evolve good mechanisms for support and prevention. This starts with the acceptance that the nurse who suffers the ill-effects of stress is not a weak, feckless, unsuitable or irresponsible individual, but the victim of a largely uncaring and unthinking system. To alleviate stress in nursing we have to change that system, and start by changing it from within.

This is an edited extract from Jane Salvage's book The Politics of Nursing *published by Heineman, London 1985. It was written with the support of the Radical Nurses Group.*

Men as midwives
Letters from readers
SR 120 July 1982
SR 122 September 1982

'MALE MIDWIVES MOVE IN'
from Maureen Edwards

Dear *Spare Rib*,
A recent DHSS circular has floated the idea of removing present statutory restrictions on the training and practice of male midwives. Few women will be aware of this move and consequently will be unaware of the urgent need to oppose it.

At an all-woman subcommittee of our local Community Health Centre we discussed this and decided:

(1) Midwifery was the only remaining area in which women retained some degree of health control.

(2) During the pregnancies, childbirth and post-natal period women see a succession of doctors and gynaecologists who are invariably men. The only constant female health worker is the midwife.

(3) Midwives are the key figure in community care. They contact women at their most vulnerable. Many women would find a man unacceptable.

(4) Whenever professions are opened up to men they take advantage of their unimpeded careers (no children, etc.) and quickly rise to the top of the hierarchy. Nursing, social work, teaching all have largely female grass root workers and male nursing officers, directors of social work, head teachers.

(5) The Sex Discrimination Act was intended as a positive aid to disadvan-

taged women, not to open up small specialist areas such as midwifery to men.

The women of our subcommittee were outvoted by men at a full council meeting. However we do intend to fight on. If you can, please write direct to the DHSS. Lobby your own MP (Joan Barnett has taken up our protest) and let your local Community Health Centre know of your views.

'MEN AS MIDWIVES – WHY NOT?'
from Elly Alexander

Dear *Spare Rib*

While I can sympathise with the concern expressed by Maureen Edwards about the possible encroachment of men in the field of midwifery, I feel the argument is muddled and, more importantly, sidetracks the main feminist issues.

(1) Retaining midwifery as an exclusive female occupation does not guarantee women control over their personal health in this area when, at the moment, as a profession, they 'manage' births, and are often defensive to women who wish to participate as at least equal partners in the event.

(2) We should not argue that because most of the doctors and gynaecologists are men that all midwives should be female, but for opportunities for more women to become doctors and gynaecologists which, of course, means a change in socialisation and education patterns.

(3) Women should not have to put up with the succession of unfamiliar professional faces during pregnancy, childbirth and the post-natal period, but should have one constant health worker to be present at the delivery with whom they can discuss how they want to have the birth, etc. Many women would prefer this person to be a woman and should have the right to be able to refuse any midwife they are not happy with.

(4) We must fight to open up the promotional opportunities in all careers to women by more imaginative childcare arrangements, etc, not divert our energy trying to preserve one all-female profession.

(5) The Sex Discrimination Act was intended as a positive aid to disadvantaged women, but if we defend the exclusion of men from midwifery on the basis of sex we are breaking a link in the person's opportunities and choices on the basis of gender – which is surely the main tenet of feminist ideology.

'AND DEFINITELY NOT!!!'
from Elizabeth Cockerell

Dear *Spare Rib*,

Thank you for publishing the letter about plans to admit men to midwifery.

As Maureen Edwards indicated, it is inevitable that, once admitted, men will appropriate many key posts within the hierarchy, and the ethos of midwifery will be masculinised.

A more serious threat is that male midwives within the practising grades will be attracted to where the action is, i.e. delivery rooms. This showed up in the pilot schemes, as the report says, 'the labour ward was popular with men, who found the work stimulating.'

It is also clear from the official discussions that women will not have the right to refuse to be attended by male midwives, except, perhaps, at home.

Knowing, as we do, the common status and conditions of labouring women, the prospect of labour wards staffed by male midwives and male (or honorary male) doctors is not a pretty one.

The history of modern birth is of the progressive infantilisation and control of women and the processes of birth. On no occasion were women consulted, on any detail. A look at any textbook shows that our passivity and silence are taken for granted, and anything else is frequently regarded as symptoms to be cured or suppressed.

I do not, of course, suggest that all is well in childbirth with a female midwifery profession. However, it would be better to re-establish womens' control of birth before men are let in.

It is ironic that, at the time when women are trying to liberate childbirth and re-learning the skills of active birth, this step could be taken without first asking us – as usual.

One predictable result of admitting men to midwifery will be to encourage home births and lay midwifery.

Male midwives
Susan Ardill
SR 131 June 1983

Restrictions on the training and employment of men as midwives in Britain are to be lifted from 1 September this year. Announcing this, the Minister for Health, Kenneth Clarke, said, 'The consultation process showed that the majority of women would accept male midwives just as they accept male doctors. However, a significant number of women would strongly prefer to be attended by a female midwife and some may be very distressed if attended by a man.

'. . . We are asking Health Authorities to ensure that women have the right to choose to be attended by a female midwife. We will also be asking Authorities to make provision for male midwives to be chaperoned as necessary.'

Accusing a doctor of sexual assault
Women from St Albans and Hatfield Women's Groups
SR 63 October 1977

On 29 September 1976 a 27-year-old student, thinking she might be pregnant, went to see her doctor in London Colney, Hertfordshire. Subsequently it turned out that she wasn't pregnant, but the doctor saw her during normal surgery hours and took a urine test. She says he told her to come back when surgery had closed and wait at the bus stop outside until his receptionist had left; he would then see her privately and 'see what he could do to help'. She claims that when she came back she was given an injection on the buttock, which the doctor later admitted was a placebo [given to humour rather than cure the patient] and practically useless in bringing on a late period unless injected in massive doses. She says she was told to undress, had her breasts felt and then was told to masturbate or a second injection would not work. She says at this point she dressed, left the surgery and went to the police who, after questioning, agreed to press charges of indecent assault against the doctor.

When questioned by the police the doctor denied the evening assignment stating he had seen the woman only once. When told that friends had both taken her to the surgery and collected her, he said he remembered seeing her but didn't recollect the injection (despite the plaster on the woman's buttock). Closely pressed in court, he justified what he'd said alternatively as a panic measure, or to protect the woman or due to loss of memory.

Because anonymity does not apply to victims of sexual assault, the newspapers went to town and the woman's previous history, which included two NHS abortions, found its way into the nationals – the fact that the father was the same both times did not – together with such gems of the defence case as 'She looks as if butter wouldn't melt in her mouth but her history tells a different story'.

More damagingly, the doctor's allegations that the woman had tried to seduce him, which in the admission of his own solicitor were not made until the case appeared before the magistrates, have stuck too. The woman has now moved from our area to Manchester where she's working as an art therapist. We've been told that she is in danger of eviction from her flat unless she gets rid of the press on her doorstep.

Although no one at any time suggested *why* such a charge should have been made without foundation, and though the woman's statements were consistent throughout, the doctor's wife, his receptionist, the district midwife and the health visitor were brought to court as character witnesses. He was eventually acquitted by a jury who perhaps felt that safeguarding the career and reputation of a long-established GP was more important than the word of a woman of 'not very high moral standing'.

During the trial we got a lot of letters in the local papers criticising the sensational way they reported it and the sexism of the whole procedure. The only reply was from a man saying we were obviously all women's libbers and biased in her favour.

Now it's difficult to know how best to be sisterly and supportive, or what actions to take. The woman concerned doesn't want to get involved in a campaign because she feels such low energy now and can't face appealing, but she would be glad if other women took it up.

Women friends and sympathisers are thinking of demonstrating outside the courts on 29 September, the day it happened last year. In the meantime we urge all women to do what they can to see that the anonymity which applies to raped women is extended to victims of sexual assault and to write to their MPs urging action on this.

It is possible to take complaints about doctors to the General Medical Council which supervises their morals. But usually a doctor, of either sex, is punished more severely for starting a voluntary sexual relationship with a patient than for undesired assaults, considered to be the imaginings of doctor-crazed women.

Lumps and bumps . . . racism and sexism
Dr K. Tandon
SR 135 October 1983

From my earliest memory I wanted to be a doctor. I wanted to make sick people better. I never had any other reason I was aware of that made me go wholeheartedly into spending many years of my life attempting to achieve the professional training that would enable me to give my best.

I have never regretted my choice of profession, but have learnt many a lesson about the individuals that go to compose it as a 'body'.

Alas, my naive, starry-eyed and idealistic motives did not account for the establishment that makes up the very heart of the British medical profession, a profession pervaded by a racism and sexism which is exercised at every level from the acceptance stage into medical school right through to specialisation at the highest possible level. It taints the nursing and allied paramedical services so that non-white workers, male and female, are subjected to its policies.

Being a non-white female doctor, I have been all too often subjected to discrimination regarding first my colour and then my sex. Most white female doctors I have met are racist and most of the white male doctors I have met are primarily racist and also sexist. The obstruction to one's training due to the attitudes is veiled in such hypocrisy, my initial reaction was one of total bewilderment; I questioned my own ability, thought I was imagining the discrimination, but over the years a systematic pattern emerged. I thought patients are the whole reason for our existence as a profession and results are there for all to see. I was soon to realise that many of the top tier of the British Medical Establishment are far more concerned with class, money and race than the quality of care their patients receive on a day-to-day basis. The whole profession is based on exclusivity and power. The climb upwards is provided with one hurdle after another, the first being acceptance into medical school. First choices go to white males often from a medical family or from an upper middle class background. I was surprised, but thrilled, when I was accepted into medical school. I was told later by a professor that it was unusual to accept a non-white woman but that being articulate in the English language, not having much of a foreign accent and being from a medical family had helped. Discussions with my colleagues revealed that my required grades for entry had been much higher than many of them had been asked for; non-white friends of mine had been rejected with equivalent grades to some of the white males that had been accepted on the course with the explanation that their qualifications had not come up to the required standard.

I was one of six women, and four non-white students (the other three were male) in a class of 80. The course was long, loaded with examinations every few weeks and totally fascinating. I was astounded at the knowledge and skills there were to acquire. I learnt to study tongues and throats, feel livers and bowels, deliver babies, remove lumps and bumps, take and give blood and a multitude of other skills. Encouragement was bountiful and all but two individuals qualified at the end of five and a half years.

It was in the postgraduate period that I found a different situation. After the period of internship when one is a 'house officer' and may work up to 140 hours a week, doing every day, one night in two and one weekend in two 'on call', there comes a time when the decision as to what field one will specialise in must be made. I chose general surgery and got a job at a junior level in a teaching hospital. After completion of one year I was told by my superiors that although I was very competent, general surgery was really a man's speciality and I would be best advised to go into a peripheral branch of surgery since I would never progress beyond a certain level. The line of argument was that the number of fully qualified women general surgeons in the United Kingdom can be counted on the fingers of one hand – why not attempt obstetrics which deals with women or eye surgery which is a little like doing embroidery?

Contracts of jobs in the National Health Service at a junior level extend for a period of six months or one year; more recently two-year rotating schemes have been introduced, but these are few in numbers and are heavily subscribed to, the number of applicants being 10 or 20 times the number of jobs available. These two-year schemes are often between a group of hospitals to attempt a varied training programme and may involve a lot of travelling in a week.

Since most jobs, however, are on short-term contracts, the possibility for setting up a stable home or having a family with a reasonably settled background is remote. Single women find it difficult to progress in certain chosen specialities, but married women doctors have a real battle on their hands – often being offered part-time jobs on a sessional basis to do outpatient clinics, family planning clinics or general practice sessions. These are often on a locum or temporary basis with poor job security, lack of holiday or sick pay and booked on a week-to-week basis; cul-de-sac jobs with the prospect of promotion and teaching being nil. The rapport with full-time 'resident' hospital staff is often minimal, the appointment being impersonal. There is a feeling of hopelessness and resentment at being treated as a pair of hands to 'clear' the outpatient clinics with no incentive to keep up with new advances in the subject and the standard of patient care is variable. I did one of these part time appointments for three months on one occasion and only spoke to the consultant in charge once, the only time he made an appearance in the clinic in that period! The bulk of the work was handled by other part-time staff, and any 'interesting' patients were whisked away by the resident doctors; and unless one maintained a very positive and active follow-up system one rarely got any feedback. I have spoken to numerous doctors in a similar position. The senior hospital posts are held by white males by and large and the odd white female; the part-time and temporary posts are held mainly by non-white males and females and married women doctors.

Being of a single-minded nature, I decided to cling on to a surgical speciality and continue with the required postgraduate examinations set by the Royal College of Surgeons. There are equivalent ones in other specialities. The exams are set in two parts, the first being in the basic sciences of the appropriate speciality. If one passes part one, after doing a further two years of the speciality in a recognised post, one is eligible to take the final part. One is charged a handsome fee for the privilege of sitting these examinations; it is forfeited in failure. Senior jobs stipulate the requirement of these postgraduate diplomas, so they are the filters for the individuals who are not considered desirable for promotion. The written papers are branded with anonymity where one is recognised by a number; the clinical and practical parts involve face-to-face meetings with senior consultants in the speciality who most certainly exercise discrimination of a racist and sexist nature. The candidates who pass average 5 to 10% of the total. On the three occasions I attempted the examination, roughly 80 to 90% of the candidates were non-white. Of the candidates who passed 90% were white and the odd one or two would be a non-white male or a non-white female. These proportions are easily discernible in the working population of the National Health Service, and seem to have remained fairly consistent since I qualified about 10 years ago. Prior to that it was worse. I now have the full postgraduate requirements to be eligible for surgical jobs at a senior level. I am still looking for one although white female doctors I taught as medical students have often been appointed to posts for which I have been turned down. I have checked my references which have been excellent; I can only come to one conclusion, that I am discriminated against on the grounds of being non-white, or a woman, or both. Temporary appointments are fairly easy to come by, covering for another doctor on holiday or maternity leave, etc. One is handling patients, performing operations and procedures as if one were doing a permanent job, but this remains elusive.

Graduates in the Faculty of Medicine are reminded that, before being admitted to their degrees, they will be expected to subscribe to the oath outlined by Hippocrates – the 'father of medicine' as he is commonly known. An important excerpt from the oath is as follows;

'I will work for the benefit of all, whosoever shall seek my service, without distinction of great or small, of rich or poor, of youth or age, of good or bad; that I will hold my knowledge in trust for the benefit of the common weal; that I will revere my teachers who have given me this knowledge which I have myself received.'

Hopes for the future exist, but are, at present, bleak. We have entered an era where increasing privatisation of health care is being encouraged. Border lines between National Health time and 'private' time are tinged with grey as consultants who practise in both areas will often steal from National Health time to attend to patients who come with a lucrative label. As monetary remuneration looms larger, how else to control the private sector than by making the very knowledge exclusive to a few who can then exploit it to their gain. The integrity of one's colleagues is highly suspect, when they block the sharing of knowledge and skills in such an orchestrated fashion. One can only hope that the spirit of the Hippocratic oath will ultimately prevail and health care for every individual on this planet is a fundamental right. Doctors and women of all races have the right to training and acquisition of the required skills so that a standardised level of care can be offered on a global scale. Only then as a profession can we hold our heads high.

NHS cuts – women bleed
Jeannette Mitchell
SR 138 January 1984

'Who will care for you while London's health service bleeds?' The GLC advert to draw Londoners into local health campaigns hints at the core of what the NHS cuts are about.

Women will care. They always have done the unpaid nursing. The NHS never properly relieved us and over the past few years cuts have intensified the burden. More cuts will take more of us beyond breaking point.

Every morning she will wash the sheets of the doubly incontinent grown-up mentally handicapped son. She will wake in the night every night to calm the screaming demented elderly parent. She will deny the pain of her own recent hysterectomy as, discharged from hospital, she copes with children and housework. She will lie awake beside the sick husband, whose condition seems to be worsening, worrying if she dare call out the doctor again. She will be sleepless, exhausted, chronically anxious. Her GP will give her valium or sleeping tablets.

The government has told health authorities to cut the equivalent of at least 5,000 full-time jobs. Three-quarters of the NHS's staff are women and it is women's jobs as nurses, domestics, laundry, kitchen and clerical staff that are primarily threatened. Many work part-time, as the number of women whose jobs may go is even greater than the official figure for 'whole-time equivalents'.

The cuts will not fall on the high prestige areas of medicine. Doctors will defend their own patch. The drug and medical equipment companies will insist loudly on the indispensability of their products. Operations will still be done. Drugs will still be dispensed. Diagnostic tests will still be carried out. What is being squeezed is what has already been deemed discernable – the basic low-status, low-paid caring which is the major part of what goes on in hospitals.

Women who work as nurses, domestics and midwives tell us that running hospitals on a factory management system leaves no time to talk to patients, no time to explain things to relatives, no time to take the time to let someone who has had a stroke dress themselves. Increasingly the intangibles of caring are just not budgeted for.

A favourite image for cuts campaigns is a big pair of surgical scissors snipping through a blood transfusion tube. But what is happening to the NHS is much less dramatic and more insidious. Most of what hospitals actually do is care rather than cure. This caring work is being gradually transferred from low-paid women workers in the NHS to unpaid labour at home. Even joining BUPA wouldn't help. It doesn't provide cover for being old, disabled or chronically ill, the conditions which the NHS increasingly expects women to deal with.

The cuts will mean more women without a job. Privatisation of cleaning and laundry will bring a deterioration in pay and working conditions for those now doing these already badly paid jobs in the NHS. For health workers still employed in the NHS there will be more work, more pressure, more worry and more sickness. Increased sickness among NHS staff will compound the pressures on those at work. For women at home there will be the work of caring for sick relatives, particularly the elderly, not just for short periods, but over months or years.

Because the NHS – which gets a smaller proportion of Gross National Product than the health care system of any other European country with the exception of Greece – has been under financial pressure for so long, the thought of another fight against this new round of cuts is very tiring. Health workers and women in health groups, community health councils and cuts campaigns have been resisting NHS cuts now since 1976.

For women involved in these campaigns the struggle is not only with a government which is cutting a service already stretched to breaking point, but with public ignorance of what the health service is about. Highlighting the real impact of cuts means taking issue with the 'Emergency Ward Ten' view of what goes on within the NHS. We are taught that doctors are the stars of the show. Their dominance blinds us to the fact that most health work is dirty routine, mundane . . . and essential. This women's work – both paid and unpaid – is invisible within the stereotype of the NHS. As women workers or future unpaid carers, fighting back means making visible our labour.

Who's zapping who?
Kim Besley
SR 166 May 1986

Greenham is nine miles around the perimeter, and is enclosed by row after row of fencing, barbed wire and razor wire. For many months after the arrival of the first Cruise missiles, there was a very heavy army presence inside the wire, and police presence outside. Suddenly they all went away – but the missiles were still there. There had to be a reason. Had some other means of guarding the base been found?

Every kind of ploy has been used, legal and illegal, to get rid of the women who watch at seven or eight camps round the base. Laws have been changed, in secret, and without recourse to parliament. Trespass has never been a criminal offence under English law but it is under American law – so the by-laws were changed to the American pattern.

Over the past 18 months there has been a gradual erosion of women's rights at Greenham Common Peace Camp in the name of 'law and order'. The state has explored many new ways of trying to destroy the peace camps. These include police extinguishing the camp fires every hour in mid-winter, strip searches on women to intimidate and attacks by unknown assailants whom the women have reason to believe were USAF personnel.

Now they may be trying something else to get rid of the women. That something else could be electronic devices designed to immobilise, disorientate and generally debilitate the women at the eight camps around the base – possibly low-level microwave radiation.

About eighteen months ago women noticed a pattern of illnesses emerging. A group of doctors and scientists began investigations – food and water sources were checked and discounted and the indications were that the symptoms were consistent with exposure to some form of low-level electromagnetic radiation. Measurements were taken and increased levels coincided with places where women felt particular effects. This could be either deliberate or incidental to the operation of the base. Interestingly enough it was possible to obtain an increase in the readings where none had previously been by the women starting a demonstration near the fence. It was also noted that visitors, both men and women, were being affected. People have been encouraged to write statements about their experiences, and currently some 50 statements are held, though many more have reported symptoms ranging widely from nose bleeds to pains in the head, ears and chest; swelling of the tongue resulting in slurred speech; dizziness; sun-burned face at night in mid-winter; palpitations; menstrual disturbances; loss of hair, impaired co-ordination; impaired memory (especially short-term); disorientation; profound depression and unreasonable panic. Headaches, sudden extreme fatigue and bouts of temporary paralysis; and in one case, apparent circulatory failure which required emergency treatment. Several women have had miscarriages rather late on in pregnancy.

When we talk about microwave radiation we are not talking about the atomic bomb kind of radiation, but the kind of energy that cooks food in a microwave oven, makes radar work or at other frequencies, makes radio work or runs building security systems.

Work on microwave radiation and its health effects has been going on for at least 50 years. Many instances of its use in situations unconnected with Greenham were documented in a film made in 1983 and shown on Channel 4. Back in 1930 the US navy did some experiments with sailors and discovered that standing in front of aerials was physically painful and caused weakness, drowsiness and headaches. Ten US marines were subjected to signals of extra low frequency (ELF) from the sanguine trans-mitter at Clam Lake, Wisconsin. As soon as it was turned on, all but one of the marines showed a rapid build-up of serum triglycerides, an unmistakeable warning of heart problems to come.

In 1955 the USAF reported that people who stood in the way of radar beams experienced ringing in the ears, buzzing vibrations and pulsations. In 1960 work at Cornell University showed that people could tell when they were standing in the way of microwave emissions. Some people could feel microwaves and also some deaf people could hear them at extremely low levels.

The discovery in 1953 that the US embassy in Moscow was being bombarded with low-level microwave radiation caused the Americans to undertake a health survey of embassy staff. That embassy staff were becoming ill at all was an embarrassment because the level of radiation was well below the safety standards which had been set by the Americans themselves. There are currently cases going through the courts by staff affected and by the ex-servicemen air traffic controllers and police officers.

In 1972 a US Department of Defence document said that the army had tested a microwave weapon, an extremely powerful 'electronic flamethrower', and according to recent intelligence reports, the US army now has a major programme and they predict that armies could use low-level microwave beams as a battlefield weapon to immobilise and disorientate opposing troops.

Far worse biologically are pulsed microwave emissions, which can be highly psychoactive and can cause neurological changes. Microwave radiation specifically affects the reproductive organs and the central nervous system. Studies in the US showed that mice irradiated by low-level microwave radiation had offspring that were severely stunted in three generations. Recent data from Sweden shows evidence that 'the normal balance between cell types in the central nervous system has been detrimentally affected by exposure to microwaves'. Brain tissue changes manifest themselves in the 'inability to perform a task, disturbances in concentration and short-term memory loss'.

You will see from the above information that the research into the biological effects has been going on for a very long time, and is well documented. What hasn't been is the effects of pulsed microwave emissions which are far more biologically hazardous and more difficult to detect.

The possibility of changing a person's mental state without them realising it has spurred on the world's intelligence services. A CIA memo commented that behavioural experiments could be used for enhancing consciousness or for re-arranging it. The theory is that if human brain waves can be turned to a different frequency, then it could be possible to change a person's mood, and ultimately their character. The CIA spent an estimated 10 million dollars on experiments with LSD and other mind-expanding drugs in the 1960s in their MKULTRA or mind control programme. Published work of Dr Robert Becker of the USA talks of specific frequencies producing confusion, fear and anxiety. His unpublished work is said to include bizarre experiments in which he has disorientated other scientists, changed their moods from elation to depression and to have shown that he can make fellow diners in a restaurant talk more loudly or quietly by emitting a magnetic pulse from a device which looks like an ordinary wrist watch.

Electromagnetic weapons are a new concept. We can't imagine the destructive power of such things. They are here with us now – off shelf technology. Is it so unreasonable that men should try their toys out on Greenham women?

'There was a pile of asbestos tiles on my sitting room carpet . . .'
Roslyn Perkins
SR 147 October 1984

I became involved in asbestos when I was exposed in my own home. The Housing Association decided to re-roof my house with asbestos cement tiles. There was no information, no warning – just a pile of asbestos tiles on my sitting room carpet, and a man sawing tiles outside my open bedroom window. Not until the work was almost complete did I learn (and then only when I chanced to overhear a conversation between the workers) that it was asbestos. Enquiries to the women's housing association and local environmental health officers confirmed this, but they added that this was 'safe white asbestos' and 'not to worry'.

They were wrong. All types of asbestos are dangerous. Even the meaningless government guidelines on working with asbestos were being contravened. There is *no* safe threshold level. The Conservative Party Chair, Mr Selwyn Gummer, has admitted that one fibre has the potential to kill.

I, like many of the women I have subsequently met, had to find out for myself – what is it? What harm does it do? Should I have been frightened by what happened in my home? Through Shelter National Housing Aid Trust I found the answers – otherwise I might have believed the lies. Because of the cover-up perpetrated at all levels of a male-based establishment this sort of truth is hard to discover. I became involved like others before me, and now it is my job.

Asbestos has been legislated for in the workplace/factory but not in the home – a workplace too! So women are affected, as are their children. Asbestos in many forms (all of which are dangerous and carcinogenic) is almost certain to be present in the post-war home and especially in the systems-built tower blocks and low-rise that comprise much of post-war public building. Older buildings may also contain asbestos, due to later modernisations, or in the form of moveable objects.

I've seen previously apolitical women become superbly militant and well organised around this issue. Moribund tenants' associations have been revived when the women realise that they have been fobbed off and deceived by Local Authority officials.

The trials and tribulations of the Adolphus Estate Asbestos Campaign illustrate how important a role women play and the extra pressure on them from the bigotry of the male officials and 'experts'.

In Adolphus Street, Lewisham (a working class area of South East London) a small group of women have been fighting for 21 months. They have been so frustrated in their attempts to gain simple information about their homes and access to those who are responsible that they are considering taking it up with the Ombudsman.

Despite the seemingly slow progress (the asbestos is still in their homes) they have been responsible for much of the Local Authority's growing awareness of the problem. These women have been educating their own public servants: they are an unpaid, largely invisible and vital part of local democracy.

It started for them with the showing of the TV documentary *All About Alice*, which played a major role in kindling campaigns nationwide. Alice with her dying breaths had decided to tell the truth about asbestos, and her courageous last statements (she was dead by the time it was broadcast) caused an outcry. Why had an industry been allowed to continue to sell this material when since 1898 (a factory inspector's report) there had been knowledge of its consequences?

After seeing this programme some of the Adolphus women called

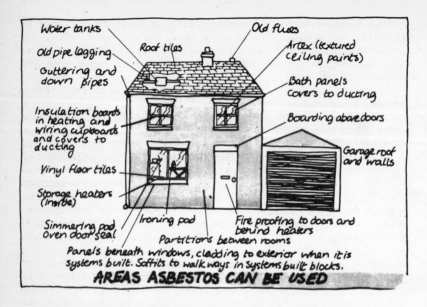

FIGURE 14 Asbestos in the home (*SR 147* October 1984)

a public meeting. Local Authority officials patronised their fears with comments such as 'You smoke anyway, so why are you worried about asbestos?' Not content with the complete lack of information they called in outside experts to talk to them, attended the first National Asbestos Conference and found support from the local Albany Health Project.

Then followed a long slog of writing newsletters, letters, meeting their MP and councillors, getting acknowledgement but no material support. They have been consistently patronised and have had to fend off misinformation. When the authorities realised the women would not be silenced they tried to mystify them with bogus science. They would be informed of meetings only on the day, so that family commitments made it impossible to attend. Tenants were issued letters supposedly advising on DIY and asbestos which contained dangerous and wrong advice. When phoning the District Housing Manager they were greeted with 'He won't speak to you'. Despite all these efforts to confuse and fatigue them, their anger grew. They exposed the lack of mechanisms for dealing with asbestos, and demanded to know why.

Recently one of their initial requests for a survey was carried out. It revealed what they had feared and Lewisham had all along denied: that 220 out of 245 dwellings surveyed needed action and 17 were in need of urgent action.

The Adolphus women are now linking up with other groups in Lewisham to make sure asbestos is dealt with properly. They are demanding that an asbestos policy be written in which they have a say, and that the asbestos be removed in an approved manner with due consultation of tenants.

Asbestos arouses more emotion than many hazards in the home, being sinister in its invisibility. The fibres can be unseen to the eye and produce no reaction at the time of exposure, yet 10–15 years later cancer may occur. There is *no* safe level and one has to work on the basis that 'one fibre can kill'. Children are more susceptible than adults and the women will often say that it is for their children's health that they are demanding its removal in such a militant way. But once questions are asked about asbestos and the myth that you have to be an expert to understand building technicalities is exposed, other campaigns tend to develop too, e.g. on the problems caused by dampness and condensation. Illnesses such as asthma and bronchitis are often related to a poor building structure, inadequate heating and insulation, but the 'experts' will often blame the tenants' lifestyle.

Asbestos is waking women up to the fact that the house is not always a haven but sometimes a den of potentially lethal hazards, which they have a right to know about and be rid of. As important is the political involvement it has given women who would otherwise be put off by the often sterile and bureaucratic traditional male organisations with endless committees and no action.

TAKING ACTION

If you suspect asbestos is present you should ask your environmental health department to check the suspect material.

For the home owner there is now help with asbestos. They will advise on safety precautions and provide a special waste-removal service. The Local Authority tenant will have to ask for their landlord to assess and ultimately encapsulate or ideally remove the asbestos in their home. Unfortunately many LAs are not responding and this is where pressure has to be applied until they develop a systematic and effective policy.

Air-tests are often used initially to 'reassure' tenants that the asbestos is not hazardous. This is utterly inadequate – a full survey is the only way to estimate accurately the potential or actual hazard. Don't be fobbed off!

Danger – women's work
Women and Work Hazards Group
SR 78 December 1978

At Aldermaston, in August this year, the Ministry of Defence closed down the laundry at the Atomic Weapons Research Establishment. Three women who worked there are suffering plutonium contamination of the lungs. The special laundry deals with protective clothing used by workers in the 'active' areas. One of the women has not worked in the laundry for some years. But she still carries a lung burden of plutonium above the permitted maximum and fears that it may have been even higher. Women in the laundry are not considered as radiation workers and are not required by law to be regularly monitored for radioactivity.

Women in factories, offices and shops everywhere risk disease and injury to their health from exposure to noise, dust, fumes, heat, stress, vibration, radiation and poisonous chemicals.

The Women and Work Hazards Group was set up to give working women information on health hazards and to support them in challenging management on technical issues. Here they give an outline of the risks women run and how to go about cleaning up the workplace.

Occupational ill-health is nothing new for women. The Matchgirls' strike of 1888 drew attention to the plight of women working with white phosphorus. Many of them contracted 'phossy jaw', the horrible bone disease necrosis. Other women, working on felt hats in sweatshops, were traditionally exposed to high levels of mercury which caused severe mental illness. Remember Lewis Carroll's 'Mad Hatter'? Women munition workers in the First World War were referred to as 'Canary Girls' because their faces turned yellow from exposure to TNT. Countless women have died from injuries, been sterilised or slowly poisoned by substances they have worked with.

Today thousands of women and men are still injured or killed from occupational causes every year. In an East London toy factory, women work so fast on the line that their fingers become raw. The little cars are hand-painted at great speed and you have to wrap your blistered fingers with sellotape to stop blood getting on the toys. But there is no way of knowing the exact figures since so many illnesses like stress, bronchitis and deafness are not recorded as occupational diseases. The statistics for women workers are particularly hard to find. Official records tell us nothing about married women workers. Often their job is not even mentioned on their death certificate, although their husband's usually is. One of the reasons asbestos took so long to be known as a killer was because in the nineteenth century it was women in the textile mills who worked with it, and relevant statistics were not collected on working women.

If we could get complete current statistics they would paint a picture of disease and chronic illness as horrifying as conditions in the sweatshops of the nineteenth century. Workers are still exposed to many of the same old hazards like asbestos and lead. But even more worrying is the fact that 19,000 chemicals are now in common industrial use, with thousands of new ones introduced into the workplace every year – and the health risks of all of them are virtually unknown. Legal limits or standards have been set for only 500 of these toxic substances and for only 16 of the 2,400 chemicals suspected of causing cancer. The standards which have been set are based on tests geared to the young, fit, male worker – usually US Marine 'volunteers'. Hazards to fertility or risks of female cancers (breast, uterus) are not criteria that scientists or the government have considered when setting limits of exposure to chemicals at work.

The women's liberation movement has always made health a priority issue. Many of us have through self-examination and self-help learnt not only to understand our menstrual cycle, but also how to identify 'women's complaints', and sometimes cure them with natural remedies. But we've made little of the necessary link between women's health and work. Stress, for example, which may cause tension, digestive disorders, depression and heart disease, occurs at high rates in women who are under pressure from two jobs: one paid and one unpaid. Or take menstrual upsets: some Eastern European studies have revealed that disturbances in the monthly cycle were very common in women whose jobs had a rhythm set by machines, like for example assembly line work in electronics factories. Our environment as well as our biology affects our health. Where we can show that sickness is related to work, we can demonstrate that as such it is preventable. As feminists we are struggling for the right to information on our health, and rights over our own fertility, but we must include control over our own body in the workplace.

Women are now 40% of the paid workforce and concentrated by and large in low-paid, dead-end jobs, doing boring, repetitive tasks – increasingly on a part-time basis, with little security. Many of these low-paid workers are immigrants who don't speak English well. Often they run more risk of damaging their health at work because management makes no attempt to help them either with language classes or with interpreters.

The more obvious occupational hazards like dusts, which harm the lungs, and noise, affect both male and female workers, and men traditionally have had some of the most dangerous jobs like mining and construction.

But women work in their millions in certain unhealthy occupations and it's these which need a closer look here. In light engineering, such as the manufacture of electrical components, women are mainly employed to do fast repetitive tasks which cause inflammation of tendons in the hands and forearms. Women packing and processing drugs are at risk from many chemicals ranging from hormones to vaccines. Hairdressers can damage their lungs and skin using toxic sprays and dyes, and harmful detergents. Office workers too, are exposed to many untested chemicals in photocopiers and stencil fluids. The very nasty trichloroethylene (trike) is used as a base for solvents in correcting fluids, inks, adhesives and dry-cleaning agents. It causes headaches, fatigue, dermatitis, and, at high levels, nausea, vomiting and confusion. Several bottles of correcting fluid open at the same time in a typing pool could result in an unsafe level of trike in the air. It can also be addictive. Office workers also suffer the hazards of noise, dermatitis, bad lighting and seating.

Many women are hospital workers. They risk infections, radiation, exposure to dangerous chemicals like formaldehyde, and they often suffer from varicose veins and backache from being on their feet for long periods. Catering workers share many of these problems. Stress from the irregular hours of shift work is also common.

Women working in the home have traditionally suffered from 'house-maid's knee' and 'washerwoman's elbow'. Nowadays, in addition to severe levels of stress from doing housework and looking after children, women working at home may be at risk from unsafe wiring or dangerous chemical sprays (aerosols) such as pesticides and polishes. In many cases it is the same sort of chemical that women are exposed to at home as out at work. For example 62% of workers in the cosmetic industry are female. The harmful effects of various combinations of chemicals inhaled or applied to the body are virtually unknown (note that some commercial talcum powders contain asbestos).

Women with a double work load are doubly at risk. Some have got severe dermatitis by handling substances when at work, and then detergents at home. Women washing men's contaminated overalls at home have contracted asbestosis and beryllium poisoning. Two jobs means an early shift and a late one. It means working a far longer week than most men. It means stress and exhaustion. Of the 20 million prescriptions dispensed for tranquillisers in 1974, three-quarters were for women.

It's a woman's right to choose whether or not to have a child and when. Yet great numbers of women abort, produce abnormal children or are made sterile every year due to exposure to anaesthetics, radiation and a host of chemicals. We must understand reproduction in a wider context than at present, and fight for our rights as women to retain our fertility if we choose.

One out of every 25 children is born with a defect of some kind; but we have no idea what causes 60 to 70% of these. Many are possibly due to work hazards. Many chemicals cross the placenta in such a way that the foetus is affected more than the mother. Research in Eastern Europe has shown that pregnant women working in the manufacture of synthetic materials and plastics, and exposed to formaldehyde, are at risk. It also indicated that some problems of anaemia, miscarriages, stillbirths and underweight babies were caused by working in factories processing polystyrene, and in the production of rayon, where carbon disulphide is used.

In Italy a state commission found that a scandalous 20% of pottery workers had aborted or prematurely given birth. These 'white abortions', as they're called there, are not recorded as industrial injuries nor are they prosecuted by penal law. This is ironic in a society which exalts the role of mother. Maternity is holy, provided it doesn't upset production.

In Britain, because of known dangers to the foetus, special protective regulations prohibit employment of women in the manufacture of some lead and radiation processes. However the vast majority of chemicals are used by employers with no thought to the health risks to foetuses, pregnant women or anyone else.

The response of some North American companies to this problem (Dow Chemicals, Esso, Dupont) has been simply to refuse employment to all fertile women. Norma Smith kept her job at a Canadian General Motors lead battery plant by getting herself sterilised. She was forced to do this after the company decided only sterilised or non-fertile women could work in the plant. This attitude threatens all women's jobs.

The British government too is currently recommending a new standard for exposure to lead and recommends that pregnant and all fertile women be banned from working with it. This means that women are in danger of being excluded from some jobs because they may become pregnant. The government is treating us all as reproductive vessels, while at the same time 'protecting' many women out of a job. This approach also ignores the fact that lead is poisonous to everyone, and ironically ignores that men exposed to lead risk sterility too. The same goes for many other substances. A higher than average rate of men working with vinyl chloride (used to make PVC), some pesticides, and anaesthetics have been found to be sterile or to be 'fathering' stillborn or abnormal children.

Making pregnant or fertile women a special category of 'worker at risk' is not the answer to the use of dangerous substances and practices. The only solution is to clean up the workplace so that it's safe for all.

The right of the foetus to be born normal must not be posed in opposition to women's right to good jobs. Foetus rights, as in anti-abortion arguments, can be held up as a banner to obliterate the rights of women when they are primarily viewed as baby-making machines.

But if you think pregnant women may be at risk in your workplace, then demand alternative jobs at the same pay and conditions (the Employment Protection Act may help here). This fallback position would not protect women who are in their first few weeks of pregnancy. It is during this time – often before you know you're pregnant – that the foetus is most vulnerable.

It's not usually in the interest of employers to abolish hazards, since this costs money and you may find you are threatened with closures when you start demanding things like ventilation systems. If you're unionised you are in a better position to bargain over pay and conditions, all depending of course on how serious the very often male-dominated union hierarchy takes demands by women. But until women are organising for safe working conditions we will continue to be completely at the mercy of industry.

The Health and Safety At Work Act (HASAWA) 1974 covers *all* workers in *all* industries and services, including offices, hospitals, laboratories, homeworkers. By law, it is the duty of employers to ensure the health of employees, to produce a statement of general health and safety policy and to consult workers' elected representatives. The loophole is that nearly everything is qualified by the phrase 'as far as is reasonably practicable' which means employers can plead poverty and avoid their legal duties. The HASAWA also puts the onus of responsibility on to producers. This means that anyone who designs, manufactures, imports, or supplies articles or substances for use at work has to ensure their safety 'as far as is reasonably practicable'.

Regulations which came into force on 1 October 1978 gave trade unionists in all industries and services the legal right to elect their own workers' inspectors. These 'safety representatives' have the same status as shop stewards and even more legal power. They have the right to inspect the workplace, receive information from management and factory inspectors about past conditions and future proposals, and to have time off with pay for training. Training should be done by trade unions or on trade union courses (e.g. those run by the Workers Educational Association). Employers must provide facilities for safety reps which may include an office and health and safety literature.

The Women and Work Hazards Group can help with information about substances and equipment which may be dangerous. We produce the *Hazards Bulletin*, a magazine for workers which contains accounts of ongoing struggles, and information about work hazards and the law; and are currently researching a pamphlet on the health hazards of office work. We also teach some trade union health and safety courses. So why not train as a safety rep? You could in fact start getting your workplace cleaned up by carrying out a small health survey. We'll help you draw up a short questionnaire, asking people about their symptoms and complaints – headaches, flu symptoms, menstrual upsets, increased deafness, depression, dermatitis. . . .

A survey like this can reveal that groups of people are suffering shared symptoms which makes it easier to find the cause than if each individual goes to her GP. (Bus drivers in Brighton found that 90% of their members were experiencing increased stress and they used the data from their questionnaires to negotiate for more staff and fewer one-person buses.) You may find, for example, a high rate of bronchial problems. In tracing the cause, check for chemical fumes and dusts. Also the ventilation system needs to be taken into account. Fungus has been found to be growing in some systems and it has seriously affected office workers' lungs. Keep a permanent record of illnesses and injuries. Demand regular medical checks and keep the results. You may need them to prove your case later. Records are essential to arm you for negotiating a better deal and to fight for compensation if necessary.

Under Section 6 of the HASAWA you have a right to know the exact contents of all substances you are exposed to at work. Either your employer or the manufacturer must provide the information. But to monitor the hazards of chemicals, the levels of dust, fumes or noise in your department, you may need outside help. You can call in the local factory inspector (even for offices, labs, etc). Inspectors vary but can be useful. However they are thin on the ground, over-worked, mostly management-orientated, and male.

You may want to call in outside advisers, for example from polytechnics or universities, or get advice from people from the various 'grassroots' health and safety groups which are springing up round the country (you can contact us for addresses). No matter who does sampling or measurement, demand the results in a form you can understand. This is your right.

When you've pinpointed the hazard you should try to have it controlled at source – whether it's noise, dust, fumes or dangerous machinery. Demand that safer substances be substituted for hazardous ones. Don't be fobbed off by goggles, gloves or masks. The onus is on your employer to provide safe and healthy working conditions. It's not on you to wear protective clothing which is usually uncomfortable to work in. These outfits are dangerous because they are restrictive and because they look safe while rarely giving real protection (e.g. dust and masks).

As a safety rep you can formulate your demands and negotiate these with employers in the form of a safety agreement – as with a wage agreement. Some workers have already won such rights as:

the right to divulge information to outside bodies;

the right to participate in the design of new equipment;

the right to 'stop the job' and boycott a process where hazards are evident.

Bargaining for health and safety is not easy. It infringes on the territory often called 'management prerogative'. In demanding decent working conditions you will be challenging management's control over workers, the production process, and your body.

When the women's movement is ideal for me as a woman with a disability
Merry Cross
SR 125 December 1982

Some months ago I went to an international women's workshop. One afternoon I led a group in exploring ways of making the women's movement truly a movement for *all* women. Before we started, I thought through what I'd learned about making a community safe for everyone. When we'd first realised that many groups of people didn't feel safe in larger groups, we would have them speak out about what it was like for them as Black people, as Jews, as women and so on. It was good for those concerned because they were able to express a lot of very justified bad feelings, but the others listening (unless they were Black, Jews, women, too) often sank into a pit of defensiveness and guilt. They were completely unable to change how they behaved.

In my experience, people can be inspired to change much more profoundly than they can be bludgeoned into change. I have found that when people share their visions (and visions can be extremely down-to-earth), others can't help but want to change and become part of that vision.

I think that the most important way the women's movement will become ideal for me is when it both *expects* and *wants* women with disabilities (of all kinds) enough to change the movement to incorporate us. How would things be different with this kind of women's movement? Well, I won't attempt to cover every possible change, but I will try to give the flavour of it, pointing out too the inevitable benefits to *all* women.

The women's movement, in all its variety, will know that without us, important perspectives, information, ideas, and understandings are missing. It will know that women with disabilities have enormous potential as a uniting force since we span every possible group of human beings: we are to be found among the young, old, working class, middle class, among all races. It will know that if there is any group who can point the way to making the world a safe place for each individual woman to flourish in, it is women with disabilities.

Women will understand that people with disabilities are an oppressed group. For example, this takes the form of the demand for us to look, act, work, as 'normally' as possible. If these are not possible, then we are excluded from society by disabling environments, overt discrimination, fearful and antagonistic attitudes.

Women will be eager to learn from us why this oppression exists, to understand how it relates to other oppressions. Knowing that only women can liberate themselves as women, they will understand that they can only back us in our liberation efforts, not do it for us. By beginning to get their own house in order women will make the sort of changes in the movement that will include us on our own terms, not as imitation able-bodied women.

Not a single piece of information would be printed that wasn't also taped and/or brailled, including 'small' things like meeting agendas. Not a single meeting would fail to cater for people with hearing loss, either through the use of interpreters, or through hearing women using appropriate communication skills. If you think such changes are simply expensive and time-consuming – well they can be, but for precisely these reasons women will learn to make their communications beautifully clear, concise and expressive, becoming in the process better able to communicate with *everybody*.

No one will ever be excluded by stairs (or included, but exhausted by the effect of getting up them.) No one will ever again get into a gathering, enjoy the first hour or so and then find there's no accessible toilet and have to choose between leaving or having to use the loo with the door open. Transport (or funds for it) will be provided for anyone who could not otherwise come along. There will be extra bonuses to instituting the more commonly considered aspects of access such as ramps and lifts.

Where a wheelchair can go, a pram can go; where someone who uses crutches can go, elderly women using sticks can go. And so on. In our wake will come other women whose contributions have also been missing.

Both listening and talking to some people with disabilities requires a slowing down; many actions take longer. This too can be an advantage as it offers a chance to stop the frantic rush and to question what really is important in life.

Many women have hidden disabilities – some of them (and some with visible disabilities) will need frequent breaks to move or go to the loo or whatever – and when those breaks are provided as a matter of course, 'able-bodied' women will realise how much longer they can stay fresh when they can chat (or laugh, or cry or . . .) about what they've just heard, during the breaks.

In an ideal women's movement, furniture would be different. Chairs, for example, will come in a variety of forms – and as we are made comfortable, able-bodied women will find themselves asking why they had put up with aching backs and sore bums for so long.

The women's movement, having learnt from its own experience of the media, will ensure that everything they put out overtly includes women with disabilities. Every ad and leaflet for gigs, workshops, for meetings, films, for jobs, will include information about access or a number to ring for that information . . . and I *don't* mean the information that, unfortunately, this event isn't accessible! Feminist theoretical literature will include a disability perspective and will be taped. Works of art will often have characters with disabilities portrayed in ways that will further our liberation. Women will be used to checking with people with disabilities that they are getting these things right.

In all its campaigns, the women's movement will seek a disability contribution and include a disability perspective, since women will assume that the issues for women with disabilities *may be* different and will want to find out if they are. As well as knowing how to support *our* campaigns, the women's movement will also be ready and happy to pass on to people with disabilities any information and skills learnt in the process of women's liberation. The ideal women's movement for me will throw its weight behind every campaign against the waste and misuse of resources in the world, whether these resources are human, other species, fossil fuels, or whatever. Campaigns, particularly around nuclear power and weapons, are an obvious example. Disability highlights dependency on resources – dependency that everyone has but most people don't recognise. As we squander and misuse resources our world becomes increasingly disabling for everyone.

EXAMPLES OF OUR CAMPAIGNS WHICH NEED SUPPORT

(1) Campaigns to institute good living conditions *in the community* for all of us and to close down residential institutions. It's easier for women to see that closure of institutions must be accompanied by good community provision of access and services, etc., because otherwise *women* are the ones who are asked to cope. This is an excellent example of two groups' liberation being tied together.

(2) Campaigns to eliminate the need for special, local voluntary provision by instituting national or nationally legislated-for, locally run public provisions for people with disabilities. Women will recognise that they too have had to devote a lot of time and energy to special women's groups (for instance, crèches) because society as a whole has failed to make the necessary provisions.

I have already suggested that the literature and campaigns will all include a disability perspective – feminist theory must too. An example will be any theory about sexuality. This will, in an ideal movement, be able to encompass the different sexual oppressions of women with disabilities which operates to deny us *any* sexuality at all, and particularly pressurises us not to have children. It will also be able to encompass in its theory on abortion a stand against automatic abortion on the grounds of foetal disability. It will campaign to give women a *real* choice in this matter by giving them good information about disability (whichever particular one – and disability in general). This is almost impossible to come by at the moment.

Any theory will particularly seek out the links between women's liberation struggles and ours. This raised consciousness will strengthen both struggles.

Women will be eager both to pass on all they have learnt and to learn from us. They will never collude with, nor create divisiveness between us. For instance by encouraging partially hearing women to come to meetings who can get by with lip reading, but not those who require interpreters or finger-spelling. Women who consider themselves to be able-bodied will no longer creep (or bluster) around, sunk in guilt about how we are treated, but will simply acknowledge that they've been hurt too by our oppression (not the least by being separated from us sisters) and need to learn lots. They'll ask what needs to be done and get on and do it!

Needless to say, in such a women's movement, women with disabilities would be different too. We would act proud and treat each other with total love and respect, as well as getting on great with all the other women.

Finally perhaps I should say that gradually the women's movement will be so full of women with disabilities that there would be lots who would readily fill in the gaps inevitably left in an article like this – and eventually *so* full that such articles would be completely unnecessary!

128

Overdose of doctors

Susan Hemmings
SR 162 January 1986

Lesbians are experts in when to come out, when to keep our heads down, and when to poke them out just a few centimetres. Nowhere do we glean more experience than in our dealings with the medical profession. Doctors, nurses, health visitors . . . you'd think that they, of all people, might be sufficiently well-informed to imagine that at least *some* of their patients might be lesbians. Indeed, many health workers must themselves be lesbians.

But no. The world of the surgery, the clinic and the hospital knows only the heterosexual norm. Well women clinics are no exception. In fact, some of us have met our worst doses of heterosexism in such venues. I promise that all the anecdotes that follow in this highly anecdotal article are true: lesbian readers will probably recognise these situations only too well.

Starting off with something relatively mild – a recent course of anti-biotics brought on an attack of thrush. I visited my (new) doctor for some Nystan, and he prescribed pessaries, telling me I didn't need the cream, 'But I'll prescribe some for your partner who must smear it on his penis.' He indicated with his hand the action he had in mind. The idea seemed so ludicrous that a sparkle crept into my eye, whereupon he told me, strictly, and twice, that we were to refrain from sexual intercourse for five days. I choked back a few snortles, while he looked on disapprovingly, obviously making me out as a rampant heterosexual. Until then I hadn't realised that these duo-packs of cream and pessaries are in fact boy-and-girl kits.

This leads us to special clinics. Again, you'd think they'd be reasonably clued up in these establishments. A friend of mine (yes, really, it wasn't me on this occasion) recently suspected a vaginal infection, and had very sore nipples. The doctor's opening questions assumed heterosexuality, so she immediately told him of her lesbianism. 'Oh, been using nipple clamps then, have you?' was his incredible response. A highly politicised lesbian of no mean punch, she delivered a short lecture about his hetero-sexist and male assumptions. She also told him not to refer to her breasts as titties. I think they parted on reasonable terms.

The thing about heterosexuals, we have learnt from our doctors, is that they do it all the time. We cannot escape this impression when we try to go for an X-ray. Poor appointment clerks just won't believe us when we insist that there is no possibility that we could be, or could get, pregnant by mistake. In despair I told one, during a phone call, that the reason I knew for sure was that I didn't have sexual intercourse with men. I could sense her choking back the thought, 'Ah, but you might before your next appointment . . .' Probably it also occurred to her that I was a nun. I sensed lesbianism was not on her list of possibilities.

Once I was asked by a doctor (testing me for abdominal pain which had persisted for months) when I had last had sexual intercourse. Knowing he must mean penile penetration, I replied that it was about ten years. Hmm. He frowned. He wrote down that I was highly stressed and anxious.

Now for well women clinics. The famous Elizabeth Garrett Anderson makes you fill in a questionnaire which pounds on about, 'Which contraceptive do you use?' and pain/difficulty on intercourse. There is no polite way in which you could make it clear on this form that you are a lesbian. I naturally wrote a few corrective comments all over mine in red pen, and posted it in. At my consultation, the doctor studiously ignored these, and her gaze never met mine. I recommend block appointments – by their fifth dyke they do begin to get the hang of it, and maybe they think it's just a local infection.

Being a lesbian, however, is not confined to 'troubles down there'. Whatever part of your body (or mind – and I'm not even going to mention all the agonies and injustices in the mental health arena), problems are acute when it comes to doctor's ignorance. Going into hospital is traumatic for anyone: for lesbians it is always bad news. If you decide not to come out to the nurses and doctors, that virtually means no visitors: not your friends and lovers, anyway. And some lesbians are very socially isolated – what about, for example, an immigrant woman whose only close relationship might be her lover living as she does thousands of miles from her family? And Black women in general are up against an even thicker wall of ignorance: at least there's an image in white doctor's minds, if you press them, of white lesbians, but they'd be totally amazed by the fact that a Black patient could be anything other than straight. All lesbians know they're in for a bumpy ride in the ward, and if you're not white, it's even more stressful and potentially isolating.

Those of us who decide to risk it and come out, either directly or by just letting our best friends in, find that other patients mainly remark not on the presence of women, but the absence of Men.

Anyway, once your friends start coming to see you, you might as well give up being discreet. One friend of mine had decided to play it straight, but after one particularly hilarious session with a couple of her mates, was horrified to see another patient, a very out dyke, came bouncing down the ward. 'So you are gay!' she yelled, delighted. 'Which of the nurses do you fancy?'

I've recently been inside for a bout of intensive nursing, following a big operation. The woman I've lived with for many years spent hours of each post-operative day helping the nurses with the intimate tasks needed for my care, since two people always needed to be on hand. At first, the nurses were a bit tense about her helping, partly out of a protectiveness for my privacy, but eventually they sensed the closeness between us. Having slowly grasped that she was not my mother, and no, not my sister, they duly remarked on what seemed to them an astounding and rather inexplicable staunchness in my friend, and on her unflinching affection. Clearly, they just could not work out what kind of relationship we have. It no doubt threw them off the scent that both of us have children, who visited. (Again, all heterosexuals 'know' that if you have a child you can't possibly be a lesbian.) The unexpected benefit was that all during that frightening time we were able to be so much closer than any of the heterosexual women were with their lovers: the reverse of what normally happens to lesbians in hospitals. All this because the doctors and nurses had a respect for women's friendship and a tolerance of women's physical intimacy in a situation of illness. But we knew, we sensed, it was too dicey to come out. We felt all that tolerance would simply fly out of the window if they really knew the totality of our relationship.

Nowadays it is easier, in London anyway, to put down your lover as next-of-kin. (You just write 'friend' where it asks for the relationship, if you don't want to come out.) And there are a growing number of radical lesbian nurses and doctors; though as yet they still can't feel professionally secure enough to come out. They must, of course, wear skirts/dresses on the ward. Lesbian identity does not depend on getting into a pair of trousers, but the pressure is on for women health workers (with the exception of physiotherapists, who mustn't show their thighs presumably, when prancing about all over us) to look 'female' in conventional terms. (God, that nurses' uniform! How could any feminist, let alone lesbian, wear it and stay sane?) Neither nurses nor medical students receive any anti-sexist or anti-heterosexist training, and boy, how it shows in most of their work.

Sometimes this seemingly wilful ignorance leads to situations bordering on malpractice. A friend of mine had suffered for a long time with lumps in her breast and other worrying symptoms. One specialist finally stumbled on the fact of her lesbianism. He subsequently wrote to her GP saying that her problem was hormonal: as a lesbian she had 'an enlarged clitoris' and 'body hair'. In actual fact, just to put the record straight, she has neither. He wanted to prescribe hormonally: fortunately her more enlightened GP disagreed.

We end with an anecdote – again an absolutely true one – which should be inscribed into the Lesbian Archives of Snappy Retorts. Another friend of mine was in the process of being thrown out of the airforce because of her lesbianism. Apparently it is common practice to give medicals before they are discharged to ensure, my friend explained, that women go out 'the same way we came in'. Bearing in mind the reason for her dismissal, she endured the internal examination with considerable reservation. 'What are you looking for?' she asked the medical officer. 'Fingerprints?'

'Elm Park Nursing Home'
Mary Dorcey
SR 99 October 1980

our hands clasped together on the white sheet
seemed to tick soft and loud as a time bomb
in the sterilised cosiness of that place.
no illness or grief here please
where wounds are freshly dressed each day
and nights are tucked in with little sleepers
in wards made crisp and bright with daffodils
aflutter with nurses who smooth every doubt
with solicitous smiles impeccably starched

the golf course stretches green and calm
outside the picture windows
gentle reminder of the virtues of health
so cheerfully guarded in the real world
while tired voices conscious of ingratitude
agree with sister that yes the lawns are splendidly kept.
husbands come and go, devotion comfortably contained
within the appropriate visiting hours
and the bouquets so dutifully presented
stare from their vases blank as photos
in a family album.

as evening comes the chatter of the colour television
shrouds our fitful conversation
but our hands embracing on the white sheet
vibrate with a violence that we know must pierce
each tactful barricade of earphone and raised newspaper
and when at last i leave, stalked by every eye
their owners caught between horror and delight
until mrs robinson the chosen mediator
exorcising any shadow of disquiet
in a voice made suave with homeliness
declares, her smile defying answer
'you have a lovely sister'.

but that last night
strained beyond embarrassment or caution
when i took your face between my hands
and kissed your mouth a slow goodbye
it seemed the bomb would explode
in a shower of brilliant sparks
that might have set the ward alight

were it not for the immediate action
of fire fighting nurses
who with the ice composure
of a lifetime's training in temperature control
drew screens, plumped pillows, inserted thermometers
and asked me to wait outside
while they changed your dressings.

but one young nurse arriving too hurriedly
with her face and her uniform not yet fully buttoned
carelessly looked in our eyes as we parted
and for once confronted too soon for defence
stood aghast as routine collapsed
her jaw shuddered and starch began to run from her lips
in thick white tears
her limp face gazed about unchecked
and in that moments stripped of her smile
she saw illness, grief and passion
undressed.

A revised edition of this poem appeared in Kindling (*Onlywomen Press, 1982), with the title 'In a Dublin Hospital'.*

CHAPTER 3

EMOTIONAL MATTERS

Within British feminism the question of how we approach and deal with our mental health has vexed us from the beginning. Women reacted angrily to men who sneeringly said that consciousness-raising groups were self-indulgent therapy sessions: we felt we were exploring the connections between our deepest personal feelings and the society we all lived in and wanted to change.

An early feminist slogan went 'Don't break down, break out'. Mental illness was produced by the society we lived in – inequality, sexism, exploitation, all made depression, even madness, quite understandable. Being part of a collective movement of women which aimed to change society, and in that process take control of our own lives, was the best route to mental health.

And yet there were feminists, more and more of them, who wanted and needed to look at what therapy or even psychoanalysis could offer. Women who *were* involved in consciousness-raising groups, and active in community or campaigning groups, still found themselves with recurring, disturbing emotional and behavioural patterns. Other women were concerned for their own or a sister's seriously disruptive mental state. They were trying to 'break out', but they were 'breaking down' too.

As well, quite a few women were already working within, or interested in, alternative therapies. The American-spawned 'growth movement', for example, had its attractions for feminists. The pages of *Spare Rib*, up until the late 1970s, contained many articles sympathetic to self-help therapy, to the experiences of women in various therapeutic situations, and to the particular conditions from which women suffer, like agoraphobia and schizophrenia. There were articles on Gestalt and bio-energetics. Feminist therapists talked, Juliet Mitchell was interviewed, and Rosalind Coward explained who Lacan was. Feature after feature explored women's personal stories of mental and emotional turmoil, and their resolution (or search for resolution) through therapy.

Only readers' letters consistently raised objections to what their writers saw as the privatization and individualization of a common pain within the four walls of the one-to-one therapeutic relationship. Some felt that therapy took women's rage and pain, and turned them away from social change and political movement, into the chimera of individual solution. And how many women could ever afford therapy – in either money or time? It was felt to be elitist.

The 'debate', long established in the women's liberation movement, finally surfaced in *Spare Rib 69*, and also brought to a close the regular place of articles on therapy and mental health which had so typified the years before. With the exception of one article of the 'old' type, and

'Deprivatizing depression' (reprinted here), there was virtually nothing of feature length in the magazine at the time this book went to press.

Sharp differences still exist between feminists about the role of therapy, its usefulness to feminists, its role in possibly diffusing women's potential anger and movement towards collective struggles. But at a time when more women who define themselves as feminists are, or have been, in therapy, *Spare Rib* is relatively silent on the issue. And at a time when Black women are organizing around the ways in which mental health is affected by a racist and sexual society, *Spare Rib* has not yet carried an article on Black women and mental health.

Self-help therapy
Fiona McKay
SR 48 July 1976

One Sunday in January 1975, at a local women's centre meeting, I nervously announced that a couple of us wanted to form a self-help therapy group, and if anyone was interested would they see me afterwards? I sat down, shaking. In fact there was a lot of interest, and a week or so later we met at my home.

From the first it was a very cohesive, very women's movement-type group. We'd all been active feminists for a number of years and we shared similar lifestyles, aspirations and attitudes to the world. One of these attitudes was a suspicion towards the psychiatric establishment, which we saw, roughly, as a way in which women were adjusted to their limited roles and oppressed position.

But at the same time some of us had good reason to be turning towards therapy. I had cracked up about a year before, and my confusion and despair had propelled me into therapy with a progressive-type therapist who worked in the 'growth movement'. Pat joined the group only because she 'was having specific problems in coping with my day-to-day life – really bad panic attacks and continuous feelings of unreality. I found it impossible to be on my own for any length of time and got really dependent on a few people I was close to.' She wanted to share her experiences with women who had undergone similar things, in a context where there was no need to feel paranoid and defensive, and she wanted to understand how and why such alarming states came about. Annie had had 'some kind of breakdown a couple of years before, and had always felt I was pretty unstable. I didn't understand why everyday life should be so hellish difficult – I felt like an invalid, a complete mess.'

Liz and Marion didn't suffer the particular disturbances which the rest of us did, nor the shame that comes from feeling you're not 'normal' in society's eyes, so their notions of what they could get from such a group were more open-ended. Liz felt it was a good idea to have such a project at the women's centre, but didn't know what to expect from it. Marion wanted 'a more structured setting than friendship where I could express fears and worries – there's less guilt at talking about worries to a small group than pouring it out to one person.'

It was hard to get established. In the first few meetings people's doubts and conflicts about the whole enterprise kept coming up. At the time I noted down: 'Marion and I were trying to convince Pat and Greta that the therapy group might help them – we felt they were being rather puritan and self-punishing about their needs. Pat said "After all, I've no way of understanding and assessing the use of therapy. It would just be a prop, something to give me hope – but such an arbitrary one." Greta argued strenuously that emotional problems could only be worked out with the people you lived with. Marion and I, as strenuously, opposed this.'

Greta in fact decided against joining, and the rest of us, having agreed that it was worth a try, had a look through a US women's therapy book called *Getting Clear* and decided to try a few of the breathing and relaxing exercises. Those who felt too vulnerable to panics just looked on, enjoying the giggles – whenever we did physical exercises there was a lot of embarrassment to break through – and picking up on the physical enjoyment. Afterwards I wrote: 'Perhaps we should try a few low-key trust games. If those of us who are panicky can relax and *play* a bit under the indulgent eyes of the group, it might be a big step forward.'

We did play trust games – specially the one where one woman goes into the centre of a ring made by the others, and lets herself be pushed gently, eyes closed, from one pair of arms to the next, lets others take all the responsibility for catching her. And we did consciously develop an indulgent and supportive atmosphere, one in which anyone could give in to tears, panic, or shakes without being made to feel ashamed. We tended to support and accept each other fully, and therefore ease conflicts a lot, rather than actually urge each other into emotional expression all the time, which happens in encounter and a lot of growth movement groups. This gentleness and reticence were partly due to inexperience, partly a response to the states some of us were in – severe states which imposed a certain cautious pace, a politeness, even, the limitations of which I'll discuss later.

At the start of every meeting, each woman would say how she was feeling, and then we'd decide whether to try exercises or deal with a pressing anxiety someone was suffering. We would give all attention to that person, letting her talk and talk, questioning carefully and encouraging her to pour out the whole thing and connect with the feelings more. Somehow, it was working. Pat recalls: 'I got really high from some of the meetings – I remember feeling really relaxed and "purged" afterwards, so that Monday was a terribly important day for me.'

For Annie, 'it was like an adventure. There was a lot of warmth, even though some of us hardly knew each other, and I found it very supportive. All of which is amazing, since three of us were in a terrible state at that

136

time, just keeping ourselves together and no more. I'm glad we took it easy and built up mutual trust. Having food afterwards was like a real treat – and then there was the swimming . . .'

Sometimes, using the same group listening technique, we would focus on someone's dream, or on an emotionally charged topic like dependence or competitiveness.

Annie: 'I remember one meeting which was really good for me, in some mysterious way. When it was my turn I was talking about a dream about my father, who's dead. The dream was very upsetting. I felt that exploring the emotions and discovering more really worked for me. Some questions that were asked made me discover things I hadn't remembered or realised. I got into the dream completely, enjoyed recreating the atmosphere; it was exciting, like a cross between writing and reading something really good. Although I got really upset, I felt unbelievably happy afterwards, as if a weight had been lifted off me.'

Some of the dream sessions were extremely creative, we inspired one another; sharing our vulnerability often tipped over into sharing pleasure and laughter. There were deeply tragic things too, deaths and fears – sometimes it seemed that the whole world and our experience of it were revealed in dream form – our individual anger at oppression, our anguish about the fact of torture, the hidden damage of class, the war in Ireland.

Yet we related to the group in different ways, and got different things from it. Pat: 'I never got much out of dreams apart from a fairly detached interest in how dreams come together. I got most out of the times when we each talked for ten minutes on the same topic – trust, passivity or whatever – you just got such a clear picture of all the different experiences, a sort of spectrum. It had a sort of seesaw effect, because – not just when I was talking but when other people were – it helped stir up associations for me.'

Marion: 'I remember a particular one. It was after a week of extreme self-hate – I didn't want to talk but the others questioned me, made me examine my misery and the talking loosened me until I cried. Then the others hugged me and gave general comfort. It was like when sympathy makes you cry. Afterwards I felt better, the weight of self-hatred lifted and hasn't returned as badly since.'

Often if I'd been instrumental in helping someone else come to grips with some emotional difficulty, discover more, and be in some way freed by it, I felt at least as good as they did afterwards. I felt happy, somehow more potent and effective – we all felt this in various degrees.

Liz: 'When it's been obvious that the person definitely felt better afterwards, I've felt good, really useful. But I don't think I've really got through anything myself. I remember being upset and coming to meetings and feeling less upset when I left, through talking and everyone listening to me, but it didn't last very long for me personally, because I don't think I ever got very deeply into the feelings.'

Since we were trying to work collectively the responsibility to play a positive, helpful role bore down heavily sometimes. Pat: 'There was a long period in which I used to feel on edge all the time because of the pressure I felt to be asking all those perceptive questions. At one level I was tuned in, really listening and empathising, but at another I was just feeling that I ought to be proving myself as a worthwhile – effective – member. A few times I was almost completely paralysed by this feeling that I ought to say something, ask a question, just for the sake of saying something.'

All of us had different needs for attention and help, and different ways of asking for it. Those who suffered more extreme states often took priority – we didn't quite achieve the sort of structure which would have ensured that each woman felt an equal responsibility for taking the time and space to explore her own emotional predicament, but which had enough fluidity to allow for sudden crises and explosions of need.

Liz: 'It's complicated working out who most needs attention, how much effort you've got to put into helping others, and how much you need to take out. It means that all the time you're in a very conscious, rational situation, trying to sort this out.'

There are certain feelings like anger which we've found very difficult to express and deal with. We're all feminists with quite a sophisticated rational understanding of the ways women are conditioned in this society, and we all want to change it. We know, for instance, that women have been forced into competition against one another in terms of sex appeal, intellect, etc., for men's approval. However, at times this rational understanding has worked against us. For instance, I came to one session convulsed with guilt and unhappiness because of the antagonism and competitiveness I felt towards Liz. I plucked up my courage and tried to tell her this in the supportive atmosphere of the group. I was lying on the bed, leaden, my chin tucked down on to my chest, my voice constricted, mumbling how I thought she never gave me any credit for things I did, always seemed to be putting me down, and so on. Merely talking and discovering what she felt about me helped to dispel some of the conflict between us – but it ended with the whole group reassuring us; collectively we explained and analysed everything away. I was left with my volcanic feelings. Whereas if the group had urged us to act out a physical confrontation, got us to yell and swear at each other, these feelings might have been able to erupt – and perhaps we could have discovered more and changed more. As it was, I stuck in more or less inhibited knots of suppressed aggression. On the whole, we've tended to tacitly avoid exercises where anger, noise, shouts and energy were released.

The gentleness with each other which was necessary at the beginning is now being experienced more often as a rather timid over-politeness, which cramps initiative and allows inertia to rule.

Marion: 'I often feel we control our irritations with each other – given a year together we should trust each other enough not to interpret criticism as a personal attack.'

Some of the friction arose from an inhibiting uncertainty about the unresolved question of leadership responsibility.

Pat: 'The way people suggest things always sounds – at least my voice always sounds – as if they're trying to be as tentative as possible, swallowing their voices. There's never an air of dynamism when we arrive – it's always as if everyone's totally weighed down.' Each of us was unsure where responsibility lay, how much of it to take, how much to urge others into doing exercises they showed reluctance to, etc.

Pat: 'When people's voices trail off at the end it's very difficult to be enthusiastic. You make this half-suggestion about trying something, so nobody responds, so you feel it was a completely pathetic suggestion. . . .' And all of this in a group where we all want each other to be able to feel, and be, as strong and forceful as possible!

As well as the uncertainty, there was an inequality in our experience and confidence. When we began, I'd had the most contact with the ways and means of therapy, since I'd done it for a year with a rather skilful and inventive (though sexist) therapist. I took an interest in the subject, read a bit, and collected techniques for use in the group. However, though I got a great deal out of sharing this and feeling helpful, as I've said, I did begin to feel trapped in the role. I began to resent what I saw as the other women's passivity – a simplistic view in fact, since the real picture was more complex than that. People were developing their confidence and experience in their own ways; my resentment was often demoralising for everyone. Quite early on I suggested we all go to a professionally led group to gain knowledge, but since only three of us did, that didn't solve the problem, which now we're grappling with anew.

Pat describes her lack of confidence: 'I find it very difficult to get any farther than listening, reassuring, giving security – I've no focus to use as a guide for suggesting things.'

Annie: 'A lot of us have never overcome our ignorance of what methods actually exist, it never occurs to us to go off and read this or that.'

Partly as a result of a discussion for this article, we've decided that each woman in turn will formally lead the group. This means doing some 'homework', working out methods, and dealing with the evening in her particular way, developing her own leadership skills and angles. We also agreed to break out of the straitjacket of endless verbalising and loosen ourselves up with physical, noise-making exercises or massage in every session. After the first and second of these reformed meetings, led by Liz, then Marion, I can only say that our inhibition with each other was greatly dispersed – apprehensiveness had given way to a sparkling expectancy. It was like a Magical Mystery Tour again.

To get a wider perspective on the use of such a group, it's interesting to look back at some of the needs we didn't meet – the people who passed through, friends or local women who were sent to us. A young student who'd been anorexic for a couple of years came and seemed to be getting a lot out of being with us, but perhaps she became fearful or alienated by our feminism, our cohesiveness, I don't know: numerous phone calls failed to get a response, and she didn't come back. Another woman who joined for a while found it rather heavy going, too help-orientated and not light-hearted enough; she wanted to do more role-exploring things, like changing into each other's clothes, or dressing up in the sort of feminine gear we wore as teenagers, acting things out, etc. We failed to integrate this, and she left, while retaining her individual friendships with us. Annie had a friend she encouraged to join – she'd moved to London from Belfast and lived in the outer suburbs with a young family. She struggled with awful fears – in the supermarket she'd be almost certain that either the British Secret Service or the IRA were after her, trailing her among the grocery shelves. In the end, fear of antagonising her husband and anxiety about travelling alone precluded her coming.

After the group, two of us had a meeting with the wife of someone we know locally. Since she seemed to be in a very bad way we talked for hours and hours trying to sort out merely what to do about her overwhelming material problems – housing, money and custody struggles. But her dissociation from us, herself, and everything around her was so extreme that we got nowhere. We felt she would need a very caring, emotionally nourishing environment for a long time to get back together. We heard that she was later sectioned, but only for a short period.

A question often asked about self-help groups is – can they ever really be an alternative for large numbers of people? In the case of therapy, we would answer that it's hardly a question of *alternatives* – the NHS provides nothing in the first place. Unless you count the services of some 50 psychotherapists for upwards of 50 million souls.

Just as the conditions of everyday life make therapy groups necessary – a matter of life and death for some people – so does the appalling lack of public, free, progressive provision make self-help necessary. The existence of our group is a living criticism of that lack, and of a system pitted with such inhuman oversights.

To preserve anonymity, the names in this article have been changed.

Forum: Therapy: reform or revolution?
SR 69 April 1978

FOR THERAPY
by Stef Pixner

Despite the women's movement, women continue to co-operate unintentionally in their own subordination. The basic psychology of the female, which is based on passivity, being nurturant and giving up one's (own) needs for nurturance, is still operating for women of our generation. (Luise Eichenbaum and Susie Orbach, *Humpty Dumpty* no. 8)

Therapy has something to offer women that action, study and conscious-ness-raising can't give. The therapy that I've done (a mixture of feminist and non-feminist, group and individual, therapy) has helped me to become less depressed, more angry, more able to know what I need and act on it, though it has been painful and uneven.

Mostly therapy is used in a way which controls women and encourages us to accept things as they are. It has developed inside the 'personal' sphere of the personal/political split, where responsibility for change is laid at the feet of individuals. Not only do you feel bad, but it's your fault. The split between home and work, between individual and social, makes it difficult to work on both public-political and personal-political fronts at once; there's a danger of going too far one way or the other . . . but that's a key problem for the women's movement as a whole and we can't afford to neglect either.

The roots of most of the problems therapy has to deal with are social and need to be fought directly, collectively. But a lot of women need individual help to be able to fight, or even to keep going. As one woman put it, 'therapy can save lives'. One in six women try to get help from the NHS at some time in their lives, and there's a growing demand for therapy amongst women in the movement. I don't see therapy as an end in itself, or something that every woman needs or should do. It can't be a substitute for collective action, for study or consciousness-raising. But there are skills and knowledge developed over the last 80 years which can be used by us, critically, to serve our own ends. We would be throwing the baby out with the bath water not to use them.

We need to build resources and experience inside and outside the NHS to help women who break down in a way that friends and family can't cope with or help; women who face persistent depressions, suicidal feel-ings, anxiety, phobias or eating problems, as well as women who just want to know themselves better, to be able to take responsibility for themselves within the limiting conditions of their social circumstances, and to change deeply held patterns of timidity, dependence, or self-hate. We can also use therapy to develop a better understanding of the psychology of oppression, of how deeply we have taken sexism into our personalities.

Why therapy? Because most therapies assume that some things can only be explained by unconscious motivation and that until you can understand the way conscious and unconscious work together or (more often) in opposition, there's a lot you can't explain or change. For example you feel dead or empty, or you can't make decisions. You're exhausted whenever you try to learn how to mend a car, or to read a difficult book. You burst into tears when you mean to be angry. You can't stop eating or smoking or hurting the people you love; you are turned on by particularly sexist men; you go blank whenever you want to speak out at a workshop; you can't remember things. The sort of things you make resolutions about, but something sabotages your good intentions over and over again, a part of you you don't know about. Therapy helps to find out what, so that you can have greater control of yourself (often by controlling yourself less).

It could be something in you that treats you as you've been treated; a voice that says you're stupid, too loud, immoral. The critical voice of your father, your mother, teachers, friends, lovers, the media: internalised oppression, the 'policemen' in your head that step on you and drive you to step on others without understanding why. It could be a deep need denied by your 'policemen' – for nurturance or achievement, or heldback anger. In the therapy groups I was in, it was very hard for most of us women to identify, let alone express, anger. It was easier to cry, criticise, reproach, or be depressed, and that was just as true for the feminists as the non-feminists amongst us.

We become the individuals we are after years of interacting in particular contexts of sex, family, class, race, etc. We respond to these givens in unique ways, taking them inside our heads, organising them consciously and unconsciously into patterns of feeling and thought which don't automatically change when social changes occur – and can't simply be changed by an act of will. Changing or breaking down the patterns may trigger off a crisis which needs reliable support from an individual or group, plus particular techniques and detective work, for getting at unconscious material and helping the woman to integrate it with her conscious feelings and self-images. The patterns are likely to be contradictory, formed at different ages and to be many-layered. The most obvious one may not be the most important. A part of you identifies with a man, perhaps. One part of you is two years old and terrified of being abandoned. Another part is 35 and independent. One part is ambitious and competitive. Another abhors success. Women's liberation can add an extra paralysing conflict. We aren't supposed to feel competitive or jealous of other women; we're supposed to be strong, angry, independent, etc. This can set up a double repression.

I think that accepting and 'owning' what you are, what your circumstances have made you, and what you have made of them, consciously or unconsciously, in all its pain and messy contradictions, is a basis both for personal change and for an honest feminist politics.

AGAINST THERAPY
by Sheila Jeffreys

In the last couple of years there has been a vast increase in the number of feminists seeking solutions by going into conventional therapy or by adopting therapy techniques into their feminist practice, even substituting them, in local groups, for consciousness-raising. It is time that the whole area of therapy was discussed very seriously, lest therapy ideas and techniques gradually take over and destroy the revolutionary potential of the movement. Is therapy a harmless sideline which could even be of great benefit to us, or is it a threat? Most of us reject traditional male psychoanalysis and growth movement therapy, because they are anti-feminist, i.e. aimed at moulding women into a 'feminine' role, and counter-revolutionary, i.e. seeking to change the person to make them fit in, rather than aiding them to launch a critique of a sick society. A feminist, who is interested in therapy and rejects these approaches, can turn to the 'Feminist Therapy Centre' where she can engage in traditional one-to-one therapeutic techniques or directed group therapy, or she can adopt growth movement therapy, e.g. encounter groups, co-counselling, gestalt or bio-energetics, for use in a group of women. I think that both these possibilities are very dubious.

Is 'feminist therapy' really much different from non-feminist varieties? Any form of one-to-one therapy with an 'expert' or 'professional' is totally non-democratic, one-way directed and, even if conducted by a woman, is precisely the sort of authoritarian and hierarchical set-up which, as women, we are trying to get away from. To qualify as radical therapy, that is, therapy aimed at changing society to make it fit for people and not the other way round, a technique should satisfy two criteria: (1) the development of awareness, from a state of mystification and false consciousness, to a realisation of oppression and its origins; (2) contacting the company of other people with whom to share these realisations and work towards change.

The first criterion could be realised in feminist therapy if each woman were to realise her situation as part of an oppressed group, with a clearly identifiable oppressor, i.e. the ruling class of men. But feminist therapy still seems very much concerned with discussing family background, individuality and uniqueness, so the oppressor could seem to be mum or dad or the woman herself. The second criterion clearly rules out all directed and one-to-one techniques.

There are no techniques of therapy developed out of the women's movement, or even by women. A technique is not simply a harmless tool which can be bent to any purpose; it is not value-free. A therapy technique is based upon certain premises about the nature of the human personality and is developed to achieve certain ends. These premises and ends emerge from the male ruling class. As we are suspicious about all other male inventions, ideologies, etc., so should we be far more rigorous in our examination of techniques concerning the mind, particularly when they are being adopted into the heart of a supposedly revolutionary movement.

The technique of consciousness-raising is the basis of the revolutionary struggle of women. Its purpose is the development of revolutionary anger and strength with others with whom we can take political action. Its method, whether speaking one by one round the group, or speaking at random, involves the pooling of the collective experience of women, in small personal groups, in order to analyse the structures of our oppression and the best way to fight them. Its purpose is not to make an individual woman feel that she can cope better with her lot, but to make her feel that she need not cope, but must struggle. That is not to say that consciousness-raising does not alleviate distress and make us feel happier. Inevitably it supplies validation and support, a secure setting for the outpouring of anger and hate, plus the joy of recognising and under-standing our situation, even though these are not its ultimate aims. None of us could feel totally happy and at ease in a patriarchal society; that would be an unrealistic aim. Satisfaction should and does come from the transformation of depression and auto-destruction into outwardly directed aggression, against the 'man' and his ways. Action with other women should be therapeutic in itself.

Clearly, consciousness-raising does not go far enough, it does not assure the well-being of all sisters, or we would not be flying towards therapy in ever-increasing numbers. It is criticised as not dealing enough with individual sources of distress, which cannot be moulded into collec-tive experience. It is also a technique which we need to polish and extend; there are difficulties in practice, in the form of hidden hierarchies and in games such as 'more feminist than thou', which can develop. However, it should not be abandoned because it has deficiencies; rather we should work on these. We must find out how to incorporate, satisfactorily, the 'cure of souls' into our feminist practice, so that we do not perpetuate the splits which have up to now been used by the male ruling-class, to divide and rule both men and women. The splits, whether between work and play, youth and age, body and mind, operate to prevent human beings from integrating their experience, from relating as whole people to each other and the world about them, and from developing total and fundamental critiques of the society in which they live. The use of therapy is such a split. It is a separation of the realm of mental health from the rest of our social and political lives.

The aims of therapy cannot be precisely the same as those of conscious-ness-raising. Apologists for therapy may claim that it can make an indi-vidual woman feel stronger about her own situation and therefore a more efficient revolutionary if she chooses to be involved in the struggle. It could equally make her a better cook or novelist. It is not the aim of therapy to create the impetus and conditions for revolution. It could be actively anti-revolutionary. One danger is the concentration on the individual rather than the collective experience, i.e. what is different, not what is the same. Is it really valuable or necessary that vast numbers of women should spend hours thinking about their dreams and fantasies and looking for individual patterns and explanations, when there is a war going on outside between men and women? Another danger is the actual deflection of revolutionary anger. That which is being thrashed out on a cushion is not being channelled against the oppressor. Those qualities which make us revolutionaries, anger, hate and fear, are our strengths not our weaknesses. Our feelings of paranoia are a clear perception of reality; we do live in occupied territory where men are trying to kill us. We need to use these emotions, not blot them out. Another anti-revolutionary tendency of therapy is the privatisation of feeling, particularly in the case of one-to-one therapy, where socialising between the therapist and client is very much frowned upon, and in some group techniques which require that group members do not meet outside the group. Most important of all, it offers a personal solution which can be achieved without revolutionary change, and without even being involved in the revolutionary struggle.

The upturn in therapy in the women's liberation movement means the liberalisation and defusing of the movement. It means the abandonment of the tenets of the movement without questioning or trying to enlarge and develop them. The implicit assumption behind the flowering of therapy is that the women's liberation movement has already failed.

The above article is a reprint of a paper presented at the Women and Mental Health Conference, October 1977

Letters Forum
SR 71 June 1978

From Linda M. Baker

Dear *Spare Rib*,
I have the feeling that Ms Jeffreys doesn't really grasp the depth or immensity of mental illness. When you're in a state where you can't recognise what a person is, you don't know where or why you are, you're living in fear and horror and pain, I fear the type of 'collective' therapy she talks about is detrimental. In my case, it was only too easy to lean on other people and push my craziness aside. When you become 'apart' from reality, depersonalised from yourself, the only way (I have found) to get back some semblance of order and become stronger is to go deep into yourself, face all those terrors and fight them yourself. It's your mind, only you can do it. With support, yes, but it's your battle.
'Is it really valuable or necessary that vast numbers of women should spend hours thinking about their dreams and fantasies . . . when there's a war going on outside between men and women?' The only way you're going to get to be a stronger, more capable person is by knowing yourself, your strengths and weaknesses. And doesn't she see that mental illness goes way way beyond dreams and fantasies. It is you, while you're feeling it.

From Carol Lee
Dear *Spare Rib*,
While I agree in general with Sheila Jeffreys's paper on therapy, it makes one or two points I should like to answer. She says, 'satisfaction should . . . come from the transformation of depression and auto-destruction into outwardly directed aggression against the "man" and his ways'. And later 'those qualities which make us revolutionaries – anger, hate, fear – are our strengths not our weaknesses.' All of this is very male-orientated and rooted in the value assumptions of prick culture. Yes, it is therapeutic for women to be angry, and it can spur us to revolutionary action. But as we used to say in the old days 'you can't build a non-violent society on a violent revolution.'

In the same way a generation of women bred only to hate and anger, and focused on their oppressor rather than on their shared potential, are far more likely to carry the politics of intimidation already rampant in the movement into the culture they create than they are likely to live out the politics of love, sharing and caring necessary to any truly democratic collective society.

From Claire Betti
Dear Sisters,
Sheila Jeffreys's article made me angry, not with men or society but with her attitudes, I'm sure that everyone is aware that therapy as an instrument to aid self-awareness, whether in groups or otherwise, happens on an individual level *to* the individual. It's also clear that there is not much room for introspection with 'revolutionaries' – there is somehow implicit in 'socialism' that there is a purity attached to thinking always of others and never about how the self is feeling. I'think this is the Left's most amazing and frightening mistake.

We, as women, have never had the space and time to even be children, being forced at an early age to take on responsibility for others and to subordinate our own needs. At the same time as being child/adults we are expected to grow up into adult/children, being passive and dependent but also caring for numerous (it feels) others. The therapeutic relationship seeks, within the context of feminism, to explore these complicated relations of power and powerlessness, how it feels to be constantly up against authority (in the case the therapist) and whether or not it might be possible ever to have power and *not* misuse it as so many parents do. Here we can question and doubt that authority and explore our anger and power without being called castrating or manipulating. For me this has been revolutioning and *not* merely reforming. Is Sheila Jeffreys really pooh-poohing the idea that therapy might make a woman a better novelist or cook?? – well why not if that's what *she* wants?

It would seem therapy is attracting more women than revolutionary politics which could be saying something about the coercive and evangelical techniques I associate with politics. After all, women have a right to choose the something they want and maybe they are choosing therapy because it's the *first* thing that's come along which gives them something for themselves – and *why not*? I get sick to the stomach of hearing how I shouldn't be so 'introspective' – why the fuck *not, for once*?

De-privatising depression
Ruth Elizabeth
SR 130 May 1983

This is an extended version of a piece I wrote to read at a radical feminist group which used to meet regularly in Lancaster. The group was formed to discuss feminist politics, in the broadest sense, starting from radical feminist assumptions – that women are a sex-class actively oppressed by men, that this oppression is more fundamental than others, and so on. Although it was not specifically a consciousness-raising group we did try to base our discussions in shared experiences from our personal lives, though this did not always work.

I had been a member of the group for over a year before we discussed 'mental illness' and, in particular, the ways in which my own frequent bouts of deep depression affected my relationships with the other members of the group and with the women's movement generally. I discovered that I was very angry with the way a wall of silence had been constructed around my experience of depression so that it was never talked about and not seen to have any political significance beyond the vague notion that 'mental illness' in women is *really* the unhappiness and pain of oppression. The article that grew out of this anger was an attempt to break through this silence by examining how and why it is maintained, and to argue that 'mental illness' is a central problem for *all* women and a crucial issue for the women's movement.

My own experience of 'mental illness' began about 12 years ago in the sixth form at school when I felt frequently overwhelmed by painful emotions which I could not control. I was expected to do very well in my 'A' levels and my family and teachers were all so sure I would sail through and cope with everything that nobody realised what a terrible state I was in. Somehow I managed to get through my exams and I went on to university. Things were no better there and I was completely unable to work. I spent most of the time hiding from people and crying. I was given some medication by a university doctor but it did not seem to make any difference, and after a term I left.

At that time it did not occur to me to think of myself as ill, though I did know that something was wrong and I wished that someone would help me. The bombshell of a psychiatric label hit me a few months later when a consultant psychiatrist I had been sent to by my GP told me he wanted me to go into hospital – and I realised he meant a *mental* hospital. I was deeply shocked.

147

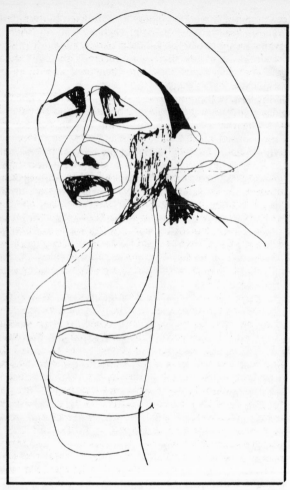

FIGURE 15 Painful emotions, *Stef Pixner* (*SR 85* August 1979)

Thus began the first of many hospital admissions – 13 in all, I think, over the next four or five years. That admission lasted six weeks, during which I spent a weekend on a locked ward after attempting to cut my wrists, and received a course of ECT (electroconvulsive therapy) as medication had failed to lift my depression. I gave my consent to the ECT because I was promised both that it was completely harmless and that it would definitely make me better. There are still gaps in my memory now as a result of this 'treatment', and after each session my friends had to introduce themselves to me because I didn't know who any of them were. After the six weeks I was told that I had received the full range of their treatment and that they considered me recovered and fit to go home. Within months I was back in again.

The following few years continued a vicious circle of home to hospital to home again, which seemed endless. I became a typical mental patient in many ways. I learnt how to manipulate my way in and out of hospital as it suited me, caused innumerable dramas by taking minor overdoses, and like many others in hospital tortured my own arms and hands with razor cuts and cigarette burns. I learnt a great deal about psychiatric classifications and what symptoms doctors looked for. (I collected a whole range of diagnoses – from schizophrenia and manic-depression to person-ality disorder.) I became a walking dictionary of drugs and their side-effects. (Over the years my medication was added to so that I was eventu-ally taking eight different drugs at once, including a barbiturate.) More than one doctor predicted that I would be on these drugs and in and out of hospital for the rest of my life. I became what was known to the staff as 'a permanent patient'. My identity had become that of a mental patient – I knew no other way of life.

The turning point for me was the 28-day 'section' (compulsory treat-ment) in a locked ward where I let rip and smashed as many windows as I could. Having gone as far away as I could go from normality and become as 'mad' as I'd ever been, I finally figured out that no one was going to come and rescue me and that unless I was to spend the rest of my life behind bars I would have to do something about my situation.

Trying to become a responsible adult in a mental hospital is a very difficult thing for a patient to do. It is much easier to play the games that everyone else plays and that the staff expect. Trying to behave 'normally' brought me into great conflict with the nursing staff and occupational therapists. I wanted to start to direct my own life and this was not allowed. I was considered 'bolshy' and uncooperative, and this was seen by the doctors as another symptom of my illness. I was put (in an open ward now) under a strict regime – denied privileges like visiting the canteen – because I was thought to be a 'difficult' patient.

I also wanted to assert my lesbian identity more strongly but had this undermined by the female psychiatrist who told me I was not a 'real' lesbian. This was harder to deal with in some ways than the male psychiatrists' voyeuristic preoccupation with the physical details of my sex life, which they liked to make notes about.

However, I was encouraged in my attempt to take back control of my life by a wonderful woman social worker who eventually got me a place in a Richmond Fellowship hostel – a 'half-way house' for mental patients. There I was at last given the space to grow, and I have never looked back.

Unfortunately though, my life now is still plagued with bouts of deep depression which my present doctors call 'endogenous' – it supposedly has a biochemical cause unconnected with outside events. I am now involved in and totally committed to the women's movement, but because of my depression I feel rather peripheral and limited in what I can do. Many women who have no experience of depression find it very difficult to believe that a mental condition can be totally immobilising. It is rarely appreciated that when I am depressed what little energy I have all goes into just getting through the routine of everyday life which is an enormous struggle. Sometimes I am unable to get out of bed, let alone leave my flat and face other people. Because of this I really do feel separated off, as if behind some sort of enclosure, from most of the women I know. Partly, this is the result of having been labelled 'mentally ill' and made to feel unfit to mingle with the rest of the world, so that it is very, very hard for me now to believe that I am acceptable, that I have a right to be here. But I also believe that this sense of separateness is perpetuated, perhaps unwittingly, by other women who distance themselves from me. I suspect that certain feelings of alienation and otherness are basic to our experience of ourselves as women under patriarchy. But I cannot accept that it is necessary for me, when I am depressed, to sometimes feel so utterly freakish and alone that I wish I could go back into hospital because that is the only place I have ever felt I really belonged.

I have noticed a variety of distancing and silencing techniques being used towards me by other women. Some women respond with looks of incomprehension and a frightened silence when I try to talk about my experience of depression and despair. Others are patronisingly 'normal' and superior and want to advise and 'look after' me. Some women feel they ought to warn me about the dangers of taking medication and want to explain that mental illness is really all a patriarchal plot and that what I should be doing is fighting to change my situation. How helpful to have further feelings of guilt and inadequacy heaped on those I've already got! Do they think I don't worry about poisoning myself? And how do you change your situation when you can't even get out of bed? Besides, I *have* changed my situation – I am no longer in hospital – but few people realise what sort of struggle and achievement that represents.

A more seductive reaction, but still a distancing technique, is the idealised view of madness as a breakthrough into an unmapped and forbidden territory. I have even been put on a pedestal in this manner and treated like a sort of prophet. I think there are situations in which 'not coping' is the healthiest thing to do. And it is good if through my 'not coping' other women have been made aware of the price they were paying in numbness, blinkeredness, rigidity, and especially in not communicating with each other, for their ability to sail or muddle through horrendously destructive situations. I have more than once been the cause of a group of women drastically changing a situation because my not being able to 'cope' with it forced them to look at what was really happening and how much they were all blocking out. But the glamourising of pain and depression is not helpful – it is simply another way for people to distance themselves from the reality, the agony of it.

A more common distancing technique is the trivialising one, comparing depression to 'off days' which 'everybody' has. A more complete silencing takes place when women pretend that my depression doesn't exist. So they never ask about it and somehow communicate that it is not the sort of thing they are interested in talking about. This makes me feel split, as if I lead a double life. An important part of me remains hidden, privatised, a personal problem I have to deal with on my own. When this unacceptable part gets out of control I have to hide myself away, feeling ashamed, so few people find out how much effort I often have to put into doing very basic daily things, and I am often misunderstood and seen as unreliable.

I would like other women to help me to stop feeling such a freak. I want to hear other women talk about *their* experiences of anguish, despair, pain, rejection, insecurity and so on, so that we can make connections. One way in which we could get away from the divisions caused between us by using medical definitions might be for us to relate the experiences of patriarchal violence I suffered in the form of 'treatment' for mental illness to other women's experience of other forms of patriarchal violence – such as rape, battering, and the oppression surrounding physical disabilities. I'm sure my feelings of powerlessness, hopelessness, humiliation, guilt, and self-hatred, if not my 'clinical depression', have been shared by other women in the hands of other male institutions. Perhaps what happens is not that I am particularly prone to these feelings but that most women block them off in order to survive, or that feeling them, they choose not to talk about them, so that they remain private and unutterable.

I believe we need to reconceptualise those experiences which men have labelled 'mental illness' so that those of us who have been so labelled can cease to regard ourselves as 'ill'. I have struggled for years to abandon that conception of myself and have found that I cannot do it on my own. If I am to integrate myself so that I am no longer split between the 'normal' me and the 'ill' me, then that 'ill' me must be acceptable not only to me but to other women as well. In fact, I cannot accept it until others do. And for other women to accept it I think means that those women must examine their *own* unacceptable, inadequate, frightened, vulnerable parts of themselves. Then together we can try to find words for these experiences, to explore their origins and understand them in order to *do* something about them. What I am advocating is decidedly *not* some form of therapy. It is precisely the experience of pain as an illness, a privatised, personal problem that I want to get away from. I'm not asking for support so much as a sense of mutual recognition, a door through which I can come in from the cold, or through which you can come out into the storm.

'Mental illness' needs to be examined as a mammoth patriarchal institution that does violence to us *all*, not only in the way I have been affected by being labelled as 'ill', but also in the way that the so-called 'healthy' have been affected by male-defined standards of normality. What exactly is happening when women behave 'normally'? Perhaps we should ask not why some women crack up after having a baby, or have nervous breakdowns at university, but why other women don't. Why do some women 'get through' the menopause or 'cope' with appalling housing conditions when others don't? When women 'cope' with, get through, and even get on and succeed in unhealthy, destructive patriarchal institutions, what is happening to them? In other words, we need to examine mental *health* as well as mental illness if those of us who have been labelled mentally ill are going to be able to stop being *ourselves* as the problem, as victims of an unfortunate personal failure setting us apart from all the 'normal' women around us. I want my struggle to be seen as important, something which affects all of us in fundamental, if different ways, something which is an integral part of the building of the women's liberation movement.

Since bringing these issues to one of the meetings our group has broken up. But sharing all this has fundamentally altered my relationships with some of the group members, and I no longer feel so apart.

Ruth Elizabeth's original article on depression, 'Deprivatizing Pain', appeared in Cat Call, A Feminist Discussion Paper, *no. 14.*

CHAPTER 4

BIRTH CONTROL: WHO CONTROLS?

One of the first four demands of the women's liberation movement in 1971 was about birth control, and some of the first organising projects supported heterosexually active women's right to free and safe birth control methods. Our ability and right to control our reproductive capacities were immediately recognised as *central* to women's liberation. Agitation for more (and more accessible) family planning facilities, for better distribution of birth control information, and a clearer spelling out of the dangers of any particular method were the initial aims.

Feminists also saw that only when women could control their fertility would they be truly free to direct energy towards other areas of life. Patriarchal control was loosened. As well, any discussion of the sexuality of fertile, heterosexually active women *had* to address birth control too. Women's choice to separate reproduction from sexuality was a fundamental challenge to male domination.

In the early 1970s the distribution and availability of the most 'effective' form of birth control, the pill, were featured in *Spare Rib*. However, the side-effects of that method and the way in which it had been originally 'tested' in the bodies of Third World women did not feature in these articles. The IUD (intra-uterine device) was also written about uncritically.

When criticism *did* come a little later, more interest in alternative methods of contraception also surfaced, for example, older barrier methods which did not carry the same perils, but *did* rely on careful use and the individual's familiarity with her own body.

Early acceptance of the pill and to a lesser degree the IUD, as liberating forces, gave way quite quickly in *Spare Rib* to a relentlessly critical voice. For one thing, who was liberated? And whose fertility was controlled? There was a confusion between responsibility for *conception*, and control of *contraception* – and ultimately the onus of both weighed ever more heavily on the woman. *Spare Rib* also pursued the dangers of the pill, condemned doctors who prescribed it irresponsibly, and condemned the drug companies whose motivating force was profit.

Within the reproductive rights movement debates around individual women's right of control over their fertility have joined or sometimes jostled with an emphasis on the role of social policy, religion and availability of information on different groups of women. The choices women make about birth control – whether to use it in the first place, and which method to use – are never made in isolation. With population control, the conflict between women's individual wishes and state (or imperialist) programmes is highlighted.

Sometimes women themselves resist the imposition of 'family planning', especially when the 'planning' is state-imposed and takes place before (or without) any meaningful changes in the economic or social role of women. There are other instances when a particular state policy seeks to increase population, again contrary to some women's own wishes. These contradictions are not always easy ones for feminists to work with. Supporting women in controlling their fertility initially seems clear-cut, and yet is there anything necessarily anti-feminist about challenging the ideology of individual 'private' choice in matters of reproduction? These questions are unresolved and raise other problematic issues around infertility, 'high-tech' babies, surrogate motherhood and AID. These issues have been debated deeply but not consistently in *Spare Rib* articles, usually through particular subjects, like the injectable contraceptive Depo-Provera, where information is given as well as the deeper issues being represented.

No packet carries a government health warning
Jill Rakusen and Angela Phillips
SR 29 November 1974

Some contraceptives can actually cause conception: this is the conclusion we have reached after examining some 14 chemical contraceptives.

Chemical contraceptives act by killing the sperm in the vagina before it reaches the neck of the womb. They come in the forms of cream or jelly in a tube, aerosols, or pessaries which dissolve after insertion in the vagina.

We bought the contraceptives either over the counter or through two mail order firms. Most of the manufacturers gave inadequate instructions, some gave none at all, many made dubious claims – either overtly or by implication – and all failed on at least one count. The area of chemical contraception seems to be particularly prone to misinformation. It seems that as long as manufacturers can fulfil the spermicide test, they can do what they like in terms of the way they market the product.

Before we go any further, we must emphasise that this is not a consumer's report with a 'best' and 'worst' buy; nor do we intend this survey to be comprehensive. Our conclusions simply point to a fundamental problem that we as women all face, a problem that is not confined within the limited field of contraception: these products are being sold primarily for other people's gain; our interests are, at best, of secondary importance.

In this country, spermicides have to undergo annual tests for spermicidal power. But the functioning of a spermicide can be adversely affected by various factors:

FIGURE 16 Never-ending problems with the pill *Williams*
(*SR* 12 June 1973)

(a) Douching and bathing: 'do not douche or bath immediately after intercourse (FPA instructing doctor writing in *General Practitioner* 22 March 1974);

(b) Age: *Which?* reported in 1971 that two products 'had deteriorated so much that they no longer killed sperms', and that suppositories and foaming tablets will deteriorate quickly if kept in hot or damp places;

(c) The time and manner in which it is inserted.

Above all, tests for spermicidal power are carried out under laboratory conditions which are far removed from the real live conditions in which spermicides are used. Thus, in the vaginal setting it is quite easy for some sperm to completely miss contact with the spermicide, whereas in a laboratory dish this is not the case. So much for spermicidal power.

The functioning of a spermicide will therefore almost certainly be affected unless the user is aware of the above factors, and as these products are not necessarily sold in clinics, it is imperative that the manufacturers provide adequate information and instructions. Many products – like C-Film – have an exclusion clause, e.g. 'highly effective when correctly applied and it is vitally important that you follow the directions carefully'. Bearing this in mind no manufacturer warned against bathing, only three warned against douching within six hours, one suggested delaying for only one hour, and Rendell's even suggest that their cream can easily be removed by douching – thereby implying that douching is a good thing and giving no warning against it. Contrary to a recommendation in the 1971 *Which?* report no product bore a date stamp.

No products gave any warning about the possible effects on caps or washable sheaths – and not all spermicides are fit to be used with such appliances. Rendell's Pessaries were claimed to be ideal with sheath or IUD – and this product was found to damage rubber in the last *Which?* report. Were Rendell's trying to imply that their product was less than ideal for the cap? (Incidentally, neither the FPA nor the DHSS Safety Committee could enlighten us about the possible effects of these products on rubber.)

Claims for the effective use of chemical contraceptives alone are numerous, for example: 'for use alone' (Preceptin and Delfen Cream); 'no further precautions need be taken' (Rendell's Pessaries); 'may be used alone when a simple (sic) method is required' (Gynomin); 'at least as reliable as the diaphragm or sheath' (Delfen). Emko gives no indication whatsoever as to what it should be used with, if anything. All this contrasts strangely with what Premier and Lamberts – the distributors – say in their booklets, which have in any case probably already been thrown away by the user; despite the claims of some women, chemical contraceptives used alone have a high failure rate (Lamberts) and for maximum protection the FPA advises their use only in conjunction with a diaphragm or protective (Premier). Either Premier or Lamberts, or both, market the above products; it does seem to be a case of the left hand not knowing what the right hand is doing, with potentially disastrous results for the women in the middle.

Statistics on efficacy are very hard to evaluate and are easily open to abuse. However, the FPA Medical Newsletter 51 (January 1974) gives a rough guide for how successful chemicals are when used alone – and that rate varies between 10 and 40 pregnancies – in other words failures – per 100 women who get pregnant in a year. This compares badly with the range of pregnancies per hundred women-years for the cap (5–25), condom (5–15), coitus interruptus (10–30), copper coil (1–2) and pill (0.2–1.5).

Variations in instructions for insertion abound; many suggest allowing an hour before as the deadline (Emko foam gives three hours); the recommendations for pessaries vary from 20 minutes to one hour . . . but an hour before what? Vague references are made to 'intercourse' but Rendell's Pessaries were the only product recommending re-insertion if *ejaculation* had not occurred within a specific time; all the others seemed to assume that 'intercourse' occurred in some split second – perhaps it does for the writers of instructions! The more independent writers in this field tend to take a more realistic view: 'the shorter the time [inserted] before intercourse the better'. *Which?* believe that 'the woman should push [the tablet] as far as possible into her vagina *when she is lying down*' for maximum efficiency and 'check that foaming starts before putting [the tablet] in – throw it away if it doesn't foam'. No firm mentioned these factors, and even Peel and Potts – a standard textbook on family planning – believe that tablets 'require no instruction apart from the warning that multiple or prolonged coitus requires plural insertion'. Rendell's also say that for a few months after childbirth, two tablets are necessary. Their logic could be concerned with the fact that the hole in the cervix is slightly bigger after childbirth – as it is after dilation of any sort (e.g. abortion, D&C). Perhaps they are subtly encouraging sales by undermining women's faith in one pessary? No other firms mention this.

The Health Education Council said in its campaign last year that aerosols were the only chemicals 'recommended for use alone', and this apparently was endorsed by the FPA. The HEC's current leaflet, however, says that no chemicals are safe on their own. Others (Peel and Potts) are more emphatic: 'the pregnancy rate was still higher (for aerosols) than for traditional methods and considerably less reliable than the other contraceptive methods described (pill, IUD, cap, condom, sterilisation)'. As we have already seen, Delfen claims to be 'at least as reliable as the diaphragm or sheath' and Emko doesn't claim or suggest anything.

It seems clear that the marketing of these products should be strictly controlled. The more obvious issues are date-stamping and the provision of adequate information. The more difficult ones are the 'undermining' techniques where double precautions are suggested if avoidance of pregnancy is 'imperative', yet the reassuring tone in the rest of the instructions heavily counterbalance this.

None of the makers seems to be breaking the law. The fact is, there isn't much law to break – and it's only recently the Committee on the Safety of Medicines has decided to concern itself with efficacy of drugs as well as safety. The Committee is not, however, dealing with the gap between efficacy and the implied claims of manufacturers.

We believe that chemical contraceptives marketed in the way we have described, are likely to cause a woman to conceive by encouraging her to rely on such products alone. Mail order and over-the-counter contraceptives are bought by the very people who are most at risk: those who are too shy to seek advice. Surely, at the very least, there is a need for a government health warning: 'This product should not be used without a sheath or a cap.'

Spermicides: DHSS to take action
Jill Rakusen
SR 40 October 1975

Since the articles concerning the marketing and efficacy of spermicidal contraceptives were published in *Women's Report* (vol. 2, no. 4) and *Spare Rib* (no. 29), the Department of Health has been spurred into action.

The DHSS is taking welcome steps to introduce regulations on advertising, labelling and package leaflets, to provide that they 'should not give the impression, either directly or indirectly, that they are a reliable means of contraception when used on their own and that such advertisements must contain a warning that the product should be used only in conjunction with another compatible method such as a sheath or cap'.

The DHSS is also proposing that leaflets should be required to carry a warning: 'When avoidance of pregnancy is important, the choice of contraceptive method should be made in consultation with a doctor.' This is a big step forward for the Department, which just one short year ago commented to me: 'The best way of ensuring that people use the contraceptive which is both the most effective and the most suitable for their individual requirements is to concentrate on education about the various contraceptive methods and supplies available.'

The Department's proposals outlined above were sent to 'interested parties' in May for comment. It seems likely that the regulations on advertising will come into effect by the end of the year. As the manufacturing and distributions process takes some time, it would be impracticable for labelling regulations to come into force as soon as that, but hopefully they will do so soon after.

Yet more pill problems

Alice Henry
SR 137 December 1983

For years, women have known that taking contraceptive pills definitely increases the risk of heart and circulatory problems and may increase the risk of breast and cervical cancer. While there has been no clear evidence that the pill provokes breast and cervical cancer, there also has been no evidence that it does not.

The guess was that taking pills for years might lead to cancer later in life – but we would have to take the pill for years, then live for years to find out. Well, we've finally done it. On 22 October, two articles were published in the *Lancet*. One found that women who had taken high progesterone pills for at least six years before age 25 were more likely to develop breast cancer by the age of 37. The other found that women who had taken pills for more than four years had a relatively high risk of developing cervical cancer.

While both studies have flaws and are not conclusive, they are quite convincing. In the breast cancer study, the number of women was small (314 women under age 38 who had breast cancer each matched with a woman living in the same neighbourhood who did not have breast cancer). However, both the length of time taking the pills and the level of progestogen in the pills were associated with a higher risk of breast cancer.

It makes sense that high progestogen taken before establishment of regular ovulation (that is, before age 23 or so) might provoke breast cancer. The researchers point out that the rate of cell division is highest in the breast during the luteal phase of the menstrual cycle when progesterone levels in the body are naturally high (a woman's breasts feel thickest and heaviest and lumpiest before menstruation as a result of breast tissue growth). Most teenage women do not ovulate every month and so do not always experience the surge of progesterone that follows ovulation. Thus, taking a high progesterone pill exposes a young woman to more progesterone than her body produces. This is probably not true for women over 25. On the average, it seems that women produce just about as much progesterone normally as there is in high dose progesterone pills. So the data seems to fit what we know about physiology. Women who took high progestogen pills only after age 25 did not have a high risk of developing breast cancer by age 37.

Of course more research is needed – after all, women who took the pill only at older ages may not yet have had time to develop breast cancer. Meanwhile, there is no reason for young women to take high progestogen pills. There are a few low progestogen, low oestrogen pills on the market – why not take the rest off the market?

The cervical cancer study was a 10-year follow-up of 6,838 women using oral contraceptives and 3,154 using the IUD. The study could not control adequately for age at first intercourse and number of sexual partners (more sexual activity is associated with a higher risk of cervical cancer). But age at first childbirth (a reasonable indicator of sexual activity) is fairly similar (76 per cent of pill users and 68 per cent of IUD users had their first full-term pregnancy before age 24).

Finding that duration of use of pills is associated with increased risk of cervical cancer is enough evidence to caution women against using pills for more than four years and to make sure that all pill users have cervical smears regularly. The study did not find any link between oestrogen dosage of pill or brand of pill with risk of cervical cancer. However, they did not test for level of progestogen dose, and this is the ingredient that is most likely to be causing cervical problems. Other researchers have noted that progestogens bind with tissue in the endocervix. It may be that a relatively rare form of cervical cancer, adenocarcinoma of the endocervix, is provoked by progestogens. The usual tests for cervical cancer look for squamous cell dysplasia and may miss adenocarcinoma.

I'm 45 and took the pill for almost ten years. After reading the *Lancet* articles, I ran to the nearest clinic for a cervical cancer test, and will get a second one immediately. One test misses a large proportion of precancerous conditions. For my next test, I'll make sure the doctor actually examines my cervix. I didn't have the guts to ask for that after he had taken the smear and withdrawn the speculum without looking. I felt I would be criticising his medical treatment – so he might either shove the speculum back up, or tell me to get lost, or both.

If you have regular cycles and are over 22, it will have little if any effect on your health to take low dose pills for two or three years. However, other forms of contraception may take a little more effort, but be safer. One possibility is to use the morning-after pill in conjunction with sheaths, caps, or other barrier methods. The morning-after pill is actually an ordinary dose pill. Doctors used to prescribe DES in high doses as a morning-after contraceptive, but that was dangerous. Now, many NHS doctors don't know about or don't tell women about morning-after contraception. After all, wide availability of morning-after pills would give women more control over our fertility.

Women, stop polluting your bodies
Letter from Jane Harvey
SR 137 December 1983

Dear *Spare Rib*,
Yet again I see someone is suffering from the side-effects of the pill and having difficulties with the diaphragm. When are we going to stop injuring and polluting our bodies? It's time we took a firm stand against the responsibility of birth control.

Either give up sex with men or get them to use condoms. Don't listen to their limp excuses of making love with a glove on, etc. They're probably not using the right rubber and should shop around until they find one. Heaven knows there are enough to choose from – all different shapes and sizes, textures and even colours. Any slight detraction they may experience in no way affects our enjoyment, and as an added bonus condoms are a perfect protection against VD, vaginal infections and cancer.

So come on sisters let's rid ourselves once and for all from the shackles of birth control.

Non-patriarchal 'rhythm'
Letter from Diana E. Forrest
SR 134 September 1983

Dear *Spare Rib*,
What has Arati got against rhythm method contraception (*SR13*)? It is true that it may not be useful to everyone, but just because the Catholic church won't allow its members any other form of contraception doesn't make rhythm methods 'serving patriarchy'.

On the contrary they have the following advantages (in situations where they can be used):
1) They do not pander to patriarchal ideas that women must *always* be sexually available to male partners.
(2) They enable other sexual activities than penetration to be explored.
(3) No patriarchal high-technology is needed, save perhaps a thermometer.
(4) They do not mess about with women's bodies or *damage their health*.

It takes a death . . .
Roisin Boyd
SR 141 April 1984

On 31 January Ann Lovett, a 15-year-old Irish schoolgirl, was found dying alone in a churchyard. Her death caused a furore of reaction in Ireland. Ann Lovett was pregnant. She had gone to a grotto beside the church in Granard (a small town) where she lived. Some schoolboys passing by saw her red schoolbag nearby and went to investigate. They found her with her dead baby and a pair of scissors beside her, unable to speak and freezing cold.

At an inquest held three weeks later the coroner returned a verdict that Ann Lovett's death was 'due to irreversible shock caused by haemorrhage and childbirth'. The verdict on the baby's death was 'due to asphyxia'. Ann's mother and father testified at the inquest that they did not know their daughter was pregnant. Her mother said, 'I never at any time suspected she was pregnant. If I did I would certainly have seen that she got proper care and treatment.'

The utter desolation Ann Lovett experienced touched and disturbed the country. It opened a wound that has been raw since the debacle of the abortion referendum held five months ago. During that referendum Irish feminists argued that it would cause even greater hardship for women with unwanted pregnancies. Ann Lovett was pregnant while the amendment on whether the rights of the unborn had precedence over those of the mother was being debated.

Ann Lovett's death opened a floodgate of response, particularly from women who had themselves gone through single pregnancies alone. These women recalled in newspaper and radio interviews how they had suffered rejection and humiliation when they went through their pregnancies. One woman said, 'Ann Lovettt gave me the courage to speak out'; another said the tragedy revealed the 'untold anguish of the women of Ireland!'.

The priest and people of Granard were furious because they felt they were being judged by the Dublin-based anti-rural media. When I went to Granard a local woman assured me she would have helped Ann if she'd come for help. 'Who could have turned their back or closed their door on her?' It's probably true but the fact is that Ann was so terrified of their judgment she chose instead to have her pregnancy alone in a church grotto. There was little reference to the man/boyfriend who was involved in the pregnancy though it appears he is known locally.

Ann had only told her close friend Mary Maguire that she was pregnant but she swore her to secrecy. However it seems likely that many people were aware of her pregnancy. They chose to remain silent. The nuns at the school she attended denied they knew although there were reports that Ann always wore her coat *during* class.

Nuala Fennell, the Minister for Women's Affairs, has ordered an inquiry into Ann Lovett's death. It will try to ascertain why the 'girl' did not seek help, why her condition was not noticed, and what steps can be taken to prevent a similar incident happening elsewhere. She said 'We can only be truly pro-life if we eradicate prejudice about pregnancies occurring outside marriage. There is little indication that a caring society has emerged fully in the wake of the three year pro-life debate we have just gone through.'

A spokeswoman from Cherish, an organisation of single mothers, said, 'What happened is an extreme version of what is happening all the time . . . We have made great strides in changing social attitudes. But the fact that someone risks their life, as this girl did, because she was so much afraid, shows we are only skimming the surface. . . .'

A spokesperson for Daybreak, an organisation that helps lonely people, said Ann Lovett's case was not an isolated one. The young women Daybreak saw were most afraid of the 'shame' they would bring on their families. The spokesman also said he knew of two people who took their own lives rather than tell their parents things they thought would alienate them.

Ann Lovett's death has succeeded in raising many issues. The fact that she felt there was nowhere she could go to have her child and that she couldn't tell anyone who could help had tragic consequences. But the fact that so many people – women and men – maintained they did not know she was pregnant and desperate indicates a more complex problem. Punitive attitudes to women's sexuality are entrenched everywhere in the world. They are pervasive in Ireland because the Catholic church still has a strong grip on institutions and attitudes. It seems it is almost impossible for individuals to break that grip when this institution controls so many aspects of your life. Fortunately someone had the courage to reveal what had happened after Ann's funeral. They rang a Sunday newspaper. Otherwise what happened to her would have been silenced and forgotten.

The 'pro-life' referendum to protect and enshrine in the Irish constitution the rights of the 'unborn' seems a terrible insult to Irish women, in the light of Ann Lovett's death.

China: fines aren't enough
Sue O'Sullivan
SR 112 November 1981

The Chinese government is at present considering drawing up and implementing a family planning law. We know how laws forbidding the use of birth control are used against women; a law which would enforce birth control is a newer phenomena.

In October 1979, when I was in China, the campaign to limit families to one child each was well underway – with strong material incentives for having one child only (best education choices, more food, best housing possibilities for the family and so on), and disincentives for those who transgressed the one child 'norm' (penalties in housing, education food, etc).

Articles in magazines and newspapers stressed the importance for the country, for women and for children of the small family. In discussions I had with officials it was always explained that no one would be literally forced to limit their family.

But these 'top-down' policies were a distinct and disturbing change from the previous official Chinese position on birth control which put great emphasis on women themselves understanding the importance of birth control.

Sometime in early 1980, a little news report came out of China . . . in a certain province an overzealous official had put undue pressure on women to have abortions in order to reach that area's population reduction target. His action was criticised. This was not the way to reach the target.

Now, more disturbing news is being published about China's population control policies, and although some of the sources are dubious (Hong Kong anti-communist newspapers aren't noted for their objectivity), one can't ignore the whole issue. From an article in China's *Guangming Daily* newspaper, it appears that the government is considering a birth control *law* which would be compulsory to follow. The article says that persuasion backed by fines and material incentives was not enough to influence people effectively.

The Chinese government argues that China's population growth if not dramatically checked, will be a disaster for the country. While this may be true, why is it so easily accepted by the government that China can force women to fit immediately into government policies on family size on the one hand, and on the other, maintain that women are not in positions of power in significant numbers because they aren't 'ready' politically? They say that as old reactionary attitudes about women are not completely changed, so 'patience' is required. Clearly expediency rules in one case (wrongly, I would maintain) and excuses suffice (wrong again) in the other.

Depo-Provera – Third World women not told this contraceptive is on trial
Jill Rakusen with help from Julia Segal and Sue Barlow
SR 42 December 1975

Depo-Provera (depot medroxy pregesterone acetate, from now on referred to as DP) is an injectable contraceptive. It's hot stuff in the commercial and family planning world, with an effectiveness comparable to the pill without the hassles of having to take one every day. 150 mg can be injected every three months, or more every six months.

The International Planned Parenthood Federation (IPPF) likes it, for 'You get people accepting injections more readily than the pill' and 'The women want contraception but they aren't sufficiently motivated to take a pill every day' (quote from a phone conversation with an IPPF doctor). Since 1968 Upjohn Co, the American manufacturers, have sold over 11 million doses.

In the mid-1960s trials began using DP as a contraceptive. In 1971 the central medical committee of the IPPF decided to allow certain family planning associations to use it for clinical trials under the supervision of the medical department which would monitor results and side-effects.

In the same year, it was found that DP could cause breast cancer in beagles. The oral form was then banned.

But the FDA allowed clinical trials of the injectable form to continue, reasoning that there were alternatives to the oral form, but that DP was the only highly effective injectable. Some reasoning.[1]

In October 1973 it declared its intention to allow the use of DP as a contraceptive in certain 'limited' circumstances, provided a check was kept on the women and doctors involved. These were (a) when women refused or were 'unable to accept the responsibility demanded by other contraceptive methods'; (b) when they were incapable or unwilling to tolerate other hormonal contraception; or (c) when they had 'repeated failures' with other methods.

In May 1974 the FDA's hand was stayed by a US Congressional Sub-committee which had been holding public hearings on experimental drugs, and had found an association (though no proof as to cause) between DP and cervical cancer.

In September 1974 the FDA tried again, having decided that the questions raised concerning delays in the resumption of fertility and breast cancer in beagles were 'not sufficiently serious' to prevent the release of the drug in specific circumstances.[2]

So the FDA published regulations and guidelines which required the manufacturer to provide informational leaflets which the woman was supposed to read before giving her 'informed consent' to the injections.

In effect, the FDA was taking the unprecedented step of requiring the woman herself to decide on the safety of DP.

However, the Chairman of the Congressional Sub-committee again stepped in and managed to embarrass the FDA into delaying its approval yet again by predicting that 'many women may be irreparably injured'. Thus, to date, the FDA has suspended its approval.

Other countries are being more cautious than the USA because of suspicion concerning long-term effects.

In Britain, for example, the Committee on Safety of Medicines has not licensed DP as a contraceptive since its rigid requirements concerning long-term toxicity trials and high-quality clinical trials are not satisfied.[3]

But while the American watchdogs sit pondering, the USA is exporting increasing amounts of DP for contraceptive purposes. An estimated one million women now use it in roughly 70 countries.

---

1. The question of DPs carcinogenic properties is very complex. For a more up-to-date assessment of the situation, see the *Evidence to the Panel on Depo-Provera* produced by the Coordinating Group on Depo-Provera (of which I was a member) available from Women's Health Information Centre (WHIC). Address in resource section.

2. Since 1975 this has been a hot potato. There have been a series of hearings in the USA following the ones referred to here.

3. More recently, the situation changed following the CSMs decision to recommend licensing the drug,and the Minister of Health's unprecedented decision, as the licensing authority, to ignore this advice. Contact WHIC if you wish to see the newsletter article I wrote about subsequent events.

It is particularly widely used in 'underdeveloped' countries, where in fact it was also first tested.

Some European countries also use it (e.g. Holland and Belgium) but on nothing like the scale of the underdeveloped countries.

The IPPF is now the largest international supplier of DP, while at the same time acknowledging that the drug is still 'under clinical trial'. In 1974 its largest shipments went to Thailand, Sri Lanka, Uganda, Kenya and Costa Rica.

The United Nations Fund for Population Activities (UNFPA) has given the UN Children's Fund a grant to enable it to distribute DP, and the World Health Organisation uses it, having made a 'careful analysis of the relative risks and benefits' (risks and benefits to whom?).

On the other hand, USAID does not use the drug because it does not supply drugs not approved by the FDA! Although Sweden has supplied DP abroad, it has stopped doing so because of reservations about side-effects. Malaysia, which previously got its supplies from Sweden, will now obtain them from the UNFPA!

In Northern Thailand, 31,780 women have been given DP between 1970 and 1974. There are few programmes where DP has been used on such a large scale and therefore this programme has been used to study 'acceptance' of side-effects, etc. Bear in mind that DP is still on clinical trial.

Women in underdeveloped countries are not informed that the drug is on trial, and it depends on the individual doctor whether or not side-effects are mentioned.

DP can affect the metabolism is similar ways to the pill. It can raise glucose levels in the blood and can cause side-effects ranging from weight gain, vomiting, dizziness, mood changes and headaches, to rectal bleeding and lumps on the chest.

Blood clotting disorders have also been noted, but the FDA is cagey about whether DP can actually cause these (for a long time it displayed similar cageyness about the pill in this respect).

In some studies, 25% of women stop using DP because of side-effects. Disruption of menstrual bleeding occurs in over 50% of users. Bleeding can be prolonged, heavier, unpredictable or completely absent, the latter being more likely to occur as the injections continue.

Unpredictable or unpleasant bleeding can make the method thoroughly unacceptable, so oestrogen is often given orally for 7–10 days on top of DP in order to 'solve' the problem. Experiments are being made with combining oestrogen in the injection.

While the more serious possible side-effects of breast or cervical cancer have yet to be proven, the possibility of infertility has certainly been shown to exist.

The FDA Drug Bulletin for September 1974 found that return of fertility after use of DP was 'variable and unpredictable, and permanent inability to conceive has been reported occasionally'. (N.B. So far it has been shown that in most users fertility has returned within 24 months.)

Despite the importance of this issue, very little research has been done on it. Nevertheless, in some countries concern about permanent infertility is such that DP is restricted to older women with completed families.

But in others, such as Thailand, the drug is being given to more and more young women (the mean age in 1975 was 27).

An Upjohn representative testified to the FDA that the dilemmas posed 'can only be resolved by exposing humans who have a high risk potential for benefit'.

In other words, clinical trials – or experimentation – are being carried out on thousands of women without their informed consent because someone else has decided that the benefits outweigh the risks.

Depo-Provera: control of fertility – two feminist views
SR 116 March 1982

HARI JOHN
Interviewed by Carol Smith

Five hundred women from all over the world met in Geneva last year for the third International Conference on Women and Health. Women organising the conference raised money from the World Health Organisation (WHO) to pay the fares of Third World women, so for the first time many of the women were from Africa, India, Bangladesh, South and Central America, as well as from Europe, USA, Canada, New Zealand and Australia. The very vocal Third World women ensured that issues of racism and imperialism informed all the discussions in the workshops. The topic which was particularly controversial, both at the conference and also in its implications for western feminists, was that of Depo-Provera. Hari John, a doctor from South India, raised this consistently throughout the conference and explained clearly her reasons for advocating the use of DP.

I was very inspired by Hari, and feel a lot of respect for her feminist, general political, and medical beliefs and practice. Her stand on DP is controversial; she is also a strong advocate of herbal medicine and the use of traditional healing methods. Her basic approach of learning from people is very different from western elitism and vanguardism. Her work and politics are putting into practice what we too often only theorise about in the west – that is, the social and political causes of ill-health.

CAROL: 'Can you tell me about your medical background?'
HARI: 'I was trained as a doctor in a highly prestigious Christian medical

school in Vellore, but the education I received there is not at all relevant to my work in rural India, and 80% of the population live in rural areas.

'The first example I had of how my training was inappropriate was that in the training hospital I was not allowed to do forceps deliveries or any operations, and my first patient was a woman with foetal distress who needed forceps delivery, so I just had to do it; and very soon after that I had to do my first operation on a woman with impending rupture of the uterus – in her kitchen in very unhygienic surroundings – I had never been taught to do these things.

'It was primarily rich people who used our services and western allopathic medicine. So my husband and I decided to concentrate on community development, and we served all, irrespective of class.

'We trained paramedics, and took women from the community who were chosen by the village; but still we made the mistake of choosing western drugs that the poor couldn't use. I think "alternative medicine" is the way that the mass of people can have access to health. Western medicine is only appropriate if a country has economic buying power; international drug companies are highly profit-orientated and hold medical monopolies over world distribution. And there is also the issue of the dangerous side-effects of drugs which increase in people who are undernourished.

'We made these mistakes for three years; then in 1976 we decided to "learn from the people". We learned many things from them, some of which were not good, but mostly good and useful things about herbs and plants that people could grow in their backyards, and things that grew wild all around. This eliminated the problem of cost, availability, and accessibility for the people. Every woman villager has a background of using herbs; they have no access to doctors, so the knowledge has been retained and passed through generations. To win the older generation, you must speak their language which is that of herbal medicine.'

CAROL: 'What are the common medical problems in the villages, and how are they treated?'
HARI: 'The women paramedics who live in the villages receive basic training in immunisation and in the diseases which are common in rural India; upper respiratory infection, gastro-enteritis, malnutrition, cuts and wounds, viral infections, whooping cough, Tetanus. We also teach immunisation of cows, animal husbandry, and simple agricultural techniques which will improve the soil.

'Perineal massage is forbidden in Indian hospitals. Also I learned the squatting method of delivery from the village women, and in a prolonged labour, a ride in a bullock cart down a rough track works wonders! – and these are the methods that are available to the people. We also teach basic hygiene to the traditional birth tenders, and train auxiliary nurses to do vasectomies, tubal ligation (tying of the Fallopian tubes as a method of sterilisation), abortion, episiotomy, if really needed, and forceps delivery.'

CAROL: 'What is the situation in India at the moment around sterilisation?'
HARI: 'India has a population of 683 million – 15.3% of the world population, yet India is only 2.4% of the world land area. At the present rate of growth, the population is expected to double by the year 2000. I am very concerned about this and although I do not approve of the Gandhi sterilisation programme, I understand it. I think there should be disincentives for having lots of children, but *not* force. The whole question of contraception in India is very complicated, and the financial incentives have reduced family planning to chaos. Women who are paid five rupees to have an IUD inserted will then go to the traditional woman and pay her one rupee to have it removed, then go and have another one fitted. It has become a source of income, with disastrous effects on women's health. IUD insertion is also used as a way of getting abortions.'

CAROL: 'The issue of Depo-Provera caused some controversy at the conference. Could you outline your position on it?'
HARI: 'I operate a contraceptives "cafeteria"; that is, I tell women about all the contraceptives and all their side-effects (condom, pill, menstrual extraction, DP, and have recently been doing some trials using herbs). I am an acceptor of DP, and use it myself. I am happy to have amenorrhoea [the stoppage of periods, which is a frequent side-effect of DP]. DP is the most popular choice that women in South India make. Women in South India choose DP because they are totally deprived, and have no say in any aspect of their lives; they are subject to constant sexual abuse; they may only eat when the rest of the family have finished eating, so don't get enough food and suffer from anaemia and malnutrition. They are subject to their in-laws' as well as their husband's disapproval, and if they want contraception their husband accuses them of wanting extra-marital sex. Most forms of contraception are very difficult to hide, and DP is the only one their husband won't know about. Using DP is the only way these women can have control over any aspect of their lives. If they have unwanted pregnancy they have no access to safe abortion so they go to an illegal abortionist with a high danger of septicaemia.

'Western feminists call for a ban on DP, without hearing Third World women's point of view. But lots of pesticides which are banned in the US are dumped in the Third World, for instance Dioxin, which has specific effects on women because it causes a higher incidence of congenital birth defects, miscarriages and stillbirths. So why aren't western feminists fighting against pesticides?'

CAROL: *'How are herbal medicine and allopathic medicine accepted by people in India?'*
HARI: 'Herbal medicine and homeopathy have a very long history in India, but the colonialists introduced western drugs, and suppressed the traditional methods. I think that is one reason why DP is acceptable as a contraceptive in India. The people have internalised their oppression; they have inherited a 'colonialist mentality' in some ways – they *believe* in injections.'

THE CASE AGAINST DEPO-PROVERA
by Janet Hadley

Many women attending a health centre in Bangladesh are refusing to accept injections of tetanus vaccine. They are convinced that the injection, a basic and vital health protection, is the three-monthly injectable contraceptive, Depo-Provera. This refusal is nothing less than a tragedy. Tetanus is a major hazard, a potential killer. Yet family planners and doctors insist that in Asia women have more faith in medicine that comes in a needle than in pills. They peddle Depo-Provera, the progestogen-only contraceptive, precisely because it can be jabbed speedily into the top of an arm or a buttock. It can be given, and often is, without a physical examination of any kind, let alone an internal. In the interests of controlling population growth, it's quick, it's simple, it's foolproof and there is a 'high return for investment of funds, time and effort', as one enthusiast put it. He added that 'once injected the medication [sic] will not be forgotten or expelled.' [all quotes from the Depo-Provera pamphlet]. Women's bodies are being assaulted with this powerful hormone compound and what trust they have put in doctors is being abused.

The Bangladesh health project, the People's Health Center [sic] at Gonoshasthaya Kendra, has now stopped giving Depo-Provera, because of doubts about its long-term effect on women's health and on their children. Also, presumably, because the women's suspicions were bringing all injections into disrepute. This sad tale gives fresh urgency to the growing debate about a ban on Depo-Provera.

As yet, Depo-Provera has not been given a safety all-clear in the United States or in Britain (though Sweden has recently backed it). It has mainly been used in developing countries, where it was also tested. The drug's American-owned, multinational and manufacturer, Upjohn, as well as the international 'aid' and family planning lobbies, have all been putting heavy pressure on the American drug safety authorities to give Depo-Provera a clean bill of health. Last time the US government drug safety agency reviewed the evidence, it took the most unusual step of acknowleding this pressure, saying, 'We recognise that the risk/benefit considerations may be different in other nations, where the alternative methods of contraception may be less available and less acceptable and where the physician/patient ratio is lower.' In other words, while the agency is worried enough about the possible health risks to keep the drug off the US market, it is encouraging other governments to adopt less stringent standards.

Death rates among women in pregnancy and childbirth are higher in Asia, Africa, Latin America and the Caribbean than in western Europe and the United States. Nutrition and sanitation are also poorer. For these reasons, Depo-Provera's backers are calling the American drug safety standards a 'luxury' and using the dismal standards of nutrition, general health and high maternal death rates among Third World women to justify the use of, 'a very powerful steroid, which disturbs body metabolism far more than oral contraceptives', with long-term risks which have hardly been researched.

The commonest side-effect is totally unpredictable vaginal bleeding. Many women have heavy, prolonged bleeding, or persistent spotting, which is often sexually and socially disruptive, and carries extra risk for malnourished women. Some women do not bleed at all and many find this very disturbing. Most women also gain weight and other side-effects can include nausea, dizziness, cramps, hair loss, headaches, irritability, backache, loss of libido, depression and feeling bloated. These can last long after the three-month contraceptive effectiveness wears off. If pills give you headaches you can at least decide to stop swallowing them. What makes Depo-Provera's side-effects different from those caused by other contraceptives is the non-reversibility of the injection, so that all you *can* do is wait for the drug to wear off.

There are also unacceptable long-term risks. Tests on animals point to possible risks of breast cancer and also of endometrial cancer, which attacks the lining of the womb. In 1970 pills containing the Depo-Provera chemical were banned in the United States because beagle dogs had developed breast tumours, yet the injectable form was not banned. There are suspicions that the drug could be linked to liver tumours and diabetes, and could reduce the body's ability to resist infection – a very important factor in the precarious health balance of many women in the Third World.

It also carries hazards for the children of users. Women who are already pregnant when injected risk having babies with birth defects. It has been shown that babies can absorb the drug through breast milk, yet Depo-Provera is often given to mothers of newborn babies and is recommended for women who are breastfeeding. Breast milk containing Depo-Provera may also reduce tiny babies' natural immunity, thus cancelling one of the main health arguments for breast-feeding.

There has not been adequate monitoring and follow-up of the thousands of women given Depo-Provera in the Third World. Studies purporting to dispel the cancer worries have been carried out over a very short timescale in cancer terms. Doctors argue that family planning staff

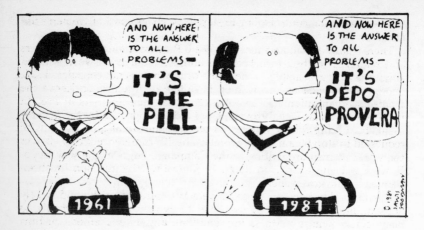

FIGURE 17 Depo-Provera *Janis Goodman* (*SR 116* March 1982)

should not 'cling too rigidly to more academic and professional standards' as to perform internal check-ups or breast examinations.

You may feel that women's safety and comfort is rated a pretty low priority for the medical profession and drug comapnies at the best of times, but such blatant double standards as have been shown in the promotion of Depo-Provera expose the racism inherent in mass population control. A drug company's sales leaflet even boasts that with Depo-Provera a doctor can be assured of 'predictability of results, regardless of patient's attitude, socio-economic environment or tendency to forget monthly schedules'. Conveyor belt contraception is the inevitable result.

I am wary of claims that Depo-Provera tops the popularity stakes among women at a particular clinic or hospital. Research shows that the most popular contraceptive 'chosen' by women attending a particular doctor reflects the doctor's favoured method, even when all the methods are explained to the woman and displayed in what is known as the 'cafeteria' system. The doctor's prejudices govern the explanations. Also the distributors manipulate the available choices. Upjohn has admitted paying millions of dollars' worth of bribes to government officials, hospital employees and others.

Feminists in western Europe and the US have in the past been too uncritical of family planning programmes which are delivered as part of aid packages to Third World countries. They have tended to regard such aid as a straightforwardly progressive step towards independence for poor women in Asia, Latin America and Africa. The male chauvinist hostility to birth control expressed by some nationalist Third World governments complicates the whole issue and has opened the way for the population control lobby to step in as 'champions' of women's liberation.

There is now enormous interest in Depo-Provera among health workers and feminists in the Third World countries. Women are very worried about the easy availability to them of a drug which is not considered safe enough for general use on women in Britain or America. In Kenya the women's organisation has complained of its 'indiscrimination' use. In India, where so far Depo-Provera is not a drug approved by the government, Hari John, who promotes its use in South India, has been twice requested to stop by a national women's health conference. From all over the world women are writing to the Campaign, angry at the way Depo-Provera is being foisted on them. In Zimbabwe the injection has been banned by the government.

It isn't hard to see that Depo-Provera is unpleasant, risky and widely abused. But why ban it? There may be women who react badly to oestrogen or whose partners interfere with any other methods such as pills or an IUD. The contention is that if Depo-Provera is banned, these women would be worse off.

However by using Depo-Provera as the answer to these or similar dilemmas a number of issues are being avoided. There *are* some women who react badly to oestrogen, or who cannot use any other form of contraception, or·do not wish to. Just because so many other forms of birth control (chemical or devices) carry health risks for women is no justification for foisting another uncomfortable and potentially hazardous contraceptive on to the market. An injection is the most passive form of contraception available. It can be administered to large numbers of women quickly and so is ideally suited for population control.

Depo-Provera may seem the 'perfect' answer for women whose partners interfere with other methods of birth control. If men do not want women to use contraception it does not follow that women's health should be endangered by birth control methods which men cannot detect. Gambling with Depo-Provera may be a short-term solution but in the long-term does nothing to change the nature of male attitudes towards women.

In its recent booklet, the Campaign acknowledges that the issue is a complex one and that calling for a complete ban sweeps you immediately to a crunch point. A ban may undoubtedly deprive a few individual women of a contraceptive which they prefer, but such a ban really is essential if far more women who have no control over their lives are not to suffer from the effects of the drug, and the political consequences of the double standards that maintain its continued distribution.

Population control is the opposite of what the women's liberation movement stands for. Population control relies on drugs and devices whose side-effects and risks are concealed from their users. By developing Depo-Provera, manufacturing it and aggressively marketing it as the next best thing to sterilisation, the real problems facing women in the Third World are being deliberately and callously ignored.

Depo appeal
Angela Phillips
SR 128 March 1983

Women can chalk up some small victories, whatever final decision is made about the licensing of Depo-Provera by the appeal panel. The panel sat for a week in April to listen to arguments by DP manufacturers, Upjohn, against Health Minister Kenneth Clark's decision to turn down a long-term licence for the drug. For the first time ever evidence from lay people has been accepted by an official review panel. The quality of that evidence has been so high that consumer groups should have little difficulty persuading future panels, looking at the safety of medicines, of the relevance of their views.

It was only a partial victory. The extensive evidence submitted by the Co-ordinating Group on Depo-Provera was accepted in written form only. Group members had the infuriating task of sitting through judicial-style hearings, in which attempts were made to discredit them and refute their evidence, without the opportunity of defending themselves.

Nevertheless it is clear that their work had an enormous impact and formed the basis of questioning by panel members. Based on close scrutiny of existing evidence in addition to anecdotal evidence from women who had been prescribed the drug, the co-ordinating group successfully pulled holes in the carefully, and expensively, structured defence of DP by Upjohn.

Through careful examination of the medical evidence, Jill Rakusen, the main contributor to the group's work, was able to show that the drug should never be prescribed immediately after childbirth because of its association with bleeding problems. On the first day of the hearing, Upjohn announced that they do not themselves believe that DP should be given immediately after childbirth and that it is better to wait until post-partum bleeding has stopped. This advice is not given in the data sheets available to doctors. Depo-Provera has been widely used, along with rubella shots, in ante-natal wards.

The group also turned up evidence that some DP users have oestrogen levels as low as that in post menopausal women. Low oestrogen levels are associated with a disease called osteoporosis in which the bones become thin and fragile. There is no evidence, as yet, that DP causes osteoporosis but since, under normal circumstances, problems would only come to light ten or more years after the menopause, there is also no room for the complacency shown by medical researchers in the only report yet done on this issue.

Much of Upjohn's case rested on the right of doctors to make decisions for patients. Dame Josephine Barnes, head of the Association of Family Planning Doctors, and an Upjohn witness, asked rather peevishly, 'Does the minister not trust doctors to prescribe properly?'

Witnesses called by Upjohn themselves were not reassuring on that point. Professor Elstein, Head of Obstetrics and Gynaecology at Manchester University, regularly uses the DP/rubella combination in ante-natal wards and was prepared to concede only that this may not be good practice for breast-feeding mothers (the DP is excreted in breast milk at the same concentration as in the mother's blood). However he felt that this was a matter to be left to the discretion of doctors. His leaflet on DP makes light of the severe bleeding problems faced by some women on the drug.

As a result of this inquiry, it's to be hoped that the use of DP on Black women, both here and in the Third World, and on women judged to be 'mentally subnormal' or 'disturbed', will gain wide publicity.

Upjohn get rough ride at Depo launch
Women's Reproductive Rights Information Centre
SR 152 March 1985

At a press conference on 5 February, Upjohn Ltd announced that Depo-Provera was now available as a long-term contraceptive in Britain. *Spare Rib* and the Women's Reproductive Rights Information Centre both asked for invitations to the press conference but were refused because we were not part of the medical press (*Good Housekeeping* was there however). So this is a secondhand report.

It seems journalists and some family planning workers who were allowed in gave the speakers rather a hard time. They asked sticky questions about the newest report from the World Health Organisation that there appears to be a twofold increase in cervical cancer in Depo users who have been on the drug more than five years (*Lancet*, 24 November 1984).

They asked why the leaflet for women who are offered the drug was being printed in nine languages spoken in Britain but only the English version would actually be mailed out to doctors, so that they would have to place orders for other languages.

One of the speakers admitted that almost all women experience 'menstrual disturbances' in the first six months of use and that 30% experience increased bleeding in that time. One doctor said she had given Depo-Provera to a woman who bled for a year afterwards and asked if that is what they meant by menstrual disturbances.

The speakers said that Depo was used by 2–3% of New Zealand women who wanted a contraceptive and that they didn't expect more than that in Britain. They also said that DP gave protection against breast cancer, as if that were some sort of balance to the increased risk of cervical cancer. Of course, we take contraception to protect us against cancer; what else is it for?

It is unfortunately easy to be sarcastic about the public relations practised by drug companies. We have managed to stall this day for many a year now, but it has come nonetheless. We may have won major concessions from the drug licensing authority but we have not stopped the licence and we have no guarantees or safeguards against the abuse of this drug that have been so widely reported.

Local monitoring is now very important and I hope women's health activists will take this up in the months to come. The licence is only for five years initially and renewal depends on post-marketing studies of cancer risks. But five years is a long time to wait for women using the drug.

In the meantime, we think two things need to be addressed by the ministers involved. Depo-Provera has not got a contraceptive licence in the USA and the data on cervical cancer with long-term use are serious. Kenneth Clarke refused Upjohn the licence once. We think he should change his mind and do it again.

Surrogate motherhood – yes or no?
Marge Berer of Women's Reproductive Rights Information Centre
SR 151 February 1985

Surrogate motherhood is again in the headlines. The first woman to be paid a fee for having a child for someone else gave birth early in January. Two major issues have emerged from this case. The first is that no one involved seems to have any legal rights. The surrogate mother was seen to be abandoning the baby so the local council, probably wrongly, slapped a 'place of safety' order on it. That meant that the people who wanted the child couldn't claim it, even though the man was the father. The child's illegitimacy gave him no rights. The child of course has no legal status at all now.

The father applied and had the child made a ward of court, taking the case out of the council's hands. It is now up to the judge to decide what happens. He could either hand the child to Barnet social services for adoption, on the grounds that the father has no rights to it or because he thinks the father and his wife would make unfit parents, or he could rule that the child should go to the father and his wife. Either way, he will be setting legal precedents that will affect adoption law and illegitimacy as well as the increasing number of people who were hoping to have a child with a surrogate mother.

The second issue to emerge is that of payments in surrogacy arrangements. Not only was the surrogate paid a fee, a private agency also got a fee for arranging the pregnancy. The adoption laws may make it impossible for the woman who wants the child to adopt it because she has paid for the baby. And the role of an agency, which made the whole thing possible, is widely condemned for charging a fee as well. The government-appointed Warnock Committee included surrogacy when it looked at reproductive technology, because it involves more than two people in having a child and because existing law and practice would be affected.

Many of us have been raised by people who are not our biological parents, but surrogacy is seen as different mainly because the surrogate mother decides in advance to get pregnant with the *intention* of giving the child to someone else. This has raised cries of immorality, comparisons with prostitution and labels like rent-a-womb.

It is increased attention to infertility, where the success rate of treatment is still low because so little research is being done to improve it, along with increased hopes that it will succeed, that have led people to think about surrogacy when it doesn't. The people who have rung us are mainly couples where the woman is unable to carry a pregnancy. She may have no womb, or a damaged womb, or may have had repeated miscarriages, or had infertility treatment that did not work, or pregnancy may be a serious risk to her health or life. All of them have tried, and failed, to adopt a child. But single and gay men might also see surrogacy as a way to have a child without a woman partner, in the same way as single and lesbian women are using donor insemination.

I often hear people ask why don't they adopt children? First of all, 'they' happen to be a large group of people, and 'they' might even be me. Second, the facts about adoption in Britain are that there are about 90,000 children in care per year. Only about 30,000 of them are available for adoption, with only about 1,000 newborn babies among them. In contrast, there are 250,000 applications for adoption each year (figures quoted by a National Association for the Childless spokesperson on radio). Adoption is clearly a hopeless cause for most people. Surrogacy is being seen as a last-resort option precisely for these reasons. These are conservative times and the media are having a field day. Surrogacy makes for great sensationalist headlines.

The Bishop of Birmingham said on Birmingham radio recently that surrogacy was 'interference in the marriage union' and therefore morally wrong. Some people who are generally opposed to the idea think it is all right if a woman does it for her sister or a friend, but they worry about strangers coming together or being brought together by an agency. Several women who phoned the Birmingham radio programme said they saw absolutely nothing wrong with it and totally sympathised with people wanting a child by any means at all.

The Warnock Committee suggested making it a criminal offence to act as an agency that brought surrogates and potential parents together, but a minority report of the Committee called for more debate first and suggested that third-party support was acceptable if it wasn't for profit.

Edinburgh Brook Advisory Centre and BPAS supported the Warnock minority report, as we did at WRRIC. Rights of Women, Women in Medicine and the Feminist International Network on the New Reproductive Technology took very negative positions. Part of their concern was the potential for exploitation of poor women who might only agree to be surrogates for the money. This follows from what has happened in the USA where some agencies are charging those who want babies huge fees, part of which they use for solicitors and doctors, part for themselves, and part for the surrogate. Do we have to imitate the worse practices in the USA?

The government seems to have overwhelming support for emergency legislation to ban profit-making surrogate agencies, though Dame Warnock has opposed it. The effect this will have on all surrogacy arrangements is unclear but worrying, because it is being rushed through without much thought for implications. And it ignores what I think are the crucial issues, the alternatives open to the people involved and the question of how their rights will be protected. This is to be left for a future date.

Did the surrogate earn the £6,500 she was paid for carrying the child concerned? Did the agency earn the £6,500 they were paid? Half of people's anger seems to be directed at the fact that the surrogate is also getting £20,000 from the *Daily Star* for her story.

It is certainly true that, with fees like that, only rich people will be able to have children that way and that is absolutely wrong. But we can equally ask if men should be paid for donating sperm, or if doctors should make profits from the practices of private medicine. Why just ban this? For me, the answers are not as straightforward as they seem at first.

As feminists, we should be looking for a perspective that supports women's needs and rights. Surrogate arrangements are going to happen; we can be sure of that. Both the people who want a child and any woman who offers to be a surrogate for them need protection from exploitation and some assurance that what they are doing will be accepted in law. There also needs to be protection for the child borne, in case the surrogate wants to keep it, in case the eventual parents can't or won't take it, in case both parties want it, in case no one does. Should we be suggesting that people are given support if they go ahead, or should they be left to get on with it without help? Which way is more likely to lead to hurt or abuse?

With all the media publicity, the demand for surrogacy will increase. People are phoning our office terrified of condemnation because they want to ask about it.

Few women have come forward to be surrogates, but then there is no one for them to come forward to, apart from the private agency in Surrey, and that is likely to be closed by the emergency legislation. But I'd be willing to bet a lot of women are thinking about whether they would be prepared to do it, and asking temselves if it is love or money that is motivating them.

Surrogacy links in to so many other reproductive rights issues, and I hope the women's movement will take a lead in trying to shape public opinion, in a way that supports women.

Infertility under fire
Emma
SR 153 April 1985

It was only this year that I started to think seriously about my infertility, although I have known about it since I was 16. I suppose because I have not decided to try for a baby yet, I have been able to avoid thinking about the implications of not being able to have one. I have not even used the term 'infertile', with its ring of doom – although many women go through periods of infertility and others are permanently unable to conceive as a result of (sometimes undiagnosed) pelvic inflammatory disease in their past. Infertility, both temporary and permanent, whether their own or their partner's, affects about 10% of women who try to conceive. And yet it is a problem about which nobody speaks.

At the conference held by the Women's Reproductive Rights Information Centre (WRRIC) to discuss Enoch Powell's current Unborn Child (Protection) Bill, I met other women like myself. This bill, as well as constituting an indirect attack on women's rights to abortion and contraception, by seeking to give the embryo 'human' rights, also has serious implications for the treatment of infertility. It would impose such severe restrictions on in-vitro fertilisation (IVF) programmes as to make them almost unworkable; at the very least extremely expensive for the prospective parent and with a far poorer chance of success than at present. It would effectively put an end to other kinds of research on infertility.

From talking to other women at the conference, many of whom have been trying to conceive for several years, most of whom are 'undergoing investigation', a lengthy process in itself, I became aware just how hit and miss many of the treatments available are. Most of the information on infertility treatment is a by-product of research on contraception. In addition, women have to undergo a kind of parenting means test in order to be considered for treatment. Which of course takes into account race and social class, but above all 'marital' situation. The legislation proposed in the Powell bill would make the situation ten times worse, delays would be greatly increased, and such treatment as was available would only be available to certain privileged women.

Most of all I would say my infertility has led me to question the idea of the 'family', the power of biological parenthood, the ownership of children. To realise that, as an infertile woman, you are simply not allowed access to children on the same level of intensity as the 'mother' (be it biological or legally adoptive). That you can spend five years getting to know a child and being like a parent, but then its mother could, for whatever reason, suddenly decide to take it away from you to live elsewhere. That's very frightening.

But what about the isolation of mothers in any case? They more or less have to do everything themselves for the baby – no one else is going to take over their responsibility. If they don't do everything, society calls them a bad mother – even if child care is entrusted to another person, perhaps as a paying service. Child care is seen as being chiefly up to the mother – if she is given this incredible responsibility, how can we blame her for taking on the power that this entails as well?

I don't feel strongly that I want a baby that is biologically 'mine'. My body has no particular desire to undergo pregnancy, or give birth – although I can see that breast-feeding might be fun sometimes. I think a relationship with a baby is what you make of it, by living with it and caring and helping that child to become its own person.

My brand of infertility is such that I might respond well to hormonal treatment: some say a 50% chance, even a 75%. . . . That is, presuming that's all that's wrong with me, and that, once pregnant, I would be capable of carrying a child to full term. But who knows when I shall feel ready to undergo this treatment; who knows if, when I want a baby, I shall be in a 'stable heterosexual couple', and thereby considered suitable for treatment? I suppose I should be glad that I'm white and middle class, in terms of my access to medical treatment. I suppose I should be glad that I already know what my problem is, that my consultant will be able to refer me to the best place for treatment.

Outside of the feminist community it is considered 'natural' to want a baby. Feminists have rightly brought into question this assumption. To what extent are women's options limited, their success and fulfilment assumed to come from rearing children? How far is 'motherhood' a social construct? 'Why do you want children so much?', infertile women are asked. Forgetting that, as they turn 30 and see the biological clock running out, many feminists do a quick turn about and rediscoverer their 'maternal instinct'. Forgetting that, even within feminism, there is the cult of motherhood as a specifically female experience which puts us in touch with our 'womanpower'. . . .

So where does that leave women who can't conceive, who can't carry a baby, or whose partners can't fill their side of the deal? It's all very fine to say that there are other ways of fulfilling oneself in life – we live in a society where the pressures are very real to have children. An infertile woman, it seems, does not have 'choice', that feminist catchword. Having spent many years fighting for women's access to abortion and contraception, control over their fertility, I find myself strangely out on a limb. Even, I could say, deserted in my hour of need by the movement which takes its strength from trying to represent all women's interests. I am positively alarmed by the strands of thought in the women's movement which say that all medical intervention in women's bodies is a male plot – I agree that there are many problems in the control of research and of 'treatment', and possible frightening implications in the genetic manipulations experiments. But I believe the feminist movement should be more aware of the specific needs of infertile women – should fight for better research and treatment of the causes of infertility, which includes better primary health care and early diagnosis, as well as techniques such as AID and in-vitro fertilisation. We should be struggling against racism and heterosexism in terms of who receives treatment (and ageism – a 37-year-old woman is not looked upon as particularly worthy of help, or of access to adoption). We have fought for years for more control over abortion and contraception facilities, and certain battles have been won – control over research on infertility is just as vital and we should ensure that our voices are heard.

For myself, I don't yet want a child. But I also don't want my life to pass without being able to help bring up a child and have a close relationship with it. In some ways I think it is better for a child to be brought up by several loving, committed adults, rather than in the intense mother-child bond. Better for the woman, also, to have a less complete responsibility for her child. But for such a thing to happen, society's whole approach to kids must change – they must become people, part of the whole social responsibility and not just the possession of the individual mother/family. Women and men must be encouraged to see children as part of the community, and the basis of parent-power must be broadened to include non-biological carers.

The infertility support group, which was started at WRRIC last year, as well as providing a space for women to meet and share their experiences, has also undertaken to fight tooth and nail this legislation, which we see as an attempt by male moralists to control male scientists without reference to women and their needs. Other campaigns are under way.

Against the might of the moral right
Jan Mellor
SR 152 March 1985

By now most people will be familiar with the best Christmas present that Mrs Gillick had ever hoped to expect. Namely, a ruling by the Appeal Court that young people under the age of 16, and specifically her own five daughters, can no longer receive confidential medical advice on contraception and abortion without the consent of their parents.

The ruling has particular implications for young women as the possible consequences of it will mainly be borne by them, i.e. an increase in unplanned pregnancies, an increase in abortions and late abortions and the possible reappearance of self-induced abortion.

The DHSS have announced they will appeal to the Law Lords (upsetting some of their own backbenchers in the process) and have requested that it be heard as a matter of urgency. However, the date for the hearing has not yet been announced and in the meantime some young women are unable to get the advice and treatment they require. It would be a mistake to see the Appeal Court ruling as the work of the one individual, Mrs Gillick, seasoned campaigner though she is. Her victory has been a victory for the 'moral' right and she has the support of groups such as the Responsible Society, Harrow Child and Family Protection Group and the Order of Christian Unity in her attempts to restore the family to its 'rightful' position. It is interesting that much of her parliamentary support comes from MPs who are already notorious for their anti-abortion views.

A constant refrain throughout has been that the provision of confidential advice and treatment for young people on contraception and abortion undermines parental rights, places intolerable pressure on the family and at the same time encourages young people to be promiscuous.

The fact that some young women seek confidential advice precisely because of abuse within the family is never mentioned, just as the evidence which points to the fact that many young women are already having sexual intercourse before seeking advice is conveniently ignored. Very little has been said about the rights of young people throughout this whole debate and yet the rights of young people to obtain the information, advice and treatment which can enable them to make informed choices about their own sexuality and sexual behaviour is what is really at issue.

If Mrs Gillick and her supporters have their way, any tentative progress that has been made in this area will have been lost and indeed their real victory will be in the fact that they will have succeeded in radically shifting the moral consensus to the right, thus opening up new areas for attack.

Gillick defeated – but have we seen the last of her?
Women's Reproductive Rights Information Centre
SR 161 December 1985

On the 17 and 18 October, the Law Lords voted 3–2 in support of the DHSS Appeal against the Gillick ruling which denied under-16s access to contraception without parental consent.

In what has looked like a one-woman crusade against the state, the evils of under-aged and premarital sex, Mrs Victoria Gillick has gone from defeat to victory to defeat.

The three in favour argued that: maturity of young people cannot only be measured by age; that some under-16s *are* capable of consenting to medical treatment; that doctors may be better judges than parents in some cases; and that parents do not have ultimate veto over a child until its 16th birthday.

Under the new judgment doctors are justified in proceeding without parents' consent on five grounds: if they are satisfied that the girl understood the advice; that she could not be persuaded to inform her parents; that she was likely to begin or continue having sexual intercourse with or without contraceptive treatment; that unless she received advice or treatment her physical or mental health were likely to suffer; that her best interest required advice and/or treatment without parental consent. Hardly the basis for doctors to 'shell out the pill like jelly babies', as Tory MP Harry Greenway and other Gillick supporters would have us believe.

If Mrs Gillick is really worried that contraceptive methods such as the pill are harmful (to all women, not just under-16s) why isn't she advocating the use of barrier methods? Perhaps it's because she doesn't believe in the use of contraception at all. Isn't she really saying that she's against sex outside marriage also?

Ignorance is no defence against abuse. Young people need more sex education, not less. And they need to know all the options, single parenthood, homosexuality, lesbianism, celibacy as well as about heterosexual sex. They need to know about relationships in general and not *told* heterosexuality and marriage is the 'norm'.

The number of teenage pregnancies since the Appeal Court ruling has tripled. The demand for contraceptive advice and treatment for young people continues to increase. The NHS cannot meet the demand because it has not got the resources to cope with the special sessions recommended as far back as 1974. Even the Brook Advisory Centres find they cannot see all the young people they would like, due to lack of funds. Ironically, the Gillick case has actually alerted young people to the fact that they can now receive confidential advice, that is, if this service hasn't been cut in their area.

Before we go overboard in thinking the Lords decision is a major blow for the right and a major victory for young women, let us remember the role of the doctor and of the courts. The DHSS, who took this Appeal to the Lords with the backing of the government, were supported by the British Medical Association. Doctors are a big lobby in Parliament and they don't like pressure groups, of whatever political persuasion, telling them how to do their job. On this count, they have worked in our favour. Where does the fight go from here?

Victoria Gillick's application for legal aid is being questioned. Normally, legal aid is only available for something of personal concern. Since her daughters will not be asking for contraception, her campaign cannot be classed as a personal concern. But she continues her crusade. Gillick has pledged to monitor doctors and any who she thinks are in breach of the

Lords ruling, might find themselves being reported to the General Medical Council. We haven't seen the last of her yet.

A substitute for nature, chance and human relations?
Brigitte Gohdes
SR 145 August 1984

The notion of artificial reproduction is a radical challenge to many of our basic assumptions about nature, chance and human relations. Reproduction is a crucial aspect of every woman's life, whether we have children or not. It is also central in theories about the position of women in society, and in strategies to change it. Reproduction has been interpreted as *the* biological difference between men and women, and as an explanation of the sexual division of labour and of male dominance. It has also been an important arena for women's struggles to gain autonomy.

The key question about reproduction is where we locate its oppressiveness to women: in the biological fact that women, and only women, give birth; or in the social and historical fact that child-bearing and rearing has in most societies been organised and confined within family forms which are male-dominated and exploitative. That women's reproductive capacity is 'exploitable' seems clear – all its aspects have been and/or are subject to control by men. The question then becomes whether women need to transcend natural reproduction through technology; or whether the economic, social, political and psychological changes implicit in women's liberation will rid us of the limiting and exploitative aspects of child-bearing. Such a 'feminist revolution' would imply social change on a scale no less futuristic to envisage than test-tube baby factories.

It is probably safe to say that most women are very alienated from science. It seems remote, we have little knowledge of its content and no sense of control over its direction and we are vaguely suspicious of its results ('what will they come up with next?'). Feminists have criticised and exposed science as male-dominated in structure and values and as something that has been used against women. But many feminists also agree that criticism from the outside is not enough to come to terms with science. (See the discussions of women and science in: Brighton Women and Science Group, *Alice through the Microscope*; Hubbard Henifin and Fried, *Women Look at Biology Looking at Women*; J. Sayers, *Biological Politics*). The scale of possible permanent and irreversible interventions in the ecosystem and in human evolution is becoming greater all the time (e.g. nuclear technology and genetic engineering). This makes popular awareness and conscious participation in science more urgent. Science is not a neutral tool that just needs to be wrested from male control, but its method, aims and direction can be reshaped, and women should play a leading role in this.

Concretely, this means engaging seriously with science on an intellectual and practical level. We must become knowledgeable about science, and this means overcoming fear of and alienation from its vastness and universality. Artificial reproduction, genetic engineering and many other issues have to be faced by women, and we should not do so from a position of weakness and ignorance.

Test-tube babies, surrogate mothers, frozen embryos, leased wombs, banked sperm – a new vocabulary which we find splashed across the front pages of the papers. It refers to a whole new technology of reproduction which is with us today. I use the term artificial reproduction loosely, to mean conscious outside intervention at any point in the reproductive process from bringing egg cell and sperm together, fertilisation, implantation in the womb to consequent cell division and development of the embryo. Apart from artificial insemination, most techniques involve the removal of part of this process outside the woman's body.

Artificial insemination (usually by donor – AID) is the oldest and simplest artificial technique. There is really very little artificial about it as the only difference with normal conception is that sperm is introduced into the vagina with a syringe. But even this simple difference raises possibilities of more intervention. Since usually sperm from anonymous donors is used, these can be selected for particular characteristics, screened for illness and genetic abnormality and matched to the woman's rhesus factor, for example. The practice of AID has given us sperm banks, where men can store their own sperm (before a vasectomy, or for whatever more oblique individual reason they might have) or where frozen sperm from donors is kept. In America, where such matters are more unashamedly commercial, sperm banks are marketing semen with particular selling points, for example guaranteed 'racially pure' sperm.

AID is practised in this country within NHS fertility clinics (as well as privately) mostly as a means of overcoming male infertility in marriage. There are few single women or lesbian couples who have succeeded in obtaining AID through the official clinics. In France, the artificial insemination service is explicitly limited to stable married couples.

But AID need not be seen only or primarily as a remedy for male infertility. It is just as much a way for a woman – lesbian or not – to have a child without heterosexual intercourse. Medical intervention is not necessary and women can do it themselves – all that is required is live sperm.

Even a simple intervention, like AID, already contains some of the implications of much more complex techniques of artificial reproduction. For example, it makes the separation of sex and reproduction complete. Heterosexual intercourse (long considered synonymous with sex) became separate from reproduction with effective contraception; now reproduction, or women having babies, is potentially separate from intercourse.

In vitro fertilisation (IVF) is the most important of the new reproductive techniques so far, if only because it is a prerequisite for other interventions. The first test-tube baby was born in England in 1978, after years of research by Steptoe and Edwards at their Bourn Hall clinic. As of early 1983 about 400 pregnancies and 150 live births have occurred through use of IVF.

IVF simply means fertilisation of the female egg cell outside the body. The procedure is as follows: egg cells are surgically removed, combined with live sperm in the famous test-tube where they will be penetrated and fertilised, the fertilised egg cells are left to undergo cell division for about five days and then implanted in the mother's womb. It is much more complicated than it sounds: removal of the oocytes required laparoscopy (instruments and a light source are inserted through a small incision in the abdomen, with full anaesthetic) and a careful study of the woman's menstrual cycle – timing of the operation has to be precise. Women are usually given hormones to stimulate ovulation so that more than one egg can be taken. Again, precise timing is needed for implantation of the embryo in the womb. It all adds up to a costly and time-consuming process. At present IVF is practised mostly in private clinics, for a fee of about £2,000 for each cycle. All clinics everywhere report very low 'success' rates (success being the birth of a baby).

The only published report on the pregnancy rate achieved after a laparoscopic operation for collection of eggs found that 8 per cent became pregnant. No one has yet reported on the number of live births resulting. However, looking over all reports published by March 1983, 400 pregnancies and 150 live births were reported. It is not possible to separate out the pregnancies still in process and those that have miscarried.

Still, the miscarriage rate may be high. Many precautions are taken to prevent spontaneous abortion. To maximise implantation, the women must stay completely still for at least four hours, followed by two days' bed rest. For the next ten days, progesterone is given to decrease the chances of spontaneous abortion.

Surrogate motherhood is a term used to refer to several different practices:

(1) A woman who produces normal egg cells but cannot bear a child can have eggs removed, fertilised *in vitro* and implanted into the womb of a 'surrogate', 'host', or 'carrying' mother. (Very complicated as the menstrual cycles and hormonal balances of the two women need to be exactly synchronised.)

(2) A variation on this is what is sometimes called embryo transfer: a woman donates an egg cell to another woman who cannot produce one but can bear a child. The donor's egg cell is fertilised through artificial insemination (not externally) and then the fertilised ovum is transferred directly to the receiving woman. The donating woman is the genetic mother, but the woman who wants the baby is both bearing and 'social' mother.

In both of the above procedures, because the genetic and bearing mothers are different individuals, three people have made a physical

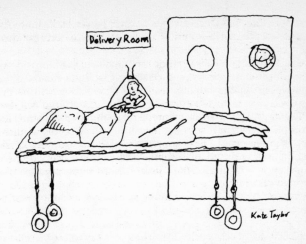

Delivery Room

Kate Taylor

FIGURE 18 Artificial reproduction *Kate Taylor* (*SR 145* August 1984)

contribution to the child that is born – the 'providers' of egg cell and sperm, and the woman who bears the child for nine months.

(3) The most widely practised form of surrogate motherhood does not involve IVF or embryo transfer. The surrogate mother has artificial insemination (presumably, if we are talking about childless couples, with semen from the partner of the woman who wants a child but is infertile). This 'host' mother is both bearing and genetic mother but she gives up the child upon birth. The 'social' mother is like an adopting mother. In the US there are now agencies specialising in finding surrogate mothers for childless couples, often for large fees.

Sex determination simply means pre-natal analysis of the sex of the embryo. The pregnancy could be terminated if the sex is 'wrong' ('wrong' is usually according to the values of the parents, although there are sometimes medical grounds for selective abortion because of sex-linked diseases). This is equivalent to sex-selective infanticide which is practised widely, both cross-culturally and historically (and we all know which sex was selected). Amniocentesis (sampling of the fluid surrounding the foetus and analysing the chromosomes of cells contained in this fluid) is a common technique now, though not completely without risk. In the second trimester of pregnancy, a small sample of amniotic fluid can be removed by a hollow needle inserted into the mother's abdomen into the amniotic sac. Cells from the sample are grown in a culture and the chromosomes can be analysed. Amniocentesis can't be done until later in pregnancy, and the later the more dangerous.

Recently, a method has been tested that can be used much earlier in pregnancy. In the first trimester, cells from the chorionic part of the placenta can be removed early by instruments inserted through the cervix. This could make sex detection much safer for the mother. External fertilisation – the fact that embryos are observable and quite testable *in vitro* for about five days, also allows sex determination, just as it provides an opportunity for intervention on grounds of other generic 'flaws'. It is theoretically possible to implant only embryos of the desired sex.

The artificial placenta is a controversial concept because of its association with futuristic nightmares and because scientists dispute whether it can ever be achieved or not.

Ectogenesis (growing a foetus outside a womb), for which the artificial placenta is a prerequisite, would raise the technical possiblity of making mothers obsolete and creating an all-male society (except for a few women as egg producers).

The very language used to describe the techniques indicates that their application is very much under medical, and therefore 'male expert', control.

The research furthering these developments is done by mostly male scientists and, more importantly, controlled through funding bodies, ethical committees, the state (law) and professional associations (codes of practice). There are pious calls for 'public debate' on the morality and implications of artificial reproduction techniques, and an official DHSS Inquiry into the ethics of reproductive technology has been set up last year, under Mary Warnock. But on the whole it is safe to say that women have very little input into policies on research and priorities, or on the way the technology will be used.

So far, both AID and IVF have been officially limited to stable heterosexual couples. The techniques are thus no threat to the nuclear family; in fact they help individual couples to reach the blissful state of full nuclear-familyhood with their own children. In this form, most people have no trouble accepting the new technology ('Two in three approve of test-tube baby projects', *Guardian*, October 1982), especially as other possible users are not mentioned much.

But the new techniques and especially external fertilisation are not just remedies for infertility. The following is a fairly random list of some of the physical possibilities and philosophical issues they raise: the freezing of sperm and embryos makes it possible for people to become genetic parents after their death; sex determination or selection introduces an element of choice (weighted in favour of males) into a natural process which so far has resulted in nearly equal distribution of the sexes through a kind of chromosomal lottery; should feminists be able to choose daughters?; surrogate motherhood makes women's reproductive capacity as marketable as our sexuality – some women's wombs can be leased outside the family but in order to uphold the family ideal. Even the *Guardian's* women's page noted the remarkable parallels with prostitution (*Guardian*, (18 October 1983); all the new techniques raise questions on the nature of parenthood – is it based on genetic or social reality?; what is the morality of infertile western couples spending £2,000 on the odd chance they might have *their own* child, while there is forced sterilisation of many Third World women?

Shulamith Firestone, in *The Dialectic of Sex*, controversially advocated that women give up reproduction altogether since she believed that biology (i.e. childbearing) creates the family (which she continually refers to as a biological unit) and oppresses women. If women no longer want to be oppressed they must transcend biology – in her view much of human history has been this type of progressive transcendence of natural limitations. Childbearing (as all menial labour!) has to be taken over by machines if women are to be equal. Interestingly, it is the 'male techno-logical mode' represented in science, and not the 'female aesthetic mode', which will set the stage for this liberation.

Andrea Dworkin, in *Right Wing Women* (1983), has no illusion about a technological solution – her analysis of artificial reproduction is perhaps more realistic and certainly more sinister. Women under patriarchy are reduced to objects for male use – sexually and for reproduction (the 'brothel model' and the 'farming model'). They are inessential to all other aspects of society. Motherhood is slightly preferable to women: in relation to prostitution/pornography it offers a modicum of respect, dignity and protection – the reason why right-wing women defend motherhood to the last. Women are reducible to the uterus but Dworkin is careful to see this status of chattel as a social, historical and political subjugation – a state of affairs which men maintain through violence and control over reproduction. This control is not always absolute or perfect – artificial reproduction would make it more so.

For Dworkin, in the final analysis, men will try to make women obsolete. I don't find the notion of a male conspiracy very helpful. We need an approach which is more pragmatic and more sophisticated in its analysis of how men, or some men, or the state, use science, and of the limitations of science itself.

A basic technology of artificial reproduction is here. Firmly under medical control and used to bolster the family, it does not contribute to the liberation of women, and might in fact hinder it if male power is increased by the new technology of reproduction. After a 'feminist revol-ution' women might choose to develop and use some new reproductive technology. In the meantime, it is the political, economic, social and psychological structures built upon the fact of biological childbirth that oppress women. It is important to break the link between women and an exclusive and life-long responsibility for and involvement in 'mothering', rather than the link between women and childbirth.

CHAPTER 5

ABORTION AND FEMINISM

'Free abortion on demand' was one of the original four demands of the women's liberation movement in Britain. It was taken up by an International Women's Day demonstration and then agreed by the second national WLM conference in October 1971. A woman's right to choose not to continue with an unwanted pregnancy has been basic to feminism and, because of repeated parliamentary attacks on the 1967 Abortion Act (comparatively liberal in its time but now coming to seem more and more narrow and restrictive by current European standards), *Spare Rib* has always covered the issue intensively, usually in the news section.

Both *Spare Rib* coverage and campaigning grew in response to an attack on the law, and then died down between attacks. There were shifts in the focus of the campaigns for choice – against private members' bills, obstructive doctors, anti-choice groups or restrictions imposed by the government without parliamentary consent – and in the attitudes, arguments and alliances of pro-choice feminists.

Abortion can be seen either as a liberal or a radical demand, as something society should provide to help women in need, or as part of women's control over our own lives. Feminists have seen it as the latter, but have had to work with 'liberal' doctors, the family planning lobby and the Labour movement, who have differing ideas about it. The law does *not* give us the right to choose – and yet thousands of us have put millions of hours into defending it against the alliance of organised Christians and reactionary MPs.

The whole issue of 'reproductive rights' – which includes the right to a free, safe abortion on demand, but is also much more than that – is now showing a huge resurgence in the WLM, free this time of any new anti-choice initiative. A debate continues in the women's movement about a woman's right to abort a foetus that appears to be abnormal. Women are taking up issues such as the question of whether a woman should be allowed to choose to abort a foetus because of its sex; or the question of whether women's right to choose to *have* a baby includes the right to concentrate overstretched National Health Service resources into facilities for *in vitro* (test-tube) fertilisation.

Black women have long criticised the abortion campaigns for ignoring the needs of Black women – indeed, for the whole idea of a single issue campaign. The campaigns are now being forced to take notice. A notorious anti-choice gynaecologist was particularly concerned that too many middle class white women were having abortions; pro-choice campaigns are now determined to uncover what sorts of pressure doctors put on Black, working class and single women not to continue with pregnancy.

One woman's abortion

Marie Arnold
SR 45 March 1976

When I left home seven years ago, one of the things I was looking for was a bloke to live with or at least have a steady relationship with. It had taken me about four years to actually 'make it' in bed with someone, after a fairly ordinary and Catholic upbringing. I started living with John and went on the pill at the same time. It wasn't so easy to get the pill then. I had to go right across London to the Brook Clinic in Elephant and Castle. Brook was the only place that would see 'single' girls with no fuss. You were simply treated as a woman – which made quite a change for me.

Xmas 1974 was the tail-end of my second 'long' relationship with someone. Paul and I had been close friends and lovers during two years of living together at a time of big upheavals in both our lives. By Xmas, after three months of fierce arguments and disagreements, he had already moved away and I was at my most miserable. I was near to tears for days at a time. During our arguments I'd often cry in the pub or on the tube. (It used to annoy me no end that he never cried once.) And when I was on my own I found it horrible that all my thoughts and feelings were focused on one person, when I wanted to be able to think and feel about all the things I was involved in. I was bitter, jealous and terribly alone.

After desperately trying to heal my impossible relationship with Paul and failing, I decided that my life and ideas had to change. I had to get to know myself, instead of continually looking for people who I could escape into.

Part of this process was going off the pill. I began to wonder whether the pill itself encouraged certain moods. I don't think this is necessarily true, as I have always had bouts of depression. But I wanted to control my own body as much as possible. I got fitted with a cap.

At the same time, I began using the 'safe' period, using a thermometer. After my period I used the thermometer again, and after about 36 days stupidly decided I must have ovulated, even though I hadn't yet had a period, and stopped using the cap.

By this time, I had a very affectionate but casual relationship with Joe, an old friend of mine. I was determined that it should be utterly equal. I was going to express my ideas and do what I wanted even if it threatened the relationship. I was no longer prepared to *try* to please. After all, I had nothing to lose since I had begun enjoying my freedom. No one to phone up, or consult with every day. Reading into the night as long as I wanted. Getting up for work in my own time. My mind seemed to take a leap. I had to determine everything I stood for by myself. I was calmer. Paul and I slept together again once or twice. For me it was half ecstatic and half total misery. A real contradiction. Ecstatic for all the old things between us and intolerably tense and miserable because my new energy and independence were just ignored.

I must have got pregnant some time in April, but didn't know. By May, I had had no period since March. I had a negative pregnancy test. My doctor thought I probably wasn't pregnant so he prescribed me Primodos, a pill which is meant to bring on late periods. For a week beforehand, I had had the most terrible cramps. like a period but much worse. The doctor offered no explanation, just telling me to take the Primodos. They give you two tablets and you have to take them on two consecutive days. I took one, and that night I slept with Joe. I was using the cap. Someone told me that Primodos gives you cramps, so I took a few aspirins and had a really nice night! Next morning, which was a Saturday – a rare chance to lie in – I took my cap out and inside it was an inch long piece of gristle. I stared at it thinking, 'What the hell is that?' Then it dawned on me . . . it must be a tiny foetus. It was fascinating. I looked at it for a long time. It was sort of grey-brown, opaque. Much thicker at one end than the other, with tiny, tiny buds sprouting at the bottom end, just like a little fish. Then I flushed it away and went and told the other people I share a flat with. I looked up *Our Bodies Ourselves* and estimated that it was a four to five-week old foetus.

That week I had a period and felt sick and ghastly. We'd organised an abortion meeting in the hospital where I work, so I stayed for that, then I took a week off sick. I still got cramps, so the doctor gave me painkillers. At no time did he examine me, neither did he particularly believe my story about the foetus. Yet I found out soon after that two women I knew had had similar spontaneous abortions.

If I had understood more about how my body worked then, I would have known something was wrong. Both the women I spoke to said that their abortions had come out in a mass of jelly and liquid – the placenta. Mine was totally on its own. I didn't think much of it as the doctor wasn't very fussed, but I started getting physically run-down and pathetic. I went on the abortion demonstration on 21 June feeling physically sick but jubilant at our strength.

Because I felt physically sick, I began to get morbid again. I felt bitter, then angry with myself for allowing these feelings to control me. I was determined not to be destructive and get cynical. I had another period and felt totally exhausted. What the hell was wrong with me?

Joe began to get concerned about me. Paul seemed completely indifferent. I felt as though to him I was an 'emotional female' so we couldn't ever discuss it. I tried talking about it with other women. In fact I approached a lot of people, mostly women. But I also held back. I didn't want to point out my confused and anxious emotions. I didn't want to be continually preoccuped and moody. I wanted to be strong, outward-looking and stable and in control of what I thought and did. I wanted the cycle of 'moods' to go away, and not to drag someone else into it.

At last Paul and I finished our relationship once and for all. It was a tremendous relief, but sad too.

During July, I felt ill almost every day. But I didn't want to keep going to the doctor. I put it down to 'nerves' and started going for long walks thinking that my body was simply run-down.

Suddenly, two weeks after my last 'period', I had a sudden rush of blood just before going to bed. Something was definitely wrong. Someone phoned the doctor for me and he told me to come in the next morning. At last, an internal examination. The doctor said, 'Well, there's definitely something there but I don't know what it is!' and sent me to the local hospital. More internals, and a urine test and the verdict – I was about three months pregnant, maybe more, but 'something' was wrong. My last two 'periods' were, in fact, haemorrhages, so was the 'rush' of blood. I had to go into hospital immediately. I was a bit stunned at all this. I phoned work to say I wouldn't be in, saying something vague about my womb.

The junior hospital doctor who took my notes and examined me was a woman, very calm and reassuring. But I was scared. I knew that I wasn't prepared to have a baby. I don't want children at this stage in my life. But I didn't want to blurt out 'Can't you just give me an abortion?'

I was relieved to have a day in bed while they gave me tests.

I was an 'interesting' case because whatever it was inside me was not at all normal. Everyone was agreed about that. After all the tests, the registrar came back with the young woman doctor and gave me the results – three to four months pregnant. I said I didn't really want a baby. So they took me on one side and told me to go back to work straight away and rush around, and that within a month I would have a miscarriage.

The prospect was daunting. They said I would know when it was coming on and I would be bound to make it to hospital on time. It seemed rational in a way. I suppose I was somehow prepared to accept the advice of 'experts'.

So I went back to work, and this time I felt all of three and a half months pregnant. My belly was definitely growing. I looked at it amazed. How could I have not known I was pregnant for three and a half months? But what about my spontaneous abortion two and a half months earlier? Most doctors I saw dismissed this as a figment of my imagination, but the ones that chose to believe me thought I must have been having twins originally!

Then I went to my own doctor. He was more shocked than I had been at what the hospital doctors had said, and told me to get an appointment for an abortion. So I went back to the hospital, but this time I saw the boss – the consultant gynaecologist.

It was clear that there was no way in which he was going to understand the way I lived, my views and what I wanted out of my life. At the same time I was saying to myself, 'Act unstable, make out you're unbalanced.' It wasn't difficult. I mumbled a few replies and tears started streaming down my face. He said, 'Well, even if I give you an abortion, it can't be down there' (meaning a vaginal abortion), 'it has to be with a drip and you'll have to wait two more weeks for that.' (This meant an induced abortion going into labour which can last 36 hours.)

I suddenly got ferociously angry and hysterical all at once. I managed to say, 'I don't know if I believe you', but I was sobbing pretty badly and got carted off to the social worker. They asked me who the father was, what my parents did, who was I living with. And I was thinking, 'I can't go on with this.' She said, 'Come back in two weeks and we'll tell you whether we've decided to give you an abortion or not'!

I walked out, sobbing like a lunatic. Luckily I phoned someone to meet me. We went home and phoned the Pregnancy Advisory Service. I went to see them that afternoon. It was completely different. I felt like a normal woman with a normal problem. My pregnancy was confirmed yet again at 14 weeks. You can usually only have vacuum aspiration up to 12 weeks. PAS said they did a special vacuum aspiration method for 12 to 17 weeks pregnancies. For me this was a combination of a vacuum and a D&C (scrape). This is a highly skilled technique, which is why many NHS hospitals don't do it, but the PAS doctor said they don't take the trouble to learn. In fact this method has been possible for 25 years.

PAS said it would cost £60 plus £7 consultation fee. I scraped the money together and had a straightforward abortion through PAS three days later. I felt as though I was paying for my sanity. Everything about it was relaxed and good except that you had to pay, and the Harley Street doctor must have been making a packet out of it. I basically disagree with private practice, but PAS has pioneered methods and clinics which should be taken up by the NHS free and as a right for everyone.

After all this, I had found out a lot more about my body. We now use the cap every time, usually with Durex too. I don't think I'd be happy with this method if I slept with someone every night. But since I don't, it has just become a part of love making. It's also been useful in sharing responsibilities for contraception with Joe and in explaining the way a woman's body works.

I waited another three and a half months for a period, but now feel much better physically and mentally.

Within 18 months, I feel that I have drastically changed my life for the better. Obviously I may get depressed again. But I am full of ideas and energy. I am more stable *in myself* and more hard-working (which I enjoy) than I have ever been.

The abortion itself was just part of this change. I learnt a lot about myself from having to cope with it alone. I'd begun to see the need to control my own life, and the abortion clinched it. It also forced me to

194

come to terms with the reasons why I don't want children at the moment. (Even though I have always vaguely assumed that I woud have kids one day, I don't want kids 'by accident'). I am committed to many other things at the moment which I want to see through. They're my responsibility.

The whole experience also made clear to me what I wanted in my personal relationships. I don't want my sexual relationships to dominate my life because I think it leads me into a situation where male/female conditioning creeps up and can't be controlled.

I am more determined to have friendships on a wide level and not discriminate against the people I don't sleep with. This has been at the back of my mind for years. It always seemed so unfair to me to invest so much in just one relationship with one man or one woman. After all, if you can make a close friend of one person, why not be equally and genuinely supportive of all the other people you know?

I see Joe once or sometimes twice a week. It's a lovely friendship. I have more time for other people and more time for myself. And more time and energy to fight to change this rotten society.

I wanted to write about my own experiences of abortion and some of the problems and pressures in my life at the time because I think it shows a lot about 'a woman's right to choose' – the slogan of the National Abortion Campaign. I think it shows that our right to choose can be about fundamental changes in our lives and the kind of society we live in, and that many women are confronted by some of the same things as I am. We want to organise the changes that are taking place FOR OURSELVES.

Abortion: the feelings behind the slogans
Eileen Fairweather
SR 87 September 1979

Only a little over 50 years ago, my grandmother died in childbirth, 'Puerperal septicaemia' is the recorded cause, a fancy term which says nothing of the conditions she gave birth in. Which was, like most women of the time, in poverty, without the help of midwife or doctor, and with a body made weak through undernourishment and overwork. She died having my mother, only 11 months after her last labour. Twins that time, neither of whom lived longer than six weeks. The good old days.

When you wash away the centuries-old gobbledygook about sacred motherhood, sacred infancy, the truth – at least in our culture – is that the generation of women now in their twenties and thirties are the *first ever* to be able to view pregnancy with something less than stricken fear. Today, only 12 women in 100,000 die through childbirth, compared with the one in 250 of 50 years ago. Medical men and male legislators would have us believe this is entirely due to their pioneer policies and technology. But whatever women have gained, we have had to fight for it every inch of the way.

FIGURE 19 Abortion demonstration: an unsuccessful attempt to place the London women's liberation banner up with the TUC banner in Trafalgar Square during the big abortion demonstration on 28 October 1979 *Jill Posener (SR 89 November 1979)*

While our elected 'representatives' (616 men, 19 women) strain their consciences over abortion, women have already had to cast their vote. From the statistics available on legal and illegal abortion over the past 50 years, probably one woman in six has had an abortion.

Why, then, don't all these women come forward to defend a woman's right to choose? The National Abortion Campaign has initiated a Campaign Against Corrie, new groups are being formed, old ones revived, a petition is being circulated and the TUC have called an autumn demonstration. But for many feminists there's a feeling of *déjà vu*. Partly, that's exhaustion. More worrying is the number who fear that the pro-choice movement cannot win the support of women overall because it does not actually reflect their experience. The women's movement was still very young when abortion first became a political football. We duly kicked back and, faced with the opposition's set of slogans, defensively came up with our own. In our rush to do that, the complexity of abortion and its emotional significance for women somehow got lost.

The National Abortion Campaign is the only nationally organised

experience for each woman is lost. This self-censorship limits our campaigns and, just as importantly, it abuses us. One feminist found herself totally unprepared: 'I was stunned by my reaction. I never thought I'd want kids and I found I wanted this one.' Debbie thinks circumstances made the decision for her, and 'what I feel now almost more than sadness is resentment . . . we've a long way to go before a woman's right to choose can mean anything.'[3]

NAC rightly says that women must have 'access to free, safe birth control; community-controlled childcare facilities; paid maternity leave; increased child benefit and more financial support for single parents . . . to enable a realistic choice'. But this doesn't come out clearly enough in the work of the campaign, perhaps because the women's movement as a whole hasn't gone far enough in fighting for motherhood to be less oppressive than it is now.

The antis use such emotive arguments about motherhood and child-hood that we again react defensively. They talk of killing life, and speak of every foetus as a baby. In response, 'NAC says the foetus is a *potential* human life, incapable of independent existence'[4] (my italics). Another much-used slogan is 'An egg is not a chicken, an acorn is not a tree, a foetus is not a baby, so don't lay that on me.'

Why do we have to make support for a woman's right to choose dependent on seeing the foetus as no more than a bunch of splitting cells? In doing so, we lost many potential supporters, and that includes those women who have had an abortion, but think of it as killing. Some women experience nothing but relief after an abortion. Others only feel guilty because they *don't* feel guilty. But for women, it's not so simple: 'I love children so much. It makes it even harder when you already have a child. This time I couldn't help thinking it was a human being, a living being. If you asked me how I felt about abortion, I would say I was against it. I feel very hypocritical.'[5]

The 'potential' human life argument implies that she is merely suffering from feminine fancy and sexist conditioning. It may seem the most 'revolutionary' position, but it is not pro-woman. How can it be, when it denies women's experience?

According to one Australian study, 60% of women believe life begins at conception (compared with 36 of men). That doesn't stop them having abortions. Countering SPUC's quasi-science with our own quasi-science is, to me, to argue in a very rational, masculine way. The only way abortion will cease to be each woman's guilty secret, and become something she is prepared to fight for publicly, is through our saying without apology – yes, if necessary, we put women first.

Many people who are normally pro-choice support the clause in Corrie's bill which imposes an abortion time limit (20 weeks, which in practice would mean 16). NAC believes there should be no time limit on abortion at all (the position in Scotland until the 1967 Act, and the one now adopted by the World Health Organisation). Any woman who needs to

199

abort at five or six months is desperate: the menopausal woman who has not even realised she is pregnant, the teenager who is too terrified to tell; the woman who has just discovered she is bearing a deformed child. A late abortion is too miserable for any woman to have one lightly. But those campaigners who insist on the non-humanity of the foetus only encourage groups like SPUC and Life, who use the undoubted distress of late abortion to curb abortion full-stop.

It is possible for people to support a woman's right to choose whether they believe abortion is killing or not. Why should we preclude that? This is not just a question of tactics; it is about making a clear choice for the humanity of a grown woman, over the foetuses she may conceive – through ignorance, accident or coercion – every month of her life, for well on 30 years.[6]

If women are denied legal abortions they will procure them anyway – dangerously, and at risk of injury or death. Professor Scarisbrick, like some other SPUC supporters, indifferently replies, 'Nobody will deny that the hag in a seedy backroom or the amateur with potion and knitting needle are horrifying . . . but agreed that the backstreet trade is ghastly, why should the answer be to bring it into the front street?'[7]

It is a mistake to see all our opponents as total woman-haters. Our aim should instead be to isolate those who are. The bulk of SPUC marchers are Catholic and, because Catholicism is mainly an immigrant religion, working class, many of them are women, and they know what a strain motherhood can be. Catholic men really practise the abstinence the priests preach. So there are many points of contact. In my experience, arguments about 'when life begins' never dissuade them – discussion about women's lives do. Many are very disturbed when you point out the consequences of their involvement. They may still say they could not countenance abortion for themselves, but are not prepared to deprive other women of choice.

Religion plays a part in the hostility of some Black women to abortion. And for women from places like the West Indies, where illegitimacy has less significance, abortion can seem less 'necessary'. But racism is an important factor. When Margaret Thatcher talks of Britain being 'swamped by alien cultures', fertility control takes on a whole new meaning. Compulsory abortions and sterilisations have already been performed on Black women here. Criticisms from Black feminists led to NAC setting up the International Contraception, Abortion and Sterilisation Campaign, which defends a woman's right to these when *she* wants them and, simultaneously, opposes the racist use of population control both here and abroad.

Many women worry about abortion because they feel it can simply be another weapon men use against us. If they have had an abortion, they may feel bitter that their partner did not offer to help them have and keep the child; some are deserted the minute pregnancy is even mentioned – with maybe just a cheque 'for clearing up' left behind. The woman who actively chooses abortion may still feel unsupported, and angry that she got 'lumbered' in the first place.

The pro-choice movement has been curiously quiet about all this – perhaps because men are involved in the campaign? The (relative) enthusiasm with which the male left adopted the slogan 'abortion on demand' may well be because abortion can mean men avoid any responsibility for the less pleasant consequences of sexuality.

At least in the past women could expect men to offer to do 'the honourable thing'. Now that is rare. This is not to suggest that men should be forced into parenting, any more than women should. Yet most women still have little real chance of economically making it on their own with a child. The 'sexual revolution' has often meant more freedom for men, with no lessening of responsibility for women.

In our fight for abortion rights, we need to stress continually that what women really need is safe and adequate contraception – 75% of abortions are due to contraceptive failure. Nominally the male left will happily go along with this because, like abortion, it fits in with their emphasis on fighting cuts and makes demands of the state. Compared to rape or woman-battering, fertility control must seem a less threatening issue; the implications of sexism can more easily be concealed. But one important element is neglected – how the hell do they think women get pregnant in the first place? Increasingly, women are rejecting the pill and IUD for contraceptive methods with fewer side-effects, but more scope for human error. How many men take equal responsibility in contraception? 'Liberated' men are often the worst offenders. Yet this aspect is hardly ever mentioned in our campaigns.

These misgivings are not reasons for feminists to abdicate the abortion campaign. If we do not want our demands to be co-opted, we must battle to change support into the kind we need. Equally, we don't need to be tied by the rules of any new-found friends.

If the laws are changed, we will have no choice but to learn how to perform abortions. The menstrual extraction method, pioneered by American feminists, is performed a few days after a period is overdue, and before a woman can even tell for certain whether she is pregnant.

Learning to perform abortions could also be a major political weapon. One strong reason why abortion was legalised in France and Italy was that women were defying the law *en masse*, through feminist-organised underground abortion networks.

Feminists have wanted to challenge previous bills with the open threat that, if the law was changed, we'd break it. But it was felt that we should hold that card until our backs were really up against the wall. Which is precisely where we are now.

There are enough nurses and medics who are feminists, or sympathetic to us, for a *safe*, illegal abortion network to be a reality. We have to let our rulers know now that we're prepared to flout their laws if forced. We must use every weapon we can. That includes petitions, writing to MPs, demonstrating – but it does not have to stop there. Those feminist actions which have been imaginative and defiant – Reclaim the Night, the blocking of Fleet Street, the occupation of Westminster Cathedral – have all won considerable publicity.

NOTES

1 Over one million abortions have been legally performed in the past ten years. In 1935 the government-appointed Birkett Committee estimated 100,000–150,000 illegal abortions a year.
2 Discussion paper, *NAC's Future Strategy*.
3 Unpublished letter to *Spare Rib*, from Debbie, Manchester.
4 *Why is the National Abortion Campaign Here Today*? NAC leaflet aimed at SPUC supporters.
5 Linda Bird Francke, *The Ambivalence of Abortion*, p. 99. Allen Lane, £5.95. The book contains thought-provoking interviews with American women who have had abortions. Written from a firmly pro-choice point of view.
6 See *Abortion: The Double Standard* by Catholics for a Free Choice, 50p from Roman Catholic Feminists, c/o 33 Arklow Road, London N21.
7 Professor Scarisbrick, *What's Wrong with Abortion* (SPUC).

Responsibility for this article is my own, but many thanks to Amanda Sebestyen, Angela Phillips and Trish Ziff for their valuable ideas and suggestions; and to Debbie, in Manchester, for encouraging me to write it.

Life: Whose right to choose?
Michelene Mason
SR 115 February 1982

I find it difficult to write a 'continuation' of the discussion about the Down's Syndrome baby case begun by Rose Shapiro in the last issue. I do not want to discuss the issue. You are speaking about my life. You wish me to discuss whether or not, as a woman born with a 'severe' disability, I think I should have been murdered. It does not sound reactionary to me to hear of people who want to put an end to the killing of babies because they have disabilities. It sounds wonderful.

The Leonard Arthur case and its subsequent publicity in the media was very distressing to me and many of my friends with disabilities. We became afraid to turn on the TV or radio in case we were landed with another dose of 'Should we let them live?' When you already suspect the world would rather you weren't there, this sort of barrage can be most depressing. We felt the overall result was to legitimise and make respectable the most appalling aspects of our oppression. Strangely enough, what cheered me up was the realisation that almost no one I heard had any idea what they were talking about. It is always easier to deal with ignorance than with malevolence.

The medical profession sees the world through the most blinkered eyes. Their discussions about 'the quality of life' left me squirming. They are part of the establishment, dedicated to Law, Order and the State. They do not like 'misfits' who may not be able to earn their living or look beautiful, who will remind them that they cannot perform miracle cures like Jesus.

Doctors, parents, people in general are notoriously ignorant about disability. Hardly any of my able-bodied friends knew what 'spina bifida' or 'Down's syndrome' meant. They, like everyone else, were caught up in the stereotyped images of helpless vegetables needing 24 hours a day care, slobbering, agonised, hopeless lumps of human flesh who ruin everybody else's life as well as their own. In fact, this is hardly ever true. It is people's fears of disability which are the problem.

These fears are fed mercilessly when the possibility of 'choice' arises. I do support the campaign for abortion to be freely available but I think it very naive to believe that any woman is free to 'choose' whether or not to give birth to, or keep alive, a baby with a disability given the climate in which she is supposed to make that decision. All the pressure will be in the direction of abortion or killing the baby, when that baby – and not the society in which it and she will have to struggle – is seen as the problem.

Rose Shapiro wrote that 'LIFE do not care about the lack of facilities and support that exist for people with disabilities and those who care for them, which must be one of the central questions involved in the decision to allow a severely handicapped baby to die'. It's probably true that LIFE do not concern themselves with facilities for people with disabilities. But, on the other hand, how do you expect things to improve whilst you accept that another simpler solution lies in the murder of the seeming cause of the problem?

There are enough resources to support everyone in a comfortable, fulfilled life, whether they live in London and have spina bifida, or live in Bangladesh and are starving. It is the big illusion of our time that it is the resources that we lack. The problem is some people control them, misuse them, and deny them to the majority of the rest of the world.

I believe that women are being manipulated into believing that it is in their interests to destroy life because it may cause problems to society, rather than seeing that it is society causing the problems by standing in the way of their right to demand and receive the support they need to raise their children, regardless of their human condition – or even to hand over their children to others who have the personal resources they may feel they do not have.

Murder, masquerading under the euphemism of 'allow to die', can never be an answer to a human problem. What difference is there between this and Nazism? The Nazis started off their concentration camp techniques on people with mental disabilities, whom they called *unnutze Esser* or 'useless eaters'. Rudolf Hess called this project *Vernichtung leber-*

sunwerten Lebens ('the destruction of life not worthy of living'). Sounds familiar, doesn't it.

It is quite normal for some children to be born with disabilities. We are part of normal life. Until this simple fact is understood, accepted and reflected in the structures of our society, the arguments about 'quality of life' and so on are utterly misleading. We will be born, we will suffer, and some will sink and some will triumph. We will not go away. Nor will we stop shouting until the right to choose to live or die is ours, and ours alone.

What future for the National Abortion Campaign?
A debate
SR 135 October 1983

It has been a long time since the Corrie anti-abortion Bill went down in defeat. The National Abortion Campaign continues to be active, but it is not the mass campaign that it was then. We have as much support in the women's movement, student unions, the labour movement and among individuals as we have ever had, and support for abortion rights remains a strong majority across the country. But the number of times we are asked 'Oh, what's NAC doing these days anyway?' is a discouraging indication that our public presence has dropped along with the numbers of women still actively keeping NAC going locally and nationally. For the last two years there has been an ongoing debate inside the campaign about what our politics should be, as we have tried to move away from a strictly defensive role. The debate centres around whether or not we should remain an abortion rights campaign or become a campaign on reproductive rights with a new name and way of working. In the following two pieces, we look at both sides of the debate.

REPRODUCTIVE RIGHTS
by Jane Marshall, Julia South (Merseyside NAC), Dianne Grimsditch, Marge Berer, Sarah Vickerstaff, Julia Goodwin, Jo Mussen (NAC Steering Committee), Helen Minett, Cathy Manthorpe (Leeds NAC), Isabel Ros (Norwich Abortion and Reproductive Rights Campaign)

NAC's main aim has been 'free abortion on demand – a woman's right to choose' since 1975 when the campaign began. All of us remain committed to that aim, but some of us feel we have become complacent about what ' woman's right to choose' means. 'Choice' suggests being able to pick from an ideal set of options. But we are deluding ourselves if we believe that women in this society can make choices about having children or not, when there are over 4 million unemployed, when the wages most women earn (if at all) are still abysmally low, when being married or not makes so much difference, when there is such a lot of very often unchallenged racism on both an individual and institutionalised level, and when we are faced with virulent anti-lesbianism.

A campaign that intends to speak for women needs a political perspective and demands that reflect women's actual needs and experiences. NAC did this on the issue of abortion in the 1970s, and at that time our demands were radical. But our experiences both in NAC and in the women's movement generally since then have made it clear that to focus exclusively on abortion rights is no longer enough. Abortion is not an isolated event in women's lives. It means something different to a woman whose doctor is discouraging her from having a third child by suggesting sterilisation, to a woman whose husband has just been made redundant, to a young woman involved in her first sexual relationship and to a woman who has decided never to have children.

As women, we all share a lack of control over our own bodies in terms of when and if we want children. But we experience that lack of control in different ways, and it is not only through abortion that control over our reproduction is felt. There is an entire climate which promotes certain women having babies and which does not favour others on the basis of prejudice and oppression to do with colour, class, marital status, sexual preference, disability and notions of the 'fit/unfit' mother. We come up against these notions when we go for contraception, if we need an abortion, if we want artificial insemination, if sterilisation is an option, if we need tests for infertility, or if we are pregnant or want to get pregnant. We come up against them precisely at the point where we attempt to make whatever limited choices are open to us, given our individiaul circumstance.

In the 1970s, abortion rights were most publicly under attack. Abortion rights are still being attacked and eroded now, much more insidiously and successfully than five years ago. The struggle to protect those rights remains crucial in a right-wing and repressive atmosphere, but for us this has become a struggle within a struggle. So much else is also threatened that to continue to focus on abortion means ignoring too many other, equally important and totally related, issues of reproductive rights. If we continue to do this in NAC, we are excluding and making invisible those of us who experience these other problems. For example:

Closure of family planning clinics has begun. If it continues, our choices of contraception will narrow because not all GPs have the training or time to provide all the methods, and many women do not want to go to their GPs for contraception. Contraception has only been a right – free on the NHS – since 1974. It could well become a right on paper only. There is an increasing backlash against whatever sexual freedom we can be said to have, especially for young women. Policies such as routinely fitting IUDs after an abortion and routinely giving Depo-Provera with rubella vaccinations after childbirth lump us together as passive receivers of contraception 'for our own good'. Contraceptive failure is defined as our failure only, and there is an increasing intolerance of accidental pregnancy. We are offered – or denied – particular methods of contraception, abortion or sterilisation, depending on who we are. And we are encouraged – or prevented – from having children on the same basis.

Our politics have changed as we have learnt all these things, and we believe NAC must change too. It has become clear to us that we ought to be campaigning for reproductive rights generally, if we are to become a politically relevant, feminist campaign again. We are therefore proposing to NAC Conference on 1/2 October that we dissolve NAC and start again with a new name, a new structure based on local groups, a broader perspective, and hopefully new energy and new women involved. We would like to work more closely with, for example, the women's health groups that have formed and with the groups who are working around our specific aspects of reproductive rights. We feel it is the only way to continue at all as a campaign, without denying what we have learnt and without ignoring the women whose experiences we have learned it from.

KEEP THE NATIONAL ABORTION CAMPAIGN
by the Scottish Abortion Campaign

The National Abortion Campaign (NAC) was founded in 1975 as a single issue campaign to fight against the James White amendment to the 1967 Abortion Act. When that particular amendment was defeated, the NAC went on to develop the aims and slogans which are still the basis of the campaign today. These are that abortion should be safely and freely available to all women who wish it, within the National Health Service.

Free abortion on demand is one of the original demands of the Women's Liberation Movement because it was recognised at the outset that, without the right to control her own body, a woman cannot control her own destiny. Of course we feel that the fight for the improvement in women's health care has been crucial in all aspects of our lives, however without the right to freely available safe abortion, we will remain prisoners of our biology. Why abandon the original demands of the campaign when we have not yet won them? It is relatively easy to obtain an abortion in London, but in many other areas of England, and in Scotland and Wales, we have great difficulty getting the limited provisions of the 1967 Act implemented. In Northern Ireland abortion remains illegal except in very extreme circumstances. It is recognised that women with money were always able to obtain a safe medical abortion, unlike women without who had to go on the backstreets.

We recognise that one of the biggest problems for NAC has been the way in which it has always been thrown on to the defensive by restrictive bills and amendments, by devious but legal back-door methods as statutory instruments, and by the smear campaign of our enemies, the anti-abortionists. Ironically these very attacks served in many ways to concentrate the energies of the campaign on the single issue of abortion. Through the constant pressure of the women's liberation movement and with the support of women in the labour and trade union movement, we managed to force the issue of abortion not only on to the agenda of trade union conferences but on the streets. Without this support we would not have defeated the Corrie Bill. It was to be the only notable defeat of Tory policies since 1979. With the prospect of more of the same policies, can NAC seriously consider abandoning what has been up till now our single-minded determination to counter all attacks on our abortion rights, whenever they occur. NAC has consistently tried to promote improvements, like NHS out-patient abortion clinics, and positive legislation, e.g. Jo Richardson MP's Ten Minute Bill in 1981. However it would be unrealistic to expect NAC to win these improvements in the next five years. On the contrary, we expect the attack on our abortion rights to become frequent and varied.

The large anti-abortion rally on 25 June in London, organised by the Society for the Protection of the Unborn Child (SPUC), and their subsequent full-page adverts in national newspapers and in *Private Eye*, mobilising support 'to get the law changed', almost certainly heralds a huge no-expenses-spared campaign. The most obvious and dramatic of these would be a further Private Member's Bill to restrict the 1967 Abortion Act. This would have massive government and Tory backbench support with a much depleted opposition in parliament. Even if we could guarantee that all opposition MPs would vote against this bill, the responsibility for organising the campaign would necessarily remain with NAC. In the event of a Private Member's Bill being unsuccessful certain aspects of the law could be changed by using statutory instruments; a parliamentary device to change the law without needing a vote. We witnessed this in 1982 when the wording was changed in abortion notification forms, thereby challenging social grounds as a reason for abortion. Perhaps the greatest threat to abortion facilities lies with government intentions to dismantle the National Health Service. Even now, abortion is the only operation more commonly performed in the private sector than in the NHS. We already know that most Area Health Authorities put the very lowest priority on abortion facilities. We would have the prospect of a woman's right to choose – so long as we could pay.

We therefore feel that to broaden our campaign out into the wider issues of reproductive rights would diminish the importance of abortion as *the* central issue. By dropping the word abortion from the name of our campaign we would be shirking our responsibilities to those who looked and still look to us to lead the fight on abortion rights. We have not yet succeeded in our aims, but the fact that we have never failed is a tribute to the single-minded determination with which the aims of the campaign have been pursued.

CHAPTER 6

THE SHAPE OF HEALTH

Because of women's opinions of themselves (and the way they are viewed by others) are so bound up in idealised images, it's not particularly surprising that many so-called little health problems can overwhelm many women's lives. It's also not surprising that women approach things which affect their health but are part of an image they desire, in ambivalent and contradictory ways.

The tyranny of size and shape, of what we look like, and how we distort our bodies, the dominance of a male-defined idealised image of woman, has been the material of many *Spare Rib* articles. The pressures which women live with and are expected to conform to can also result in intolerable internalised frustration and anger. Again, it's not surprising that these erupt in physical and mental pain.

Women's bodies have been the justification for their subjugation and a means of maintaining it. Women often express their distress through their bodies, trying to fit a physical pattern imposed upon them. Feminists attempt to uncover how women have been psychologically controlled through the dominance and internalisation of body image which in this society is almost always white, young, slim and able-bodied.

Spare Rib was one of the first newsstand magazines to look at women's eating disorders, and the first to carry major features on anorexia through interviews with Susie Orbach, author of *Fat is a Feminist Issue*. These early articles were primarily concerned with the psychology of women, food and weight, and almost entirely devoid of any discussion of nutrition and health.

Later articles on women and food have stressed content of diet in relation to health, as well as taking more account of class and race. Most recently, vegetarianism as a feminist issue has been raised. But in all diet/food/shape articles there is a distinct absence of any awareness of the politics of 'Fat Liberation'. Only letter-writers have challenged the presumption that healthy eating will eventually mean thin, or at least thinner.

Spare Rib has also looked at fashion, and tussled with the attractions which it holds for any women, feminists certainly included. Although no one yet has written a book called *Is Fashion a Feminist Health Issue?*, *SR* articles indicate clearly the power of image, and the extent to which women seem, spontaneously, to agree to their own manipulation through fashion. Ten years ago, some feminists probably thought that stiletto heels had been consigned to history's dustbin by any woman who was touched by feminism. Yet today the attitude is much more tolerant even among feminists.

Feminist concern with all these issues has raised dilemmas. Certainly many of the problems addressed are historically and culturally specific to western women living in capitalist countries. Some women have reacted angrily to the angst others express about too much hair, too little hair, spots and weight. Women with physical disabilities have felt that their own difficult struggles to be accepted for who they are – not in spite of their disabilities – are mocked by essentially able-bodied women's inability to come to terms with minor problems which are so bound up with male-defined images.

Yet as feminists we try to understand the way in which how we feel about ourselves is shaped by the society we live in, even as we commit ourselves to changing it. To be able to 'admit' how influenced any of us can be by dominant images of ideal womanhood can be a step towards consciousness-raising, sharing our distress, and moving towards accepting all the differences between us.

Hairy Story
Alex Balsdon and Eva Kaluzynsha
SR 66 January 1978

We've been questioning why we make ourselves look the way we do for years now. In the women's liberation movement we've discussed the images we have of ourselves, and though we can't claim immunity to the influences of fashion, we have become more aware of them and of the role 'looks' play in most women's lives.

We've also learnt a lot about the way our bodies work. Their specifically female functions have become less of a mystery to us as we've demanded the right to know what's going on inside us, how and why our natural rhythms and cycles affect our lives, how they can go wrong and how contraception, for instance, interferes.

But one aspect of our bodies has eluded a thorough public reassessment. Many of us still have to come to terms with our body hair. Why are we so sensitive about it?

The media – particularly women's magazines – have much to answer for. Even an early *Spare Rib* carried an article about 'natural' ways of 'coping' with body hair! But this July *Woman's Own* outdid them all with a really disgusting hair scare story.

Work hard and you'll grow hairy was the threat the magazine made to millions of readers in an article supposedly based on research by Professor Ivor Mills, billed as 'top endocrinologist and Professor of Medicine at Cambridge University'. The equation was crude: man's work equals man's hair. To compete in a man's world, you've got to *be* a man!

Ivor Mills also happens to run a clinic for women suffering from hormone imbalance. They provide him with the raw material on which to conduct his research. So he's drawing conclusions about all women from a highly selected sample, many of whom come to him specifically because of hair problems.

The *Woman's Own* article described a variety of disorders from which women may suffer if their hormonal balance is disturbed. It then claimed that when the 'strain on a woman's brain and her coping powers' becomes too great, she may respond by producing more male sex hormone, androgens, than she should – in a physiological effort to make up for her incapacities perhaps?! Or she may have a disease in male hormone production, in which case she'll become frigid.

Woman's Own put all the symptoms down to the stress of over-work – outside the home that is. They implied that housework and typical women's jobs aren't really work. But a *career* is dangerous if you want to keep your femininity.

Take the item 'Changing sex' for instance. The context implied that this too is a hazard of 'man's work'. 'In some very rare cases, increase of male hormone causes an enlargement of a woman's clitoris and vulva.' True. It's also true that in some very rare cases (and some less rare, following alcohol abuse) increase of female hormone causes an enlargement of a man's breasts (gynaecomastia). In neither case are people suffering from such disorders changing sex; we suspect *Woman's Own* would hesitate to blame excessive zeal for washing-up and nappy changing for gynaecomastia!

Most women would find the idea of the 'disorders' *Woman's Own* describes distressing, largely because they would be unable to argue back with a clear idea of what constitutes 'normal' hair for a woman. Almost everyone has their idea of 'normality' and tries to conform to it. But is one woman's idea of normal anything like another's? Do we pluck and trim ourselves because we fear we're abnormal?

As a basis for at least discussing these questions, this article describes body hair and the changes it usually undergoes at puberty in both women and men. We've added outlines of the main disorders which can provoke abnormal hair growth as one of their symptoms, in the hope that most women reading this will be reassured that they don't have any of them.

Everyone has hair almost all over their body. This hair is of two types. There is the fine down type called *vellus*, which covers the whole skin surface except for the palms and soles. Most of this down is almost invisible, though some women may find the vellus on their upper lip is darker. Vellus also grows all over the forehead, nose, back and other places we think of as hairless.

Terminal hair, such as that on the scalp and in the armpits, is coarser, thicker and pigmented. There is non-sexual terminal hair, such as eyebrows, eyelashes and scalp hair, which does not change significantly with puberty. Some of the sexual hair is similar in both sexes, for instance in the armpits and lower pubic regions. But men have additional sexual hair, on their faces for instance. Differences in body hair between men and women are quantitative, not qualitative.

The relative proportion of vellus and terminal hair, their distribution and the extent that one changes into the other at puberty is affected by an individual's hormone balance and also by genetic factors. So Mediterranean women tend to have more, darker hair in more places than do Scandinavian women.

Women have, however, been thoroughly persuaded that all hair except that of the scalp and eyes should always be invisible, at least in public.

Women's magazines recommend to us remedies for what they call our 'excess' hair, with the effect of making us hairier than we might otherwise have been, since vellus is converted into terminal hair if removed with razor, wax or depilatory chemicals. The more you remove it, the faster and coarser it grows. The fair-haired woman can induce coarse, dark hair on her legs if she persists; the Mediterranean woman living in this country can become convinced she is abnormally hairy by our standards and aggravate what she supposes to be her personal problem. Interestingly, in Latin countries it is only 'upwardly mobile' women who remove hair.

Few women in this country have managed to resist removing body hair at sometime. This means that many women don't know how much hair might have been 'normal' for them had they left it alone; neither do their sexual partners or doctors.

HIRSUTISM – WHAT CAUSES IT?

There are some conditions to which the body responds by growing hair, either in a specific place or all over. Such growth is commonly described as hirsutism.

The skin protects itself from persistent chafing by growing hair, as people who regularly carry loads on their backs know. Local hair growth may also occasionally be associated with birth marks.

Hirsutism can be due to an alteration in the normal amount of sex hormones circulating in the blood, but this is rare. An excess of body hair, whether confined to one area of the body or all over it, is not a 'disease' in its own right anyway. It is usually only one of several symptoms produced by a disorder elsewhere in the body.

Cysts

The most common cause of generalised hirsutism is known as the polycystic ovary syndrome. In this condition, the ovary has on it a large number of cysts which stop it producing its hormones in the normal way.

Excess hair production is one symptom of the condition; others are scanty or absent periods, infertility, and sometimes obesity. Cysts tend to develop in the late teens or early twenties, but may appear for the first time in the late thirties.

Tumours

Tumours of the ovary or adrenal, a gland lying above the kidney, are very much rarer causes of hirsutism. Male hormones (androgen) are normally produced in both the adrenal gland and the ovary, but a so-called 'virilising' tumour on either of these glands may produce greater than normal levels of androgens.

The symptoms in these cases usually appear suddenly and include signs of 'virilism' such as acne, altered muscle bulk and strength, and clitoral enlargement as well as excess hair. The presence of such a tumour in no way means that a woman is changing sex.

There are other glandular disorders which can result in similar disturbances of hormone production, but they are all rare.

Drugs

All synthetically prepared drugs prescribed for the various ailments from which we suffer have a variety of unwanted effects, called 'side-effects' by the pharmaceutical industry. One of the unwanted effects of certain drugs may be to cause excess hair production in some people, and then probably only with long-term use.

The known offending drugs include:
• androgens – which may be included in the 'menopausal mixtures' of hormone replacement therapy
• ACTH – a hormone found in certain preparations used in the treatment of rheumatic diseases, bronchial asthma, adrenal malfunction and allergic conditions
• corticosteroids – widely used for rheumatic conditions, allergies and skin complaints
• phenytoin – an anticonvulsant drug used to control epileptic fits
• diazoxide – used to treat high blood pressure.

Hormonal imbalance

Hirsutism sometimes occurs after menopause, because of the considerable hormonal upheaval taking place. And hormones can be imbalanced after childbirth, while the system is readjusting to a non-pregnant level.

Anorexia nervosa

Food refusal to the point of emaciation in adolescent girls can sometimes cause excess hair production. This is rather ironic, since the current trend in psychiatric thinking is that anorexia is a subconscious attempt to delay the process of 'growing up', with which sexual hair is associated.

All of these conditions have one thing in common: the hirsutism is just one of several symptoms, probably the least of a sick woman's worries.

Excess Hair – You're not the only one
Letters from Spare Rib Readers
SR 136 November 1983

'COMING OUT' AS HAIRY
from J.

Over the past six months we've received a spate of letters in response to ones we published on the subject of body hair. All these letters reveal just how much confusion and pain 'unacceptable' body hair causes for women, feminist or not.

They say, in different ways, that even as we assert our right to be our 'own' women in the world, we continue to be plagued by images, attitudes and reactions within ourselves and from outside which define us as different, abnormal, unattractive.

As feminists begin to engage more and more with the vast areas of oppression and exploitation which exist all around us based on race, class, age, disability, as well as sex, these 'small' individualised, debilitating worries and realities about our bodies such as weight, too much hair, too little hair, acne, breast size, still cloud our lives and sap our energies. Taking these areas of our lives on board isn't a luxury . . . the way we feel about ourselves, the way other people respond to us doesn't just drop out of the sky; it comes from the kind of society we live in – a society which exploits and demeans women on every level and one we must understand and take seriously on every level too.

Dear *Spare Rib*,
The more people who 'come out' and admit they have what is known as 'excess' body hair, then the less abnormal people will feel. I've had 'problems' with nipple hairs, stomach hairs and a moustache for about seven years and after all this time have only just begun to accept myself as being 'normal' (what's that?).

It must have been the worst time of my life when my moustache arrived when I was 16 years old. My mother repeatedly advised me not to remove it, though I very nearly did so on a number of occasions. Her argument was that any hair removed will regrow twice as fast and thick. This has been borne out by the thick crop that now sprouts from my stomach! My moustache is still soft and fine and the way I cope is to use cream bleach.

At one stage I went to a doctor for a contraceptive cap and he sent me to the hospital for a series of tests as he suspected hormone imbalance.

After blood and urine tests, X-rays, etc., I was told I was quite normal. When I asked if the hair was caused by the pill, I was told that nothing was certain!! At this point I'd been on and off the pill for approximately five to six years.

I did go for electrolysis for my nipple hair at one stage but it was expensive and I was put off because the electrolysist wouldn't tell me how long it would take before the hairs were permanently removed. I felt exasperated by the situation, assuming it might take 10 to 20 years before I had bald nipples!

A big turning point in my life was when I told my then boyfriend about my hairs (I'd hidden the 'problem' previously). I couldn't believe his understanding attitude – it made me feel free (oddly enough) and liberated in the sense that I didn't have to hide away the hairs any more. We actually felt closer after that because he was able to tell me a couple of his own embarrassing and guilty secrets too.

I don't feel guilty about shaving my legs, bleaching my moustache nor plucking hairs from my nipples. Why should I? It makes me feel OK and that's what's important. Being a feminist doesn't mean to say I have to pretend not to be embarrassed about something – if I blatantly am embarrassed.

In conclusion, then, the point I've reached is to accept myself as I am but also to accept that I feel better removing some of the hair.

ELECTROLYSIS CAN WORK
From M

Dear *Spare Rib*,
I find your last correspondent something of a mystery. Whilst I sympathise totally with her experiences (many of which I shared, except that when, at enormous personal expense, I finally plucked up courage to go to my doctor, I was told to 'learn how to shave every morning'), I find her ability to divorce her hairiness from the rest of her life has not been my experience at all. I must say here that I not only have hair on my face but, like the second writer, I am heavily covered on my legs and stomach as well.

On the practical front I have had 'success' with electrolysis on my face, i.e. after 20 years of painful and expensive treatment my face is now just about normal, although I still go about every six weeks for cleaning up and have also started treatment on my stomach. I must say that I have almost without exception found the operators to be kind, gentle and competent – it is just that it *is* a long and painful process, and as it is still regarded as a 'beauty' treatment we pay the prices such frivolous and, of course, *totally* ideologically unsound luxuries demand!

I have also fairly recently discovered leg waxing, which has almost changed my life! Suddenly I am able to go swimming and even, if I time it right, walk bare legged in a skirt on a sunny day! Such bliss has been an impossible dream for most of my life – indeed, most of summertime is a misery with the double-edged sword of covering up my own body and being surrounded by so much smooth bare skin which the owners seem to take totally for granted. How I felt for the writer who remarked on the scorn of feminists who do not *need* to shave their legs! My own CR has done much for my self-esteem, but nothing is going to take away the years of cowering and misery as I lived the life of a 'freak' when I should have been concentrating my efforts on more worthwhile things. My confidence was non-existent. Every aspect of my life was governed by my physical appearance. Sex was to be one-night stands in the dark – what hope of a relationship developing when looking and feeling were tortures of embarrassment.

It is only in the last few years, when I have begun to feel 'normal', that I have been able to take a hard and deep look at myself, and any feelings of relief are mixed equally with resentment and anger at the waste of all those years. I am sure (indeed your letters prove it so) that there are many of us 'closet shavers' and although the solution can only be treatment of the hair itself, I think we can (and should) gain strength and comfort from knowledge of each other. I also hope that in the future girls will be helped to get treatment early enough for it not to blight their lives.

Underarm hair and light legs hair *are* OK now thank god, but believe me, bearded ladies with legs like gorillas are just never going to make it as an accepted minority!

FIGURE 20 'Ride on, sisters', from Wonder Wimbin – everyday stories of feminist folk *Cath Jackson* (*SR 140* March 1984)

Alopecia: courage to be yourself
Angela Cheetham Wilkinson
SR 122 September 1982

Dear *Spare Rib*,
I am an artist. Female. 33 years old. Largely ignored. I am divorced. I
have two sons aged 13½ and nearly 9. I am living (?) on supplementary
benefit. Prior to my divorce I had given six days a week support to my
husband in his business. Any time left I painted pictures. Then my
husband ran away to Canada when his business was in great debt,
sending a note and a bunch of keys from the airport. The business was
closed. My house was sold to meet the debts. I had previously signed a
second mortgage agreement with the bank. My children and I now live
in a council house on the very edge of Taunton.

I worked for my husband for nine years and during all that time I
managed to keep my own work going. When I first went to the DHSS I
told them I drew and painted pictures, the reply was:

'That's OK, if you have a hobby on which you spend four or five hours
a week like other people may knit, for instance, that's fine. But if you are
working on these pictures daily then you are self-employed and will not
be eligible for supplementary benefit.'

It seems strange to me that I am allowed to perform perpetual housework and receive SB, but I must not work to try and improve my situation.

As a result of the problems *vis-à-vis* my marriage I have not much hair
left. I am going to talk to you about this because I think it is a problem
which many women suffer in silence.

Let me explain – when a woman loses her hair and the specialist
pronounces 'no hope' she is then given the most dreadful wig courtesy
of the NHS. My wig was given to me in a dark cupboard of a room by a
man with a suitcase of wigs. There was a tiny mirror. I wore the wig until
I could afford a better one. For two years I hid under my acrylic hair until
I could stand it no longer.

I think it is probably impossible to describe the difficulties which arise
from wearing a wig to hide the fact that you have no hair – the overwhelming feeling of 'falseness' – this is not me – I am not like this – of
being a split-person, the image presented to the public and the real me
in the mirror, in private. There is always a very real fear of having the
wig knocked off – in a pub, for instance, as someone raises their pint to
their lips. You are at home, there is a knock at the door – is it a friend
who knows you are bald, or a stranger whose face will show immediate
shock as you open the door – maybe your wig is upstairs and you have
to creep past the front door to rush upstairs and don the ghastly lump
of plastic which makes everyone else feel uncomfortable.

Of course, before a woman takes to wig-wearing her hair is extremely
thin and when she wears the wig and goes off to the shopping there is
always someone who sees her and exclaims:

'God, what *have* you done to your hair, it doesn't look like you at all, I never imagined you to be a person who would spend hours in the hairdressers.'

You see, it is impossible to purchase a wig which looks like an ordinary, messy hair with all its wonderful imperfections. Wigs are for 'feminine' ladies and if you are most definitely not one such person it's quite horrid to go around looking like one. One's usual jeans and T-shirt look ridiculous topped by this obscene nylon creation.

Women suffer dreadfully concerning their sexual attraction. Of course I could write much more.

One year ago when my husband escaped all responsibility and left me holding the baby I took all my wigs and burned them – yes, I think it was when the bras got dumped too. Jesus, it took some doing. It was some time before I felt brave enough to venture forth unaccompanied. It has made all the difference to my life and freed me from all the anxieties I experienced whilst wearing a wig. There have been new difficulties to face. Wherever I go I am laughed at, often quite openly, some people actually wind down their car windows for a better look. There is no hiding as there is with a wig and going out always requires a moment's squaring of shoulders to face the giggles, gawps and sneers.

Taunton is a town of 40,000 inhabitants and I am able to perceive that there are many women with the same problem. Some of them are poor and with an NHS wig only available at the rate of two a year, it makes them look tatty and ridiculous.

Then, a few weeks ago, I advertised a sofa for sale. One evening a woman came round to look at the sofa. She became nervous and agitated. The deal was done but she did not appear to want to leave. Suddenly she said, 'I am so relieved to meet someone with the same problem.' It took me some moments to realise what she was talking about, her wig was so good and well-fitted to her well-dressed image. She wept. She came back the following day and wept some more. She told me she was happily married and that for the four years she had been wearing a wig.

Her husband had never seen her without it, nor had her children, not even her 16 year-old son, so sure was she that she was totally unacceptable. She wears a headscarf in bed, secured tightly with yet another headscarf. Sex is a wash-out. Her young children never have the pleasure of sharing her bath. She lives in a perpetual state of anxiety.

I think alopecia is a feminist issue. Men are allowed to go bald. They may walk the streets with out being jibed at. The image many women feel they must present, their belief constantly reinforced by a media so strong with its urging of physical 'perfection' in women is threatened to the core by baldness.

Any advice would be most welcome and you are more than welcome to print this letter. Good luck for the future.

Women and sport – the paradox
Jenny Thomas
SR 151 February 1985

In a year when women have at last been allowed to compete in the Olympic marathon and 3,000 metres events, it is paradoxical that rhythmic gymnastics and synchronised swimming should also have been introduced for the first time.

These contrasting types of activity exemplify the paradox with which women in sport have to contend. The latter events assume that females should be graceful, aesthetic, non-aggressive, and 'feminine' and, together with the massive increase in aerobics classes, have only strengthened gender stereotyping. The social construct of the restrained, passive, servicing, nurturant, non-competitive female endures. Participation in all but graceful activities threaten a woman's femininity, and it is only 'attractive' athletes such as Catherine Tanvier, Chris Evert Lloyd, Kathy Cook and Shirley Strong who do not invite hostility and distrust.

Women are being encouraged to take part in sporting activities by such initiatives as the Sports Council's current campaign, but the insidious cultural message that sport is for men (or surrogate men), has not diminished.

On the positive side, the popular misconception that women's reproductive systems are vulnerable to injury has been largely confounded, and the only accepted difference in physiological make-up is that women's bodies are less powerful and slower than men's. So improved women's athletic achievements, that it has been suggested that the absolute difference between performance levels for women and men may only be 5%, rather than the 10% which it averages today. Women are venturing into new areas, such as rugby, soccer, long-distance running, solo marathon sailing, weight lifting, horse racing and mountaineering.

Paradoxically, at the same time as women who are successful in sport are challenging the traditional sporting ideas, they *still* have to face the misconception that sports de-feminise them, and cope with insinuations about their sexuality. Competitors dye their hair blonde, wear jewellery and sexy sportswear to collude in the femininity game. In sport, women are either sex symbols, freaks or butch.

Newspapers and journals perpetuate the assumption that the sporting woman is either not serious or else a deviant, by describing women competitors by their role or looks ('blonde mother of two', 'woman inside the body of a man'), rather than their athletic prowess. No top sports*man* can ever have received such continual derogatory media attention as Jarmila Kratochvilova ('the surrogate man'), and Martina Navratilova ('the dyke'). If a woman is successful at sport, her sex is questioned, and her muscular body, which is the instrument of her success, is viewed with disgust.

There is minimal television coverage of women's sports, inadequate facilities, coaching and sponsorship, and sporting hierarchies are male-dominated and controlled. Women's achievements are constantly compared to the qualitatively different achievements of men.

There is little socialising, support or encouragement for women in sport. Men see the qualities associated with it as the antithesis of those they expect to value in women. They seem to fear the prospect of the development of Amazons living in a matriarchal society. Even sporting women criticise one another for any lack of femininity, and blame their sport for any failure in socialising with men.

Despite all the changes for women at all levels of their lives, sport remains obviously male. There are still only 73 all-female events in the Olympic Games, compared to 168 all-male, and women competitors number only one-fifth of the total.

Women are patronised and tolerated in sport, but not taken seriously; their place is thought to be in 'female appropriate' activities. Until the conditioned prejudice that successful sportswomen have in some profound, symbolic way become men, is erased, the paradox will persist, and there can be no wholesale entry of women into such an institutionalised male domain.

76.1% of women take no part in outdoor sport, and 84.8% do not participate in indoor sport (General Household Survey, 1980), particularly mothers with young children, and older women. Having children imposes more than physical constraints upon a woman. Even if she has not been absorbed into the traditional paradigm of a privatised home-based life and has preserved her career and interests, she will probably feel guilty and selfish at desiring and taking time for self-fulfilment. Involvement with the family can subsume a woman's personality, so that she finds it difficult to see herself as an individual apart from it.

Only those who have had children can really appreciate the tremendous loss of identity experienced by a mother. The focus of attention suddenly passes from the woman to the child. People talk to, and look at, this new individual in such a consistently uniform way, that the mother feels like a shadowy being, who ministers to and propels the real person. Her own identity disappears, the feelings of 'me', and with it the awareness of self.

Women who have lost their feelings of self are *afraid* to exercise, *afraid* to expose their legs to the stare of the passer-by, class or group. They hide behind their clothes and quite successfully forget about their bodies.

Lack of confidence and a positive identity, lack of encouragement for women in sport, self-consciousness and acceptance of the traditional role are some of the complex and fundamental reasons why women's leisure tends to be home-based, servicing and private, unlike that of the majority of men.

Women and migraines
Barbara Boyton, Alison Fell, Lucy Goodison and Sue Lloyd
SR 85 July 1979

More women than men suffer from migraine. It's been defined as an affliction of hysterical women, dismissed as hypochondria or regarded fatalistically as an inherited condition. Here, a group of women provide a very different approach. They trace the causes of their migraines, linking them with particular pressures on women, and suggesting self-help ways of working with the pain.

SUE: 'I can remember my first migraine. I was 19 and had cooked dinner for three friends – lots of cheap wine. One of the friends was a man with whom I had an uneasy, worrying relationship. The next morning I had a headache with a horrible intensity at one side of my head. I was brought coffee to drink – two sips and I retched into the wastepaper bin. I lay there shaking with the intense pain, almost too fearful to sleep. By the afternoon the pain had dulled to the point where I could get up and walk around. My head felt heavy, but I stopped feeling so sick and I thought, OK just an aspirin and I can face the rest of the day.

'We went out in the car to visit friends and suddenly in the middle of the road I experienced intense pain again in the side of my head. My vision seemed to slip sideways and for the space of seconds disappeared into bright silvery flashing light. I pulled to the kerb, got out shaking, and retched. We drove back slowly, delicately – I didn't dare turn my head suddenly because the stabbing pain would push right across the centre from one ear to another. Back home I managed to sleep and woke feeling light-headed, tired and shaky – totally drained and unable to respond comfortably to those around me.'

LUCY: 'A strange feeling of being very dreamlike, high, moving slowly, intensely aware of light and sounds. My whole body became electrified – I tingled and shook all over. My migraine was in some ways similar to acid trips with the same super-sensitivity to people. I look at people and it is like receiving them on every wavelength at once. I'm aware of their smallest movements and expressions, and very aware of what I feel about them. The similarities come down to little things, like the acute difficulty and slowness of speech I get during migraine and trips – as if my voice comes from very deep down and had a long way to get out.'

Most people seem undecided as to exactly what is happening in the body during migraine. They write variously about intestinal toxaemia; digestive pressure leading to retention within the body fluids of toxic wastes which should have been eliminated; low blood sugar; contraction followed by swelling up of blood vessels in the head. These different physical malfunctions are not incompatible with one another and can be linked. Some see these physical symptoms as 'causing' migraine, but many recognise the importance of the emotional element in contributing to migraine.

SUE: 'I learnt to accept that I would get them after eating chocolate or drinking alcohol, but I read that these were 'common causes' of migraine, so a vicious circle of expectancy and fulfilment was established in my mind. Also I worry about my weight so that when consuming chocolate, sugar and alcohol I was suffering from intense feelings of guilt, and would become agitated and emotional after eating. Tiredness, stress, emotion and food are all connected – I stuff myself, sleep badly (stomach discomfort and guilt) and wake up with a headache.

'Other women I have talked to mention monthly cycles, the pill and other distinctly feminine reasons. I feel that emotions and hormones are in a fine balance and can be upset – but a question remains. Is migraine a condition of woman as she has been physically created, with her great capacity for emotional depth and experience? Or is the stress that brings on migraine a reflection of our social position – our striving to find a place, and the social, economic, and sexual pressures that society's double standards still impose? Is migraine a result of such pressure, do we create it, or does the world impose it? Sexually we are too often castigated as frigid or 'easy' – sluttish. Economically we must learn to support ourselves but too often get the lowest-paid jobs. Or else we are told to stay at home and care for the children we ought to be bearing. We make our own stands and are told not to be so aggressive – then we are told not to be defensive. We face social, economic, legal, biological and sexual pressures – and we develop our own reactions. Migraine is such a reaction.'

BARBARA: 'I think I had them as a result of putting myself under an amazing amount of pressure; trying to do things because I felt I ought to do them, because I felt it was expected of me. I tried to live up to an image of what I felt I ought to be. I used to worry a lot about whether I was doing things "right". I didn't want people to ever think I was stupid. I remember waking up on the first day of college once with a terrible migraine. My anxiety seemed to be not so much going back to college, but whether or not I had the correct date for starting. I didn't want to look foolish by turning up a day too soon, nor could I ring anyone up and admit that I didn't know. I solved the problem for myself by having a migraine.'

ALISON: 'Often when some strong emotion is triggered off in me by a relationship or by some day-to-day event, and can't be released – I suppose because I hardly feel safe enough to release it, except gradually in one-to-one therapy – then the acute, bulging, blinding headaches result. I think a lot of the feelings are massive anger – remembering a particularly bad situation in our household at the moment alone can bring one on. Extreme rage is powerful and scary to express. Apart from anger, I believe my migraines are connected with a need for nurturing – wanting to be cuddled and loved, wanting an ideal mother rather than the real sort I had. I think it's something to do with having been a daddy's girl; you model yourself on him in terms of competence, putting firmly behind you all sorts of needs and feelings for your mother. Then those try to erupt and you try to keep them under control.'

221

It is said that certain foods (cheese, chocolate, peanuts, orange, glucose) bring on migraines. Apparently these are all foods whose fat or sugar content makes your blood sugar rise a lot suddenly, and then the body overcorrects the balance so you actually end up with not enough blood sugar. Low blood sugar is believed to lead to migraines. These 'physical' explanations do not conflict with the 'emotional' explanations. It seems rather that there is always a precarious balance between suppressed feelings which want to erupt and the controlling mechanisms of the body. Anything which upsets the balance – feelings being stirred up more strongly on the one hand, or control mechanisms being weakened by diet or tiredness on the other, brings on the conflict and crisis which is experienced as a migraine.

WHAT BRINGS SOME RELIEF?

BARBARA: 'Most important for me in the long term was a women's self-help therapy group where I was able to explore the pressures I put on myself. I gradually began to learn to say "no" to people without feeling guilty. I realised that I personally could not be responsible for everything, and I gradually began to give up some of my commitments. I know that I did a lot of things because I felt I ought and not because I particularly wanted to. I began to believe that it was OK for me to spend time on myself, doing things for my own enjoyment and pleasure. I started taking care of myself, getting more rest, eating regularly with more fresh vegetables, fruits and grains. I had long since discovered that red wine and sherry could trigger off an attack, so steered clear of them, and I cut down on cheese and chocolate which I love.

'I began doing yoga to loosen the tensions in my body, but yoga on its own was not enough to shift my terrible backache which worsened with migraine. I decided to go to an acupuncturist who said my pain was a physical manifestation of my anxiety. After the treatment I often used to feel high. I had a glimpse once a week of how I could feel when completely relaxed and resolved to try and change my attitude to life – to try and approach a new day openly instead of which the gloomy determination that I seemed to carry round with me. It sometimes works!

'As part of slowing down and taking myself more seriously, I had time to notice that migraines coincided with the start of my periods. I was also on the pill for most of the time I suffered from migraines. I have come off the pill but I don't know if there's a direct correlation between that and no longer having migraines. Both are signs that I have made significant changes in my life for the better.'

ALISON: 'Some of the things I try are:
- lying in a hot bath which means I'm looking after myself and being nice to myself.
- writing endlessly in my diary, free association until I can find out what the agglomoration of emotion is that is bothering me, and get to a point where I can cry and release a bit of it.

- loving attention and acceptance from someone I'm close to can often clear it. Not always.
- managing to concentrate on something outside my own head. Sometimes television works wonders, films almost always, in fact anything that lets me flow past the knotted up feelings. These sound like avoidance techniques but I have to carry on with life, kids, relationships, and I usually can't get at what is bringing on the tension and headaches – at least not quickly and not alone.'

LUCY: 'When I get a migraine I have found that by deliberately exploring my emotions and letting myself express them I can get rid of one in two or three hours whereas they used to last days. Once I had realised that my headaches were to do with repressed feelings, that they were about something, it still took me a long time to discover how I could use that understanding to deal with the headaches. But I did start to try and investigate what feelings were going on behind the headaches. I knew that friends of mine have migraines which are about feeling angry, but the main feelings which seem to come out for me are hurt, usually about being left, and neediness and love. Whenever things went badly in a relationship and I felt abandoned, when pressures on me to cope increased, when my defences were worn down by tiredness, the same feelings would come up.'

Contributions extracted from a pamphlet Women and Migraines *which provides more detail on this approach to migraine, and includes body and awareness exercises for treating and preventing it. Information on how to order the pamphlet is included in the chapter references at the end of the book.*

FIGURE 21 It's good for you *Christine Roche* (*SR 85* July 1979)

One small horrid word
'Unknown woman' (Kathryn Johnson)
SR 89 November 1979

Dear *Spare Rib*,
I have been a reader and supporter of *Spare Rib* since its instigation, and when each new issue arrives, I immediately look for the health article, in the hope of finding that *this* month it will at last reassure me that I am not the only one.

That it isn't just me who is recoiled from (that it isn't just me who imagines she is recoiled from?).

That it isn't just me who is in constant physical pain.

That it isn't just me who 'blows it up out of all proportion'.

That it isn't just me who makes regular, embarrassing trips to the doctor.

That it isn't just me who cringes every time certain everyday words are spoken at home, school, on TV, film. Words like complexion, skin, smooth, healthy, glow, soft. . . .

That it isn't just me who has tried every product on the market.

That it isn't just me who is unable to look people in the eye.

That it isn't just me who feels utterly ashamed because, although an ardent feminist, I recourse to mascara and make-up.

That it isn't just me who feels so ugly, inadequate and completely weary that nothing can be done to help. . . .

Your awareness, sensitivity and practical help has been a relief to so many women with so many health problems. But the time has come for me to write the article myself. I can wait no longer. I cannot bear to be misunderstood, nor advised by people (including, I'm afraid, sisters at conferences, meetings, etc.) who are blissfully ignorant of the devastating effect on a woman's psyche, her resultant personality, her consequent relationships, and her final life-pattern that one small horrid word has . . . gulp . . .

I fear so much that you will all find it foolish, please don't. The word is *acne*. The courage it has taken me to say it, to 'admit' it! If only that would exorcise it! But no – it doesn't. *Nothing does*. Please believe me, it is isolation. It is hell. And it is made so much worse by your never writing an article about it – for that is indicative of your thinking it a minor problem, insignificant, trivial.

May I show you that you are wrong? Next time you see one of us with acne, do not say, 'I used to be spotty until . . .', or 'Don't worry, you'll grow out of it.' I'm 27 – have had it for 12 years now. Or, 'Have you tried . . .? Please:

(1) Appreciate that the sufferers will have tried: Clearasil, witch hazel, Phisohex, Phisoderm, Phisomel, medicated soaps, Topex, TCP, face packs, Swiss bio-facial, Neutrogena, DDD, Valderma, Torbetol, Quinoderm, anti-biotics, Neomedrone, Actinac, Toracsol, Dome-acne, white

spirit. They all work for a while, but soon lose their effectiveness. Then there's the side-effects of papery, tender eyelids, chapped lips, dried hands . . .
(2) Appreciate the joy of washing your face, neck, chest, back and not feeling dozens of lumps, bumps, ridges, holes. . . .
(3) Appreciate the joy of not dying inside when your lover runs his hand over your skin and finds to his consternation. . . .
(4) Appreciate the joy of not feeling everyone thinks you can't be clean, or careful.

I am a vegetarian.
I do eat health foods.
I am clean.
I never eat chocolate, chips, ice-cream, licorice, rich or spicy foods, though I like them.
I do take a lot of exercise.
I have plenty of rest and fresh air.
I never touch my spots.
I always use a clean towel, pillow case, tie my hair back.
I know it's hormonal! I know it's nervous!

But if you have acne, you feel that people think you *can* help it, and/or that they are repelled. And who can blame them? One is so repelled by oneself. It's just impossible *not* to be disgusted by endless greasiness, pus, scars – will you ever print these ugly words I wonder? Susie Orbach (*Fat is a Feminist Issue*) please note – how does one (a) 'eat exactly what you feel like' when some things make us much worse? (b) love a body which produces such vile things?
Readers, before you condemn me as unliberated or vain or self-pitying or pathetic for being so affected by my acne (honestly, I wish I did regard it as insignificant, compared to all the atrocities being committed all over the world), believe me: I don't need to be pretty, nor to have an 'attractive' body. I just wish I could do something about this acne which *hurts* me so much as it destroys the tissues of my skin, and which twists me inside as it destroys my self-regard, my confidence, my peace of mind, and worse of all, my love for my normal-skinned sisters.
Thank you for listening. I'm sorry I can't sign my name on this article. An unknown woman.*

---

* *After a stream of supportive letters in response to her article, 'Unknown Woman' came out as Kathryn Johnson as the following letter section reveals.*

Spots . . . a sequel
Letters from *Spare Rib* readers
SR 92 February 1980

From L
Dear *Spare Rib*,
I felt I had to write in response to a letter in *SR 89* from a person with whom I totally sympathise – that is, the letter about that 'one small horrid word'. I started with my affliction at a very early and horrifying age – 11 years old, a time which is vitally important in one's life. Before 'acne' I was a happy, contented, reasonably well-balanced person. I am now 21, and it is still with me, and it is only recently that I have been able to come anywhere near able to cope with it.

Like your reader, I have tried endless remedies, and made endless trips to doctors, hospitals, dermatologists, beauticians (yuk), etc. etc., with little or no effect. My worst experience ever was a visit to a beauty salon in Manchester (very reputable!) when I was about 16 years old. I was lain down on a bed – all protective layers (make-up) stripped off – you just can't imagine the vulnerability – and then a cluster, of petite ultra-feminine, sweet-smelling, perfect-skinned, newly engaged trainees all peered at me, prodding and poking my stricken face. I began to sob hysterically, and they all said how sorry they felt. At that moment I wanted to take a knife and cut up every one of their faces.

One of my major problems in adolescence was that of feeling 'no one will ever love me'. I have never been closer to suicide than when at 18 a three-year relationship was ended by my partner. Suicide has been contemplated many times, usually after one of my self-persecution sessions. I would wash and sit in bed with the light on and bring a magnifying mirror right up to my face. Then I would cry and scream for hours. I have now learned to avoid mirrors at all costs. Many times I have emerged from dressing rooms in shops in tears without even trying on the garment. The sight of my own horrific face in the mirror would be enough to once again convince me that I could never look nice in anything.

I used to be a really good swimmer at school. Everyone said I could have been better, but it got so that I couldn't bear to go – guess why. The water would wash off all my make-up, and worse – everyone would see the spots on my back. More restrictions include:
(1) Never going in places with bright lights – hating going shopping.
(2) Dreading going to discos, because the lights might suddenly come on at the end of the night.
(3) Crossing my legs for hours when I'm out drinking or socialising because I can't bear to go to the 'ladies', as when I get there I might have to pass a brightly lit mirror, usually clustered round with nice-skinned people.
(4) Never being able to go on holidays like camping, or stay at a friend's

unexpectedly, because I may not be able to attend to my face properly or I may not have my stuff with me.

The list is literally endless!

I feel I must stop this letter now – I could go on for ever – I've always said to my mother that perhaps one day I'd write a book about it, but who would want to read about spots? Anyway, I do hope the anonymous woman becomes unanonymous. I'd like her to know she's not the only one.

From J
Dear Sister,
I wish I had a solution to your problem and could offer more than sympathy and support. But I don't and am not sure that letting you know 'you are not alone' is of any real use. All I can say is that reading your letter to *Spare Rib* was a tremendous relief for me. It is exactly what I would have written if only I could have found the courage. So I write mainly to thank you for writing it for me.

What angers me as much as acne itself is the way doctors will not explain things properly. When I persist for explanations I am made to feel either stupid or a damn nuisance. (I should explain that I suffer badly from PMT also.) I feel helpless and completely out of control of my body.

I am plagued by doubts about my commitment to our movement because of my skin and other problems – am I ugly and a man hater, etc. etc.? I am sure it stops me from getting more actively involved. I want so desperately to be 'ordinary' and a women's liberationist. It is so easy for more fortunate sisters to be able to say we should not worry about how we look. They cannot know the hate we sometimes feel for our bodies.

I have no idea how many other women have acne and could benefit from contact with sisters in the same position, but I suspect the problem is much greater than we realise. The trouble is that it is so isolating and will remain so if we don't speak out. I hope that something positive can come out of the step you have taken. In my own experience, acne goes hand in hand with other health problems so a group might encompass other issues besides skin. I think we must explore the causes of acne ourselves, with the help of feminist doctors if there are any. I am fed up with being told that it is due to hormones/endocrines/nerves or whatever as if knowing this is a solution in itself.

From K
Dear Sisters,
I read with indescribable relief and gratitude all your helpful, trusting and empathetic letters to my anonymous article on acne. I only wish you could all read each other's letters, to support you too. But, what can we *do*? There were a few suggestions of cures that I haven't actually tried, would you believe – and of course I view them with great wariness, but

of course I shall try them. . . . However, just in case they don't work (ha ha) I'm writing this to encourage and reassure other women with acne, who haven't yet got the confidence to contact anyone about their anxiety, self-hatred and fears.

A lovely lady who wrote to me suggested it: could we not form some sort of group to enable us to share our experiences, and get the best out of medical help?

I'd really love to hear from anyone who is suffering in anguished silence, and will reply personally with, hopefully, contact from others like us – it was certainly a tremendous help to me – and makes a nice change from being advised to 'purify my blood' with rhubarb, or to get pregnant!

Feminists of the world unite, you have nothing to lose but your spots! Love and sisterhood,
Kathryn Johnson

Apart or a part
Pat Duncan
SR 168 July 1986

After reading a wide selection of women's magazines, I found myself wondering where, or if, disabled women fit into this sisterhood or whether others find themselves, as I do, light years behind the discussions contained in these magazines. Disability is not and should not be the main focus of life but more and more – despite a good and interesting job, many acquaintances and a few close friends – I am being forced to acknowledge the impact and consequence of disability.

Childhood and teens passed in a haze of being 'done to', being cheerful and grateful and learning to manipulate people. Being cheerful and grateful was obligatory to the stereotype; without this, you soon found yourself alone. Only a few years ago was a new-found friend honest enough to say that this eternal cheerfulness was boring. What a relief; freedom, at least with this friend. Manipulative you had to be: 'You can play hopscotch without hopping,' you said firmly to your pal; 'Look at that,' you said to teenage friends so they would stop and allow you a short rest from struggling to keep up – skilfully done and amicable but even in adulthood, a habit hard to break.

Dependent on parents, you dressed as they dictated, behaved as they wished, because physically you were unable to put on the trendy head-band, colour your hair purple, anger was not part of you for anger drove away the company you desperately needed.

In hospital, you learned to switch off when people probed and handled you with scant regard for the embarrassment of a developing child. You felt the violation, the lack of privacy but had neither words nor freedom to express it. Your mind became your haven of privacy so you were called 'stubborn, awkward', for nobody realised you were scared and offended. As an adult, you now shrink from physical closeness while longing for someone sensitive enough to break a barrier you don't want. Displays of affection are not part of you – it's off-putting, not to say off-balancing, to hug someone round the knees from a wheelchair or to strangle them because your stiff arms have locked round their neck!

A curious aspect of disability is that, apart from parents who have the divine right, you are seldom criticised – instead, allowances are made for you so you long for some reality, for someone to say 'No, I don't like . . .,' 'You're wrong. . . .' You retreat, for there are no boundaries. You set your own and they are more rigid, more self-critical than need be.

Childhood and teens were not necessarily unhappy. Rather, they were unthinking and the resultant adult was without form, undeveloped, with a personality compiled from the expectations of others. Continue in this cocoon and you finish with an adult of 60 with the eager subservience of a child, never outgrowing the shelter of disability. If, however, you start to think, to examine and explore who and what you are, the effect is traumatic and there is no turning back. You want to be part of the scene but you find new and more impenetrable barriers.

Your peers have gone through and discarded experiences which you have never encountered. Your language, dress, thought processes, are worlds apart. Not for you the screaming madness of a pop concert, the casual invitation to a party, the walk over the hills, going to see a film, the growing awareness of the opposite sex, the gatherings where friendships are formed and forged, the pain of a breaking friendship and the pleasure of a new one. Somewhere along the way the message has been given and received that you did not form part of this life – not through any maliciousness but simply because you seemed content and self-contained and the hustle of youth never found time for the slowness of disability. You learned to keep smiling, go to Daffodil Teas with the pensioners and wash away the growing awareness of loneliness with tears trickling into your ears in bed. Determined to make a life, you get involved 'doing', being busy. 'There's always someone worse off,' you mutter with determination. Getting your own back?

By now, you know your real friends but you treat them with care for they are precious. You select yourself out of things for fear of putting a burden on that friendship. The invitation to a meal or an outing throws you into a panic such as that felt by a youthful teenager – when will you grow up? Self-awareness grows but so do the agonies. Many are common to other women but the impact is often greater for the reality of disability is different.

Pressure from the media emphasises the perfection of 'normal' but, though commonsense questions what is 'normal', you are faced with the reality of your own ungainliness. With it, you wear a pendant which, with your swinging walk, gathers momentum like a pendulum, threatening to knock out your front teeth; 'scarves are in,' state fashion experts – you look as though you have a sore throat.

Sexuality is discussed and put under the microscope. While your peers have worked through this area of their lives and are now defining their own level of sexuality, you are wondering if you understand the word. So long have you been neutered by society and your own low self-image that to define yourself as woman is too hard – to be referred to as such comes as a shock. Along with this, you have another barrier to break – the knowledge that disability can repulse people. While others discuss and worry about their relationships, you bury such thoughts for experience has taught that, in most cases, the male ego cannot cope with the embarrassment of a disabled woman and too often women feel compelled to mother rather than mingle.

The physical rather than the emotional barrier, however, is often what finally determines the loneness of disabled people – female or male. By definition, a 'loner' opts for that state – being or doing, by choice, alone. The disabled person does not make that choice. Steps, stairs, parking can all prove impossible barriers to the desire to be part of a group, a club, a party. Instead, you say you're busy, it doesn't matter . . . and you watch 'Dallas'.

Do others feel as I do? Do you too come to the women's world from a different direction, on a different level, chasing different devils? It is not that I or my friends do not want to be a part of the issue which concern other women. Our problems are different but the same. We know the strength and comfort to be found in the company of women (and the support from those men strong enough to give it), but we need self-acceptance as well as acceptance from 'differently-abled' women before we too can take our place in that sisterhood.

Herbivores
Jenny Muir, De Voce and Susan Ardill
SR 149 November 1984

Bricks through butchers' windows, midnight raids on cosmetic laboratories, declining meat sales. The more 'sensational' aspects of animal rights activists are becoming everyday news. But there is, too, a growing body of thought among feminists which links the cruel treatment of animals with the subjugation of women, and considers what we eat to be a political tool for change. Well, is it? Are you what you eat, or, more to the point, do you *condone* what you eat? Here, a few women have their say.

EAT UP YOUR GREENS!
by Jenny Muir and De Voce

We are vegans because we object to all ill-treatment and slaughter of animals and refuse to participate indirectly in it by eating animals and animal products. To us, the idea of 'humane' slaughter is a contradiction in terms.

There is a connection between the way animals and women are treated in a violent, patriarchal society. Animals are exploited in the manufacture of cosmetics and drugs which oppress women. Female animals are particularly abused in factory farming – battery hens are cooped up in tiny cages which prevent them from stretching their wings, cows have their calves taken away from them within days of giving birth, sows are imprisoned in stalls in which they cannot turn around. Women are sexually abused, from being called animals' names – bitch, cow, chick, etc. – to being treated as non-human objects (pieces of meat).

Women are seen as existing for the (often violent) use of men; animals are used solely for the (questionable) advantage of the human race. The abuse of women and animals is linked to the false dualism which opposes woman to man, human to animal, the flesh to the spirit, nature to culture. Women and animals are identified with nature – therefore to be dominated – while men are identified with the 'higher' realms of abstract thought and the spiritual.

Consciousness of one form of oppression should lead to an awareness of other oppressions. Human animals who have become conscious of sexism, racism, class oppression, heterosexism, etc. should not ignore the suffering of millions of non-human animals.

VEGANISM
by Jenny Muir

I have been a vegan for nearly a year now, and before that I was a vegetarian for three years. My reasons for giving up meat and fish were based on the argument that it is wasteful to graze animals on land which could be used to produce cereals and vegetables, and that the seas are over-fished. I was not concerned at all about the way in which animals are treated, but when I stopped eating them my awareness in this direction increased. So when I gave up eating animal products it was out of disgust at methods of egg and milk production. I was also attracted by the idea that it isn't necessary to eat animals in order to survive. I think it's important to question things we take for granted and what we should eat to stay healthy is rarely looked at critically. Of course, being a vegan doesn't in itself mean you will have a healthier diet – it's still possible to live on chips or beans on toast! But you do have to find out a bit about nutrition and I found that interesting.

I have never been involved in the animal rights movement as it isn't a political priority for me. This makes what I do on a personal level very important to me, as it is my sole contribution. My political outlook is based around feminism and women's issues, and I am a member of the Labour Party. I meet a lot of people for whom the idea of animal rights is a standing joke. But I've met this attitude before. I get it from men who think it's amazing that I'm a feminist. I get it from politically uncommitted people who don't understand why I'm a socialist. Recently I've encouraged it (among other things) from the general public when collecting for the miners. It's a defence put up by people when confronted with something they've never had to think seriously about before. They don't know where to begin.

The most important misconception I came across is that, since I am concerned about the sufferings of animals, that concern must be at the expense of my feelings for human beings. I know of no other area of my politics which is considered to operate in this mutually exclusive way. My support for animal rights is complementary to my support for other oppressed groups and my revulsion at the amount of needless suffering in the world. At the same time I'm not a pacifist and I accept that it is sometimes necessary to kill in order to survive.

I think most people who haven't thought carefully about the ill-treatment of animals assume that animal suffering is either trivial or unavoidable. Trivial, because animals don't feel pain like we do, an argument that doesn't bear close examination. Unavoidable, because we are dependent on animals and animal products for our survival. In the past this may have been true, but a growing number of people are now disproving it either as a principle or for health reasons.

I have found it much easier than I expected it would be to stick to a vegan diet, although there are times when I eat dairy products, for example when I'm eating out. I don't demand vegan food from my friends but I often find that they're prepared to provide it anyway. I'm more interested in cookery and nutrition than I used to be and my health has improved. I suppose I've got to the stage where I don't understand what all the fuss is about. Animals are ill-treated and murdered for our supposed benefit. We don't need this – so stop eating them. Simple, isn't it?

FOOD IDEAS JUST HALF BAKED
by Susan Ardill

I've been a vegetarian for five years now and I don't really think it's got much to do with anyone else. No – I'm not putting forward the ultimate individualist argument ('what you eat in your house is your business'). It's just that thinking about this whole subject of vegetarianism and meat-eating underlines for me the futility of 'pure' lifestyle politics.

At the point where any individual takes a bite to eat, a whole range of factors comes into play – class, culture and gender, certainly, but also age, health and personal choice determines where, why and how food is eaten. The same forces operate in the *production* of food, and it doesn't take much investigation to discover that the food industry runs on the profit motive, gross exploitation of people and animals, racism, chemical manipulation, etc.

As a socialist feminist, I want to understand how these things connect with my own situation in life. It almost goes without saying that I want to see an end to the present system. But I reject as misleading the idea that changing that system rests on individuals changing what they consume. Taking that sort of tack seems inevitably to lead to the sort of moralism which reminds me of the 'victim-blaming' inherent in 'lifestyle' politics. (There are various strands of this, ranging from 'to get cancer you must have repressed certain emotions' to 'women wouldn't need abortions if they didn't sleep with the enemy'.) Enough of all this stuff about meat-eating being collusion with murder. Do we collude with the chemicals industry when we buy vegetables grown on fertiliser? There are many deaths hidden in that transaction too – human ones. Conjuring up images of animals with mournful eyes and tying that to meat-eating is emotional manipulation of the sort which especially ties in with the pressures on women to *feel* everyone else's pain.

I should make it clear that I don't think there's anything fundamentally wrong with killing animals for meat. How they're treated when they're alive *is* of concern to me. But I want to see changes come from political campaigns that don't pivot around personal choice. And I want those campaigns to make connections with the entire food industry and economic system. So far the priorities displayed by animal rights activists seem fairly dubious to me. I don't want to deal in stereotypes – but the abusive and emotive tone of letters received at *Spare Rib* on the subject haven't helped much.

My vegetarianism has some political dimensions in the sense that it's part of a movement to break through the restrictions of much of western diet, and in the beginning, was very much linked for me to questions of health. Now, five years on, I'm much more sceptical about my own capacity for eating non-meat junk food, *and* sceptical about the healthiness of most 'health food'. It seems to be dwindling more to a question of taste – (I still have no interest in eating meat) – and a bit of stubborn rejection of social mores (my unconscious insists on meat as a symbol for the nuclear family). I realise that my position might seem contradictory – I'm tempted to say 'that's life'! As with most other political issues a balance between the specific and the general is hard to find, and requires a constant balancing act.

Yet I remain worried about the growing power of animal liberation ideologies amongst feminists, as so often no attempt is made to examine where they come from, what they're saying about culture, and who is producing these ideas. And most of all – why *now*? It's not trivialising the subject (or animals) to feel that this is a handy repository for certain emotional conflicts felt by those of us in privileged positions in western consumer societies. So far, nothing I've seen has convinced me otherwise.

Fat – not an eating issue
Letter from Tina Jenkins
SR 150 January 1985

Dear *Spare Rib*,
I'm glad that you finally published a piece by a fat woman about fat oppression, but I was wondering why now? Why is it in the special 'Take-away' issue on food (*SR 149*)? I have already written a letter to the Spare Rib Diary Collective complaining about the way Fat Liberation is tagged on to 'eating issues' in the Diary listings. Fat is not an eating issue in the way that compulsive eating and anorexia are. First and foremost, fat is a political issue. By correlating it with food in the way you do you both depoliticise it and contribute to stereotypes of fat women as eating too much and as having a 'problem' with food. As a fat woman, eating has always been an issue for me – not because I ate compulsively, but because I felt I did. I felt guilty about food, guilty about my own appetite. If I ever ate too much it wasn't what made me fat in the first place – it was because I was already fat and depressed about it, because I had starved my body on yet another diet. I was made to believe the myth that it was all a matter of personal control, that my oppression was my own fault. But it was never, and is not now, my 'problem'. Food is not my 'problem'. It's society's attitudes that have to change, not me.

I also object to the word 'obesity' on your front cover (a) because it is coming out of a box of food (once again making the correlation) and (b) because I don't like the word. It's a doctor's word – used to classify us as a 'medical problem' and to justify their abuse of us. Fat is what we are and it's what we've reclaimed both the word and the right to be fat. Fat women of the world unite . . . you have *nothing* to lose!

CHAPTER 7

CRISES

When Ann Scott wrote about her mother's illness and death, it was a first for *Spare Rib*. In a movement made up mainly of younger English women, death had not yet affected many of them directly.

But also there is a reticence in speaking openly about death; for the majority of white English people any open, ritualised display of grief has been taken over by a 15-minute cremation ceremony. There seems to be a profound if unspoken hope that those 'nearest and dearest' will pull themselves together as quickly as possible after the funeral.

Cancer was another difficult subject which brought *Spare Rib* writers face to face with an illness imbued with even more fearful meanings than the disease itself carries. Cancer has become, as tuberculosis was for earlier generations, *the* western metaphor for decay, evil, perhaps even retribution. Sure cures for many cancers remain elusive; with some types chances of survival remain no better than 30 or 40 years ago. Yet the medical profession still practises the most extreme intervention – surgery, chemotherapy, radiation – in its attempt to destroy the disease. When faced with an unknown outcome and the uncertainties of alternative treatment, most women and men opt for the dominant medical approach.

In all the articles which *Spare Rib* has published on death or dying, and on the crisis which a very serious illness presents, the writers have attempted to use their experience to open up and make possible discussion and change around hitherto silenced or choked back parts of life.

Spare Rib questioned many of the traditional views of illness, the images of women which illness contradicts, and addressed issues of power and self-help. Women alone, or groups of women, have been forced to go through internal and external searching and struggle to find the courage and strength to pursue their own path, to dare to demand answers, to speak when it was assumed they would be silent. They have highlighted the importance of support, love and friendship in periods of physical and emotional turmoil.

What defines a feminist approach to death and dying, or to a serious health crisis? Are feminists basically saying the same thing as any other critic of western ways of dying? Is a feminist wholistic approach to serious illness any different to a male-dominated one? There are cross-overs and similar themes, but it's instructive to recognise the importance of feminist sensibilities around these issues. It is the extension of the principle of control of our bodies, control of our lives, into the arenas of death and life-threatening illness which is essential to understanding a feminist approach. Women are rejecting a sentimentality which refuses to look at the reality of our lives in crisis. They are also revealing the connections between our 'ordinary' lives as women and the more extreme times of crisis: the same old sexism, heterosexism, racism and class divisions inform what we face in crisis.

Confronting serious illness or death can cut through a lot of accumulated bullshit. But fear, and lack of information and control, can lead to passivity and depression. Women have acquired, sometimes through feminism, a *way* of gaining the strength to take an oppositional stance even while in distress. To be robbed of this possibility in illness and when facing death makes a mockery of radical feminist attempts to achieve some control over our lives. Deprivatising the individual nature of these events is part of the process of making them both political *and* meaningful.

Joan Scott: living her dying
Ann Scott
SR 57 March 1977

Joan Scott, who reviewed a television play about breast cancer for *Spare Rib*, died last June. The play had been controversial within the BBC on the question of patients being withheld information, and Joan was one of several women asked to read the script before transmission. 'I would not only argue,' she wrote in the magazine, 'that one has a right to such vital information about one's own body, but also that one develops strength to face it. To deny a fellow human being the opportunity of finding and working on inner resources is to belittle and underestimate her/him.

With her characteristic sense of purpose she wrote that review during one of many hospitalisations for bone cancer. She sat up with her glasses and her biro, writing and rewriting, asking me to read each draft, angry when the nurses got her painkillers wrong, DF118, Distalgesic, she always knew the names and had preferences.

'It is not enough that when we are having surgery we are suffering and scared. We must also rally our wits and defend ourselves against the consequences of other people's incompetence, uncaring attitudes, or reluctance to face our needs. When we can get out we can start/resume agitating for a better health service; but while "in", if we want to take responsibility for "our bodies, our selves", we can't afford to be passive.'

That familiar slogan, originally the title of a North American book about women's health, had a particular meaning for Joan. She was in her late fifties when she got involved in women's liberation, a couple of years after her marriage ended. She was 62 when she died; and that meant childhood after the First World War, adolescence before the pill or any ideology of sexual emancipation.

In an essay written for a Workers Educational Association summer school four years ago, Joan described 'Three Generations of Women': her mother's, her own and her two daughters'. 'There had been a son before me, but he had died. Three more daughters were born in an effort to replace him and a family legend, no doubt founded on fact, is that the doctor (also a friend) reproached my father when delivering the youngest: my mother was over 40 by then. Of course he had never been able to give them any contraceptive advice: in those days, at any rate in Guernsey, it was abstinence or nothing.'

Joan's subsequent experience of a marriage in which domesticity was the only socially acknowledged role for women like her – educated women, genteel women who might go to the theatre – made women's liberation an imperative. Silenced by the demands of her class and sex, she had lived as a competent housewife. 'I put up with the usual domestic oppression, blaming myself for resenting it. When my first child was born I gave up paid work and became a captive wife and mother. I knew it was foolish, and resolved that next time I would go out to work and pay someone to look after the baby. But when the younger one was born I had so internalised the maternal duty that I could not bring myself to hand her over to a stranger, and stayed where I was.' She did volunteer work for the Family Planning Association, entertained neighbours and her husband's friends. Never showing anger. Rarely laughing. Rarely time to read.

She had been active in the pacifist, almost conventionally feminine setting of the Women's International League for Peace and Freedom. It was when she began living on her own that she felt a need to act fast. 'I must look for an outfit working to change the society,' she wrote me in 1971. She would look for women's liberation and socialist groups 'as near home as possible, and latch on to them,' urging me, too, to 'develop some empathy towards a woman who is only now, in middle age, struggling to be liberated'.

She stopped wearing her wedding ring, she bought her clothes in boutiques, went to women's conferences. 'The Anti-Discrimination Bill comes up in the House of Commons tomorrow evening and once more we rally to the lobby,' she wrote early in 1973, ending with the casual postscript: 'Now I'm going to do about a fortnight's dishes.' But she was conscious of her age and full of doubt about her worth; she was glad when the women's group met at her flat, for touches like this made her feel accepted. Feminism came to have a real relationship to everyday experience: she had some people to dinner; the men talked, the women fell silent. I was much more critical of the men than Joan was, and she wrote to me the following week: 'I have thought a good deal, intermittently, about the dinner party. . . . Your observations on it have made me aware that I can and should do something, even in what appears to be a minor and purely superficial setting, to bolster my sisters' egos and raise the consciousness both of them and of their men.'

Not everything could change, and I think there was always a tension between the demands of her generation and those of the movement. She had learned to be polite, and caring, and discreet; to gauge her meaning

237

as a person by her success as a woman. Irony was possible; convalescing after her mastectomy she wrote: 'Today we have had fun watching the Queen's (wedding) anniversary celebrations and toasting her in vodka and orange juice, wondering how many other middle-aged women whose marriages had gone awry were doing exactly the same thing! . . . From which you will see that I am coming back to life.' And shortly before her bone cancer developed, she laughed when she described her fantasy of opening an FPA sex education seminar with, 'Well. One of my daughters is a lesbian and the other's an unsupported mother.' She was discovering defiance.

But there was always a poignancy to her freedom. However much she knew that her needs had been shaped by the culture ('I was thankful to be married – to "fail" to "get" a husband would have been intolerable'), she had been a wife and mother far too long to discard that culture without unease. If she rejected femininity, wasn't she also rejecting years of her own experience, of her sense of herself? In Joni Mitchell she found a singer who spoke to her condition, but inspired her to go on letting go:

Papa's faith is people
Mama she believes in cleaning
Papa's faith is in people
Mama she's always cleaning

Mama thinks she spoilt me
Papa knows somehow he set me free
Mama thinks she spoilt me rotten
She blames herself
But Papa he blesses me
It's a rough road to travel
Mama let go now
It's always called for me

The sadness of Joan's cancer was that it interrupted the delicacy of that transition. Letting go became more and more difficult as illness undermined her independence. To find her own autonomy, then, to be her own person, she took responsibility for her body. She fought for control in the only territory that was open to her: her relationship to her illness, her hospital's relationship to her.

It was a very definite fight. 'I had to make clear that I was determined to know everything,' she wrote in reply to Gill Loveday's 'Facing up to death', a letter in *Spare Rib*, 'and that I wanted my daughters to know too. They were interviewed separately [by her doctor and social worker] and since then there are no secrets.' Access to information gave her a way of affirming herself within rather than against her cancer; it was her only defence against the bitterness and humiliation of dependence. She experienced the loss of self-esteem that goes with eating from a feeding bowl with a spout because she had to lie flat on her back for a week. She wished she could walk to X-ray: it felt 'psychologically damaging' to go on a stretcher day after day. She was often too depressed to talk, let alone to cry.

Six weeks later she had learned to walk, first with a frame, then with a stick. She felt there was a bit of a future, the possibility of pleasure. 'It's bone cancer now,' she wrote to her sister-in-law in Vienna, 'and yet, strangely, if one must have cancer, there's something to be said for this brand. Soft tissues rotting means surgery whereas I'm treated with radiation and hormones, and the race is on between the disease and the steroids that are being packed into my bones to strengthen them. . . . I'm resigned to having no long term – perhaps a couple of years – but I'm just speculating. The excellent people here can't commit themselves. As Dr Johnson said, it [the prospect of death] concentrates the mind wonderfully.'

Leaving the hospital was quite hard. 'I felt so odd driving away,' she told me the day after her discharge. She had been in for two months. 'I knew the nurses would set to, scrubbing my room – they'd soon forget me – and somehow I had to live in the real world.' That determination gave way to despair, anger and loneliness. Joan had deposits at the base of her spine and couldn't bend. She couldn't stand or walk for more than a few minutes. Cooking and cleaning were impossible. She hadn't the strength to go in to work more than two or three mornings a week. 'How I wish I could help you,' her letter to Gill Loveday continues, 'but how right you are when you say what a debilitating disease cancer is and how one's own need is *for* support from others, there's no surplus energy to give. I live on a razor's edge, trying not to conceal this from family and friends, and yet at the same time trying not to be a drag on them and make them feel that I'm a hardly bearable burden.'

The sense of that razor's edge is explicit in two descriptions of the same week. To her sister-in-law she writes: 'I have had to devise occupational therapy for myself – I now *knit*, I who was utterly handless, because I was almost literally twitching as I sat listening to the radio or "relaxing" in some other passive way. . . . So you can picture me sitting like a Madame Defarge, feverishly clicking away with big needles.' My own account is rather different. 'My mother knits long scarves as therapy. Fingers shaking, sits watching TV programmes she's not interested in. Is irritated by her listlessness, is pernickety and fastidious, has no pain, wonders whether she'd be better dead. And we have cathartic talks where we cry and hold hands.'

The loss of energy – 'I haven't the physical or psychic energy to initiate anything' – contained an ambiguity for Joan. It was a release from trivia – at times of relative calm she would remind herself of Dr Johnson – and an opportunity to discover what really mattered: to talk to friends, to read when her concentration allowed it, to be active where it was physically possible. Three weeks before her death she was planning to go to the

London Region women's liberation conference; had she gone it would have been her first excursion in three months.

But that loss also meant abdicating her ability to control her environment. Her women's group organised a rota 'so that there is always someone at the end of the telephone ready to come, do anything, spend the night, simply provide moral support – or drive me somewhere if I need to go.' And yet it was very hard for her to acknowledge the extent of her needs: 'To have to be on the receiving end all the time isn't always easy after learning to be independent.' At times when I would have liked to sit and talk she would force herself to put the dishes away. It was a way of establishing herself as competent. But living on her own had to change, and a friend of mine suggested that Joan have her own flat in the house we were going to buy. We asked her what she thought of this and she burst into tears. But that same day she talked about a holiday in Italy a few years before; she could link her past with a possible future.

It was when the illness was weakening her and she became susceptible to infections like pleurisy that Joan began to talk more about dying. She was in hospital last March; I remember her floral nightie and an angora shawl. She was writing in her notebook when I went in. She lay musing for a while. She had been thinking about a memorial meeting for herself.

She mentioned the song 'Bread and Roses' and a poem of my sister's. She wanted statements to be made about her work in the Family Planning Association and the women's movement. She moved her hands a little, stared ahead of her. 'And there are some lines from Keats' "Ode to a Nightingale",' she began, "though lots of it isn't relevant, of course. . . . "To cease upon the midnight with no pain" . . .' And then, faltering: ' "I have been half in love with easeful death" . . .'

We cried for a while. Then we laughed when I teased her for deciding what people would say about her in advance. She wanted to give her body to a medical school and enquired placidly about the students' work: did they need both breasts? I mentioned the dissection room in Cambridge where I have begun to study medicine. No, you often saw bodies where surgery had been done. She nodded. Thinking all the time.

Darling I listen; and for many a time
I have been half in love with easeful Death,
Called him soft names in many a mused rhyme,
To take into the air my quiet breath;
Now more than ever seems it rich to die,
To cease upon the midnight with no pain,
While thou art pouring forth thy soul abroad
In such an ecstasy!

That deep sadness, that recognition of loss could find expression only in metaphor. By remembering the poem Joan was able to externalise her fear, to find acceptance of her death in a kind of magic outside herself.

But those meetings of ours had to be ephemeral, almost invisible. The acknowledgment of imminent severance created the very intimacy that would have to be loosened if her death wasn't to become a struggle against itself.

A month later Joan was barely able to move. She was losing her resilience, feeling sick from the painkillers. 'I don't know how much longer I can go on being ill like this . . . I don't know how much the human frame can take.' I helped her to get undressed. There were her bruised arms, her scar, the pain on moving, the nervousness when she cleaned her face, the anxiety when she looked in the mirror. She started to cry. 'It's so hard for you,' I said. 'For you, too,' she replied. 'Why for me?' She sobbed louder – at first her words were indistinct, and then: 'It's so hard for you to see me like this.' She looked at me, as though she were terribly ashamed of herself. And then I understood how hard it was for a mother to be a child, to let her daughter look after her, and how hard Joan had battled to let me go.

She still planned to go to Vienna for a fortnight. Her doctor told her that if she felt as weak when she came back, she should come straight into hospital. She spent that time in Vienna in bed and went into hospital the day after her return, too tired to talk. But a couple of days later she was cheerful again: she'd been told she'd had a mild viral hepatitis. A tangible illness, it seemed to explain everything – the loss of appetite, the depression, the loss of weight.

In fact Joan was dying. The cancer had spread to her liver, and as her next of kin I had been told. It was a real betrayal. Had they forgotten that she was 'determined to know everything'? By deceiving Joan they were denying her right to live her own dying.

A hospital will tend to deny the reality of death and dying so long as medicine's social role is defined as one of curing disease. 'The current culture of the hospital, which emphasises the disease process and the diseased organ, is counterproductive to the needs of the dying patient.'[1] In the work of dying[2] there is no need for the very resources – technical knowledge, diagnostic and therapeutic procedures – which legitimate medicine's control of physical experience. The dying patient, then, represents a particular kind of threat.

The medical management of death itself creates estrangement. 'The patient's alienation from his own body is increased at just the time when it needs to be broken down: since medicine defines dying as a doctor's failure, not a patient's task, the dying person is prevented from accepting death and allying himself with it,' David Ingleby wrote.[3] 'As in childbirth, mind and body are disconnected by drugs, machines and social pressure . . . and as in childbirth, nothing could guarantee a worse outcome: only those who can let themselves go *with* the natural process of dying are able to find in death a completion of life.'

But a denial of death also undermines the kind of therapeutic communication that can go on between people when both know that one of them

241

is dying. When the patient is ready to accept the reality of dying, those around her must show they are ready to share her acceptance. But the dying person's acceptance exists alongside envy and resentment towards those who will go on living, however much support they have given; there is also guilt at 'leaving people behind'. Nor does acceptance cut out fear. What matters is that communication be allowed to go on; that the dying person experience that ambiguity, that it be acknowledged as real; that the feelings related to death be accepted.

Joan herself understood this. 'One is overwhelmed with sorrow for Simone's mother,' she had written me five years before, after reading de Beauvoir's *A Very Easy Death*, 'and at the same time one enters utterly into Simone's conflict of feeling, so lucidly expressed, between suffering and the detachment that the living must feel for the dying. And an added pang for me, as perhaps you can imagine – twenty years on, will it be you and Miriam and me?'

There was a great deal of conflict over the handling of Joan's last illness. The hospital staff kept saying different things. Her doctor: 'It's the disease, you see. Patients do change. I see a lot of patients who say they want to be told everything; and they *don't*?' Her social worker: 'I've never lied to my patients and I'm not going to start now.' Her ward sister: 'She's so calm now. It would be a tragedy to make her distressed.' And in the middle of it all was Joan herself, irritated that the nurses kept measuring her fluid intake, but confused by her own behaviour: sometimes relaxing with *The Times*, sometimes dissolving in tears. She rang me one morning: 'Oh . . . I feel so limp; I can hardly rise from my chair – the nurses keep telling me I'm doing very well . . . but I wonder whether they say that to everybody. . . .'

I was very angry. I asked to see the medical team together – consultant, senior house officer, house physician, social worker – to discuss Joan's rights in the situation. How much did they think she knew? What did they think she thought they knew? What would her needs be? How could we co-operate better in meeting them? What was the physiology of dying? We went through the ways in which I felt she was being deceived. Her consultant asked me whether I'd thought of the possibility that she herself knew she was dying, but wasn't yet ready to communicate it. 'She isn't asking us any questions about her illness, you see,' he said, 'and she always has – always.' No, she wasn't on the sort of euphoriant dose that would confuse her. I began to see that I had to show her I could let her die.[4] 'If she asks you a question that you don't feel you can answer, come and ask us to help you.' Apparently it was the first time a relative had challenged the department like this.[5]

A couple of days later, then, I took her a volume of Keats's poems. Joan looked at it, sighed, and began to cry. I asked her what she was thinking about. 'The process of dying . . . is this it?' she whispered. 'Is it here one minute and gone the next?' I asked her what kinds of anxieties she had about dying; she hesitated – stayed silent.

'You might think I'd be too frightened to talk about it,' I said. 'But I'm not.' It seemed to reassure her; then I said, 'Do you have other anxieties?'

'Yes.' But she couldn't say them.

'That you'd be on your own?' She nodded, closing her eyes.

'But you won't . . . because I'll stay with you.'

She looked at me, smiled, held my hand; there was the relief of openness but an agitation too. She said she was scared that she wouldn't be able to breathe. I suggested she talk to her doctor the following morning.

When I saw her the next afternoon, she was much weaker but seemed less anxious, almost unself-conscious. She told me she'd had 'a good long talk' with her doctor, but then she started to drift. 'People keep asking me what my feelings are . . . I wish I wasn't the focus of people's attention . . . I just want to be left alone.'[6] Joan was separating herself now, and she died the following day.

'An added pang for me,' she had written five years before. 'I want to concentrate on the main impression [de Beauvoir] has made on me – that when one is in one's terminal illness it is too late to talk about one's feelings, past and actual – one is simply too tired to bother . . . one is sunk fathoms deep in self-absorption – it takes a long time "to come to the surface of one's eyes" – as Simone describes her mother doing, and see the people around, who once were all-important to one.'

The night before she died the woman who had suggested she live with us came to see her. 'Cathy's here. Will you see her?' Joan smiled with great joy. Cathy came behind the curtains. There was a scent of summer flowers, a feeling of peace. Joan lay her arm on the table; it was a languid gesture – her death was very close, for her body was getting colder. She tilted her head to one side – said Cathy's name – looked up – and towards Cathy again; and that moment, which was one of the sweetest, was soon gone, for Joan was weary. Too weary, as well, to say more, to respond or withdraw. Limbs thin with cancer have a quietness which can be calming.

We held her memorial meeting on Midsummer's Day. Of the letters that I got afterwards, one caught its meaning exactly. 'I was especially glad that you talked about Joan's feelings about having such an illness and preparing for death. Like most other people I find it all very frightening, and it is a great help forward to hear people who have been very close to the experience being able to talk about it . . . as you did. I suppose that is what I meant by consciousness-raising, because it is in an ever-present way a component of so much of my thinking – that hope and desire that when it comes one may be able to die among friends and struggle through to an acceptance of what is happening. So though perhaps it is paradoxical, I had a lovely time.'

A month after she died I was looking through Joan's copy of *Away With All Pests*, Joshua Horn's account of his work as a surgeon in People's China. The custom of holding memorial meetings for rank and file comrades who die while serving the revolution, Horn wrote, started in

Yenan in 1944 when Mao Tse-tung made a speech at the funeral of a charcoal burner named Chang Szu-teh. Memorial meetings should be held so that what was worthy of study could be brought out and placed before the people and so that they could express their love, their gratitude and their sorrow. 'In his speech, Mao quoted a Chinese historian who, two thousand years before, had written: "Though Death befalls all men alike, it may be weightier than Mount Tai or lighter than a feather." He said that the death of anyone who had truly served the people was weightier than Mount Tai.' Joan had underlined those words.

NOTES

The title of this piece comes from *Living Your Dying* by Stanley Keleman, an American bio-energetics therapist (Random House, 1975). Joan's review of 'Through the night' appeared in *Spare Rib 45*, April 1976.

1 Hans O. Mauksch, 'The organisational context of dying', in Elizabeth Kübler-Ross (ed)., *Death, The Final Stage of Growth*, Prentice Hall, 1975.

2 See Sigmund Freud: 'Towards the actual person who has died we adopt a special attitude: something like admiration for someone who has accomplished a very difficult task,' in 'Thoughts for the times on war and death', 1915.

3 'The politics of depth psychology. Part II – nature, culture and capitalism', Unit for Research on Medical Applications of Psychology, University of Cambridge, 1976. You can check out the analogy with childbirth in Ann Oakley, 'Wisewoman and medicine man: changes in the management of childbirth', in Juliet Mitchell and Ann Oakley, (eds), *The Rights and Wrongs of Women*, Penguin 1976.

4 Elizabeth Kübler-Ross illustrates the complexity of this exchange in *On Death and Dying*, New York, 1969. The seminar on the psychology of dying that she initiated in Chicago ten years ago has involved doctors, nurses, medical students, social workers, physiotherapists and chaplains. It is an attempt to 'refocus on the patient as a human being, to include him in our dialogues, to learn from him the strengths and weaknesses of our hospital management of the patient. We have asked him to be our teacher.'

5 A couple of weeks after her death Joan's consultant wrote to me: 'Did our meetings before she died help? I do hope so. I think we all came to understand things a little better.'

6 'When our patients reached the stage of acceptance and final decathexis (detachment), interference from outside was regarded as the greatest turmoil and prevented several patients from dying in peace and dignity. It is the signal of imminent death and has allowed us to predict the oncoming death in several patients where there was little or no indication for it from a medical point of view', Kübler-Ross, *On Death and Dying*.

Strong love, strong grief
Daphne Mimmack
SR 134 September 1983

The decision to write my personal feelings about grief came to me because there seems to be very little written on the subject.

Unlike grief, everyone is prepared for love in so many ways. Hundreds of books and poems, plays and songs have been written on all different kinds of love. Perhaps even knowledge of grief would leave us totally unprepared for the way it takes over our minds and bodies.

Being 'in love' can give those involved great confidence in themselves and their abilities. Everything seen through the eyes of love can be beautiful. Grief to me has an opposite effect. I have become introverted and inward-looking. Although I see things very sharply, I am seeing with grief, and this makes me different from other people.

My daughter, aged 27, died from suicide, after fighting two terrible disabilities for ten years. She was paralysed from the armpits downwards after breaking her neck in a car accident. At the end of the first seven years of her disablement, just when she was beginning to make a 'tolerable' life for herself she began to develop some allergic symptoms, first to dust and smoke and pollen. By the time of her death she became allergic to everything, including food, and to antibiotics which were essential to keep her free from urine infections common to paralysis. She became anorexic, and became so weak that the allergist felt that had she not taken her own life, she would have died very soon. The medical profession gave up and left us to manage the best way we could. Julie took the only way open to her with characteristic courage and honesty.

My uppermost feeling was she is not in any more pain mentally or physically; and she has no more worry about her long-term care if anything happened to myself or my husband. This I still feel very strongly, but it fades into the background, because the immediate shock of losing someone you love evokes such pain it is impossible to feel anything else.

A friend lent me a book on grief. I found it too academic, although relevant to many stages through which grief takes you. First it was the devastating physical and mental breakdown of my body. In retrospect, 15 months later, I think nature is so clever. It made it impossible for me to think or feel strongly about other things as I was so concerned about my own needs. Everything required supreme effort. To make a cup of tea left me exhausted. The effort of getting out of bed every day was so exhausting that it was necessary to rest between each little daily task. Every day was a horrible nightmare, the basic chores took so long and required all my attention so that my body and mind just felt numb.

I went to 'work' with my husband, who was having the very same feelings, because it was impossible for me to stay at home on my own in those first months, or to visit people on a social basis however kind they were. Everything I did was totally meaningless and seemed to have no relevance to living at all. When I spoke about Julie to other people I got, and still get, a feeling of breathlessness. I thought I had some form of heart trouble.

I experienced the same feelings when my mother died over 30 years ago. I remember going to my local GP because of feeling so exhausted, even though I was sleeping well. He prescribed sleeping pills and 'purple hearts'. I only took one of each and learned my first lesson about drugs. It is no use trying to blot out reality. I did not go to a doctor following my daughter's death.

To get through the early weeks of dealing with the 'establishment' like coroners and all the other things that had to be attended to, I found a small bottle of brandy kept in my handbag helped me cope with all the people and going over the same ground with each of them. I was able to do without the brandy after a few weeks.

In those first weeks of exhaustion I had another awful symptom: restlessness. Although I was exhausted I couldn't stay still. I had to keep taking the dog for a walk. Then after a short while I would have to go out again even though I was totally drained. That has now settled, but it was very distressing at the time.

I get great comfort in being near to people who physically cared for Julie, especially her most recent and previous boyfriends, and her most recent girlfriend. I felt I could draw on their closeness to Julie. I also got comfort from playing her music tapes. I missed the sound so much. I liked having her things around to touch them. I also like to wear a sweater of hers: it is all I have left beside memories.

There are so many mixed emotions: anger directed at everything and everyone. Contempt: especially towards people who would not acknowledge Julie's death. A great many of those people have hurt me terribly. Ironically they are the same people who hurt Julie when she was alive.

I received great comfort from the many people who wrote to me. It was an acknowledgement that Julie once lived. I felt they had taken trouble to sit and think of her. It was much appreciated.

Healthwise I have had what I call the seven plagues, a series of boils, rashes, sore throats, urine infections, broken nails, annoying things which made me even more 'uptight'. But the feeling of not being able to remain home on my own has now eased. I still feel totally exhausted. I know now that actual rest does little but I still have a sleep sometime during the day even if only for a little while.

Socialising is a painful experience. Unless I know the person extremely well, I can only tolerate very short encounters. I made a rule very soon after Julie's death not to allow myself to get into company where there is no escape. After one painful experience I was quite ill when we got home although the people concerned were very kind and it was no fault of theirs.

Anniversaries and holidays are an especial nightmare. At such times I just want to vanish into the ground. It is impossible to spend Christmas at home or with other people however kind. I take a self-catering place somewhere and hibernate. On Julie's birthday I visit the crematorium and send some money to a cause that interested her and hope the rest of the day passes as quickly as possible.

There is another side that is difficult to put into words. To me it has no religious connotations. During these long endless months I have great comfort from the feeling that Julie is very close and near. This has receded slightly now but it is a definite and tangible feeling. I believe many people have this experience, and it is a great help in getting through the day.

Outwardly my appearance seems much the same, but inwardly I feel hundreds of years old. I am surprised when I find I can laugh at the same things I used to but it takes longer to reach the core of humour. My mind tends to slip, I can forget things even as I speak of them. In company I find my mind has totally wandered and it requires great effort to come back to 'earth'. Visiting public places where we enjoyed ourselves is especially difficult, and although I do not easily cry, I do so on revisiting those places.

I do not allow myself to think too deeply about Julie as this again drains me. I cannot want her to live as she did those last months. I grieve not for Julie, but for myself. Grief to me is totally selfish. Love I can spread around, grief I hug to myself.

To be occupied and to keep my mind busy does help, but until quite recently my body has not allowed me to work physically or mentally. This is only just beginning to change. Everything seems to go in slow motion. To keep myself occupied I joined two outside associations. Experience has led me to speak of Julie as I have been told that I look as if I have not a care in the world. I take the initiative in these circumstances. People I have not seen for some months I tell immediately to save embarrassment. The greater majority of people find it difficult to speak of the dead. This makes social intercourse quite impossible for me as it creates an 'unreal' situation, and I feel it is a denial of Julie having existed.

I think I am coming to terms with the hardest part of grief. Because life is relentless and doesn't wait for anyone. I am having to re-shape my future. It is unbearable that I am now planning, buying, and doing things about which Julie has no knowledge.

Death is so final.

Daphne's daughter, Julie Mimmack, was a Spare Rib *contributor. One of her articles appears in chapter 11 of this book.*

Surviving cancer, facing death
Nicolle Freni and Tierl Thompson
SR 100 November 1980

NICOLLE

On Thursday 3 May 1979 I was 30 years, nine months and ten days old, and apart from flu I'd never had a serious illness in my life. Emotionally I hadn't been so lucky and there were two periods in my life when I labelled myself as having had a nervous breakdown: once when I was 20, and the second time ten years later in November 1978. I came through this second fire with more ease because six years' experience in the women's movement gave me the confidence to deal with it.

I began to feel physically ill in January 1979 but as this feeling followed what I consider a nervous breakdown, it didn't really surprise me. I thought my body was responding to my nervous problems. As the months went by I didn't really get better. In April my lover Tierl and I went to Oaklands, a women's holiday house in Wales. At one point Tierl was chopping wood with ease and strength. I remember feeling angry at my body for letting me feel ill and I forced myself to chop wood. I chopped a few logs and nearly fell down!

Within a week of coming back to London the pain I was feeling was much worse but I still didn't want to go to a doctor. I felt I could deal with my own problems as I always had before. In the end Tierl made me go and the doctor told me it could be a strained muscle. I got some painkillers which I took morning, noon and night as the pain got worse and worse and worse – like knives twisting inside me. Finally I went back to another doctor in the surgery who was actually very good and suggested an X-ray. But it was weeks before I could get an appointment for one.

Through Tierl's insistence and a lot of pushing I finally got an appointment at the hospital. I went along that day with my lunch packed so I could go off to school and teach the way I normally do. When I walked into the X-ray room I felt completely confident that absolutely nothing was *really* wrong with me. I never dreamt that after a short wait I would be called in by a doctor and told point blank, 'You're a very sick woman. You're not going home. You're not going anywhere!'

I was completely shaken, taken by surprise and shock! This doctor turned out to be the biggest creep in the hospital and he couldn't explain anything to me properly. I burst into tears eventually although at first I was very hostile and told him, 'don't give me this bullshit – just tell me what's wrong.' But when he started talking in medical jargon I found that I was out of my depth; I didn't know enough about my own body to understand his words. So he brought me to the nearest woman, a social worker, who was wonderful. She gave me a lot of sympathy and

248

explained to me in terms I could understand what they thought might be wrong with me. I had no idea at that time of the real danger or that I had cancer. That came about a fortnight later.

I didn't leave after that. I didn't see the outside world. It was like suddenly being arrested and put into prison as if I'd done something bad or wrong. I had no choice because I didn't know enough about my own body to choose any other alternative.

I felt strange about being a lesbian in the hospital world. Much as I could relate to the other women on the ward, and we got along extremely well, my life was completely different from theirs. The nurses found it difficult to know how to respond to me. I'd put Tierl down as my next of kin and I could see everyone was wondering about me from the very first day because she came in immediately and she was there every single day.

After a few weeks I found out that I had cancer. I had a very rare form of the disease which is almost never found in women. Men get this particular cell structure in the testicles. If women have had it before it's rarely been diagnosed. It appeared in my chest as a germ cell tumour of the thymus gland and it pressed against the left lung on the top causing the lung to fill with water. Having a form of cancer usually found in men's testicles makes me laugh now although at the time it felt weird. I had fantasies that if the doctors knew I was a lesbian they'd concoct a theory about my strange hormones and deduce that all lesbians have the same formation in their chests as men have in their testicles!

Because medical experience of treatment was with men, I can't help but feel my dosages of drugs and treatments were a bit hit or miss. They probably gave me too much at times and the drugs they used are still at a research stage. In any case lots of chemotherapy is hit or miss. The treatment is a form of poison: they're purposely poisoning your body in order to kill off the cancer. The danger is that the patient gets killed off in the process.

During this time the support I got from the women who were close to both Tierl and me played a tremendous part in my strength and ability to deal with the illness. Facing operations, facing chemotherapy, facing tests and treatments – a lot of it is based on your state of mind. You can almost goof up a test if you're hysterical and frightened. You can't handle it if you don't have a certain confidence and if you don't feel love and support from others. I think this is something hospitals and doctors certainly don't know enough about – treating the whole person, not just the disease and symptoms but everything about how a person feels about the illness.

For 24 hours a day the only people around are other women on the ward and thank god they were so wonderful. Some of the talking on the ward was the deepest and most emotional I've experienced because it happened immediately after facing such awful things. I remember such

249

a time when I'd just been told by a group of doctors that my chances of living were 50/50 and I was filled with terror.

However the most important thing in the world was knowing Tierl would be there every single day and knowing that my women friends would come and see me. I didn't know I would need and get such tremendous support from my friends. What would it mean to die? I can't imagine nothingness. What does it mean? But I was part of a whole group of women, feminists, close friends, including some men, my lover, a whole circle of people so that I didn't feel I faded away into nothing. I never felt my life would be over and forgotten in a shot. Somehow the idea of dying is less terrible if you're *part* of something.

Then came a point in my hospital experience that Tierl calls The Crisis. I had a blood transfusion and they sent me home. They'd done a blood test but hadn't got the results back. Suddenly the hospital phoned up and said GET HER IN HERE. It turned out they should never have sent me home. In fact I had a 0.1 white blood cell count which meant I was on the border of living or dying. The slightest germ, cold or virus would have killed me. For a week I was at my weakest physically and emotionally. I could think, couldn't communicate. I didn't have the strength to smile let alone lift my head or take in any food.

I was slung into an isolation ward where no one could come except the doctor, the nurse and Tierl who was allowed in for 15 minutes a day. This was a very important judgment on the part of the doctor. Covered in plastic from head to toe she was allowed in every day and if she hadn't been I just don't know if I would have had the emotional strength to stay alive. I was freezing cold in the middle of the summer and covered with blankets. Tierl wasn't allowed to touch me but she would put her plastic covered hand on top of my hand which lay under the blankets. It meant so much to me; the slight pressure of her hand was the only time I *felt*. It was like a morsel of food to a starving person. Physical nourishment wouldn't stay down. But this person wanted me to live and was communicating that to me in the most tangible way.

In the autumn I got out of the hospital for good, nearly dead from the treatment. The support from my friends continued and intensified. When I was out of the hospital during my illness and in recuperation I lived mainly at Tierl's house except when my friend Ev had me to stay in her council flat where she coped with me and her family! At Tierl's there was a rota of people to look after me 24 hours a day. Those friends had to take me to the toilet, hold the bucket when I was sick, feed me. Sometimes they just held me and soothed me when I got terrified because I couldn't stop being sick and the pain was so strong. In hospital nurses can be very kind but they're trying to be objective. They're not people you know or who particularly love you. But that's not to say it's easy for friends. Your confidence about your own health is threatened and you become vulnerable by seeing someone else in such a position. But the closeness that can come out of that relationship is very special.

When I came out, I was fairly emaciated, bald, and a certain shade of green. My body had changed colour because the chemotherapy changed the skin pigmentation. My back in particular was all scored with marks from that treatment and still is. My legs were swollen. I had no eyebrows, no eyelashes. I looked hideous, like a monster. But no one made me feel that way. They touched me and sometimes I needed that. When a friend would lovingly bath me, that was something which was sensual in a completely loving non-sexual way. A friend gave me a massage and I could feel in tune with my body no matter how wrecked I was. Tierl and I now joke that for us the link we two had was perhaps like a mother and child.

My check-ups were once a month and now are less frequent. I try to get them further apart all the time. My doctor has been very kind in many ways but I'm torn in my feelings about him. On the one hand I'm grateful and even like him because apparently this man saved my life. But on the other he's part of what I feel played a role in my illness. I can't help but feel that in his huge authority and important position he has a place in my undoing. So patriarchy gave me the illness and patriarchy helped cure it, the way they always seem to cure (if they can) their own lousy symptoms without changing the causes.

After all my experiences one thing both Tierl and I have got really acute about is all the environmental factors, the pollution and stress of living in a city. We hadn't given it much thought before. Now I'm incredibly against women smoking. I have a huge no smoking sign outside my flat. We get conditioned into wanting to smoke, and if it's conditioning, then we of all people know we can break it.

TIERL

It was really the last thing I expected. Nicolle and I were having the usual problems of work, relationships, living collectively, too many meetings, all those things. But this was something else altogether. Nobody close to me had been threatened with death. Old people died. Other people got cancer. Not my lover.

The whole experience has been both negative and positive. At worst it's made me terribly depressed about the possibility of being whole and healthy in this society. I feel angry that the fundamental things we need to be healthy are so polluted and destroyed. There is more and more evidence to suggest that cancer is caused by bad food, toxic substances, nuclear waste, imbalances due to stress. Nicolle being ill has made me feel how dire the consequences of that can be in a very personal way. There isn't anywhere you can really escape the consequences of male-dominated exploitation of life.

I pushed down a lot of my feelings of fear in order to cope. My feelings surfaced when Nicolle was getting better, perhaps because I didn't have

251

to have such a tight rein on them. Having to think that you might lose someone who is an enormous part of your life has changed me and unnerved me, but it's a whole side of life that we must sort out somehow. That's been the hardest thing really – having to deal with something so mysterious, so threatening, actually extending your consciousness to include death without getting morbid or paranoid.

It dawned on me with horror after Nicolle's treatment had finished that she was radically changed, and would be for a long time, physically and emotionally. I was impatient to know the old Nicolle, to be reassured. A year later she's seeming more like that person, which is wonderful but we've both been irreparably damaged in some ways. At times the illness put a great strain on our relationship.

Still there are positive things. For us as women it's meant trying to cope with areas totally controlled by men. Death and illness are so removed, depersonalised, unreal. We have no context for death and it's hard to find one without resorting to male religions. I think it's important that as feminists we value life and care for it – though not in the old self-destructive way. We have to somehow place death in a context of care, not impersonality.

Although objectivity from other people sometimes helps this isn't what you get from the hospital; the hospital treats you and then you get handed all the problems. I needed to try and make sense of it all with women. I needed to get ideas and information. I needed to share my shock. Although a lot of the time I felt totally unable to express the enormity of it, there were times when I really needed to talk. Surely that's one very positive thing we can do for each other. Although I feel terrified at the thought of anything happening again I know somehow we'd cope.

Nicolle and I are extraordinarily close in some ways because of the whole experience. I know we're not unique, but I've never been through that with anyone. Somehow we're both very determined to be positive. We both wanted her life so much. Relationships had never been about that before, about just trying to *live* as well as wiping up sick, and waking up all night. We were very close during the illness. We dropped old conflicts. I willingly wanted to give this enormous commitment. I would get hysterical at the thought of her dying but somehow facing day-to-day things wasn't hysterical. The same was true for everyone else who cared for her.

The Women's Theatre Group with whom I work gave me a lot of support and time off. We were very lucky. What do people do without a community? How could one person ever cope with looking after someone in that way? My levels of exhaustion were terrific. There were difficult times when there was no one around to help while people were away. Sometimes I felt guilty about asking people to do things for me and Nicolle sometimes guilty about being ill! And coping with the DHSS is a full-time job!

I think as women we have a great responsibility to inform ourselves about our health, to wrest information from men. I think we have to be open to alternatives. Nicolle and I chose straight medicine – at the time it seemed like the only security. That's such an irony.

Still, the thing that overwhelmed me the most wasn't the physical inadequacies, it was the whole medical ethic, the sheer incompetence at dealing with personal life. The first hospital Nicolle was in was good. Some of the nurses were able to give emotional as well as physical care and we were befriended by some gay nurses who took a special interest. But the doctors were a little elite group in white coats. It used to make me really angry at how subservient the nurses are made to be because in fact they would patch up all the holes the doctors left behind. At the next hospital no one seemed to have the faintest idea. I got so wearied by chasing them around trying to get information. I don't know whether they would have volunteered more if I had been 'family'. The idea of someone needing information who isn't a relative, let alone in a lesbian relationship, seems to be anathema to the medical profession.

The doctor thought it was some quirk of Nicolle's that she wanted to know things about her illness and he made jokes about being American, she liked to let everything hang out.

It wasn't even that they were nasty. I wasn't ever prevented from seeing Nicolle. Just this incredible casualness which I'm sure can't be the only way of coping. People say that doctors and nurses can't afford to think about illness and death too much in a personal way. But we have to cope. It's just irresponsible. They hand you all the consequences of their treatment, give you the most enormous problems to deal with when they've told you nothing. I know they did good things and are supposed to have cured Nicolle but I feel ungrateful and antagonistic towards them because of the mistakes they made, because I had to fight them the whole time. Then they congratulate themselves for helping you.

We never once had any information on diet. Given the links that are emerging about food and cancer that is quite staggering. It shows you how single-minded straight medical research is. Nicolle was their guinea pig. She was treated with their chemicals, instruments and tests and handed back a physical wreck.

Breast cancer: power vs. prosthesis
Audre Lorde
SR 122 September 1982

On Labor Day, 1978, during my regular monthly self-examination, I discovered a lump in my right breast which later proved to be malignant. During my following hospitalization, my mastectomy and its aftermath, I passed through many stages of pain, despair, fury, sadness and growth. I moved through these stages, sometimes feeling as if I had no choice, other times recognizing that I could choose oblivion – or a passivity that is very close to oblivion – but did not want to. As I slowly began to feel more equal to processing and examining the different parts of this experience, I also began to feel that in the process of losing a breast I had become a more whole person.

After a mastectomy, for many women including myself, there is a feeling of wanting to go back, of not wanting to persevere through this experience to whatever enlightenment might be at the core of it. And it is this feeling, this nostalgia, which is encouraged by most of the post-surgical counselling for women with breast cancer. This regressive tie to the past is emphasised by the concentration upon breast cancer as a cosmetic problem, one which can be solved by a prosthetic pretence. The American Cancer Society's Reach for Recovery Program, while doing a valuable service in contacting women immediately after surgery and letting them know they are not alone, nonetheless encourages this false and dangerous nostalgia in the mistaken belief that women are too weak to deal directly and courageously with the realities of our lives.

The woman from Reach for Recovery who came to see me in the hospital, while quite admirable and even impressive in her own right, certainly did not speak to my experience nor my concerns. As a 44-year-old Black lesbian feminist, I knew there were very few role models around for me in this situation, but my primary concerns two days after mastectomy were hardly about what man I could capture in the future, whether or not my old boyfriend would still find me attractive enough, and even less about whether my two children would be embarrassed by me around their friends.

My concerns were about my chances for survival, the effects of a possibly shortened life upon my work and my priorities. Could this cancer have been prevented, and what could I do in the future to prevent its recurrence? Would I be able to maintain the control over my life that I had always taken for granted? A lifetime of loving women had taught me that when women love each other, physical change does not alter that love. It did not occur to me that anyone who really loved me would love me any less because I had one breast instead of two, although it did occur to me to wonder if they would be able to love and deal with the new me.

In the critical and vulnerable period following surgery, self-examination and self-evaluation are positive steps. To imply to a woman that yes, she can be the 'same' as before surgery, with the skilful application of a little puff of lambswool, and/or silicone gel, is to place an emphasis upon prosthesis which encourages her not to deal with herself as physically and emotionally real, even though altered and traumatised. This emphasis upon the cosmetic after surgery reinforces this society's stereotype of women, that we are only what we look or appear, so this is the only aspect of our existence we need to address. Any woman who has had a breast removed because of cancer knows she does not feel the same. But we are allowed no psychic time or space to examine what our true feelings are, to make them our own.

Ten days after having my breast removed, I went to my doctor's office to have the stitches taken out. This was my first journey out since coming home from the hospital, and I was truly looking forward to it. A friend had washed my hair for me and it was black and shining, with my new grey hairs glistening in the sun. Colour was starting to come back into my face and around my eyes, I wore the most opalescent of my moonstones, and a single floating bird dangling from my right ear in the name of grand asymmetry. With an African kentecloth tunic and new leather boots, I knew I looked fine, with that brave new-born security of a beautiful woman having come through a very hard time and being very glad to be alive.

The doctor's nurse, a charmingly bright and steady woman of about my own age who had always given me a feeling of quiet no-nonsense support on my other visits, called me into the examining room. On the way, she asked me how I was feeling.

'Pretty good,' I said, half-expecting her to make some comment about how good I looked.

'You're not wearing a prosthesis,' she said, a little anxiously, and not at all like a question.

'No,' I said, thrown off my guard for a minute. 'It really doesn't feel right,' referring to the lambswool puff given to me by the Reach For Recovery volunteer in the hospital.

Usually supportive and understanding, the nurse now looked at me urgently and disapprovingly as she told me that even if it didn't look exactly right, it was 'better than nothing,' and that as soon as my stitches were out I could be fitted for a 'real form'.

'You will feel so much better with it on,' she said. 'And besides, we really like you to wear something, at least when you come in. Otherwise it's bad for the morale of the office.'

I could hardly believe my ears! I was too outraged to speak then, but this was to be only the first such assault on my right to define and to claim my own body.

A woman who is attempting to come to terms with her changed landscape and changed timetable of life and with her own body and pain and beauty and strength, that woman is seen as a threat to the 'morale' of a breast surgeon's office!

Yet when Moishe Dayan, the Prime Minister of Israel, stands up in front of parliament or on TV with an eye patch over his empty eye socket, nobody tells him to go get a glass eye, or that he is bad for the morale of the office. The world sees him as a warrior with an honourable wound, and a loss of a piece of himself which he has marked, and mourned, and moved beyond. And if you have trouble dealing with Moishe Dayan's empty eye-socket, everyone recognises that it is your problem to solve, not his.

Well, women with breast cancer are warriors, also. I have been to war, and still am. So has every woman who had had one or both breasts amputated because of the cancer that is becoming the primary physical scourge of our time. For me, my scars are an honourable reminder that I may be a casualty in the cosmic war against radiation, animal fat, air pollution, McDonald's hamburgers and Red Dye no. 2, but the fight is still going on, and I am still a part of it. I refuse to have my scars hidden or trivialised behind lambswool or silicone gel. I refuse to be reduced in my own eyes or in the eyes of others from warrior to mere victim, simply because it might render me a fraction more acceptable or less dangerous to the still complacent, those who believe if you cover up a problem it ceases to exist. I refuse to hide my body simply because it might make a woman-phobic world more comfortable.

Prosthesis offers the empty comfort of 'nobody will know the difference'. But it is that very difference which I wish to affirm, because I had lived it, and survived it, and wish to share that strength with other women. If we are to translate the silence surrounding breast cancer into language and action against this scourge, then the first step is that women with mastectomies must become visible to each other. For silence and invisibility go hand in hand with powerlessness. By accepting the mask of prosthesis, one-breasted women proclaim ourselves as insufficients dependent upon pretence.

In addition, we withhold that visibility and support from one another which is such an aid to perspective and self-acceptance.

As women, we cannot afford to look the other way, nor to consider the incidence of breast cancer as a private or secret personal problem. It is no secret that breast cancer is on the increase among women in America. According to the American Cancer Society's own statistics on breast cancer survival, of the women stricken, only 50% are still alive after three years. This figure drops to 30% if you are poor, or Black, or in any other way part of the underside of this society. We cannot ignore these facts, nor their implications, nor their effect upon our lives, individually and collectively. Early detection and early treatment is crucial in the management of breast cancer if those sorry statistics of survival are to improve. But for the incidence of early detection and early treatment to increase, American women must become free enough from social stereotypes concerning their appearance to realise that losing a breast is infinitely preferable to losing one's life (or one's eyes, or one's hands . . .).

Although breast self-examination does not reduce the incidence of breast cancer, it does markedly reduce the rate of mortality, since most early tumours are found by women themselves. I discovered my own tumour upon a monthly breast exam, and so report most of the other women I know with a good prognosis for survival. With our alert awareness making such a difference in the survival rate for breast cancer, women need to face the possibility and the actuality of breast cancer as a reality rather than as myth, or retribution, or terror in the night, or a bad dream that will disappear if ignored. After surgery, there is a need for women to be aware of the possibility of bilateral recurrence, with vigilance rather than terror. This is not a spread of cancer, but a new occurrence in the other breast. Each woman must be aware that an honest acquaintanceship with and evaluation of her own body is the best tool of detection.

The greatest incidence of breast cancer in American women appears between the ages of 40 to 55. These are the very years when women are portrayed in the popular media as fading and desexualised figures. Contrary to the media picture, I find myself as a woman of insight ascending into my highest powers, my greatest psychic strengths, and my fullest satisfactions. I am freer of the constraints and fears and indecisions of my younger years, and survival throughout these years has taught me how to value my own beauty, and how to look closely into the beauty of others.

There is nothing wrong, *per se*, with the use of prostheses, if they can be chosen freely, for whatever reason, after a woman has had a chance to accept her new body. But usually prostheses serve a real function, to approximate the performance of a missing physical part. In other amputations and with other prosthetic devices, function is the main point of their existence. Artificial limbs perform specific tasks, allowing us to manipulate or to walk. Dentures allow us to chew our food. Only false breasts are designed for appearance only, as if the only real function of women's breasts were to appear in a certain shape and size and symmetry to onlookers, or to yield to external pressure. For no woman wearing a prosthesis can even for one moment believe it is her own breast, any more than a woman wearing falsies can.

Attitudes towards the necessity for prostheses after breast surgery are merely a reflection of those attitudes within our society towards women in general as objectified and depersonalised sexual conveniences. Women have been programmed to view our bodies only in terms of how they look and feel to others, rather than how they feel to ourselves, and how we wish to use them. As women, we fight this depersonalisation every day, this pressure towards the conversion of one's own self-image into a media expectation of what might satisfy male demand. The insistence upon breast prosthesis as 'decent' rather than functional is an additional example of that wipe-out of self in which women are constantly encouraged to take part. I am personally affronted by the message that I am only acceptable if I look 'right' or 'normal', where those norms have nothing to do with my own perceptions of who I am. Where 'normal' means the 'right' colour, shape, size, or number of breasts, a woman's perception of her own body and the strengths that come from that perception are discouraged, trivialised, and ignored.

Every woman has a right to define her own desires, make her own choices. But prostheses are often chosen, not from desire, but in default. Some women complain it is too much effort to fight the concerted pressure exerted by the fashion industry. Being one-breasted does not mean being unfashionable; it means giving some time and energy to choosing or constructing the proper clothes. In some cases, it means making or remaking clothing or jewellery. The fact that the fashion needs of one-breasted women are not currently being met doesn't mean that the concerted pressure of our demands cannot change that.

Some women believe that a breast prosthesis is necessary to preserve correct posture and physical balance. But the weight of each breast is never the same to begin with, nor is the human body ever exactly the same on both sides. With a minimum of exercises to develop the habit of straight posture, the body can accommodate to one-breastedness quite easily, even when the breasts were quite heavy.

Women in public and private employment have reported the loss of jobs and promotions upon their return to work after a mastectomy, without regard to whether or not they wore prostheses. The social and economic discrimination practised against women who have breast cancer is not diminished by pretending that mastectomies do not exist. Where a woman's job is at risk because of her health history, employment discrimination cannot be fought with a sack of silicone gel, nor with the constant fear and anxiety to which such subterfuge gives rise. Suggesting prosthesis as a solution to employment discrimination is like saying that the way to fight race prejudice is for Black people to pretend to be white. Employment discrimination against post-mastectomy women can only be fought in the open, with head-on attacks by strong and self-accepting women who refuse to be relegated to an inferior position, or to cower in a corner because they have one breast.

Within the framework of superficiality and pretence, the next logical step of a depersonalising and woman-devaluating culture is the advent of the atrocity euphemistically called 'breast reconstruction'. It should be noted that research being done on this potentially life-threatening practice represents time and research money spent – not on how to prevent the cancers that cost us our breasts and our lives – but rather upon how to pretend that our breasts are not gone, nor we as women at risk with our lives.

Any information about the prevention or treatment of breast cancer which might possibly threaten the vested interests of the American medical establishment is difficult to acquire in the country. Only through continuing scrutiny of various non-mainstream sources of information, such as alternative and women's presses, can a picture of new possibilities for prevention and treatment of breast cancer emerge.

The mortality for breast cancer treated by conventional therapies has not decreased in over 40 years (Rose Kushner, *Breast Cancer*, Harcourt, Brace & Jovanovitch, 1975, p. 161). Since the American medical establishment and the ACS are determined to suppress any cancer information not dependent upon western medical bias, whether this information is ultimately useful or not, we must pierce this silence ourselves and aggressively seek answers to these questions about new therapies. We must also heed the unavoidable evidence pointing towards the nutritional and environmental aspects of cancer prevention.

Cancer is not just another degenerative and unavoidable disease of the ageing process. It has distinct and identifiable causes, and these are mainly exposures to chemical or physical agents in the environment. In the medical literature, there is mounting evidence that breast cancer is a chronic and systemic disease. Post-mastectomy women must be vigilantly aware that, contrary to the 'lightning strikes' theory, we are the most likely of all women to develop cancer somewhere else in the body.[3]

Every woman has a militant responsibility to involve herself actively with her own health. We owe ourselves the protection of all the information we can acquire about the treatment of cancer and its causes, as well as about the recent findings concerning immunology, nutrition, environment and stress. And we owe ourselves this information *before* we may have a reason to use it.

It was very important for me, after my mastectomy, to develop and encourage my own internal sense of power. At all times, it felt crucial to me that I make a conscious commitment to survival. It is physically important for me to be loving my life rather than to be mourning my breast. I believe it is this love of my life and myself, and the careful tending of that love which was done by women who love and support me, which has been largely responsible for my strong and healthy recovery from the effects of my mastectomy. But a clear distinction must be made between this affirmation of self and the superficial farce of 'looking on the bright side of things'.

Last week I read a letter from a doctor in a medical magazine which said that no truly happy person ever gets cancer. Despite my knowing better, and despite my having dealt with this blame-the-victim thinking for years, for a moment this letter hit my guilt button. Had I really been guilty of the crime of not being happy in this best of all possible infernos?

The idea that the cancer patient should be made to feel guilty about having had cancer, as if in some way it were all her fault for not having been in the right psychological frame of mind at all times to prevent cancer, is a monstrous distortion of the idea that we can use our psychic strengths to help heal ourselves. This guilt trip which many cancer patients have been led into (you see, it *is* a shameful thing because you could have prevented it if only you had been more . . .) is an extension of the blame-the-victim syndrome. It does nothing to encourage the mobilisation of our psychic defences against the very real forms of death which surround us. It is easier to demand happiness than to clean up the environment. The acceptance of illusion and appearance as reality is another symptom of this same refusal to examine the realities of our lives. Let us seek 'joy' rather than real food and clean air and a saner future on a liveable earth! As if happiness alone can protect us from the results of profit-madness.

Was I wrong to be working so hard against the oppressions afflicting women and Black people? Was I in error to be speaking out against our silent passivity and the cynicism of a mechanised and inhuman civilisation that is destroying our earth and those who live upon it? Was I really fighting the spread of radiation, racism, woman-slaughter, chemical invasion of our food, pollution of our environment, the abuse and psychic destruction of our young, merely to avoid dealing with my first and greatest responsibility – to be happy?

The only really happy people I have ever met are those of us who work against these deaths with all the energy of our living, recognising the deep and fundamental unhappiness with which we are surrounded, at the same time as we fight to keep from being submerged by it. The idea that happiness can insulate us against the results of our environmental madness is a rumour circulated by our enemies to destroy us. And what Woman of Colour in America over the age of 15 does not live with the knowledge that our daily lives are stitched with violence and with hatred, and to naively ignore that reality can mean destruction? We are equally destroyed by false happiness and false breasts, and the passive acceptance of false values which corrupt our lives and distort our experience.

The idea of having a breast removed was much more traumatic for me before my mastectomy than after the fact, but it certainly took time and the loving support of other women before I could once again look at and love my altered body with the warmth I had done before. But I did.

Right after surgery I had a sense that I would never be able to bear missing that great well of sexual pleasure that I connected with my right breast. That sense has completely passed away, as I have come to realise that that well of feeling was within me. I alone own my feelings. I can never lose that feeling because I own it, because it comes out of myself. I can attach it anywhere I want to, because my feelings are a part of me, my sorrow and my joy.

I would never have chosen this path, but I am very glad to be who I am, here.

30 March 1979

This article was excerpted from Audre Lorde's book The Cancer Journals.

Resisting useless prostheses
Letter from Merry Cross
SR 128 March 1983

Dear *Spare Rib*,
On the whole I say a resounding *yeah*! to the articles by Angela Fisher and Audre Lorde about rejecting prostheses to cover up altered bodies. I would be proud to know either of these women.

But, I want to point out that this is a major issue for people with disabilities too (particularly women) and Audre and Angela have in fact been experiencing part of our oppression.

We are pressurised constantly to both look and behave as normally as possible and excluded if we don't or can't . . . denied jobs, access to pubs – you name it. . . .

And, Audre, you're wrong about other artificial prostheses; many, many of them are forced on us to make other people feel better despite their being functionally *useless* and despite excellent mechanical alternatives.

I have been lied to, and pressurised by 'most young women' stuff, in efforts to make me choose 'normal'-looking prostheses and I'm sure thousands of other people with disabilities have had similar experiences.

So, it's not just about sexism, it's also, perhaps even more fundamentally, about normalism.

The picture of health
Jo Spence
SR 163 February 1986 (Part I)
SR 164 March 1986 (Part II)

PART I

Three years ago I was diagnosed as having breast cancer. Like so many women before me I submitted myself to the medical machine, going along with the treatment as far as to have a lumpectomy performed on me. The feelings generated in the circumstances surrounding this were so totally negative that I felt, come what may, that I had to get off the production line set up by the medical orthodoxy. So I did. I wanted to write here a 'happy ever after' story, but unfortunately this is not it. Nonetheless I feel it is worth writing about what has happened in between then and now.

I am not better, in spite of beginning to take responsibility for my own health, and working out an integrated programme of health care with others. On the other hand, although I still have active cancer, and my general health is not good, I feel more in control of my life than at any other time previously. This has come about because of the questions I have been forced to ask myself about my belief system, my lifestyle and my attitude to my mind and body. As a result I see myself neither as 'heroine' or 'victim', but merely as a person in struggle, changing and adjusting daily, and trying to keep a state of equilibrium which will allow me to function optimally, at the same time as I strive to regain health.

When I first realised I had breast cancer I felt that I had been stricken and marked in some way which left me outside the experience of everybody else. The labelling of the disease was tantamount to having a curse put on to me. I went home and waited to die. Fortunately, friends were unable to accept this passivity on my part and plagued me with literature which seemed to offer other ways through the illness and initially I took myself off to the Bristol Cancer Help Centre. Here I was introduced to a philosophy of patient-centred medicine, whole mind and body therapy, and the idea that we can begin to be involved in trying to have a say over how we become well again, or manage our disease to our own satisfaction.

Apart from the fact that 13 years ago, my own mother died of liver cancer six weeks after a mastectomy (a fact I had completely disavowed, of which I had no real memory, in spite of being present and an accomplice to her euthanasia), I had no knowledge of the disease apart from a few anecdotal horror stories from friends and relatives, and the media coverage of various 'victims' of the disease. In spite of having earned myself a first class honours degree as a mature student, I still had no clue as to how my body worked, or even where my liver was situated.

I wouldn't say that I ever saw myself as an 'ill' person. Yet in retrospect, illnesses of one sort or another have dogged most of my life – most especially asthma, hay fever, eczema and bronchitis. These don't sound much but were like a long-running soap opera, appearing regularly at times of stress, exhaustion, over-indulgence, environmental extremes – always being treated by drugging or surgery. At 28 years I developed an ovarian tumour (14 lbs weight at the time of my operation), as a result of the 'side-effects' of steroid treatment for asthma. And still I didn't learn. Years later, after two attempts to detoxinate myself through naturopathic medicine (my liver having practically packed up), and each time running out of money to continue with such private treatment, I eventually had breast cancer diagnosed.

The treatment offered for this was mastectomy, and, if necessary, a further mastectomy if it developed in the other breast. Nothing more or less. It never occurred to me until I was in hospital waiting for the ward rounds with the results of the needle biopsy that I have any rights in the matter. That I could just put my clothes on and go home. Refuse their treatment. That is, until the incredible insensitivity, lies, evasiveness and uncaringness began. What happened to me is hardly any different from what other women have told me, so it was fairly 'normal' procedure it seems. To me it disgusted me so much that I finally found voice to refuse a mastectomy, after bedside arguments at the last minute with 'my consultant', who finally conceded that I have only the tumour removed, and that we'd take it from there.

Since that time I have not been back, but pursued a path which led me towards alternative medicine. However, in spite of my care and attention to diet, stress levels and lifestyle, always under the vigilance of either a naturopathic, or (latterly) somebody who practises traditional Chinese medicine, the tumour has grown back on the site of the previous operation and steadfastly refuses to budge. But I feel this is hardly surprising as my body is still trying to throw off the years of toxins held in the tissues, and I am still trying to work through any number of self-destructive patterns of eating and behaviour in therapy.

Because I am a practising photographer, having worked within the education sphere for many years, I began to ask myself questions about how disease and health are represented to us. Given that women are expected to be the object of the male gaze, are expected to beautify themselves in order to become loveable, are still fighting for rights over their own bodies which are very fundamental, it seemed to me that the breast itself can be seen as a metaphor for our struggles. The fact that we have to worry about its size and shape as young women, its ability to give food when we become mothers, and its total dispensability when we are past childbearing age, should be explored through visual representation, as well as within health care itself. The two should not be separated out in any way, as our concept of sexuality and our social identity both stem from lived experience and our own imaginary self carried in the mind's eye. Just as the female body is fragmented and colonised by various advertisers in the search for new markets for products, and through pornography is fetishised and offered for male consumption, so the body is similarly fought over by competitors for its medical 'care'. There are no departments of 'whole body' medicine in any hospitals I have ever attended. The concept is quite alien at any institutional level, although individual doctors and nurses are clearly interested in such a type of medicine.

How, then, do we begin to see and experience ourselves 'holistically' when we have always been dealing with 'body bits' which we perceive as deficient in a variety of ways?

In the system of medicine for which I finally opted (traditional Chinese Medicine – TCM), the patient is encouraged to begin to take some responsibility for getting and staying well. At the very least this means more work for the patient, and the necessity to make informed decisions; at its best it means a complete change of outlook on the world and the shattering of lifelong habits in relation to food, drugs, exercise, breathing, and the awakening of the knowledge that the body cannot deal forever with a completely unharmonious relationship with one's psychic, spiritual, social, economic living and loving conditions. In plain English, for me, this meant that I learn to love myself better and get more in touch with my actual needs and feelings so that I could start to try to change things wherever possible.

It is my belief that traditional Chinese medicine offers me the best chance of survival as a cancer patient, or at least a better 'quality of life'. It does not pretend to offer me a 'cure', but is a way of managing the illness, putting it at bay, or perhaps slowing it down. It involves long-term planning and care, making great changes in my daily routine, does not build up toxins in the body and mobilises the body's own resources and defence system. There is also continuity in medical care.

With a radical change of diet (details below) my long-term depression began to ebb away and my general health improved considerably. I lost four stone in weight, could breathe better, asthma and hay fever virtually vanished and I went through the early winter bronchitis-free. The scar tissue from the operation was rock-hard but within months began to soften.

However, within 10 months on a naturopathic regime my breast began to swell (like mumps) and there was extensive pain between my shoulder blades. I decided to change to TCM with its integrated system of herbs, exercise, diet and acupuncture. Within four months my back pain had more or less cleared, though the breast continued to increase in size and the lump enlarge. Now, after 15 months on this continuous regime the lump has softened and begun to break down, though it has a long way to go. Every time there is another kind of crisis in the body (e.g. a bad cold) the breast tends to harden and remain inactive. Throughout the treatment I have been able to continue to work part-time, though my energy levels fluctuate wildly if I do not rest enough. There has been a lot of acute pain in different parts of the body, coming and going as the liver copes with the detoxination process, the intestine takes on new bacterial fauna, and the body settles into new posture from exercising.

My TCM practitioner is Yana Stajno, whose partner David Lurie prescribed herbs to me on a weekly basis, taking account of my total condition at any point when he prescribes. I see Yana as a traditional female healer, in that she uses her hands and her medical skills and counsels me whilst she is attending me. We have a totally professional relationship yet, within it, we discuss ways in which I treat her as a surrogate mother, but in which she returns that power to me continually. I have experienced love and care from both her and David which is without parallel in my years of continuous medical treatment by general practitioners and hospital personnel. They charge me on a sliding scale at their lowest fee as such medicine is not available on the NHS. Traditional Chinese medicine is either picked up as a medical commodity (e.g. acupuncture), or else is sneered at by western cancer specialists, who thereby display an alarming degree of ignorance (and racism), believing that their recently evolved systems of treatment are far superior to thousands of years of cumulative health care within TCM. In China both traditional and orthodox treatments are available for cancer and patients can (in theory at least) have access to either or both systems. The regime for rebalancing my whole body and my psychic life is as follows:

Long term change of diet to a macrobiotic diet, occasional white meat or liver – which needs to be organic; plenty of fruit and vegetables, some nuts and seeds, fresh sprouted seeds and beans, freshly juiced fruit and vegetables. No sugar, salt, gluten, dairy products, most animal products, no preserved, tinned or processed food at all.

Daily Qi Gong exercise (routinely part of treatment for cancer in China, which helps circulation, breathing and general energy distribution, as well as strengthening the body).

Twice weekly acupuncture.

General health care through Chinese medicine.

Occasional lymphatic massage.

Daily megadoses of Vitamin C and mineral supplements.

Herbal intake daily (brewed up from raw dried Chinese herbs in my kitchen).

Monitoring of stress levels.

A loving relationship and reciprocal counselling sessions with David Robelts, my partner in life.

Plenty of cuddles and bodily contact with others.

I work part-time as a secretary, as well as continuing with my work as an educational photographer (on the proceeds of which I would starve). I receive local government rate and rent support, sometimes draw supplementary benefit and am supported by my partner financially if there is absolute necessity. There have also been intermittent donations from friends towards my health costs for which I have been grateful.

Even whilst I was in hospital I began to try to represent to myself what was happening to me by using my camera. But how to represent *myself to myself*, through my own visual point of view, and how to find out what I needed and to articulate it, and make sure I got it? Ultimately wanting to make this visible to others. And, eventually, how to deal with my feelings about myself, and give them visual form.

During the course of my illness I came to the conclusion that one of the major absences in my own family history and archives was any knowledge of what had happened to other members of my family in terms of mental and physical illnesses.

In looking through my family photographs (even though I had already done extensive work on them in *Beyond the Family Album*) I now realise that they actually hide any evidence of illness or ageing, as photographic conventions encourage us to always show the 'bright side', or to 'smile' for the camera, and the lack of clarity in small images prevents us from seeing any fine detail. I finally made up a health chart of my own life, including banal snapshots of me, as against details of diseases and treatments, which crystallised for me the paucity of family records. This led to my deciding to visually document my own struggle for health, and to try to see how that allied itself to struggles that others are making.

I believe it should be everybody's right to take photographs inside all state institutions. So, on the last two occasions when I went into hospital, I photographed a lot of what happened around me. Using delayed action

265

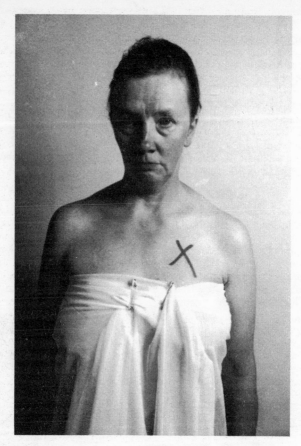

FIGURE 22 Powerlessness: 'From a phototherapy session on powerlessness – a reconstruction of the moment of confrontation between me and "my consultant" when I was told I needed a mastectomy' *Jo Spence and Rosy Martin* (not published in *Spare Rib*)

on my shutter in some instances I was able to include myself in the picture, but I never had the nerve to photograph anything happening to *me* directly, least of all my appalling treatment at the hands of consultants, which in any case would have warranted a video camera with sound.

I am continually asked 'what is phototherapy'? It means, quite literally, using photography to heal ourselves. As part of my health project I have been working on my stress and anxiety levels, reviewing my life in general and trying to understand the part that psychic life (phantasy/fantasy) plays in my well-being, or otherwise. Particularly, I have worked with Rosy Martin, a sister co-counsellor, who shares similar interests in cultural politics with me. Phototherapy should be seen within the broader framework of psychoanalysis and its application to the photography of family life, but should always take account of the possibility of *active change*. We drew upon techniques learned together from co-counselling, psychodrama, and a technique called 'reframing'.

Using this technique, Rosy and I began to work together to give ourselves (and each other) permission to display 'new' visual selves to the camera. In the course of this work we amply demonstrated to ourselves that there is no single self, but many fragmented selves, each vying for conscious expression, many never acknowledged. We created a range of portraits which were the visual embodiment of our fragmented selves, which still continue to emerge every time we meet to have a phototherapy session. We have found ways of having a dialogue with ourselves about the conflicts and constraints of marriage, or of health, education, ageing, class economics and oppression for us as women, and working 'against the grain' around dominant definitions of sexuality and love.

Ways in which I have used the camera therefore include taking natural-

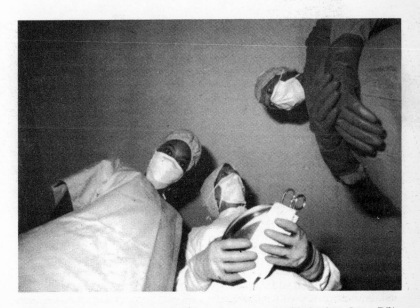

FIGURE 23 Patient's point of view *Jo Spence* (not published in *Spare Rib*)

istic photographs as things happened to me and around me (what is called documentary photography); staging things specially for the camera; using old personal photographs as a starting point and re-investigating what they mean. The whole technique depends upon expecting photographs to help us to ask questions, rather than supplying answers. Using this framework for photography it is possible to transform our imaginary view of the world, whilst working towards trying to change it socially and economically.

As a newly emergent middle class woman who is involved directly with ongoing cultural and ideological struggles, rather than economic ones (though at the moment I live on an average of £50 a week, out of which I have to pay for my health care), I feel it is still most useful that my time and energy be deployed within the institutions of education and the media. I believe that I can best intervene in the place in which I find myself, not look outside (as a photographer) to 'help' others.

In future I want to work more to help open up criticism around 'amateur' practices in photography, rather than (as in the past) to criticise and problematise 'professional practice'. Much of this will now revolve around 'the body politic' – concentrating on what could constitute a more social and pleasurable (through being critical) practice within amateur photography, particularly in photography within the family, of power relationships. This is where photo therapy becomes so important, to an understanding of our social identity, gendered, classed and racially determined. Questions integral to health identity, what we feel we are capable of doing and changing in relation to our well-being.

PART II

I offer here some questions and ideas for consideration. Some of these came up during the course of orthodox treatment, some afterwards during my investigation and moving into, then enjoying, my new health regime. I would emphasise that I have found no evidence to contradict the notion that cancer is a complicated process to reverse or rid ourselves of, and whatever is offered here is merely information, not a way for anybody else to proceed. If women decide to combine orthodox and supplementary treatment they will of course be supervised by a doctor. But if, as in my case, there is a rejection of orthodox medicine, it is still nonetheless vital to be supervised at all times by a qualified medical practitioner. Because the treatment I chose, traditional Chinese medicine, is still in its pioneering days in this country (though it is regularly used in China), it is not easy to have access to a network of practitioners. I was lucky in that I found a practice where they were willing to take me on as a patient, in spite of the fact that it is illegal for anybody who does not have an orthodox medical qualification to treat cancer.

However, as they are not treating the cancer, but my entire condition, this seems to be a way round the double-bind that those of us who wish to choose to proceed outside the NHS are in. Of course there are private health insurance schemes which one can negotiate with to have a range of treatments for cancer, but as I am opposed to this in principle, I have had, of necessity, to find a way to move forward outside the NHS, whilst operating on a very low income. Because I am a socialist I support the idea of a national health service within a welfare state, but because I am also a feminist I will fight with others against patriarchal medicine as it is currently practised in this country. Also, concentrating on the whole woman is in no way in opposition to group struggles over the social and political causes of illness.

In using the term 'orthodox' throughout, I mean the dominant system of medicine as practised within the NHS. In using the term 'supplementary' I mean the other 66 therapies which exist in the private sector which need to be paid for, but can be used in combination with orthodox medicine. In using the term 'alternative' I mean all therapies which are practised outside orthodox medicine, most of which have to be paid for.

Before you go to a doctor or to hospital it is important to know that you have the right at all times to refuse treatment (unless you are considered to be insane, suffering from an infectious disease, or considered incapable of looking after yourself). A patients' rights leaflet is obtainable from the National Consumer Council, from Citizens' Advice Bureaux, or from your local Community Health Council.

You have the right to ask that a friend or partner of either sex be present during examination or consultations. You have the right to refuse to sign a 'patient consent' form if you are not happy about surgery offered to you.

We should have the right to know not only 'side-effects' and survival rates for treatment but also what non-orthodox therapies, or complementary treatment is available on the NHS. (Important to note that the Homeopathic Hospital in London offers orthodox treatment for most cancers, although iscador (mistletoe) injections are considered suitable for some types of breast cancer.)

If opting for mixed treatment (i.e. orthodox and complementary therapies as in combination), it is important to establish with your doctor that this is *your* decision and you don't expect it to be undermined in subtle (or unsubtle) ways.

You do have the right to know if you are part of a 'trial' in which pairs of patients are double-blind computer-matched via their similar symptoms and then each given different treatment, which is monitored. There are least six major trials going on in this country in different regions. What does being part of a 'trial' mean in relation to your right to make decisions about your own body? I was (unbeknown to me) part of a trial in the Nottingham area and was never told until I attended another hospital who 'didn't believe in such trials'.

We should have the right to know that different consultants actively oppose one another's treatment for the same set of conditions (in some hospitals mastectomy is still fairly automatic, in others not so; sometimes consultants in the same hospital have different methods of treatment.)

You should make it clear if you wish to refuse to have your disease progressively documented by a medical photographer for use as teaching materials, lecturing, the writing of papers or the illustration of books (most consultants ask to have two sets of slides done of 'interesting cases' – one for the patient's records and one for their own private collection). Why don't we document our own health, keeping an inventory of all chemical intake throughout our lives – this is often requested of you if you decide on naturopathic detoxination programme.

Try to keep copies of all letters you handle which are about you (open them – nobody can do much about it). Ask for the right to read your notes and ask as many questions as you feel you need to. There are 'management techniques' for handling awkward patients – try to watch how you are being 'handled' if you are not too frightened. Some people have even managed to make tape recordings of their consultation which are very useful later for a variety of reasons.

Try to get advice from the welfare rights people on the difficult decision of whether to sign off from work (or unemployment) as 'sick' or not, which often mucks up payments to you for weeks on end. Also whether or not to have the disease named on certificates (do you want personnel to have you marked out as a potential health risk)? Part of the whole syndrome of the 'victim hiding the problem', also linked to the compulsion for you to conform and wear a prosthesis after removal of a breast. To get rid of the evidence of what has been done to you.

You should have the right to know just what your NHS doctor is 'allowed' to prescribe for you if you opt for supplementary alternative therapies which include massive doses of vitamins or minerals. The MIMS guide to prescribable medicines is held by all pharmacies and you can ask them to look things up for you. In my experience, the nearer a patient is perceived to be to death the more likely the GP is to co-operate with complementary prescriptions.

If you are interested to know your rights in relation to making decisions about your death then contact the Euthanasia Society. Far too much fear around breast cancer resides in our inability to face the fact that either the disease or the treatment might kill us.

If you suspect that you may have lumps in your breasts but are afraid to go for immediate screening it might help to visit a naturopath and go on to a very strict cleansing diet for four to six weeks. This may clear up non-malignant lumps and might mean the avoidance of an awful lot of pain and anguish.

The breast screening process will not indicate your general bodily condition, nor the presence of other tumours. If disease is fairly advanced then the lopping off of a breast will hardly help the overall condition. Other testing and screening is sometimes done after an operation, but not always. Beyond that you are recalled for regular breast screening, but the rest of your body is ignored until something manifests itself as a symptom.

It is important to consider the cost effectiveness, from the state's point of view, of NHS treatment. Removing a breast is often cheaper than 'staging' the treatment (i.e. removing lump, then radiotherapy, then perhaps chemotherapy). Not only is it cheaper to have body bits removed but it is often considered unimportant for women to want to 'cling to' their ovaries, wombs and breasts once they are past childbearing age. Often different treatment is offered to younger women.

Beyond breast screening, hardly any hospitals do any follow-up work for breast cancer patients once you are 'cleared', and there is no notion of the prevention of recurrence. Most people go back to exactly the same circumstances as brought them there in the first place. Then we hope for the best, or live in terror of the next outbreak of our bodies. Why are we not encouraged to try to help ourselves more? Six-monthly screenings won't encourage us to change the circumstances of our daily lives.

More and more evidence is being accepted that cancer is a systemic disease (i.e. the entire system is involved). If this is so, and we are not merely a set of signs and symptoms which can be read off tumours and cell conditions, how is it possible to talk of breast cancer as a killer? The term is inaccurate and misleading. Women do not die of lumps in their breast, they die because there co-exist with lumps other conditions, either in the lymphatic system, or in other parts of the body. Some breast cancers are slow or fast-growing, others are already linked to lymphatic cancer – how can we begin to educate ourselves to look for a fuller and more long-term view of the disease?

When you go into hospital a brief history of family health patterns is usually taken (which in my experience is never referred to again). How can we seriously talk about hereditary tendencies between generations of women? As the non-orthodox have pointed out, we inherit diet and stress patterns and patterns of repressive, 'being good' behaviour as women, which are as important as any genetic structures. How can we denaturalize what seems to be a common-sense view of breast cancer, and feel it is possible to change our lives to be different from previous generations of women? Long-term depression is the norm for breast cancer patients, treated with mood-changing drugs, yet other forms of therapy would be far more effective in helping us to change our lives.

It is generally accepted by alternative therapists (and in particular the Gerson therapy) that chemotherapy or irradiation can prejudice your chances of survival. If you opt for orthodox medicine and it fails you, and you then turn to alternative therapies your chances of survival will be jeopardised by the previous treatment. It is important to bear this in mind from the very beginning when trying to sort out the best way to proceed through treatment. Once the immune system has been broken down it is very difficult to build it up again so that it can help you survive.

In all cancer treatment it is really important to emphasise *management* rather than 'cure'. As diabetics take daily precautions to keep their bodies in a state of dietary balance, so most non-orthodox regimes strive in the long term to balance the mind and body for optimal functioning. If this balance is lost then the physical or mental state deteriorates again (in any number of ways) as the body moves into 'disharmony' and illness.

What is the importance of nutrition to breast cancer? Firstly it has been found that low animal fats are helpful, and secondly that excess weight is detrimental. On a fruit, vegetable and grain diet weight just drops off until the body finds its own optimum weight. Dieting in this sense is nothing to do with calorie counting but is about maximal nutrition from minimal intake. For those of us who are compulsive eaters we have to do work on the emotional roots of our eating problems, so that we can actually enjoy new eating habits, rather than experience them as a continual misery.

If you have been told you have cancer I feel it is important to read all the *positive* stuff on how to survive you can get your hands on. Reading death statistics will cripple you emotionally unless you somehow manage to turn it on its head and say to yourself, 'I intend to be a survivor.' Alternative bookshops are good stockists of books and pamphlets on alternative health and critiques of orthodox medicine. If you can't afford to buy the stuff, once you have located it then you can order it from a library. If you are reading for 'prevention' of cancer then the order in which material is read seems to me to be very different and might even include quite a lot about orthodox practice itself.

You need to cold-bloodedly sit down (on your own or with an ally) to work out what resources you need, what you can afford, what you will have to ask to be given, and what dearly held previous benefits about yourself and your invulnerability as superwoman will have to be examined pretty quickly. Also finding a strategy for letting others know you have needs so perhaps theirs will need to be deferred for a while!

In the hospital where I was, all the women were going straight back to their jobs and/or looking after their families as if nothing had happened. The turn-round time for mastectomy then was three to four days if all went well.

Such needs might include the following:
(a) A network of support (even if such a network doesn't perceive of itself as such).
(b) Some kind of counselling (some regions have voluntary counselling schemes through the hospitals, or else these can be located through Cancerlink).
(c) Money! You need to maximise your resources and assets.

If you feel you want to investigate alternative approaches to breast cancer, to try to put together a 'package deal' for yourself, which might consist of orthodox treatment, plus (say) acupuncture or diet, then this is relatively easy to do if you have an income of your own. This can be nigh on impossible for working class women who are on low incomes or whose income becomes part of the family income, and who, anyway, are more used to 'doing what the doctor says', and perhaps less articulate in a situation where they are in a sub-dominant position. The Bristol Cancer Help Centre is a mine of information here.

All alternative therapies have to be paid for by somebody. Many practitioners have a sliding scale of charges. Within whole body, or holistic medicine, this would include preventative/curative treatment in the form of herbs, acupuncture or naturopathic treatment, change of diet, and various forms of exercise. It would also involve looking at the psychological side of our lives and perhaps going into some form of therapy. Most therapies cost money, though some less than others (co-counselling for instance costs little to learn and nothing to practise, beyond your own time and commitment). 'Therapy' is much more likely to be on offer if you are middleclass, whereas chemical drugging and/or psychiatric treatment will be seen as 'solutions' for working class women.

In alternative cancer therapies there are various approaches – all of which aim to build up the immune system. These range from mucousless diets, Gerson detoxification therapy, nutritional therapy, vitamin C therapy, to the system I opted for in traditional Chinese medicine. I have listed some institutional bodies and books which I feel would be useful to help you deal with these various approaches.

Perhaps you will decide that you want a non-invasive form of diagnosis. Iridology is the reading off of your bodily conditions from colour configurations within the eyeball and iris.

Try to think of your body as your major resource in life. Do you want high technology which attacks the system like a war machine, or low technology which helps to convince the body that you are willing to listen to its warning signs, and to care for it better? (Read Rachel Carson's *Silent Spring* for analogies with the maltreatment of the land by 'experts'.)

It is very important to understand the difference between the terms orthodox/non-orthodox and supplementary/alternative medicine. Especially their complications in relation to:

(a) How do you get access to monitoring resources at low cost or no cost if you opt for alternative treatment? It is usually assumed that most people who purchase their health care are rolling in money. If you don't want to run the gamut of hysterical consultants every time you refuse their treatment, where do you get then?

(b) There may be problems with certification for absence from work for the recovery period after operations/treatment, or for long periods off work. Only a registered doctor is legally entitled to treat cancer, therefore, if going to an alternative practitioner, how do you describe the illness? Important to know how to get invalidity benefit from the DHSS if you are entitled to it. Long-term illnesses can qualify for payment at a higher rate than normal sickness benefit, but who is qualified to sign the certificate?

I feel it is important to think about different holistic health approaches as *systems*. Western medicine treats all other systems as commodities, i.e. they will lift a bit off the shelf and insert it into their own system of medicine. There is a constant struggle going on for definitions of health care between orthodox and non-orthodox practitioners, as to who will have professional status, who can prescribe treatment, who can be employed by the state as part of the NHS – but e.g. India and China each have their own philosophies of medicine, and medical sub-cultures. When looking for treatment for cancer I feel it is useful to know how other cultures have dealt with it – not all miracle drugs are seen as miraculous in other cultures, though some have revolutionised health care.

We should realise that if we opt for alternative treatment for cancer this means alternative treatment for everything, including headaches. Herbal and non-chemical remedies are readily available in most towns from registered herbalists. If we opt for alternative treatment what do we do in emergency situations?

It is important to know how to separate the disease from its treatment. Possibly getting in touch with others who have gone the alternative route will help. (I did it by putting a letter into the magazine *Here's Health* which brought forth dozens of replies. They also list health groups in various towns.)

There are sometimes problems of how to deal with secondary infection after treatment or operation. Because the immune system is invariably damaged by orthodox medicine, or because it is actually dealing with fighting the disease, the rest of the body is much more prone to anything else going wrong. Often people coming out of hospital after surgery have a major round of colds, flu, shingles, etc. If they are also dealt with chemically it compounds the problem. If undergoing radiotherapy then large doses of vitamin C are said to help the side-effects.

HINTS FOR THE DAILY ROUTINE

How can you evolve methods of stopping people treating you as a victim or a heroine? Telling you shock/horror stories of other people's cancer and treatment? Initially when I was ill people were in full flight with their anecdotes before I could stop them. The images of horror and death piled up at an alarming rate and it was only when I went to Bristol Cancer Help Centre that I realised the importance of having positive (even Utopian) images to aspire to.

If you are on a strict diet then it is important to find strategies to stop other people encouraging you to break it. Most people's notion of a diet is in relation to calorie control, which is different. How do you persuade friends it is not a social disaster or failure on their part to serve you baked potato and salad while others gorge themselves! At home I was lucky because my partner offered to share my new eating habits.

Think about the problems of meeting others who have the same or similar problems to you. Do you want to mix with people who are having orthodox treatment (this often happens in a therapy group), people who are trying to combat degenerative illnesses in general who have a good pool of information about systemic diseases (e.g. multiple sclerosis, arthritis)? Do you want to meet survivors or people already half-dead with chemicals?

Important not to become undernourished and anaemic through very strict forms of dieting and detoxification. This must never be undertaken lightly or without qualified supervision.

It is important to know where to buy food in bulk, and survive on a low income – especially sprouting grains and seeds for alive food with maximum nutrition.

If you opt for a new cleansing dietary regime then you need to reorganise your kitchen so that you have everything you need to hand, including herbs and spices for flavouring. If you intend to carry on with a mixed kitchen (i.e. cook one diet for yourself and another for others) then this needs to be thought through. If you intend to strive for a different attitude to health this will include new patterns of food preparation and eating, so you might as well get used to it from the beginning. If you have had bouts of compulsive eating throughout your life (as I had) re-organisation also makes life a lot easier. It is useful to colonise existing cookery books, especially vegan and vegetarian, as most so-called health diets are very bland. Also read cookbooks from other cultures.

If you change your diet suddenly to one which is mostly fruit and vegetable then your internal eco-system of stomach and intestines will feel like a battlefield, with excessive production of body gases. Very embarrassing and uncomfortable initially, and you can't tell if you are getting better or worse!

There is a need for some sort of assertiveness training for those of us who feel totally intimidated by the medical profession.

How do we deal with the abject loneliness of the long struggle for health (the most boring of subjects to other people who are 'well')? How to present yourself as a subject in daily struggle? People are used to the 'narrative resolution' of illnesses like cancer. (In the media's terms you are either 'dead' or 'better'. The actual *struggle* over many years to regain health is not good box office. It is more like soap opera with its continual peaks and troughs and minor resolutions for most of the time.)

Cancer may mean restructuring your life *and* society, but when you as an individual have it, the struggle is usually on your own! You have to get your priorities sorted out – if you are a feminist or a socialist it probably means that you are involved in half a dozen struggles which are no longer *immediately* relevant to your day-to-day life. Cancer research and 'self-love' must take priority in my opinion at this stage. This can cause a lot of internal conflict if not sorted out from the beginning. (I lay in bed worrying that I could not go to a rally at Greenham the day before my operation!) The amount of solidarity among people around cancer is very limited (and breast cancer terrifies most women) – and though people are 'supportive' – they can't take on our burden for us. It is often up to very close friends and/or our partner to shoulder the main burden with us. But what do we do if a partner rejects us because our 'body image' is no longer tenable to us or to them through having breast cancer? Who do we turn to?

A basic problem for me as a socialist feminist was that I had a 'conflict' model of the world. How to mesh this up with needing to be more 'harmonious' in order to begin to be well again. For instance, initially I took on the medical profession rather than the illness itself!

How do you deal with the problem for us as 'new' women of 'over-performance' in order to prove ourselves, often burning ourselves out (something I continue to witness to my horror)?

How do you deal with your own bravado/rebellion? Being the 'naughty little daughter' is all very well when facing up to doctor/daddy, and nurse/mummy within the cancer field (where most top jobs are held by men) but what we need is knowledge of how to begin to take responsibility for ourselves and have a say in defining our own bodies. A well-trod path in feminism but not in relation to breast cancer.

The problem of love and sexuality for us in relation to this particular illness? How to redefine 'love' and move towards a less phallocentric type of sexuality. Many women see their sexuality as totally destroyed through mastectomy and hysterectomy . . . a good prosthesis might help us to pretend to the world that nothing has happened, but for many women the scars will remain in memory long after the others have faded. Good counselling can help here.

Time scales? If it took 20 years to get your body in the state it is now, then how can you expect a few 'magic bullets' to sort it out? We need a different philosophy of our body's needs in relation to cancer therapies. It might take many years to get the body back on to an even keel – it might never do it. But, as has been said many times, the 'quality of life' may be vastly improved.

Not only is there a 'cancer industry' where (as in America) more people are involved in researching and treating the disease (and whose standard of living may depend on it) than are actually being treated at any one time, but it is important to note the continual orchestration in the national media of various 'breakthroughs', 'miracles', 'new discoveries' (always on the horizon), etc. The public relations of the British Medical Association is quite phenomenal, and this orchestration should be examined for its sub-text in the ways in which it constructs 'the truth' of cancer. In an inverse ratio to this is the limited mileage given to alternative (and less miraculous and more long-winded treatments) in its onslaught against the cancer orthodoxy.

Some people have theorised that cancer is just another form of slow suicide. Whilst this might be highly contagious I feel that for some people life might be so stressful and apparently unchangeable that legalised death is the only way out. However, in my own journey through illness I seriously considered my rights to suicide or euthanasia and found the literature of the Voluntary Euthanasia Society very useful.

Finally and on a positive note, I feel it is *important* to try to help others to share a new philosophy of health. My partner, David, asked if he could attend the same practice as me, which he now does. I am quite happy that our general health is openly discussed between all of us, and that he is taking the same long-term (good ecology, whole body, *mind* and body *integration*) route as myself.

CHAPTER 8

ACROSS BOUNDARIES

The initial confidence of white feminists that sisterhood was global, that patriarchy was the common oppression, led to a genuine interest in the situation of women worldwide. *Spare Rib* articles reflected this early enthusiasm. However, the right questions were often not asked, and any self-consciousness about the way in which white western feminists were approaching the lives of women in Third World and socialist countries was almost completely absent. A women's liberation movement, specific to a particular historical moment and culture, was being used as the measure for the aspirations and lives of all women in very different situations. Too often the priorities and cultures of these women were dismissed as being 'not feminist enough'.

Black women 'at home' challenged these assumptions. An attack was mounted on Eurocentrism as anti-imperialist women maintained that the privileges and choices of white western women were connected to the exploitation of Third World women. This was hotly denied by some – imperialism had nothing to do with them, it was a 'man-made' phenomenon. But others drew back in confusion, not sure what it all meant or how they should react.

On *Spare Rib* in the late 1970s and early 1980s, the collective agonised. Articles were offered to the magazine but more often than not these came from white western visitors. The desire to publish articles which would inform, educate and inspire women reading them conflicted with the seeming difficulty of getting submissions from the 'right' women.

In 1980 *Spare Rib* carried a long interview with Nawal el Sa'adawi in which she briefly discussed clitoridectomy. The collective wrote an editorial addition (reprinted here) which attempted to provide a British feminist response to the issue of female circumcision. Although it is a careful piece, it still angered some readers because it included uncritical reference to work being done around clitoridectomy by white American women. The desire to learn and support women in other countries and also look critically at one's own 'backyard' still can get mixed up with condescending meddling.

Now, even though the *Spare Rib* collective believes in an international feminist perspective and regularly carries international articles, the problems of how to *get* representation from women in other countries, or *how* to represent them if that proves difficult, remain.

Most *Spare Rib* international articles are not specifically about health. Some, like a major one on health in China, were outdated very quickly, in this instance by the rapid changes which followed the death of Mao. Often international health information appeared in the news section of the magazine. Many feminists on the Indian sub-continent, in Africa,

Central America, and many other countries are deeply involved in projects around women and health, so hopefully we will see their work as feature articles in the pages of *Spare Rib* in the near future. As health issues so often open doors to understanding the ways in which British society works, so the health concerns of women in other countries, and how they approach them, open up direct and accessible ways of learning across boundaries and developing long-term solidarity.

Nurse in the middle
Sithembile Zulu
SR 118 May 1982

'I am a Black woman, born and brought up in a rural area of South Africa. Most men from this area work many miles from their homes in one of South Africa's industrial centres. The following story is very much part of my own experience.

'I trained as a nurse in the Transkei and worked there for three and a half years. I then worked for a short time on the Ciskei before training as a midwife and working in this field in Zululand for just over a year. I spent a further two years at a mission clinic on the edge of a large African Reserve in Mid-Natal running a maternity clinic. I was also a member of a mobile clinic unit which served the arid Reserve area, from which the vast majority of the men were away working in the mines around Johannesburg. Finally, I spent two years in a small town Provincial Hospital in North Natal working mainly in the children's ward.

'Thus I had in South Africa experience of different geographical areas of the country, and also different environments – I worked in rural areas, in tribal reserves, and in town. I had lived in the countryside, where my home is situated, in small town "locations" and in large African townships'

Sithembile Zulu

MY STORY

'Bring in the next patient please!'
I moved away taking the mother whose baby had just been examined, explaining to her the importance of giving all the antibiotic to the child even if he showed signs of improvement before the bottle of medicine was finished. As the mother left the surgery, I poked my head into the waiting room. There was only one patient left, but the waiting room still held a familiar smell, a combination of smoke from the open aloe fires used for cooking in the kraals which impregnated the clothing of the local

residents, together with the clean pungent aroma of the red ochre which the tribal women used to dress their hair.

Although it was only 10 in the morning we had already seen and treated about 30 patients. In the summer patients arrived from 7 a.m. onwards, and surgery started at about 7.30 in the morning. The surgery was part of a small maternity clinic which admitted, when full, 25 patients. It was situated at the lower end of the clinic near the dirt road used by traffic from and to the village about a quarter of a mile away.

'Woza ma' (come in mother) I said in our language to the woman who sat with her hands under a blanket. It was a hot sticky morning, especially in the surgery where we kept most of the windows closed in order to keep out the dust from the dirt road. I puzzled as to how she could feel cold to the extent of using such a large blanket instead of the usual small one used by the women in the area. I concluded that she must have had a nasty cold from which she was recovering. Although the clinic itself was specifically for maternity patients, in the surgery we were inevitably consulted about everything. With the next hospital four hours' walk away, it had to be so.

The woman stood up clumsily still keeping her arms under the blanket. Her face looked drawn, tired and anxious, as she sat on the chair facing the doctor.

'Uphethwe yini, Ma?' (What is the matter, Ma?) I asked.

'No, it is not I who am unwell. It is the baby.' As she spoke she removed the blanket revealing an extremely dehydrated baby about nine months old. He was lying limply in his mother's arms. His eyes were closed and the eyeballs sunken in his skull. The mouth looked dry and was slightly open. The breathing was shallow and irregular. His skin too was dry and hung loosely on his dehydrated body.

The doctor started to examine the baby. Eventually he looked up, his face red and angry: 'Staff nurse, ask her why she kept the baby at home for such a long time. Why didn't she come earlier with him?'

I hesitated, looking at the mother who was trying to force the breast between the baby's opened lips. The doctor was new to this field of medicine having just joined the clinic a month ago. Previously he had worked in an all-white provincial hospital. Until his appointment at the clinic he had had no contact with Black people and knew very little of the problems they faced in their daily lives.

I knew the answer to his question without even asking the mother but I still went through the pointless exercise of asking the question just so the doctor did not think that I had made up an answer. Her reply was as I had expected: 'The baby had not been ill for a long time. He only started yesterday. By evening time he had vomited so much and had had so many loose stools that he had become very weak and was refusing the breast. If it were possible I would have come yesterday evening but there is no transport from our place at that time of the day. Tell the doctor I couldn't have come earlier than today.'

As I translated the information, the doctor shook his head incredulously. He did not believe what the mother was saying. As I finished he said: 'Tell her that her baby is very ill. He needs a lot of water to replace the fluid he has lost through vomiting and diarrhoea. We cannot give the water through the mouth because the baby is too ill to take it, but even if he did drink it at this stage he would just vomit the whole lot out again. The baby must go to hospital. The doctor there will put a drip in the baby's vein and replace the water directly to the body whilst the child is being given the antibiotic to kill the infection.'

The woman listened with no change in her expression. When I finished she said quietly: 'I understand what the doctor is saying. But I can't take the baby to hospital without letting them know at home. I must also write and let his father know. I must go home now and I will come back with the baby tomorrow perhaps.'

The doctor was already writing the letter of introduction to the hospital. He stopped writing when I told him what the mother was saying.

'Tell her there is no time for her to take the baby home. If treatment is not started immediately the baby will die. There is a chance to save her baby, but only if she agrees to taking him to hospital now.'

As I spoke to the woman tears just rolled down her face and she clutched her baby to her breast.

'I don't want my baby to die. Please God don't let him die. I have waited so many years to have him. Don't let him die.'

The doctor's voice cut in anxiously:

'What does she say?'

'She doesn't want her baby to die.'

'Of course she doesn't want her baby to die. Neither do we. That is why we want the baby to go to hospital. That is the only chance we have of saving her baby.'

I just stood there saying nothing. My mind was on previous occasions when we had successfully persuaded women to take their children to hospital and they had died. How could I tell this woman to do the same? The doctor's voice came through: 'Aren't you going to tell her what I have just said?' he demanded.

'No.'

'Why the hell not? You are a trained nurse. Surely you must know that the hospital is the only place where this baby has a chance of surviving.'

The doctor was a German missionary and had done his training in his own country. During the month he had been in the clinic he had shown genuine care, and his treatment of patients was humane, unlike that meted out by many South African white doctors. It was precisely this background which encouraged me now to speak quite openly to him.

'If I knew that I would have no hesitation in encouraging her to take her baby to the hospital and I am sure that if we could guarantee that the baby would be well in hospital the mother would go now. But we cannot be sure that the baby will be cured in the hospital.'

The doctor was getting more angry as he listened.

'Of course we cannot guarantee that. It is her fault for not bringing the baby here earlier in the first place. We are now offering her a chance to save her child.'

'It is not her fault and what we are offering her is not a chance of survival but a graveyard.'

I was getting very angry and my voice must have communicated my feelings to the doctor. Looking at his confused face I realised that he had no conception of the problems facing the woman he wanted to help. I turned towards him feeling slightly ashamed for losing my temper. After all he was ignorant about the problem he thought he could solve.

'I am sorry. I know I am not making much sense but perhaps I could explain if you could spare a few minutes.'

Turning to the mother, who was getting ready to take her baby home, I explained: 'Can you please wait for a few minutes. The doctor and I are just discussing if there is any other way to make the baby better.'

Addressing the doctor I continued: 'The situation facing you at the moment is only part of the whole problem of my people in this country.'

'At the moment I do not give a damn about the problem of your people. My concern now is the life of this baby in front of me. You explain to me why the baby should not be given a chance in hospital and I am willing to listen.'

'I do believe that you are genuinely concerned about the baby. But the fate of this baby is the fate of a thousand more children which you are going to see in this clinic, and the dilemma facing the mother is the dilemma of all the women you will be trying to persuade to take their children to hospital. Unless you understand at least part of the problem you will neither be able to help this baby nor many more who will be in his position.'

'Well I have read a lot about the system of separate development and the Bantustans but I still don't understand what that whole problem has to do with taking this baby into hospital.'

'It has a lot to do with it. Under the system of apartheid women and children must remain behind in the poor and arid reserve whilst husbands spend months 300 miles away in the mines in Johannesburg as migrant workers. Although women spend a lot of their time planting in the fields they get very little return in food because the soil is very poor. The money that husbands send home is negligible because they themselves get very low wages. The result is consistent unremitting starvation. The most vulnerable are children. Because they are already weak from malnutrition any disease they get hits them very hard. A child who was taken ill only yesterday looks as if he has been ill for months.'

'But why doesn't the mother bring the child in as soon as he gets ill – on the same day?' asked the doctor in some exasperation.

'Most of the people who come to the clinic are from the top of that mountain', I pointed out. 'The only bus serving the area leaves at 7 a.m.

to arrive here at 10 a.m. People who live across the Tugela river must leave their homes at 5 in the morning in order to catch the bus before it leaves the terminus. If the baby gets ill at 8 a.m. after the bus has left the mother has to wait until the following day to come here.'

'Yes, I see the problem,' the doctor said musingly. 'But now she is here, why won't she let the baby go to hospital?'

'Because in our custom, the decision to take the child to hospital is a family decision which must be approved of by the father of the child. In his absence his parents or brother must be consulted. But a lot of mothers would be prepared to ignore this restriction if they were sure that their babies would get better in hospital. There would be less recrimination about taking unilateral decisions provided the baby got better.'

'But there is a chance in the hospital,' the doctor insisted.

'It is not a chance that is worth taking. I have worked in that hospital. There is only one children's ward in which babies from one month old are admitted with children of 14 years of age. Children with infectious diseases cannot be effectively isolated. The number of children in the ward rarely falls below 50. Babies share cots and bigger children share beds with little ones. There are only four nurses to look after all the children and, at night, sometimes only two. This baby will have no chance at all. With the risk of cross-infection he is bound to die of some other disease even if they checked his gastro-enteritis. Should the baby die then the mother has to face the problem of taking the body home possibly without much help or sympathy from the members of the family she did not consult before taking the baby to hospital. To meet the expense she might have to borrow some money which the husband may refuse to pay when he hears that his wife failed to obey the orders of his community. Not only would she be blamed for disobeying the unwritten laws but also for the subsequent death of her child. There will always be people who are wise after the event whose comments will be "she should never have taken the baby to hospital when it was so ill, unless she wanted it to die of course. Maybe that is why she did not even tell her parents-in-law. Maybe it is not the husband's baby." From the mother's point of view, when she knows from other women's experiences, the risk is not worth taking.'

'But what can I do? I cannot change the system.'

'Perhaps not but we can start by treating this baby now, here in the clinic. By 10 in the evening we shall have given enough water through the vein and at least four doses of antibiotic to see the baby through the night. We can take both mother and child home in our ambulance. If the baby shows signs of improvement the mother will bring him back tomorrow. All we need to do is to borrow the necessary equipment for the treatment from the hospital and if the treatment works we can start ordering our own stuff. Once mothers have confidence in the treatment they will not hesitate to bring in their children. They may even agree to leave them overnight. If they chose to they could stay here or come at 10 in the morning, spend 4 hours with their babies and take the bus back home at 2 in the afternoon.'

The hospital we had talked about was 45 miles away and had no facilities for mothers. Transport to and from the town in which the hospital is situated is very poor. To visit a mother has to leave home at 5 a.m. and will not get back home until afternoon the following day and all that for half an hour's visit.

'All right,' the doctor said slowly. 'I'll ring the hospital. Could you please ask the ambulance driver to go to the outpatient department. I'll borrow all the equipment from there. Meanwhile we could start with the antibiotic treatment.'

After giving the message to the driver, I came back and sat by the mother. I explained in Zulu: 'The doctor will try and treat the baby here. I will just give the baby his medicine first and I will discuss the arrangements with you.'

As the baby swallowed his first dose, he gave a little cough and the mother's expression lost its hopelessness. 'My baby, he is getting better already.'

He did get better. By the time I left the clinic we were giving similar treatment to many more babies. Although it still maintains the title of clinic it is in effect a cottage hospital. One tiny change. But the basic cause of that baby's starvation remains and will until apartheid is destroyed.

Bhopal – dangerous effects on women's health
Susan Ardill
SR 154 May 1985

There is strong evidence to suggest that the Bhopal gas leak disaster has caused an epidemic of gynaecological diseases.

Until recently, any effects on women's health had been judged in terms of pregnancies alone. But a recent study in field clinics in the gas affected slums revealed an extremely high proportion of gynaecological diseases. Of the women examined, 94% had leucorrhea (a white vaginal discharge), 79% had pelvic inflammatory disease, and excessive menstrual bleeding was found in 46% (with possible consequent severe anaemia, reduced working capacity and aggravated respiratory problems). Other effects noted were suppression of lactation (which could lead to malnutrition in the infants of these poor women), impotence in husbands, still births and abortions.

What was found is probably only the tip of an iceberg. Medical relief so far has been given via polyclinics and hospitals – the crowded facilities discourage women from attending, and they have complained that doctors are not paying attention to their symptoms and not carrying out gynaecological examinations.

Some gynaecologists have dismissed the findings, saying that these diseases are due to poverty and poor hygiene. It is clear that a research project needs to be set up immediately; but also there is a strong need for more field clinics and training of women paramedics; and for women's organisations to bring pressure to bear on the authorities to implement full-scale treatment and investigation of the insidious problems caused by this gas.

Women and health in India
Caroline Rees
SR 163 February 1986

The struggle of Indian women against oppression, about health in particular, was the subject of a talk organised by the National Abortion Campaign in London in December. The speaker was Trupti Shah, a co-founder of Sahiyar, the first autonomous women's group in her home city of Baroda in the north-western state of Gujarat.

Child labour still exists and male children, who can supplement the family income, are preferred. There is no social security system, and work practices make it more likely that sons will provide financial support for ageing parents. Dowry payments when a woman marries, although officially illegal, are common practice. Many parents would prefer to avoid this burden.

The Indian women's movement has only comparatively recently taken up health as a major issue. The most recent census indicates that for every 1,000 men, there are 935 women. It is no accident, according to Trupti: 'There are social and economic reasons for this. It is not some strange demographical feature. It can be explained by infant mortality, life expectancy, and the preference for male children among parents'.

The abuse of amniocentesis tests (which were intended to detect foetal abnormalities), turning them into sex determination tests, is too important to ignore. The result of these has been that, on discovering they are carrying a girl, the majority of women have opted, under enormous pressure, for abortion – and at a dangerously late stage too, as results are not known until the 18th week of pregnancy.

The test costs between 80 and 100 rupees (around £6–8) and is wide-spread in urban areas like Bombay. In rural areas, abortions are often self-induced – and dangerous. While women are taunted and humiliated for giving birth to girls, especially if it amounts to two or three, there are still strong taboos against abortion, despite it being legal and free on demand. The weapon used against them is double-edged.

All too often, says Trupti, 'health' has been seen in terms of population control rather than as a woman's right to control her own body. Mrs Gandhi's forced sterilisation programme during the State of Emergency in the mid-1970s was a 'burning issue' for the women's movement. Often, poor women were used as guinea-pigs for contraceptives banned in other countries; often, they had no idea what it meant, going to doctors later to ask why they were unable to conceive.

Today, sterilisation incentives are offered to both women and men – 250 and 100 rupees respectively – and in return for persuading others to take the plunge. 'People are rather scared of population control, because it is enforced. To have more children is economically advantageous to the *family*. . . . It's a question of survival, not of having a better life.' A 'better life' for women would be to have fewer children of course, or at least to *choose* whether to.

Compared to men, three times fewer women visit hospitals and health centres. 'The values inculcated are that women have no right to be ill. They have to work all the time.' Going to hospital means losing a day's pay, so women are expected to neglect their health.

In the 1960s and 1970s, the women's movement waged some successful, and quite militant, campaigns around issues like price rises, deforestation, sexist films, gang rape (often at the hands of policemen), and wife-beating. Usually the groups were led by educated middle and upper class women and radical students. Autonomous groups were formed as a result of political disinterest from parties on the Left. Today, with the increased strength of the movement and with greater involvement amongst political activists and the working class, the situation is improving, says Trupti Shah, 'slightly'.

Baby foods – formula for abuse?
Fiona Lumb
SR 99 October 1980

Massive advertising campaigns by infant food companies have brought about a worldwide decline in breast-feeding – especially in Third World countries. Lack of facilities often means mothers having to use dirty water with the formula milk, or overdiluting it to make it go further because it is so expensive. So thousands of babies fed on artificial milk either die or suffer malnutrition.

'The problem of infant formula versus breast-feeding is not limited to Third World countries – it is here and now,' said La Donna Harris, President of Americans for Indian Opportunity, at the opening session of the Infant Formula Action Coalition's Fourth National Conference in Washington DC, last March. Ms Harris urged conference delegates to continue their efforts to eliminate the influence of infant milk companies on the medical system and consumers, but to avoid focusing only on the Third World. In the US, for example, the poor still bottle-feed while middle and upper class women have access to information which encourages breastfeeding. On Indian reservations, infant mortality and illness are disturbingly high. She stressed: 'This is one world. Women in the US and in other nations need a system which supports what is best for them and their children.'

The promotion and marketing practices of multinational milk companies throughout the Third World have received increasing attention in recent years. In 1975, *Spare Rib 34* documented how milk companies such as Nestlés, and Cow & Gate, aggressively advertised their products in highly inappropriate situations. Examples are given of parents who could not afford the correct amount of milk powder and the fuel to boil water, who were dependent on irregular or contaminated water systems and who often could not understand the instructions on cans of powdered milk. This led to the death or extreme malnutrition of thousands of Third World children.

The promotion and sale of infant formula is deeply rooted in sexism. While there are women who physically cannot breast-feed (estimated at less than 5%), women in all countries are constantly told it is to their advantage to bottle-feed. By implying that breast milk can be insufficient, the industry makes women feel inadequate. Artificial milk is also given a more modern, western, 'clean' image. With aggressive hospital promotion, the industry restricts women's choice of how to feed their babies. The image of the passive, elegant, sex-object mother is successfully communicated, with firm breasts which must not be allowed to sag.

Yet both milk powder company personnel and nutritionists acknowledge that breast milk is *better* than artificial infant milk. It protects against infection, has some contraceptive value for the mother, and is cheap. However, to expand their markets and increase profits, companies take advantage of poor standards of consumer control, especially in the Third World. Pressure from action groups and individuals across the world has made some changes in the last five years, bringing this issue to the floor of the United Nations and to the attention of many Third World and western governments. In consequence, multinationals *appear* to be modifying their practices, but in effect this can simply mean altering their image, not withdrawing their products.

From 1970 to 1975 awareness of the issue grew through statements by concerned nutritionists, through publication of an article in the *New Internationalist* (August 1973), and the War on Want publication *The Baby Killer* (February 1974). The film *Bottle Babies* (Teldok 1975) graphically depicted the enormity of the problem, while Nestlés' court action against the Swiss Third World Action Group (June 1974–June 1976) gained wide publicity in European newspapers. Baby Food Action groups were formed in Britain, Europe and Australia.

Between 1975 and 1980 pressure has been stepped up. In 1975, eight infant milk companies formed their own council (International Council of Infant Food Industries), established a code of ethics and reluctantly began dialogue with their critics. In July 1978 Nestlés claimed to have stopped all mass media promotion – though countless reports proved otherwise.

FIGURE 24 Boycott Nestlé products (*SR 108* July 1981)

Companies broadened their promotion through health personnel while reducing mass media advertising.

In the USA in early 1976 church shareholders began to pressure US companies (Bristol Myers and American Home Products). Two companies (Barden and Abbott) changed their promotional practices. In mid-1977 the Infant Formula Action Coalition was formed to begin a national US campaign including a boycott of Nestlés' products. In May 1978 Senate hearings began to investigate the behaviour of American formula companies.

Meanwhile, in September 1977 the Papua New Guinea government set a precedent by passing legislation banning advertising of infant milk products and the sale of feeding bottles and teats without a prescription.

In October 1979 the World Health Organisation and UNICEF convened a four-day meeting of company representatives, national governments, action groups, health workers and UN bodies at which it was recommended that a code of ethics for the marketing of infant formulae be established. The meeting was declared 'a remarkable concession for an industry like ours' by one representative, though no code was adopted and most companies continue to defy the recommendations put forward by the meeting.

During consultation in February 1980, the infant food industry submitted the following proposals to WHO and UNICEF. They virtually ignored the October meeting's recommendations by:

(1) advocating mass media advertising of an 'educational' nature (October meeting: 'There should be no sales promotion . . .');

(2) permitting company personnel to give demonstrations and lectures to mothers, advocating free sample distribution to health staffs and in some cases directly to mothers (October: 'Facilities of the health care system should never be used for the promotion of artificial feeding');

(3) allowing numerous forms of promotion to the medical profession (October: 'Promotion to health personnel should be restricted to factual and ethical information').

At the close of the October 1979 meeting, activists from the Third World, Europe and the US formed the International Baby Foods Action Network to co-ordinate research monitoring, and resource development worldwide. At this year's World Health Assembly, the statement and recommendations of the 1979 meeting were endorsed, and the Director-General of WHO was empowered to continue working on the code. This will be presented to the 1981 World Health Assembly for final ratification.

But what, if any, changes have been made?

Malaysia, November 1979: Nestlés catered for the Infant Nutrition conference in Kuala Lumpur, hiring ten attractive women to serve refreshments, wearing aprons with 'Nestlés' written across the breast.

Western Samoa, November 1979: The Managing Director of Glaxo (British) admitted that his company would not abide by the WHO/UNICEF recommendation to halt direct consumer advertising.

Pakistan, January 1980: Glaxo newspaper ads promoted Glaxo bottle feeds.

Such examples of promotional tactics occurring since the October 1979 meeting do not encourage optimism. Certainly the fight is not over. What, then, has a decade of consumer awareness and action achieved?

The fact that the issue reached WHO and UNICEF and that for the first time non-governmental organisations were full participants alongside national governments, experts and UN agencies can be seen as a unique, precedent-setting recognition of the role to be played by consumer activists. More importantly, the meeting showed that forceful consensus exists 'in support of strong measures restricting the marketing activities of the infant food industry.'

The industry should stop pushing infant milk products and co-operate

289

in developing low-cost weaning foods. Even in undernourished mothers, the quality of breast milk remains remarkably high, so any 'supplementary feeding' should be aimed at lactating mothers rather than their babies. Third World governments need international support in controlling the influence of commercial companies, through such means as placing products on a prescription-only basis (as in Papua New Guinea), nationalising infant food industries or imposing import or price restrictions. At the same time, government programmes actively promoting breast-feeding are essential.

Britain: Oxfam is encouraging its local groups and supporters to take up the baby food campaign by lobbying MP and health workers about the code of marketing. The UK Baby Milk Action Coalition has begun to put shareholder pressure on Glaxo, and a British Nestlés Boycott Campaign with supermarket leafletting has begun.

Australia: Australian baby food groups are monitoring hospital sampling practices with estimates that 80–90% of the country's small hospitals give samples to all mothers (mostly Nestlés and Wyeth). The February 1980 issue of the Australian Consumers Union magazine exposed the Australian Dairy Corporation's involvement in the marketing of sweetened condensed milk as a baby food in Asia. Research is about to begin into the infant feeding situation among Aboriginal communities.

Research and action goes on as well in Panama, South Africa, USA, Kenya, West Germany, Canada, Japan, Holland, Norway, Switzerland and Malaysia. As a joint action, Oxfam, War on Want and Infant (US group) have circulated a questionnaire to contacts in Third World countries asking about: types of baby food promotion; breast feeding practices; and any government action being taken.

Warning: breast-feeding may be hazardous
Mary Phelan
SR 134 September 1983

Breast-feeding went out of vogue for at least a generation, especially in the United States and Britain, and has only seen a revival during the past 20 years. Women who wanted to breast-feed often attempted it in a hostile environment – in hospitals nurses and doctors were often unhelpful and pushed the bottle, in public breast-feeding mothers often met disapproval in parks, restaurants and stores. Even at home some men were jealous, feeling that 'their' breasts had been taken over by the baby. Many women, themselves inundated with images of breasts as the embodiment of female sexuality, rejected breast-feeding.

Feminists support women wanting to breast-feed. They also oppose Baby formula companies attempt to break down traditions of breast feeding in Third World countries in order to market their goods for profits.

But breast-feeding is not a timeless or heavenly act and any woman who decides she does not want to breast-feed is not condemning her child to a bleak future, as some breast-feeding proponents imply. Women must have information in order to make the choice which suits them best. This article looks at the way environmental toxins affect women's breast milk. Toxins affect most of what we eat and drink and this should be remembered when weighing up the possible dangers of breast-feeding.

The last couple of years has seen a revival of interest and enthusiasm in breast-feeding. It therefore comes as quite a shock to realise that breast milk has been proved in many countries to be highly contaminated with many of the chemicals which pollute our present-day environment. It has been established without doubt that several highly toxic chemicals are passed via a mother's bloodstream on into her milk and that these toxins, known to be responsible for miscarriages, birth defects and cancer, are found in concentrations high enough to give cause for serious concern.

Toxins are absorbed from the environment and through the food chain, and are then stored in the fat cells of the body. These are the very cells which are mobilised in the body of a lactating woman for the production of breast milk.

In the USA, as far back as 1951, DDT in excess of the level permitted by the World Health Organisation (WHO) was found to be present in 94% of the human milk samples tested. These concentrations were found in human milk tested apparently regardless of geographical location or population size.

In 1976, another study, undertaken by the USA Environmental Protection Agency, showed that the milk of virtually all American mothers is likely to contain detectable levels of polychlorinated biphenyls (PCBs) and in such quantities that the average level present would give nursing infants 'seven times the amount permitted in cows' milk by the Food and Drug Administration'. Similar figures have been reported from other parts of the world including Norway, Australia, Holland and Canada. And what about Third World countries where breast-feeding is often a necessity, not a 'choice', for the survival of babies?

In 1981 a number of breast-feeding women in Freiburg, in southern Germany, worried by results of German research, sent samples of their own milk to be chemically analysed at the university research centre. Their milk was found to be contaminated with the following toxic chemicals:

HCB hexachlorbenzene
Environmental sources: 92% from industrial wastes, oils, etc.; 8% from fungicides.
Potential health effects: can deform the foetus in pregnant women; liver and kidney damage.

HCH hexachlorcyclohexane
Environmental sources: agricultural and domestic insecticides, wood preservatives, detergents.

Potential health effects: carcinogenic (cancer-causing); damages liver, kidneys and immunisation system.

DDT
Environmental sources: pesticides.
Potential health effects: liver damage; long-term reproductive effects; proven to be carcinogenic to animals.

Heptachlorepoxide
Environmental sources: highly toxic pesticide with very long life:
Potential health effects: carcinogenic, also a nerve poison.

PCBs – Polychlorinated biphenyls
Environmental sources: until very recently contained in varnishes, glues, softeners, pesticides, flame retardants, carbonated paper. Major current use in the electricity supply industry – transformers, etc. Have a very long life and present as a global contaminant at present time due to large range of uses in the past.
Potential health effects: cancers; birth defects; affects metabolism and nervous system.

Traces of **heavy metals** were also discovered.

On the basis of internationally recognised 'acceptable daily intake' values these women should not have been breast-feeding their babies at all, so highly contaminated was their milk. If their breast-milk were sold as infant food, or indeed as normal drinking milk, it would have been withdrawn from the market because of the high levels of toxic residues.

In many places it has been officially suggested that women stop breast-feeding altogether in the light of this disturbing data. And among those women who have the financial choice or conditions to be able to, many have. Among the Freiburg women however, many didn't want to stop feeding their babies.

Groups were set up all over Germany to alert women to the dangers discovered. Concerned mothers have held a protest outside the European Parliament in Strasbourg with the slogan, 'Breast milk, the newborn's first human right', and although their fears and their anger have been noted, very little concrete action has been taken.

The women in Freiburg are, understandably, not willing to wait for years and years until these dangerous substances have been banned. The groups they have inspired throughout Germany demand an immediate end to the production and use of all toxins that endanger the human body; a total ban on the import of all goods containing these substances; that the chemicals contained in all products must be accurately listed; that their producers must be obliged to prove that they present no threat to human health and well-being; that agriculture be immediately reorganised along biologically correct lines; and that the state subsidise such a reorientation.

It is obvious that it's not breast-feeding itself, but the contaminating chemicals which are currently threatening the most basic form of human nurturance which should be examined. The dismaying fact that toxins are currently being recorded in breast milk is an unambiguous indication of the extent to which our world has been poisoned and the ultimate indictment of current political, industrial and agricultural practices.

How can we support our sisters?
Editorial
SR 92 March 1980

If we are allowed to hear of clitoridectomy at all, it is as the custom of faraway tribal people. Our horror and anger are set at a distance; we are taught to see 24 million circumcised women as victims living in some unimaginable Dark Age, not sisters in exploitation. Yet the last known clitoridectomy in the west was performed as recently as 1953, in Kentucky, on a girl of 12. The operation was popularised in the nineteenth century by a British doctor, Baker Brown, as a cure for 'hysteria' – autonomous sexual desire, leading to every other form of rebellion and 'moral leprosy' in a woman. The mortality rate from Baker Brown's operations was high, but not once did the medical profession oppose his right to kill a patient. He was finally expelled from the BMA for advertising, and for performing surgery on one woman without her husband's permission. But the operation went on, and reached obscene variations within the American Orificial Surgery Society, whose hatred and prurience towards the female genitals make truly frightening reading.

Today the same doctors might be performing brain surgery. Chemical and physical lobotomy are our cures for female 'hysteria'. In Arab societies, the word is 'fitna' – sexual disruption – and the cure is clitoridectomy. The west has its purely sexual mutilations too: almost half the hysterectomies in the US are now performed not from proven medical need but 'in case' something might later go wrong with a womb that is seen as disposable. (One quarter of all North American women over 50 have lost their wombs.) There are also the routine episiotomies to facilitate a quick convenient delivery for the doctor, often with horrible side-effects which last for years; the 'voluntary' facelifts, and the breast implants that have caused women's deaths.

At this moment, a Dr James Burt from Ohio is making a fortune with a new form of sexual surgery. 'He has developed a $1500 "reconstruction" of women which changes the angle of vaginal access so that during intercourse the penis stimulates the clitoris.' In doing so, he mutilates a major muscle, creates a high risk of infection and incontinence, makes unaided childbirth impossible and forces the woman to remain underneath at all times during intercourse to experience her newly constructed vaginal orgasm. These are our modern, progressive versions of clitoridectomy . . . new aspects of that long hatred of women's bodies stretching back to our segregation in the tribal menstrual hut and the Christian churching services to rid us of the 'filth' of childbirth.

In finding parallels, we are not saying that oppression is everywhere the same. We do not suffer the agonies of a Sudanese woman undergoing circumcision, but we are part of the same system. When we met Nawal el Saadawi last year, she spoke about what she called the psychological clitoridectomy of women in the west: 'Sometimes you think you are free, but still you are not free' – how many western women do not even know that they *have* a clitoris? Some of the feminists she'd met abroad had seemed to miss connections – not only between Arab women's oppression and their own, but between Arab women's oppression and the conditions of their countries as a whole. Women like Saadawi cannot afford to separate their fight against clitoridectomy from the deliberate 'underdevelopment' and near-starvation of most communities where it's practised. Nor should we.

So far moves against clitoridectomy have come mainly from progressive doctors, health workers and psychiatrists, in Third World countries and the US, putting pressure on international bodies like the World Health Organisation. For a long time these organisations have resisted making any commitment to change in this 'sensitive area' of 'traditional custom' – while seeming to feel no worries about other modernising moves like campaigns for sterilisation, or for replacing breast milk with the powdered milk marketed by multinationals which has caused so many infant deaths.

The conference on Traditional Practices affecting the Health of Women at Khartoum in Feburary 1979 was a turning point. A resolution was passed condemning clitoridectomy and urging campaigns for its abolition in all the countries of Africa and the Middle East where it is now performed. Within the conference there was a battle between those who wanted the practice stopped altogether and those who wanted to 'clean it up', bringing it into the hospitals to be done in sterile conditions and under a local anaesthetic. This is already beginning to happen in some cities, and could lead to clitoridectomy becoming even more firmly entrenched, as hospitals would have a vested interest in keeping it going. Fortunately those who absolutely opposed the operation won at Khartoum.

But the future fight will be difficult. It is overwhelmingly women who perform the operation. Esther Ogunmodede, a Nigerian nurse, has written in *Drum* magazine: 'Most African women have been through it but if the truth were known none would thank their well-meaning relatives for the deed. Why then do we subject our own daughters to the same horrors?' As everywhere, mothers have to teach their girl children chastity and submission in order to survive. The main opponents of clitoridectomy at the moment are among the educated elite – people influenced by western ideas, people who have studied western medicine. It is in the villages that people cling to the practice, particularly the women. And with good reason. In the Sudan, for example, a public health education campaign with support from the government has succeeded in moving public opinion against the cruelties of infibulation. But now reports are surfacing that men in the more modern villages have started to pass over the infibulated women of their own age and look for a younger girl to marry, one who has undergone a less extreme operation.

As feminists we believe that societies can only be transformed willingly, from the grass roots, if change is to be deep and lasting. While we oppose clitoridectomy, there may be other rural traditions of women that we would support against western influences and would hope to learn from ourselves. For instance, we oppose the way western medicine interferes with female control of childbirth. It seems clear, too, that decrees from above are often ineffective. In India the government abolished child marriage and the dowry by law, but they still exist in practice; with their deep roots in the social system, they cannot be waved away on their own. Clitoridectomy too fits in with a whole social system, denying female sexual pleasure to ensure the safe inheritance of male property and the continuance of women as an essential part of that property.

But Esther Ogunmodede points to the abolition of tribal scarring as an example of what can be done. She sees the most effective way to fight as a broad-based health campaign. First and foremost, it must be pointed out that clitoridectomy and infibulation kill – young girls die from loss of blood and septicaemia, mothers die in childbirth and their babies die too. Innumerable other women are crippled for most of their lives. In some parts of Africa the health campaign has already begun with caravans going round rural areas showing displays, leaflets and tapes.

In the meantime, some women are already making their own fight. This account comes from Mali: 'When my daughter was 5, she said to me, "Mama, I'm not like the others. I want to be circumcised." She cried and pleaded with me. So I bought all that was needed, the black loincloth and so on. I picked her up, told her to sit with her legs apart and be brave. I pinched her clitoris very hard and pressed a very cold blade against it and told her, "There you are, it's done." Now she is 23 and knows she is not actually circumcised, and can think about the question as an adult.'

Now women are breaking through from these isolated acts of resistance and organising in the open. The Women's Federation of Upper Volta is an inspiring example, taking on their own government as well as the force of traditional opinion. What can we do in support? One western feminist campaign has been underway since 1973, when Fran Hosken began her long work of research, discussion and organisation around clitoridectomy. Her strategy is to put pressure on the international agencies – the UN, WHO, UNICEF, the International Planned Parenthood Federation. A small but militant demonstration calling for the Khartoum decisions to be implemented by UNICEF was held in New York this winter by a group called Women Against Mutilation. Since UNICEF and the other bodies are western funded and staffed, what they do is very much our business. At the same time, Third World women have reason to be suspicious of these agencies. In the name of education, health and modernity they have often introduced dangerous drugs like Depo-Provera, or farming techniques that oust women from their traditional hold on the land. We want to force changes in these areas too if our outrage over our sisters' mutilation is to become part of a great movement of solidarity.

Spare Rib decided it was important for us in Britain to have more contact with the people working against clitoridectomy *inside* the countries where it is performed. We hope that by writing to these sisters we shall learn all the different ways they may want us to support their struggle.

Against circumcision
Efua Graham
SR 161 December 1985

Only five years ago, it was practically impossible to hold a meaningful discussion on the issue of the sexual mutilation of African girls in and outside Africa.

Since 1980, however, grassroots work on the issue has been progressing remarkably, albeit at non-governmental level, in countries where there was a dead silence on the issue, e.g. in Ethiopia, Nigeria, Ghana, the Gambia and Djibouti.

The Foundation for Women's Health Research and Development (FORWARD) which became a part of the African network on Detrimental Practices on Mother and Child, is presently supporting work in Ghana and the Gambia. Recently the Department of Health and Social Security in the UK has made a significant contribution towards FORWARD's programme of education and counselling of mothers in the UK against circumcision of girls, as a back-up to recent legislation banning such operations. For the first time in five years, FORWARD will be able to have a fully backed team of workers to take information properly to mothers.

Non-governmental organisations (NGOs) have helped in this development. For example, a *sister-to-sister* programme introduced by FORWARD provides an avenue for cross-cultural exchange of views on a variety of themes on development, and support for the campaign against female circumcision. Through its quarterly development publication *Sister Links*, African and British women are learning from each other.

The practice of circumcision is a huge problem and thousands, if not millions, of girls are cut each year. We need not just NGO action but pressure on governments to take specific action against the problem. This pressure may come from the United Nations Human Rights Commission which has just completed a report on the subject. Again NGOs with consultative status with the UN Human Rights Commission have been instrumental in preparing the report.

AN IMBALANCE WITH MOTHER EARTH: An interview with Winona La Duke
Ruth Wallsgrove
SR 90 December 1979

'In 1974 the International Indian Treaty Council was formed to bring the issues of our survival as the indigenous peoples of North and South America to the United Nations, and to talk to other liberation movements and indigenous peoples in the same situation. Working within the Council, we realised we needed something for just the women – a network between the women at home or working on the reservations or doing our organising work, but also between us and the women's community internationally. For us it's really important to realise how *attacked* indigenous women are – what it means that one quarter of Native American women living in the United States are sterilised, that one out of every three Native American children is taken from its home and put into a non-Indian foster home, that there's an increase in breast, uterine and cervical cancer attributed to radiation from uranium. The women have to have a way to voice what is happening to us, within the context of our liberation as nations.

'Under our treaties with the United States government we're guaranteed certain things – rations if we can't get the food we need through gathering or growing it, health and education facilities. We're not in control of any of those things – the government is. Their Indian Health Service is responsible for sterilising Indian women. A study done in 1976 by Senator Abouresk found that in one series of five hospitals in Oklahoma 3,406 women were sterilised in two years – the youngest had been 14. You have to understand that a lot of Indian women don't read English – they speak it, but we have an oral tradition, so they don't read. They didn't know what the forms were. A lot of women have been having a child and were drugged; they were told to sign a form they thought was to get them out of the hospital. Or else they'd go in for another operation and were sterilised then. On the Cheyenne Reservation almost 50% have been sterilised.

'We've been trying to get some justice from the United States for 200 years, and you just can't. There were a couple of cases taken to court where it was found that the woman had been sterilised and had her children taken away against her will, but there were still said to be "socio-

297

economic" reasons to take them away – that means you're poor and not white.

'Under international law we are sovereign nations; but the United States has so effectively colonised us that very few people understand that. Few people even know that there *are* Indians any more. Where we live, it's like islands; they keep us isolated, and there's no press on the reservations. There's no way to get word out about what's going on there. So they can basically do whatever they like to us. We used to be under the Department of War – now we're under the Department of the Interior, who manage rights over fish and game. They treat us like animals.

'What is central to our lives is the land, and we don't have much of that left – 4% of our original land base. We're sitting on two-thirds of the uranium and one-third of the coal in North America, so they want to take the rest of our land away. Mining destroys the land, and so it destroys us.

'The first place in the US they found uranium was in the South West, where the Navajo and Pueblo people live. They started mines there in 1952 and 1953. The companies and the government told the Bureau of Indian Affairs – our Great White Father! – and the tribal councils (installed to the approval of the Department of the Interior) that there were good jobs in mining uranium. Navajo and Laguna Pueblo Indians worked in the underground mines without ventilation. The companies ran the mines for 20 years and then they ran out of ore and moved out. They left the mine shafts and, on the Navajo land, 71 acres of mill tailings – that's the waste from the processing – sitting in the middle of the town. Uranium is in the water, it's in the air, it's in the land.

'Uranium gives off different kinds of radiation that cause cancer, leukaemia and birth defects – they could show up this generation or the next. But they have a lag time, and don't show up immediately. The Navajos didn't know what was happening until 1974, when 18 miners had died of radiation-induced lung cancer. 100 of the miners are being watched – and out of that 100, 25 are dead and 45 have lung cancer. And small children are showing up with leukaemia. Kerr McGee, the company found guilty of negligence in the poisoning of Karen Silkwood, has refused all responsibility, so it wouldn't pay any medical expenses. One spokesman said, "I couldn't tell you what happened at some small mine on an Indian reservation, we have uranium interests all over the world."

'A study done by the Senate said there have been 100 birth defects in the last five years at Laguna Pueblo – that operation is now the largest uranium strip mine in the western hemisphere and, we believe, in the world. Now in the one area of the Navajo Reservation there's 36 uranium mines, six mills, six abandoned mills, five coal strip mines, and they also want to make a national nuclear disposal site there. There's one word for what they're doing there – genocide.

'In July this year there was a spill at one of the uranium mills, and 100 million gallons of radioactive water spilled into this Navajo community.

The company (United Nuclear) and the government never bothered to tell the people – they heard it on the radio. They can't eat their food, they can't drink their water. The company hasn't cleared it up yet – they don't know how. It's going all the way to the Gulf of Mexico but there's been total censorship on the press.

'I work with the American Indian Environment Council. We talk with the anti-nuclear movement, to make them understand that for us it's not a one-issue thing. They're beginning to understand – but for the American people, it's very scary to have to think about Indians. First thing is, it doesn't matter to us whether it's uranium or coal that's mined. Uranium and coal are contained in the same geological formations, so when you take out one, you take out the other. When they burn coal, there's uranium in it, it's sent into the air, so you breathe it in anyway.

'But what's really basic is that we're talking about centralised, highly profitable, highly technological energy systems controlled by an elite group of men that sit in their little skyscrapers and make decisions for everyone. They have effectively programmed all of the people – in Europe it's the same – to think we have to depend on these companies, that we should leave it to technology and the corporate state. But the corporate state doesn't have anything in mind but its own interest.

'The American Indian Movement is talking to our people, so that they understand that what is about to happen is the final genocide. We have 'survival' schools, run by and for Indians, where they teach children about our languages, religion and culture, and the basics of economic planning for self-sufficient reservations. We're also setting up co-operatives, so that we don't have to eat the food the government gives us. It contributes to the 85% malnutrition on the reservations, the basics being white flour, grease, coffee, and white sugar. You can't fight unless you're feeding yourselves, that's pretty basic. But after we've fought things at all levels of the state and region, we're often left with no recourse. That's why Wounded Knee happened (when a group occupied the trading post on their reservation in 1973). They had tried every other thing they could think of to stop that trading post from ripping them off. I'm definitely not against, I don't know what you'd call it, armed struggle. Because when all you've got left is 4% of your land, you've got to stand up for it.

'What we're fighting for is to have self-determination of our land and our future. We want to return to a way that's as non-exploitative as possible. It's called "walking in balance on mother earth" – it's very simple.

'It's taken women a long time to say why nuclear power is a women's issue. We are the first affected by it, and that's why we have to take it real personally. I speak a lot at anti-nuclear rallies – I get up there and I'm (1) the only woman and (2) the only non-white – they get two birds with one stone! Women have got to demand that we speak, because men are doing all the talking at the moment. We have a saying – Women are the backbone, and men are the jawbone; and it's true in every society.

299

I'm not saying that we should be the jawbone, but that men be a little more of the backbone.'

Nuclear horror in the Pacific
Tsehai Berhane-Selassie
SR 153 April 1985

Two indigenous women from the Pacific are now touring Britain, campaigning against nuclear testing and nuclear waste dumping. Their first public meeting was at a press conference on 1 March in the House of Commons, on Bikini Atoll Day commemorating the 31st anniversary of the Bravo nuclear test at Bikini in the Marshall Islands, Micronesia. On 1 March 1954, despite weather reports that winds were blowing towards inhabited islands, the US exploded its largest above ground hydrogen bomb at Bikini, severely contaminating 1,600 Marshalese, 28 US servicemen and 23 Japanese fishermen and producing a lethal cloud which eventually encircled the globe causing worldwide fallout. Over the past 40 years, 250 nuclear tests have been exploded in the Pacific, causing thyroid cancers, miscarriages, birth deformities and other severe health problems.

Chailang, a Chamorro woman from Saipan, spoke about the 2,000 old Micronesian islands, where the US has been carrying out their atmospheric and underground tests. The French and the British too have been carrying out tests more recently. The Japanese are dumping nuclear waste without any hesitation about life in the islands. Speaking with feeling she said: 'We are islanders, and we eat fish . . . once they contaminate the seas our lives are threatened.' Titewhai Harawira, a Maori woman from Aoteaora (New Zealand) added: 'We are like dogs . . . like guinea pigs . . . One hundred and fifty years ago, my ancestors signed a treaty with your people, to respect my land, forestry, fishing and people. That has not been honoured. . . . In the Pacific, we are people too; you should not carry out your nuclear tests on us. . . . We want to be independent from that.'

Both women pointed out that the women's movement in the Pacific derives its strength from their determination to expose the nuclear warfare that is actually going on now in the region; the number of their membership does not matter that much. Both women have very strong grassroots support, despite the fact that the islanders have been subjected to racist abuse by the US army, which in a press statement in 1946, said: 'The natives are delighted, enthusiastic about the atomic bomb which has already brought them prosperity and a new promising future.'

The talks Chailang and Titewhai gave were augmented by a slide-tape presentation which showed horrific scenes of islands disappearing from the face of the earth, people being removed by force, children born deformed, people losing their hair and skin, etc. Chailang pointed out that the people have been made dependent on US food stamps, and parts of their lands have been rendered unusable because of long-buried bombs.

Peace campaigners in Britain see a link between themselves and the experiences of the Pacific islanders as 'we share concern about US bases and missiles' and grass roots protest against these and Britain's multinational, neo-colonial interests in the Pacific. The visit of the two women has generated useful exchange and dialogue.

Famine in Ethiopia
Tsehai Berhane-Selassie
SR 146 September 1984

The frequency and number of births by Third World women has been a matter of concern to many observers. Some organisations such as Population Concern and the UN Food and Agricultural Organisation even blame the present food crisis in Africa on the increasing size of the population. The crisis is so acute that in more than 20 African countries emergency food aid camps are already set up by governments and foreign non-governmental organisations (NGOs). Women constitute the majority of those who come to these camps. Women and their children are dying in their thousands because of the famine the causes of which are more complex than the mere number of population.

British NGOs have just launched a campaign to raise funds to help starving people in Africa, and in documentaries shown on television some of the causes behind the famine were brought out. The Ethiopian famine was used to illustrate the gravity of the problem as well as highlight some of these causes. Drought over an extended period of time and warfare which has been going on for more than two decades have greatly hampered the process of food production in the whole region of North East Africa. The Ethiopian government spends the bulk of its energy and financial resources on war efforts, fighting against Somalia in the south east and trying to suppress rebellions in most of its northern territories. The guerrilla warfare in the north is, by its nature, designed to create incessant pressure without giving victory to either side. In that part of Africa, therefore, peasants, especially women, children and the aged, live in a man's world of the battlefield, where crop cultivation takes second place. The fertility of women has very little to do with the problem of famine in that area.

Nevertheless government, NGOs and guerilla leaders are trying to do all they can to help the victims of famine. British NGOs working in the region are caught in a dilemma as to which side is best for channelling aid to the most needy. For, as Oxfam put it, 'damned if you do and damned if you don't'. Women and peasants generally need the help, and they do say so whenever they have the opportunity.

According to conflicting reports about five million people are affected by the famine in Ethiopia alone. Similarly large figures are quoted for other parts of Africa. A large part of Southern Africa is also affected because of the international conflict ensuing from the pressures exerted by the apartheid regime of South Africa.

In all regions women are reported to treat the early symptoms of famine like any other illness, so that they do not encourage 'families', which means themselves and their children, to seek food aid in time to save their lives. In Ethiopia, as elsewhere, by the time they arrive at the camps they are already at advanced stages of starvation, physically weakened and dying. One woman explained that even though she was able to acquire food from the emergency food camp she would not be able to return to her home because it would be too much for her to carry her three children and the food aid. She had travelled from a distance of 60 kms, and as her husband was dead, she alone was responsible for the children. Generally men are said to have migrated in search of employment long before the famine got worse, which is one explanation for the preponderance of women in the camps. Whether men escape the famine by running away is another question, but the women are left to bear all the responsibility. Migrant labour and single women parenthood is a familiar story in the states of Southern Africa. According to my own findings, in some parts of Ethiopia women are prevented by tradition also from using the plough or planting certain crops, so that when the men migrate cultivation of crops necessarily drops.

Both the present government and the rebel leaders are trying to change that tradition. The women follow suit, and sometimes they take the initiative to help themselves against all odds. Needless to say, they have not been able to prevent the wars; only the men involved can. Everyone is trying to acquire means of easing the additional problems that add to their misery.

CHAPTER 9

DISCUSSING CHILDBIRTH

Many women involved in the early years of the 'second wave' of feminism were already mothers of young children. From 1969, in small often local groups (later known as consciousness-raising groups), women got together to talk about their varied experiences of being female in a sexist society. For women who had found motherhood a contradictory and isolating experience, one which brought frustration and anger as well as joy, breaking through the image of perfect motherhood was a liberating relief.

Childbirth itself was often the first focus of our personal 'mother' stories. How was it for each of us? What had we expected? How were we treated? Did 'natural' childbirth work? Was home birth better than at hospital? Experiences differed: some women loved giving birth, others were shocked by the duration and pain of their labours. But whatever the variations, the indifference and arrogance of the medical profession drew us together. Treated like cattle, assumed to be unable to manage without the 'experts' ' control and interference, resentment and anger rippled near the surface.

A common refrain took shape as women saw more clearly how the medicalization of childbirth designated pregnancy as an illness, and therefore in need of doctors' care and control. Some women hankered after a total rejection of technology in childbirth, a return to a more 'natural' past. Others, not believing a return to the past was possible or desirable, wanted the possibility of support and help from the medical profession, not the powerlessness and alienation so often experienced in male-dominated hospitals.

These early concerns of many women involved in women's liberation, women in their twenties, mainly white and middle class in background, were not reflected strongly in the feature pages of *Spare Rib*. Except for an article on epidurals, nothing else on childbirth surfaced until a eulogistic appraisal of the childbirth methods of the French doctor Leboyer appeared. Women's experiences and feelings about birthing tended to figure primarily in the letters pages.

The first major article on childbirth was in *SR 36* and it forms the basis of this chapter. It's a sustained critique of 'painless' childbirth and a thought-provoking argument in favour of a new kind of hospitalization for birth. The article produced a flood of letters, a sample of which are reprinted here. Some writers were upset at what they saw as an attack on natural childbirth, others were inspired to write of their own experiences and develop their own opinions. Although later articles in *Spare Rib* have looked sympathetically at home births or individual women's good or bad experiences, this was the article which created the most response and which has stood the test of time.

More recently there has been a powerful resurgence of the natural birth movement, and an almost obsessive feminist interest in if, when, and how to have babies. But *Spare Rib* has not matched these developments with any major articles. Is it because it's a topic which has been taken up enthusiastically in many other magazines and books? Or is it an issue which patiently awaits a *Spare Rib* writer? Now the news pages carry regular reports on different aspects of childbirth, and the new 'Parenting' page gives a bit more space to the topic.

Birthpangs
Valerie Charlton and Annette Muir
SR 36 June 1975

Childbirth is in the news again. Almost every day there is an article in a magazine or newspaper on the latest developments. There was even a television programme ('Horizon') which graphically brought childbirth into the living room, scandalising us with the dangers of pain-killing drugs and induced births. A number of letters have been sent to *Spare Rib* from which we shall include points.

Medical opinion is divided about the advantages of certain drugs and 'aids' to labour. The research seems scanty and inconclusive. At the same time, the women's movement has given many women the confidence to question authority and the wish to make informed decisions for themselves. There are women who have had bad experiences in childbirth and rightly begin to look at ways in which the hospitals may have contributed towards this. Others, however, would go further and argue that births should take place at home. We want to look at these issues more closely.

When women talk about their childbirth experiences, the most noticeable fact is the wide variety of experiences they have had. They range from the fortunate woman who feels discomfort and some slight pain to the woman who is shattered and shocked by the birth. It would be useful if we could say that one particular characteristic of the hospital or the woman, for example, fear, made this difference – but clearly there is no such simple answer.

If we are going to talk about childbirth the question of pain is central. We *must* talk about pain. Many of us contribute towards a conspiracy of silence, partly because we think we may alarm expectant mothers, thus creating the anxiety which will make pain inevitable. This silence is no way to get the problem of pain in childbirth examined and a frank approach is long overdue. Quotes from two letters sent to *Spare Rib* show how pain can dominate the memory of giving birth.

'The pain I suffered when I had my two children was so terrible that I suffered nightmares for ages afterwards and even now, whenever I read or hear anything on this subject, I get terribly depressed.' Frances Sinfield.

'I didn't realise just how unbearable the pain was compared with other pains, until the day before my last baby was born. I had an accident where I spilled scalding hot liquid all down me. Yet, while suffering labour pains next day, I thought, "Goodness, the pain of having scalding hot water poured over you is nothing compared with this." ' C. D. Haines

Contrast this with another statement:

'Whatever the discomfort may be, do remember that it will never be allowed to become unbearable.' From *You and Your Baby* (Part 1), the British Medical Association Handout to all pregnant women.

In the absence of any survey of women's experiences in childbirth, we talked to some women we knew.

Sue

Sue had her baby in a large teaching hospital and, after attending ante-natal classes, was fairly familiar with the wards. At the classes she had been asked if she wanted an epidural anaesthetic. This is an injection into the spine which blocks off all sensation below the injection. During labour she had a medical student with her all the time. It was a short labour for a first baby, four hours, and at no time was the pain unbearable, although in fact she did not have the epidural as there was not enough time. She was given an episiotomy, a small cut in the pelvic floor given during the last stage of labour, but did not have too much discomfort. Her whole experience was happy.

Mary

Mary had a 'grim' first childbirth lasting 12 hours. The second was very quick, two hours, because she took castor oil. This can be a very dangerous thing to do. With her third child she was in labour for 16 hours, starting in heavy labour at 9a.m. After seven hours she was given the epidural which she had asked for repeatedly during her ante-natal visits to the hospital.

'I was numb from the midriff to the ankles. I let them know as soon as I felt it wearing off even slightly. I didn't wait for any pain. It was topped up three times at two-hourly intervals. I was sick every time but that wasn't too bad. They had to send for the anaesthetist each time and I was worried in case they'd take too long to get back as they had five casualties that evening. The contractions were monitored on a machine but I was also able to judge when to push, there was just enough sensation. When it was time to push, I only pushed twice and the baby came out. The labour was very long because the baby, although head first, was facing the wrong way.

'Although I had no pain I had nightmares for several nights afterwards.'

Mary was in a large London teaching hospital and had no complaints about the way she was treated. She said the doctor at the delivery spent half an hour talking to her afterwards.

Mary-Ann

Mary-Ann attended classes run by the National Childbirth Trust which teach psychoprophylaxis, the breathing and muscular exercises intended to help one keep control of one's body during labour.

'It turned out that I had a very difficult labour, ending in a caesarian. (This is an operation where an opening is made into the womb through the wall of the abdomen.) Despite my preparation and confidence I found it an ordeal and was quite shattered. I welcomed the caesarian at the time because it meant an end to the ordeal but, in retrospect, I'm very disappointed that I didn't give birth to the baby normally.'

Jane

Jane had taken the psychoprophylactic preparation for childbirth very seriously during a pleasant and relaxed pregnancy. She was in control during the first stage of labour but then the contractions weakened and a forceps delivery was necessary. Forceps are metal instruments about the size of a hand. With these the baby is pulled along the birth canal.

'I was first given an injection which felt as if it was being given from the inside. I felt it scrape against the bone and this was incredibly painful. I had an episiotomy which wasn't painful but as the forceps were put in I felt as if my bones were being pushed apart. The pain from there on until the baby was born was beyond description.'

We think it is important to take women's subjective experience very seriously. All too often doctors are dismissive of the woman's assessment of her own pain.

There is a school of thought which assumes that pain in childbirth is related to the attitude of the woman and is therefore controllable by her. This is the root of the natural childbirth theory as expounded by Dr Grantley Dick-Read. He thought that childbirth should be painless because it was a 'natural' function and he saw relaxation as the answer. But it worked for only a very small number of women.

Psychoprophylaxis, which we have already mentioned, is another method of preparation for childbirth but one which maintains that relaxation is not enough and advocates the learning of neuromuscular disassociation, which means keeping most of the muscles at rest while some are working. This is complemented by a series of controlled breathing exercises.

In neither method is 'pain' referred to as anything but that which is caused by resistance to the 'natural' function of childbirth on the part of the woman, be it due to ignorance or fear. The psychoprophylactic method as described in Erna Wright's book *The New Childbirth* is supported by a comprehensive description of the childbirth process, thereby attempting to remove the ignorance. But, to remove the fear, it relies heavily on the suggestion that pain will be minimised, if not removed, by careful following of the method.

Unfortunately, many women experience a degree of pain during even normal childbirth which is beyond relief by neuromuscular control or relaxation. The most disillusioned women we spoke to, and this in no way pretends to be a survey, were those for whom these methods had failed.

As we have repeatedly referred to pain we thought it necessary to look more closely at the nature of pain. It is a little understood phenomenon in spite of a great deal of research. We talk of people having different pain thresholds, assuming people to be phsyiologically different in this respect. Ronald Melzack in *The Puzzle of Pain* says that there is now evidence that all people, regardless of cultural background, have a uniform sensation threshold. This, however, only holds true in precisely controlled laboratory experiments in which all environmental conditions are kept constant. Once outside this situation the experience of pain can be affected by numerous other factors.

Pain is a highly personal, variable experience, influenced by cultural learning, the meaning of the situation, suggestion, etc. (It is also a highly complex physiological process.) However, whereas it is one thing to observe the complexity and power of these factors on pain perception, it is quite another to attempt to *control* pain by intervening at a psychological level only, especially when we don't even know how the central nervous system functions to permit such powerful psychological/cognitive control over bodily sensations of pain. There are simpler societies where suggestion may be more reliably used because it is supported by the whole culture and possibly religion. But we are the products of a diverse, fragmented and contradictory society and there is no way of knowing what forms of suggestion will work for each individual. But the preparation for childbirth methods which we described earlier are based on a notion that we can control pain in childbirth at a psychological level precisely because they assume the pain to be psychological in origin. This is particularly insidious for a woman because it puts the responsibility for pain squarely on her psyche.

Confusion may lie in assuming a function for pain rather than a cause.

'The National Childbirth Trust believes that pain is valuable to a woman who knows what it is for and is prepared to accept it.' 'The vital first hours' by Louise and Oliver Gillie, *Sunday Times*, 24 October 1974.

FIGURE 25 The waters breaking *Pen Dalton* (*SR 38* June 1975)

But what is it for? In a straightforward childbirth, pain fulfils no apparent purpose as it is not necessarily a warning of malfunction. Yet if we think of what is happening physiologically during childbirth it is not too hard to see why it is often a very painful process, be it 'natural' or not. It is indicative of the depth of sexism in our ideology, regarding motherhood, that so much confusion surrounds the question of pain in childbirth. Would the National Childbirth Trust say, for instance, that pain is valuable to a man with a broken leg if he knows what it is for and is prepared to accept it?

We must accept that, for the majority of women, childbirth is a phsyiologically painful process and that there is no virtue in suffering pain. Indeed, many women develop severe problems from having intensely painful experiences. Frances Sinfield, in her letter to *Spare Rib*, suggests that 'shock' after childbirth may be one of the main causes of post-natal depression.

With this in mind we now want to look at what drugs are available to most women who have their babies in hospital. There are two most commonly used painkillers, firstly, inhalation gas, of which there are three types. These will cut down sensory awareness but not usually produce unconsciousness. And secondly, pethidine or pethiliform which are injected and take about 20 minutes to become effective. Complaints about these vary widely. Some women were given them against their will and others were not given them when they were needed. The most important fact is that, according to a study by the Royal Post Graduate Medical School in London, pain relief with pethidine was only satisfactory for one in four women: there are women who enjoy these drugs and get quite high while others become confused and frightened and can hallucinate. So we cannot regard this as an answer to pain in childbirth.

The other method of anaesthesia which is becoming more widely available is the 'epidural block' which we have mentioned already. This completely numbs the lower part of the body and can produce a painless childbirth while the woman remains conscious. This is not yet offered in all hospitals because it requires the attendance of an anaesthetist. All the women we spoke to who had had epidurals were entirely satisfied with the result and it works for 90% of women. Sometimes, though, it may mean that a forceps delivery is necessary as the woman might not know when to push due to the reduced sensation.

The disadvantage of all these drugs, according to some members of the medical profession, is that they can enter the baby through the placenta and may make it sleepy and slow to suck. It is also suggested that this can jeopardise the relationship between mother and child. When the effects of the drug are by no means proved and the research is not totally convincing, we find these suggestions undermining and guilt-provoking for women who are being made to feel that relief of pain can only be at the cost of harming their baby. The long-term effects on a woman of a painful delivery could be far more important than a temporarily sleepy baby and it is far more likely, if this is the defining factor, that a woman who has had a painless delivery will have a good relationship with her child.

Another controversial issue is that of induction. For many years now

309

births have been induced for medical reasons. The methods most frequently used are the rupturing of the membranes (breaking the bag surrounding the baby) or the introduction of a hormone into the vein of the arm or hand by a drip over a period of hours. The snag is that the amount of hormone varies greatly from woman to woman and in any case is greatly in excess of that occurring naturally in the body during labour. If too much hormone is given the resultant labour may be very rapid and the contractions more painful. Obviously rupturing the membranes is preferable to the introduction of a hormone into the body, but it does not always start labour, hence the need for other methods.

More recently, some hospitals have started to induce labour for the convenience of the hospital and this practice has been widely attacked in newspapers and on television. If left to themselves the majority of babies are born at night, which is when hospital staff are more difficult to get and doctors often have to be woken up. Shortage of night staff can lead to the unfortunate situation of a woman being left on her own during labour.

As far as we could gather no hospital induced births for its own convenience against the will of the woman, although it must be said that for many women a suggestion from a doctor would be regarded as an order. The arguments in favour of convenience induction were put quite clearly by one woman we talked to. She wanted her husband to be present at the birth and there were only two dates when he could be off work, so she decided on which of these days she would have her baby. She also preferred a time when the hospital was less busy so that she could be assured of the best available attention.

Other aspects of a hospital confinement that worry some women arise from insensitivity or an unquestioning attitude to tradition on the part of the hospital staff. Some common complaints are that women are left alone and frightened during their labour, that the hospital staff fail to communicate with them, that they were given drugs against their will, that they were given no anaesthetic and were treated clumsily while being stitched up after an episiotomy. These criticisms must be taken very seriously by those who work in hospitals though low pay and consequent staff shortages put many doctors, nurses and hospital workers under unreasonable stress. Hospitals, like all the institutions in our society, reflect the patriarchal and class structure. Nowhere could this be clearer than in the rigid hierarchy of the National Health Service. Inevitably, in this situation, women, especially working class women, will be prey to sexist and class attitudes.

In response to these difficulties in hospitals some people are now suggesting a return to home confinements, thus reversing a trend to hospital confinements.

'The whole process of childbirth today has been taken away from the women who actually bear the children into the clinical world of male obstetricians, and it is getting progressively harder for a normal healthy

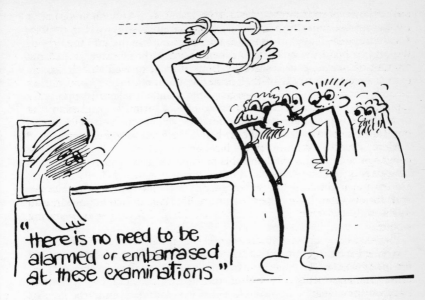

FIGURE 26 Examination time *Pen Dalton* (*SR 38* June 1975)

woman to experience a normal, healthy childbirth.' Christine Beales to *Spare Rib*.

'For the 80 to 90% of women whose pregnancy is normal, the experience of childbirth could be a much more natural one. Obstetrics has never been very much interested in normal childbirth – which has always been left to the midwives – but has concentrated on the pathological. The result is that by degrees normal childbirth in hospital has become pathologised.' 'The vital first hours' by Louise and Oliver Gillie, *Sunday Times*, 24 October 1974.

These two statements indicate the thinking behind the movement towards more home confinements. What is most worrying however is the assumption that a 'normal' birth can be predicted. This is certainly not the case. A birth can only be described as 'normal' after the event. The following description of an intended home confinement shows what can happen.

Ann

Ann had made all the arrangements for a home confinement for her first baby, but because she had a haemorrhage, she was taken into hospital as an emergency case. The bleeding was caused by the placenta partially

311

covering the entrance to the womb. Had it been a total covering, a caesarian section would have been necessary. There was no way of predicting this during what had been a normal, healthy pregnancy. She was discharged from an overcrowded hospital 12 hours after the induced birth, to the care of the midwife whom the hospital had failed to notify and who could not be contacted until the next day.

'It was then the panic set in. I felt desolate and totally unsupported. I had no idea what to do with this tiny baby. I hadn't even tried to feed him. Eventually the midwife did come, but never at the time she said because she was needed at other deliveries. Although she was very good when she did come, she was just too busy.'

At that time in that city no woman under 30 could have her baby in hospital unless complications were expected.

Sometimes proponents of home confinements say that domiciliary midwives, free of the atmosphere of the hospital, will be more sympathetic. But:

'I was determined to have my second baby at home. However, the midwife treated me terribly. She forgot the gas and air (until the last ten minutes). She forgot the pills and injections I was supposed to have and was only able to give me one injection. She told me afterwards I wouldn't have found it so bad if she'd been able to give me another injection towards the end. She left me when I was about to give birth to go and collect the gas and air from her house a few miles away. I was holding back waiting for her to return, which of course made the pain worse. She herself administered the gas and air in the last ten minutes. She kept pressing it over my face so making it difficult for me to push.'

This whole area of discussion touches on the difficult question of freedom of choice as it is organised that we should be able to choose between a hospital or home confinement. But when we demand freedom of choice we have to remember we live in a class society and that freedom of choice for one individual may limit the choice of others.

In practice, when we demand the right to home confinements, what assumptions are we making? (Incidentally, we could also discuss the right to a hospital confinement that is denied to women in some parts of the country.) We are assuming adequate home conditions, someone to help the mother, sufficient midwives and a back-up emergency service. The first two conditions are far more likely to be satisfied by those women with higher incomes. As in similar situations in education, when a service is used more by vocal, better-off people, that service is improved at the expense of others. It is necessary to improve the conditions for *all* women. Home confinements may be preferable to confident, leisured women, but we cannot improve facilities generally without medical technology and for this we need hospitals.

There is an element of back-to-nature and away from medical technology about the arguments for home confinements. But in societies with few hospitals and little medical care, childbirth remains a hazardous business. Undoubtedly, hospitals with all their faults are the safest places in which to give birth. For this reason we think we should press for improvements in hospitals rather than support a move towards more home confinements.

If hospitals fail to reach our needs, the reasons are political, and the lack of development of satisfactory medical technology for women in childbirth is an indication of the power of the sexist ideology which dominates this whole area, completely exposing the way society *really* views impending motherhood. The following quotes are taken from the British Medical Association handout *You and Your Baby* and the leaflet for *Expectant Fathers* by the National Childbirth Trust.

'Of course she will think of clothes and what women wouldn't. . . .'

'A woman should continue to take meticulous care of her appearance during pregnancy, this is a wonderful time in a woman's life and a happy woman is a beautiful woman. Conversely in the first few months she may feel off colour, but at such a time carefully applied make-up and a new hair-do proves a tremendous morale booster, and the end result is appreciated more than a little by the father to be.'

'Try to keep your feet as smart-looking as possible for a woman's appearance counts from the feet upward as much as from the head downwards.' BMA.

'One of the earliest signs of pregnancy, particularly in a girl who is having her first baby, is that her breasts change in appearance in a subtle and beautiful way.' BMA.

(For expectant fathers:)

'A woman is inclined to link the big moments in her life with clothes so when she is going to have a baby her thoughts run on "little garments". . . Your wife may well be attracted by a pram that either looks like her neighbour's or is the exact opposite [!] depending on whether she is an individualist or the reverse; it will be up to you to see that the brakes work and the handle is the right height for easy pushing. Don't forget that you may want to take your child out yourself sometimes!'

'Caring for a baby may have little in common with a manufacturing process but your wife's gratitude will repay you if you simplify feeding, bathing and cleaning routines with intelligent application of a little time and motion study.' NCT.

It is extraordinary that such generalisations are actually made about the way *all* women feel. Not only are women seen as frivolous creatures whose thoughts turn to clothes at the drop of a hat, but also as half-witted idiots. How can the nation trust the rearing of its children to such incompetents?

Diversion on to clothes and appearance has many effects. It distracts from fear and anxiety. It helps to make women see themselves as passive objects thereby ensuring their powerlessness, and also pregnancy, birth and childbirth provide a huge area of commercial exploitation. As long as women can be lulled into this 'cotton wool' view of pregnancy and

"breast feeding gives the mothers a fierce joy"

FIGURE 27 The joys of breast-feeding *Pen Dalton* (*SR 38* June 1975)

childbirth, the real work necessary to make childbirth a truly safe and painless experience need not be done and the doctors will go on wondering what on earth post-natal depression is all about.

We are intelligent, thinking beings and our expression of pain and distress must be taken seriously. This is a necessary condition for the application of medical science to the problem of pain in childbirth. The tendency to dismiss accounts of real pain as exaggerations or the complaints of neurotic women is found not only among the medical profession and those who have not had children, but also among women fortunate enough to have had an easy birth. There is an element, even among those who recognise the existence of pain in childbirth, of believing that 'women should bring forth children in suffering' in the true Judaic-Christian tradition, or alternatively, that one has to suffer for anything worthwhile. We reject these attitudes totally and think that it is the right of every woman to give birth painlessly.

Some complaints made by women arose out of this ideology but others were caused by unsatisfactory physical conditions in hospitals. In the main, these are caused by shortage of staff. Better pay and working conditions for hospital staff will remedy this and it is up to us to support the struggles that many hospital workers are already involved in to this end. We need to recognise that our interests coincide in many areas, for example the National Union of Public Employees (NUPE) present campaigns against paybeds in National Health hospitals.

We have covered some of the points usually raised by women when they discuss their childbirth experiences and inevitably this leads us to politics. At this time anything to do with the National Health Service is intensely political. Whereas it is necessary to criticise the NHS constructively, we must acknowledge that its existence is fundamental to a civilised society. We have tried to indicate practical areas of change but nothing can happen without change in the way women are viewed by society as a whole, which includes the way we view ourselves and each other.

Childbirth
Letters from *Spare Rib* Readers
SR 38 August 1975

HARD LABOUR
from Sue O'Sullivan

Dear *Spare Rib*,
I liked the article on childbirth in *SR 36*. The emphasis on the variety and validity of women's experience struck me as important. I'd like to add a few points.

My first child was born after approximately 30 hours of labour (not counting the first nine hours of 'little' contractions after the waters broke). What I felt so acutely during this long haul was that I was being worked to death by forces I had no control over. My serious application of psychoprophylaxis began to falter because of exhaustion and when I had hours of confusing transition (supposed to be a brief period in labour), I just wanted it over in any way. In fact I was knocked out and when I woke up started up again wherever I'd left off. In the end the actual delivery with forceps was nothing compared to the long struggle to get there, and my shock – and believe me it was shock – came mostly from the fact of literally being worked so hard by labour which *happens* whether you are in control, whether it 'goes well', or whatever. I think this idea of losing control is very important. My pre-labour idea was that I could face pain, discomfort, etc. if I knew what was happenimg and was 'on top of it' or in control of myself. In my case labour was a whirlpool in which I was unable to consciously control how I responded or even ride out for all my preparedness. My consciousness of myself as a distinct person was tossed in and sucked under.

When I finally had this first baby my pain came from dreadful cramps in one hip joint because my legs were hoisted up in stirrups. When I tried to explain I was totally ignored. They assumed I was complaining

315

about labour pains! In fact the doctor said to the students (oh yes, I had them feeling and standing around during the whole process), 'they always swear and shout at me but the next day they've forgotten it completely and before you know it are lining up to have another one.'

I had another baby two years later (without forgetting), and labour took in total about four easy hours. By the way, I really suffered from post-natal depression after the second 'easily' born child.

The other thing I wanted to raise was about home deliveries. In ideal conditions I guess every woman should have a choice of home or hospital but I tend to agree with the article that primary importance should be put on changing, improving and extending the facilities and attitudes in hospitals under the National Health. I had to insist on having a full eight-day stay in the hospital after my second baby was born. I was determined to take advantage of being in the hospital to rest, get a few nights' full sleep and not worry or feel guilty about *anything* at home. And my home situation is relatively supportive, secure and flexible.

With the exception of a few communes and women's houses, the home birth advocates, without actually saying so, rest their case on a 'happy family' base. Mum lies in her comfy, soft bed while loving, curious but considerate children, and adoring, helpful father, and kind, under-standing midwife, home-help etc., quietly circle around and do all the housework, cook the meals, etc. The mother lets them take care of her and they are knit together *as a family* by this wonderful experience. Well – maybe.

But what's all the stuff we talk about in the women's movement about families not necessarily being such simple, happy units? What about guilt, tensions, etc. – do they all magically disappear? If we have criticisms of the privatisation of 'family life' and particularly of women's place both in day-to-day life and in the way women are presented as being *in* families – defined by them, why this glorification of the 'happy' family at childbirth?

CASTOR OIL, EPIDURALS AND HOME BIRTHS
From Cindy Harris, trainee National Childbirth Trust teacher. Marianne Scruggs, trainee midwife

Dear *Spare Rib*,

We were very pleased to finally find an article which attempted to discuss women's subjective experience in childbirth, but we think you missed some vital points on the question of pain in labour.

Certainly doctors often underestimate and dismiss complaints from 'neurotic' women patients, but also very often, they will administer anal-gesia or barbiturates indiscriminately to women in labour irrespective of their own individual needs and occasionally against their wishes.

There are other specific points we would like to take up.

We think you are wrong in assuming that the various methods of natural childbirth interpret pain in labour as a purely psychological phenomenon. On the contrary it is generally recognised that it is necessary to cope physically with the physical (probably painful) process of giving birth. In this situation, pain can be increased by physical tension and decreased by controlled relaxation. Fear and ignorance do play a large part in the anticipation of unknown situations which, as you say, can 'raise the level of anxiety and thereby the intensity of perceived pain'.

On the question of epidurals and other painkillers, your article seems to give the kind of whitewash that is positively dangerous for a critical, sensitive women and health movement. A woman who has an epidural is virtually assured of a low forceps delivery which in turn leads to an increased risk of complications. Once intervention is begun, control is taken out of the hands of the mother and midwife; more intervention still becomes necessary – it becomes a doctor's procedure. Also you do not mention the possible harmful side-effects of epidurals, e.g. bad headaches which can last for days afterwards. It is important for women to realise that research on epidurals is only just underway and that in fact they may be serving unknowingly as research subjects.

There is a lot of evidence that pethidine and barbiturates given during labour do make for a sleepy baby. This can make breastfeeding extremely difficult and have a potentially very detrimental effect on the mother-child relationship. Many studies have shown the beneficial effects of immediate mother-baby contact, which is hampered by sleepy babies – and sleepy mothers! Induction for reasons of convenience, even if all the parties are willing, can hardly stand as a valid procedure given the increased risk of distressed premature babies, and the number of mothers who don't have a chance to control their own labours because of the increased strength and frequency of the contractions.

You gave a very distorted picture of home confinements by just noting one case in which something went wrong and the mother had to be admitted to hospital. In the vast majority of home confinements, the woman is confident and relaxed in familiar surroundings, the birth is normal and in many cases shorter than hospital births (many women's labours stop suddenly when they go into hospital).

Women should feel free to have their babies where they feel most secure. We in the women's movement should be backing a move towards home confinements for non-risk women (backed up by emergency flying squads) as part of the extension of women's freedom to choose. We must also give our wholehearted support to midwives who are gradually being undermined. Surely the answer is not for more women to deliver in hospital but for midwives to learn to be able to do more.

Please, no more of your reactionary thinking, *Spare Rib*.

CHAPTER 10

ADDICTING FORCES

In recent years, the increase in female addiction to alcohol and smoking has been the subject of concern in the popular press and media. Flurries of attention have been given to the huge numbers of women using tranquillizers and other doctor-prescribed psychotropic drugs. The addictive quality of these drugs was not recognized at first, and even now does not appear to have made much of a dent in their use or prescription. Most recently, heroin, as the 'evil scourge' of British youth, has hit the headlines.

For women, addiction to chemical substances often stems from the particular circumstances we are in – many of which are viewed as 'normal' and 'natural' for women. The rate of female addiction – to cigarettes, alcohol, 'hard' drugs and tranqs – is not decreasing. It is only among women, manual workers, and Black people, for example, that cigarette smoking is increasing.

In the United States there has been much more feminist discussion and action directed at *why* women drink, smoke, take drugs, and consequently there is a stronger move to provide support and promote 'substance-free' activities. In Britain it is still common to meet hostile resistance to 'smoke-free' feminist conferences or public socials.

In Britain we have not publicly addressed the particular problems of lesbian alcoholism. So far none of the articles published in *Spare Rib* do this. But clearly one of the reasons that American lesbians have 'come out' about alcohol is because of their analysis of the way in which lesbians are pushed into ghettoized pubs and clubs where alcohol is the social norm. They also recognize that the homophobia of their society is to one degree or another internalized by many lesbians; alcohol dulls that self-hatred. And it temporarily lifts the weight of a heterosexist world which presents such real danger to lesbians on so many levels.

When feminists write about addiction in *Spare Rib* it has often been to describe their own experiences, or those of someone close to them, and to try to understand it from the perceptions they have gained from feminism. However, for many women, breaking an unwanted addiction relies upon more than understanding its causes. For some, feminism and the existence of a women's liberation movement have provided both the basis for understanding *and* the possibility of being part of a collective movement for changing those causes.

Your money and your life: their profit
Bobbi Jacobsen
SR 148 October 1984

So you can stop smoking any time – and you're only a moderate smoker.

The classic woman smoker's defence. It's a view which stems from 40 years ago when 'ladies' were not supposed to indulge in unbecoming male habits. Yet today, teenage girls have caught up, and in many countries overtaken boys.

Today's young women are by no means moderate smokers. The most recent British survey showed that among 15-year-olds, girls have overtaken boys with nearly 30% smoking compared with just over 25% of boys. It is hardly surprising, then, that there has been a steadily rising female death toll in smoking-induced diseases. While lung cancer rates in women rise inexorably, and will soon overtake breast cancer – the biggest cancer killer in women – the peak of the epidemic is over for men.

Aside from the well-known big killers, smoking imposes further special risks for women. Women under 35 who smoke and also use the contraceptive pill are three and a half times more likely to die of a heart attack, blood clot in the veins, or certain kinds of stroke than non-smoking, non-pill users. The older you get and the more you smoke, the bigger the risk. If you don't smoke, are under 35, and take the pill, the risk is very low. If you smoke you *multiply* the risk.

The risk of smoking and the pill is quite different from the long-term risks of lung cancer which occur predominantly in older people. The casualties of the pill and smoking – although fewer in total – are among *young* women who are often under 40.

New evidence is mounting that smoking may play a role in causing cancer of the cervix which kills 2,000 women each year. Smoking, of course, is only one of the many factors implicated in cancer of the cervix. Unlike lung cancer, it is a disease which can be completely cured if caught at the pre-cancerous stage when you have a smear test. But if stopping smoking helped to prevent it, it seems worth a try. It's probably easier to do than staying celibate – which is another factor that protects against cancer of the cervix!

It has been drummed into us for years that smoking in pregnancy can harm the unborn baby. Pregnant women who smoke are more likely to miscarry or produce a lighter, less healthy baby than non-smokers. Although smoking may not be one of the most important factors which can affect the unborn child, it does impose a real risk, and it makes sense to stop if you are planning a pregnancy. It makes even more sense to do it *for yourself* as well as for the baby.

So you're smoking the odd cigarette – but you'll never become a regular smoker.
If only this were true. More than 90% of children who smoke do so regularly, and 80% of these do not escape the pull of the cigarette in

319

adulthood. This is why cigarettes are so profitable. The tobacco companies know it is worth investing in your future ill-health. So much so that they have made young women a key 'market target', designing special women's brands such as Virginia Slims ('You've come a long way baby'), and more recently KIM, aimed deliberately at young women.

Their aim is to implant the notion that it is liberated to smoke. Cigarette dependence, empty pockets and ill-health are not my idea of emancipation. Will you really lose friends if you say no when they next offer you a cigarette? You may gain their respect as an independent thinker. Try it.

So you've chosen to smoke a low tar cigarette – and you're only a moderate smoker.

Your 'moderate smoking' can still cause lung cancer 20 years later, although the risk is reduced for low tar cigarettes. Did you know that smoking low tar cigarettes does *not* reduce your risk of heart attack? Naturally, the tobacco industry will do its best to persuade you to smoke low tar cigarettes – their biggest 'growth area' also aimed at women. And we kindly oblige with twice as many women smoking low tar cigarettes as men. Why swap one health risk for another when you can be free of both?

So you smoke 10 to 20 cigarettes a day – and you daren't stop

It is now well known that women often find it harder to stop smoking than men. Cigarettes fulfil different needs for women than for men. Women often smoke *instead of* expressing those prohibited emotions such as anger and frustration. Unlike men, most women have to deal with the double burden of home and family as well as paid work. Smoking for women is but one symptom of the stresses we must absorb. And so it is harder for us to stop smoking.

Young women, especially, are worried that if they stop smoking they will gain an unacceptable amount of weight. Unacceptable to whom? To a society that forces women to squeeze themselves like toothpaste tubes into a size 8? Ironically, men gain more weight than women when they stop and a third of women who give up actually *lose* weight. The secret of success is believing, like women who have stopped successfully, that your well-being and your future health are more important than the cosmetic strait-jacket society has designed for you. Once you have done that the rest is easy.

Coming off drugs and alcohol
A member of the Essex Road Women's Health Group
SR 39 September 1975

My mother is a suburban housewife and always has been. Six months ago she gave up barbiturates and alcohol to which she'd become addicted. She didn't feel confident enough to write anything herself. First I'll explain a bit about the barbiturates.

Barbiturates are used for treating various mental conditions and sleeplessness. The long-term dangers of taking them have been recognised now that enough people have suffered from them. The ease with which you can take an overdose has recently caused some doctors to panic.

Each year 1,800 to 2,000 people die from taking barbiturates – two-thirds are said to be suicides. Many of those taking overdoses have been young addicts who inject barbiturates straight into the vein. The quieter, less spectacular sufferers are mostly housewives, often of my mother's age (60 this year) who have become addicts through no decision of their own. Doctors, never warning them of addiction, continue to provide prescriptions for years and years. Deaths in these cases are often accidental, the person just forgets how many pills they've taken that day, and takes another. . . .

Three years ago, the Advisory Council on the Misuse of Drugs set up a working party to look into the problem of barbiturates. It discovered that 8,500,000 prescriptions are given out every year. This means that control of the drug would be very difficult and expensive. Instead they are organising CURB (the government-financed Campaign on the Use and Restriction of Barbiturates) to educate doctors in ways of reducing prescriptions, of the dangers of sudden withdrawal, about less habit-forming drugs to use as alternatives, and so on. It's hoped that CURB's activities will gradually cut down the use of barbiturates.

Anyone being given a course of barbiturates should be warned not to drive or to drink. The drug can impair the judgment of time and space. The effect of alcohol is more dangerous. Alcohol acts on areas of the brain which are first stimulated and then depressed. Usually the chemical form of alcohol is changed in the liver. But the barbiturates are also changed in a way which competes with the alcohol. This means that less of the alcohol can be converted and it continues its action on the brain. Together they dampen down the electrical activity which controls breathing and heart rate. Eventually the body stops breathing because the 'messages' are no longer telling it to do so. Unconsciousness is common through an overdose. Choking may occur and then vomiting. Some people die suffocating on their vomit.

In the future doctors will have to act more responsibly. Sudden withdrawal from the drugs can cause convulsions, unconsciousness and the shakes. You can't just tell people to pull themselves together. The cells of the body have come to depend on the drug and it can no longer be simply a decision in the person's mind to stop taking them.

I'll describe a bit about how my mother came to be taking barbiturates and how she decided to come off them. She had really devoted support day and night from my father, his sister and my sister. It was a terrible struggle for all of them and I think it would be very difficult for someone to do alone.

The London Hospital originally prescribed sodium amytal and at the same time told her, 'Guinness is good for the nerves.' This was 26 years ago. She had been attending the hospital because of a nervous state that had built up over several years through the behaviour of a neighbour.

This neighbour was 'mad'. I remember one day her calling me and my sister mud pies. She couldn't have kids herself and was jealous of all the women round about who did have them. My mother got it worst I suppose because we lived a few doors away and my gran lived next door to her. She used to throw bottles at our door and chase my mother down the road and round the milk van. I was toddling and my sister was in a pushchair. My mother was terrified when she was alone in the evenings.

She also always met me from school when I was 5 or 6 because she was afraid this woman would come and take me. When we saw her coming we had to duck behind walls or hedges. I remember nothing of this at all. Eventually my mother and other women round about had meetings to try and decide what to do. They asked the woman's husband along because he wouldn't believe what they were saying. Finally she was taken away to the 'loony bin'. She stayed there 15 years and had some sort of brain surgery. The whole thing sounds really terrible for everyone, and my mother had a kind of nervous breakdown.

What I do remember from childhood were the endless pill counting sessions – 'Where's mother?' 'She's upstairs counting her pills.' There were outings started then abandoned because she had forgotten her pills, or was terrified once we left home. She couldn't bear to be in open spaces nor in strange enclosed spaces. She couldn't cross fields without something to hold on to. When we wanted to take the dog for a walk, she'd take the bike so she could lean on it. She told us kids that we took it to put the dog in the basket so it wouldn't get tired.

I never questioned any of this as I had nothing to compare it with – I thought every woman rested in the afternoon and took pills if she felt a bit miserable. I took some of hers and they certainly cleared up my miseries. One pill put me asleep for a solid 14 hours. My father sometimes took them too. In the end they used to hide the bottles and rifle each other's supplies when they could. My mother took up to eight a day as well as three or four pints of Guinness. 'Not all at once,' she says, 'I spaced them out.'

The pills didn't all come from one doctor. She went to a private doctor to increase the supply. This shows just one of the evils of allowing private practice. For most of the 26 years the same two men, her own GP and the private doctor (a GP ten miles away who had some private patients), prescribed drugs for her. At times her GP made half-hearted attempts to cut down the dose, but he hadn't much in the way of alternative treatment to offer, and her persistence made him give in. Same with the Guinness man.

It never struck me as odd, until recently, that she should go down to the off-licence at eight in the morning, long before it opened. She had some arrangement to go round and knock him up at the back door or he'd leave the bottles on the step for her.

In the last couple of years things got worse. I noticed the bickering and nagging a lot more. Her face looked very droopy and her eyes glazed, her speech was getting slurred and she shook quite a lot. She didn't seem to concentrate or listen. I dreaded going home as both my parents seemed more and more miserable.

Just over a year ago she had a number of strange turns where her body just sort of collapsed and she had to more or less crawl to her room, and to the bed. So she decided to see a psychiatrist and through talking to him, and to me and my sister and father, she began to realise she was addicted. Until then she'd always claimed that she needed the pills and drink for her nerves. We had also been ignorant for far too long about the effect these pills have. Now she began to see that they were making her ill.

'It's the doctors' fault. They shouldn't have given them to me. They should have told me they were poisonous,' she says now.

'You're not a drug addict, we call it dependence,' said her psychiatrist. And for a while the situation dragged on and her feelings of never having done anything, being no good, not being liked and so on worsened. At last she decided to give it all up.

The psychiatrist suggested both NHS and private hospital treatment, but the family talked about it, and then, in her determined way, she said she'd do it at home or not at all. She says being at home made a difference.

'I don't like to go away, never have. I'd've been worrying all the time about what was happening here.'

So . . . a day was set when she was to stop drinking and taking the pills. All at once, just like that. It's unusual to take someone right off instead of decreasing the dose gradually. Sudden withdrawal can be very dangerous. The doctor has not explained why he did this, and he is ill in hospital just now so I couldn't ask him about it.

She was immediately switched on to another batch of drugs said to be less dangerous, but it's a formidable list.

This long list amounts to 30 pills a day, all low dosage but it seems pretty hit or miss. Although pharmacists understand the chemical responses these different drugs will produce in the body, they do not know who will respond and feel better from having their chemical levels altered in one way or another. A more common approach to barbiturate withdrawal is to slowly take the dose down and to replace it with *Mogodon* which is a less dangerous sleeper.

'He said it would be like going into a black tunnel but that there'd be light at the other end. The first few weeks were very difficult – very very difficult. I was shaking all over for three days. The whole bed was shaking. I had no sleep – I couldn't get to sleep. There was this hot burning right through my head. I thought, oh well, something must be happening. I felt like I would just have to scream out, but I didn't.'

She stayed in bed for nearly two weeks.

Father: At that time the doctor said to ring whenever we wanted to check what was happening. I'd ring three or four times a day then, wouldn't I, to check the effects.

Mother: Then how the bed shook. And I didn't want to eat. I wished I hadn't done it.

Father: And all you wanted was a drink, wasn't it?

Mother: Oh, I kept saying, 'If only I could have a glass of Guinness, I'd give up the pills.' I don't think I'd drink Guinness again now. I'd go for ale. [This is six months after stopping.]

Father: You went for it all before didn't you? Come on now.

(Mother laughs. She often laughs now when she's talking. I realised that I hadn't heard her laugh so heartily like that for years and years, and I asked, 'Did you drink other things as well as the Guinness?')

Mother: Yes, I did – not spirits though.

Father: I know, I marked the bottle.

Mother: I know you did, that's like you.

Father: Well, it was for your own good. I'd get a bottle of wine and it'd all be gone – that was as well as the Guinness and the pills.

Mother: (laughs again)

Me: Would you advise other people to give up like you did?

Mother: Oh yes, I'd advise anyone to do it.

Me: Do you think the hospital did wrong to give you the pills in the first place?

Mother: Well, they didn't tell me anything, did they? They didn't pay much attention.

Me: What about all these other pills you're taking now?

Mother: He [the doctor] says he'll get me off them all, but I think, well after 26 years, I can't see I'll ever be off them *all* now.

Me: What really made you give it all up?

Mother: Well, I knew I was doing wrong. I was sleeping so much – sleeping all the time. I shouldn't have been sleeping like that, I don't know. If anyone asked me how I was, I'd say I felt rotten, really rotten. [I remember that, whenever I saw her she'd say, 'I don't feel myself.' She hasn't said that the last six months, it's always, 'I feel much better, if only I could stop the shaking, but that's going gradually now.']

Mother: I wanted to do things but I had no interest in them, you know I

324

couldn't do them. And I was increasing the Guinness and increasing the pills at the same time. I could tell it was them making me feel bad. I wanted to feel different, and I do now.

Me: Wasn't there anything you kept in mind – you know, something to get you through the first days when you stopped?

Mother: Well, no, I can't think of anything, the strength was just there. The strength was just given me somehow. I knew I wanted to feel better. I knew what I was doing wasn't good for my health and I was just determined.

For years there'd been problems, mother saying she'd do things and not doing them. It used to drive my father and her friends crazy. Now she says she's interested in things. She doesn't like to be alone at all, although she always sleeps alone. My father is retired so they take things easy and just go out and enjoy themselves in a quiet way.

For so long it was painful for me to go and see them. We would all argue and nag and someone would cry. It always seemed over nothing. I felt torn apart between them, my mother's paranoia and my father's patience, their dependence on each other and their continual bickering and arguing because the other wasn't how they wanted them to be. My stomach felt tense and knotted, and I would hold back the tears seeing them so unhappy and feeling there was nothing I could do. I was all wrong too. I really thought the problems were so deep and so many that stopping addiction wouldn't really alter much. I was worried by my father's desperate clinging to the idea as if a miracle was going to happen and as if the years of problems would just disappear. Well, they didn't disappear, but the change is far greater than I thought possible. Her face is completely different, her behaviour too.

Doctors' treatment of women and their particular problems is often irresponsible, as this story shows. Instead of admitting their own helplessness and lack of understanding when confronted with such cases, they pretend they have the answer, the cure, and prescribe drugs that may hide the problem (or create another). The women patients are encouraged to have complete unquestioning trust in the doctor's methods, and no trust in themselves.

So much of my mother's behaviour must have been drug-induced, creeping up on her slowly over the years. How different could all those years of her life, our lives, and loads of other people's have been, if only medicine was a more honest and caring part of our society.

Amytryptylin – an anti-depressant. This has side-effects like a dry mouth and blurred vision. It should not be used with alcohol or by a person who has high blood pressure. Only 8% of people given it are said to respond to the treatment. It's been in use since 1964.

Stelazine – a more recent tranquilliser often used after addiction, for toxic psychosis, chronic alcoholism and anxiety states. The main difference between these two is that the first treats depression and the second anxiety. Both states are pretty much mixed together and doctors are often just guessing.

Valium – an anti-depressant and muscle-relaxant. It's now widely used for states of tension and anxiety.

Equinal – another muscle-relaxant.

Orovite – a special vitamin often used for a while after alcoholism.

Disipal – used to counteract the shakes which have often been drug induced.

Heaven in a bottle

An interview with Liz by Marsha Rowe
SR 22 April 1974

The alcoholic finds heaven in a bottle and then finds she doesn't want to give this heaven up. The difficulties arise when the alcoholic realises the heaven is indistinguishable from hell, or that her heaven makes life hell for others, or that these moments of heaven leave her as lonely and life as difficult to cope with as before.

Liz is an alcoholic striving to remain an active feminist socialist and cure her alcoholism.

My mother used to give me hot toddies to comfort me when I was sick or upset. When I left school I joined the Young Socialists for a while, but none of it made much sense to me and I left it when I got to university. I really enjoyed drinking, it got me over my shyness when I went to parties. But I couldn't afford to drink that much on a grant. I didn't go out to get drunk then. Bob and I got married when I was in my third year. The rationalisation for it was that we weren't allowed to live together because of college regulations which was a hassle. I brought to the marriage all the preconceptions about wanting it to be forever and always and a great relationship. I remember saying I don't want to get divorced and his saying, 'That's bloody ridiculous'. We've rather changed roles now.

I don't think I can honestly say I ever needed to go to pubs in order to meet people. Not like some of the others in AA, people who've obviously done all their socialising in pubs. When I got married I was still hung up on this being taken out for nice meals bit. I thought that was the height of sophistication. In fact, I always had this thing, that I would really have arrived the day I had a well-stocked cocktail cabinet and could say, 'What would you like to drink?' It never arrived, and it never will, because every time I bought anything I drank it as fast as I could.

Then we came to London and that was a sort of nadir of my life. I started supply teaching and I got pregnant. By this time I felt a complete write-off and thought I was bound to be infertile, it's so clear now, looking back on it. I decided to find out. I found out pretty quickly. It was pretty miserable, but I got closer to Bob and decided I wanted to carry on. I thought I'd have perhaps three at the time but when I did I found it was ghastly. Two kids are just a hell of a lot of work, they get jealous of each other. I remember I began to have morning drinks to sort of anaethetise the mid-morning feed because it was such a strain having to cope with a bawling child while the other was feeding. Then I'd get sloshed you see, and it really used to be quite nice once I was sloshed, the housework and the children were all quite bearable. This was not drinking to get drunk, it was drinking to get into a state where I didn't mind things too much. I don't know whether Bob noticed. I think I told him. He took a very cavalier attitude to the whole thing.

But then I remember I stopped. There was half a bottle of whisky left and I thought, 'I've got to stop because I'm never going to do anything except look after the children and get sloshed,' and then I started painting. That was the first time since being an adolescent. Then I thought, 'Well, that's all right. I've stopped for three months and I've got it under control.' So I started drinking again just in the evenings, but there were days when I got very sloshed because I remember once being very, very drunk on a bottle of Greek sherry and weeping to a friend that I couldn't go on. That's when we moved to where we live now. I know every off-licence in the area, the hours they're open, every single one. I can tell you where to go at what time of day and I'd do the rounds so none of them would know about my drinking. But then there's the problem of empties, that's ghastly. You buy all this stuff, usually in quarters or halves. I was topping up bottles by this time to make it look I hadn't drunk much. I drank anything I could lay my hands on, but mainly whisky. We always had a joint account so it came out of 'housekeeping'.

By this time it began to get ugly. I've always lost my temper easily when I drank a lot, and Bob and this other guy who was living with us would come home and suggest we go out for a drink. I would have a couple of drinks with them on top of all the other drinks they didn't know about. Then I would suddenly snap and all this shit would come out and later I felt dreadful about it. Bob used to hate the rages but I think he quite liked comforting me through the hangovers.

Then we went abroad for a year. I was pregnant again. It's interesting the way one has all these mechanisms towards good health built in because I couldn't drink the last three months of my pregnancy. I'd get this terrific heartburn which was very painful. Although I got plastered the day we left because there was a hell of a lot to do. After we arrived there was no money to spare but then a cheap gin came on the market and I got stuck into that. That was about four months after we left England, and I was discussing women's liberation then. I do think it is a terrible indictment both of me and the group I was in that I didn't talk about it with them. It wasn't a proper consciousness-raising group, it was sort of half consciousness-raising and half study. Drinking escalates very quickly. Well, it was only 11/- a bottle, a small bottle would fit into my bag. It smelled foul. And brandy, I drank, and beer, in the morning or the lunchtime. Then I'd take the kids out in the afternoon to the swimming pool and I'd be pretty plastered then usually. I dunno.

I don't think I showed that many signs of it. Yet I would not remember things. I started having these memory lapses, blackouts they're called, and I didn't know who I'd been talking to or what I said and sometimes I wouldn't know how I got from A to B. I'd lost 12 hours, that's when it starts getting frightening. Bob would notice and I would ask the kids if I'd put them to bed the night before. I was scared I'd leave the kids in a locked car or something.

It's a nightmare because nobody understands. People say drink less, that's the usual. But the minute I've had one drink it's just not enough. By this time I was saying to people on an individual basis I've got a drinking problem, I'm an alcoholic, but nobody knew what to do. I tried to stop drinking again as a result of being involved with somebody else. I remember on the tail of a really awful hangover him saying you've got to stop drinking. I couldn't keep going round with half my brain knocked off, and feeling so ill. I said I wouldn't have another drink, which I'd said frequently before. Next time I was with him I said, 'Right, I'll have a beer.' He said, 'No, you won't.' I was absolutely livid, really furious. I flounced out of the flat and that was the first time anyone had stopped me taking the first drink. He didn't know about alcoholism but he said you are psychologically dependent on this thing and you've got to break this dependency, and that means coming off alcohol for quite some considerable time, like six months. And I thought I'll show you mate, and after this initial thing of flouncing off I thought, he's right, I won't drink for six months. I still haven't made it six months without a drink but I didn't drink for about six weeks after that.

The first thing that happened when I stopped, it was awful, it was really awful, like hanging on a cliff. I really didn't think I could manage it, I hadn't got any AA philosophy at this stage, knowing that you're only supposed to try and cope with a day at a time. It was six months here we come, which is a terrible mistake. After about three or four weeks I was feeling better, not suffering gastritis, and I didn't have cramps in the night, visual disturbances and I didn't get up vomiting. I could remember there were good things about not drinking. I'd remember what I said to people, I hadn't hit anybody and forgotten about it. But I was living on a knife edge.

Then things began to go wrong. He broke off the relationship. But somewhere, deep down, I knew I mustn't drink then; that I had to stay stopped, not to show him, but myself. I was only able to sustain that a couple of weeks. Then I was off on these periodic benders. First I wanted oblivion, then I'd think, 'Oh well, I haven't really stopped at the moment' and have another drink. It's like snakes and ladders.

AA groups help because people have been through the same thing. In terms of character types, I think there are a lot of people who've been very shy, self-conscious, inhibited, often really successful but inside just a quivering mess. Nobody knows how many alcoholics there are, except there must be some people suffering with nobody knowing anything about it, realising they've got a problem. Women are reputed to be more difficult to treat than men. They are more secretive as drinkers, and I think, because of the economic facts of life, women stick by alcoholic men longer than men stick by alcoholic women. And women usually drink in their home environment, which means that they are back in the drinking environment as soon as they leave hospital or whatever, it's not like the pub, which a man can just avoid. At first, I got into a terrible state about the spiritual side of AA, but I think maybe if I've got to depend on something, it's better to depend on a belief which may or may not be false than to depend on alcohol.

Some people say the power of the group is the higher power, the power of AA and it's true that it works.

So I've stopped thinking of myself as the centre of the universe which I always did before, or I'm trying to stop.

It's very weird, because now I can go around thinking bloody men, they're always putting me down, and look at the differential between my earning power and Bob's, and the fact that I look after the kids and nobody ever counts that in an incremental scale. It's all bloody unjust and I could go round feeling that and get myself into a terrible state over all sorts of things. I learned to switch really, and think well, I've got the kids and I know where the next meal is coming from and you know, I'm bloody lucky, and I've got somewhere warm to live. I feel this is difficult to discuss with some women in the movement. You're not supposed to take one step back. Well, I don't think that's true, in order to survive with any sort of equanimity at all. This whole thing AA has about resentment. In a women's liberation group, you're looking at the things you're feeling angry about and validating your anger really, saying, 'Yes, I'm right'. But, in the end, unless you can actually go and change a situation, do something, you have this cancer inside you eating you away. It's not the man who's put you down, or won't give you a job, who's discriminating against you, who's suffering, it's you. Unless you can actually take action. AA has this prayer: 'God grant me the Serenity to accept the things I cannot change, Courage to change the things I can and Wisdom to know the difference.' It seems to me that what's crucial is the wisdom to know the difference, because I differ from a lot of people I've met in AA about what that is – perhaps I've just been unlucky.

I don't have a straight environmentalist line about alcoholism. There are alcoholics, I'm sure, in every society. I really feel I ought to stay in AA but I feel pulled in two directions. What do I do when somebody makes a joke at an AA meeting, like I'd rather be watching a Miss World competition on the telly than being at an AA meeting. I don't ever say anything in these situations. I'd be odd and isolated and I don't fight it because it just upsets me, because I need to be there. I'm a socialist but one doesn't talk about politics at AA, it's all on this personal level and I suppose I feel isolated because I do connect the personal with the politics and nobody else does. Anyway political arguments upset people and so it's an area that isn't discussed and the connection isn't made. I really do feel I'm picking up where I left off about 12 years ago, before I started drinking. I've anaesthetised myself. There's this terrible wilful bit you can't control. When I'd go shopping, I'd walk straight over to the drinks counter in the supermarket, the number of times I've said half a dozen coca cola and a quarter bottle of whisky, and it's just been out, just like that, and I feel this part of myself, reason has nothing to do with it. It might have rational beginnings, but now it's totally irrational. Alcoholism is the third biggest killer. Society keeps bloody quiet about it, look how much money they're making out of it. They put a government health warning on cigarettes, but they don't on alcohol. It really is the opium of the people.

Alcohol: what's it doing to our bodies?
Ruthie Petrie
SR 82 April 1979

According to Alcoholics Anonymous, ten years ago the ratio of women alcoholics to men was two to seven: now they claim it's one to one. Other statistics show a less drastic leap in ratio, and no doubt each uses a different measure to define alcoholism. But whatever the figures, new medical research shows that women's upper limit of daily consumption – 100 grams – can affect our bodily health, whereas men can booze on up to 200 grams. And evidently this difference in response can't be explained away by weight variances between men and women. Women appear to have higher blood alcohol levels drink for drink, pound for pound. So far, though, it is *how* our bodies react differently rather than *why* that has been documented.

Cirrhosis and serious disease seem to hit women whose average daily consumption is lower than men's, and if we continue to drink with liver disease, our survival rate beyond five years runs at 50% compared with men's at 80%.

How does alcohol affect us during and at the end of our reproductive cycle? Medical research points tentatively to hormonal connections, but still leaves huge questions unanswered. For example, our blood levels are higher just before menstruation – but does this relate to alcohol damage? And what happens after the menopause? Christine Doyle, the *Observer's* medical correspondent, noted that in pregnancy, many women go off drink, but heavy drinkers 'risk some degree of physical and possibly mental handicap in their babies' and that 'a hormonal influence is among the possible reasons for a higher than expected incidence of breast cancer among alcoholics'. All this evidence, even if still scanty, does indicate the areas of suspected *specific* damage to women, and those other areas of damage which can affect women more acutely than men.

So what can we do besides pushing for more research? If, like me, you worry that you drink too much, but reject that worry by not doing anything about it, maybe it's time to try to overcome it. Why not ask your GP for a liver function test, check your breasts as a matter of routine, and try not to drink when you're depressed, as alcohol is a known depressant. These may seem small measures, but they can be a positive start for those of us who decide to ask ourselves whether we ought to have 'just another little drink'.

Heroin addiction: beyond the stereotype
Sara Jeffries
SR 132 July 1983

I originally wrote to *Spare Rib* from an increasing feeling of frustration, loneliness and desperation. I've been desperately fighting a seemingly never ending battle against the tyranny of heroin addiction.

I've been reading *Spare Rib* regularly since the first issue and it's been the only contact for my rapidly rising feminist consciousness. But the fact that I've never read anything on the subject of addiction has increased my feelings of alienation from other women. I found it very difficult to actually admit to having a 'problem' with addiction. I feel I'm missing the support of other women who may tend to dismiss drug addiction as a somewhat hedonistic tendency unrelated to feminism. This feeling was reinforced when I made tentative efforts to form a women's conscious-ness-raising group which, though it alleviated my desire for participation with other feminists, fell short of my goals. I couldn't be myself and admit to being a drug addict. Obviously this may say something about my personality, but I also think it reflects the attitude of society in general towards addiction – that it's not talked about as if it involves 'real women' and instead is ignored or sensationalised in lurid Sunday newspaper articles. I believe that heroin, like alcohol and tranquillisers, is a valid feminist issue.

It is only in the last few years (since I've had children) that I've realised how women are manipulated and that using drugs is an extension of this. Women start using drugs for various reasons; mainly because it is pleasurable, a pleasurable escape from our daily lives. It also enables us to desperately attempt to conform to a way of life which is becoming increasingly intolerable with its unnatural forced values and expectations, especially for those labelled 'wife and mother'.

Drugs give you confidence, energy, an exquisite feeling of well-being and contentment. We are able to use heroin and function 'normally'. It's a myth that a heroin addict can't lead a normal existence, hold down a job, behave as the next person. Heroin just gives us the means to perform these things without question.

I am 30 years old now and it's ten years since I had my first taste of heroin. For the last six years I've been totally addicted to either heroin or methadone, an opium substitute. I really enjoyed my first hit of smack (heroin); there was that wonderful rush of warmth and contentment. I'm not really a very talkative, outgoing person but once I was stoned I suddenly had all the confidence I'd ever lacked. After my first hit I used smack intermittently and always relished it.

I went abroad for a while and began to use heroin regularly in an unreal situation: Amsterdam in the early 1970s, a drug user's paradise. I was always able to come back to England and suffer a period of readjustment while I went through the frustrating and discomforting experience of withdrawal. I had no worries about not being able to come off. Without the lubrication of opiates, though, I gradually began to feel more and more dissatisfied with myself, lethargic, apathetic and depressed.

I started living with a man who was using regularly and rapidly embraced his habit. The responsibility was taken from me: he did all the scoring and I happily shared his highs. It's impossible to live with someone who's a junkie and not be one yourself. It's extremely difficult to have a close relationship if only one of you is using. I would get furious when this did happen: partly because I was jealous of his high but also because it's difficult to communicate on two different states of consciousness.

I continued in this way for five years. Suddenly, last year, I was 30 years old, had two babies and was living in London away from family and friends. I'd accumulated huge debts and had a £10-a-day heroin addiction. It was intolerable, unbearable, yet it was something that had crept up on me and I could see no way out. When I'd first moved to London John and I had been relatively stable though we were using methadone daily: John was a registered drug addict. We began to use heroin occasionally. I was amazed and pleased at how cheap and readily available it had beome: there was never any difficulty scoring. It made me feel better about being in a strange city with a new baby.

Then things started to go wrong. John lost his job and we couldn't find anywhere to live. I got pregnant again when my first baby was only four months old and, for various reasons, decided against a termination. John's methadone was stopped and it became necessary for us to score every day. Our lives became ruled by the daily securing of and using smack. All our friends were junkies and life was smack-orientated. Being stoned was the only way I could function. There was no way I could go 'cold turkey' and be a mother ('cold turkey': extreme withdrawal symptoms as a result of stopping drug intake *immediately*, rather than gradually) with a young baby. There was no one I could leave him with while I recovered. Mine and John's relationship was changing entirely. I couldn't exist without a daily fix, that soon became two or three. John did the scoring whilst I waited at home with the ties of baby and pregnancy.

I found it very hard as a woman to actually go out, make the connection and score, though I was surprised at the number of women dealers in London. Most of the dealers we've been scoring off have been women. There exists the myth of the rich dealer living in luxury off the backs of desperate junkies. I've never come across anyone like this. All the dealers I know are junkies who sell smack to maintain their own habit. Many of the women dealers are unsupported mothers who have no other way of providing for their children and maintaining a habit. They've usually been living with a man who turned them on to heroin and then either over-dosed or simply left.

Maybe I'm being over-sensitive in deliberately underplaying the 'seed-iness' aspect of drugs. I want women to understand that women addicts can be just the same as anyone else. Obviously if a woman with an expensive habit is desperate for money there is always prostitution: personally, I know no women in this situation. I know quite a high proportion of prostitutes do use drugs. I wonder whether they began in order to pay for their habits or started using in order to 'escape' from an unacceptable existence. Also drugs do go hand in hand with most illegal activity simply because in order to obtain them you have to go outside the law. I know a lot of people reading my piece will think that I've had an 'easy time'. Certainly a £10-a-day habit is nothing compared to the amount some people use and I do know women who shoplift to pay for their drugs.

Women have a different relationship with drugs. Men tend to glorify the whole thing, get into the so-called drug culture and socialise with other junkies. I can't get it together to clean the house, or do the washing, until I've had a fix. The main reason I'm finding it so hard to stop using drugs is the presence of the children. I can never relax my responsibility to them and that never-ceasing guilt that comes with motherhood is exacerbated by the stigma of drug addiction. More and more I got to need the energy drugs gave me just to care for my children.

It was during my second pregnancy that my use of heroin escalated and I was fixing every day. My fear and guilt about this was enormous. Not much is known about how the developing foetus is affected by heroin. It's possible that a baby born to a woman with a habit can go into withdrawal about eight hours after birth. The medical answer to this is to immediately remove the child at birth and wean it off on some kind of barbiturate. This has happened to a child of one of my friends. Although I didn't want to take any chances with my babies' health I wanted to, and felt I could, control the situation myself. I also don't think the medical practice is necessarily the best thing.

I was really depressed throughout my second pregnancy. We still had nowhere to live and the guilt and fear about not being able to come off increased. Being put on a methadone programme was unacceptable to me. I desperately wanted to admit my addiction whilst pregnant but couldn't bring myself to face the moral indignation of the medical profession. I'd been a student nurse myself for a while and I'd seen that junkies were treated as contemptible. I was also terrified of being declared an 'unfit mother' and running the risk of having my child taken into care as had happened to another friend of mine. In the end I went into premature labour and gave birth six weeks early. The baby was born slightly asphixiated. He'd had the chord around his neck and the foetal heart monitor malfunctioned so his distress wasn't picked up early enough. He was taken to special care for observation where he developed respiratory problems. It was then that I admitted my addiction and the child was administered largactil for a fortnight from which he then had to be withdrawn.

I felt a strange, but certain, relief that it was now all out in the open alongside apprehension about initiating a chorus of social workers. Fortunately a supportive health visitor accepted that I could look after my children in spite of using drugs. I was so traumatised by the whole experience that I stayed off drugs for a month after the birth. Although he was now in perfect health doctors constantly stressed that he would only remain healthy if I kept off drugs. This was ridiculous and another attempt to make me feel even more guilty using my baby. Throughout this time John had continued using smack. Although he professed a desire to come off there were no pressures on *him* to do so. It was hard to accept a situation where he could use without threatening the baby and I was made to feel completely guilty about everything. After a while at home, coping with the pressure of two young babies. I succumbed again to using. It was too difficult to resist, all our friends were still using. It made life so much more acceptable.

In the past I'd never made a total commitment to coming off. I had assumed it was something which would come about one day; now I was desperate for some way out. I was getting increasingly into debt and living in an intolerable situation.

I'd wake up in the morning withdrawing, unable to function until I'd had a hit. Then I'd have to wait around half the day whilst John went out to score. As your body begins to need the warm glow of heroin, it becomes a state of abnormality to be without it. You feel sub-human and have a lack of concentration, coldness, depression and pain. Movement becomes an effort and sleep is impossible. After a while a fix doesn't create the soporific ecstasy of first usage. When using, however, it's possible to function normally and adequately. I not only had more energy and confidence, I could remain undetected as well. When I was fixing daily I even managed to do a part-time job. I was working in a restaurant, ostensibly as a straight housewife and mother. One day a junkie friend turned up for a job. She hadn't had a fix and was a little wide-eyed. My boss refused to employ her and then confided in me that she thought she was 'on drugs' and added that I shouldn't let her near my children.

At the time I'd been working there for six months and was only able to go in week after week because I was using.

Finally, last year, I decided to go to University College Hospital and become a registered drug addict. I felt very ambivalent about this. On the one hand I'd be receiving methadone every day which would lift the financial burden, but I was very sceptical about it being a cure. Methadone is used by addiction clinics as an alternative to heroin. It's no less dangerous or addictive but it doesn't have the stigma of heroin which, incidentally, was first formulated and lauded as a cure for morphine addiction. The actual treatment consists of being allocated a daily prescription of methadone which is gradually reduced over a six-month period until the patient is finally drug free. Compulsory attendance of a weekly group therapy session consists of about eight patients and two social workers and usually revolves around disgruntled male addicts moaning about not receiving an adequate amount of methadone. It's generally accepted that it's more difficult for women to stop using than it is for men. Along with alcohol and tranquillisers, it's an emotional crutch for women when life becomes overwhelming. This makes giving up much harder, especially when we're coping with children and are expected to remain even-tempered and instantly available to the demands of child-rearing.

I found the male-orientated regime of the hospital extremely difficult to cope with. There's no provision for the care of children whilst you attend the meetings and I found it impossible to have my children looked after for a couple of hours every week. This is not only completely disregarded, it's also considered an excuse for not being committed to the programme. If you miss three meetings in the six-month period, your treatment is terminated. You also have to pick up your methadone daily. In my case this involved a bus journey with two babies in tow – no mean feat when you're feeling like death until you've taken the methadone. All this is supposed to give the patient a sense of being 'in control of her own cure'. All it really comes down to is being manipulated with your life totally controlled by the clinic. It's impossible to hold down a job while you're on the programme (how many employers are going to give you a few hours off every day for six months?) and there's no provision for evening attendance. You can't go on holiday for a week as you're not trusted with more than a day's prescription at a time – except, of course, on bank holidays, when you're suddenly capable. The entire regime becomes a punishment for having become addicted in the first place. The whole, nasty, patriarchal staff/junkie relationship reduced me to tears on many an occasion. Finally, I failed the allowed three meetings and my treatment was terminated, but I can go back and try again . . . and again and again.

I find myself now in a never never land of trying to come off, no longer a fully fledged junkie (i.e. scoring every day) but getting by on bottles of codein linctus and, when I succumb, heroin every few days. The days I

335

have nothing are a blur of depression and lethargy. I don't want to be like this. I want to wake in the morning and be able to function without chemicals, but now I watch people walking down the street and wonder how they can do it without drugs inside them. I've got quite a sympathetic doctor who initially prescribed me valium to help me come off heroin, but then he worried I'd become dependent on *them*, so now I live on codeine, hope and despair.

The frustrating thing is I know I can come off, but not without lots of sisterly support. Unfortunately there are very few groups for women drug-users. I'd like to get one going myself but I only have the energy and enthusiasm when I'm high. I hope my tale will encourage other women who are in the same situation to start talking about it. Perhaps together we can help each other. I would love to hear from any women who have overcome addiction, who have suggestions about alternative medicine and from any women, like myself, who are still struggling.

CHAPTER 11

SEXUALITY AND WOMEN'S LIBERATION

From the minute we are born – male or female – we get messages about the 'proper' sexual behaviour to go with our biology. As women, the message builds up insistently: our biology gives us a 'special' destiny, therefore 'special' responsibilities as well as 'special' weaknesses. Of course, it is assumed that sexuality means *hetero*sexuality, which is not only 'natural' but *healthy*. It is only relatively recently in most medical circles that lesbianism, for example, has ceased being seen as a pathological, antisocial disease.

Sexuality figures in a particularly intimate and intertwined way with women's physical and emotional health. The way our individual sexuality is constructed, in different ways for different women, greatly affects the health care we get, the way we approach the health of others, the way we experience ourselves as female. Just think about menstruation, pregnancy, abortion, vaginal infections, AIDS, breast disease, birth control, menopause, depression, mental illness, and you have to think about sexuality too. Conversely, think about sexuality and you have to remember the influences of class, race, disabilities, age. And although society deems a healthy female to be heterosexual, we might ask if heterosexuality actually *damages* women's health. Women experience their bodies, their sexuality, in a social context and there are contradictions between body and culture; how can it be otherwise when the body is female and the culture is predominantly male?

The articles in this section attempt to address questions of female sexuality directly or as a major aspect of the article. Assumptions still exist within them – certainly Black women have been traditionally excluded from white feminists' discussions of sexuality. Within the pages of *Spare Rib* this has been changing slowly, but in the process some Black feminists have stopped even wanting to give time and energy to *Spare Rib*.

Also, although *Spare Rib* carried an early editorial on lesbianism, there was an absence in the first years of any sustained discussion or description of lesbian sexuality. In the early days of the magazine women wrote primarily about heterosexual sex; articles on vaginismus, solutions like masturbation and women's pre-orgasmic groups, guides like 'Unlearning Not to Have Orgasms' feature strongly. But heterosexual dissatisfaction mingled with heterosexual optimism. The tensions of sexual relationships with men went deeper than being able to come. Even among the 'achievers' resentment rankled. Clearly learning sex techniques didn't solve the deeper issues of female sexuality.

After the early rush, articles on sex and sexuality in *Spare Rib* are few and far between. When they do appear they are addressed to a specific experience, like pregnancy or disability. They bounce off a particular focus and attempt to generalize about sexual politics. Or they address sex education for young women. They tend not to be about how to 'do' sex, or how to get individual pleasure. The reign of the confident technician gives way to the need to spell out the thorny bits, suss out the ground, face the contradictions.

Spare Rib has never recaptured the confidence exuded by its early articles on sex and sexuality. As lesbianism came out more and more within the women's liberation movement, heterosexual feminists displayed a variety of uneasy reactions – sometimes defensive, sometimes cynical, sometimes silenced. Sometimes coming out themselves. Yet lesbianism, although more visible in *Spare Rib*'s pages, has hardly taken over, as an editorial in *SR* 116 pointed out. And many articles still assume heterosexuality.

Other important criticisms have been made about the magazine's coverage of sexuality by Black, Third World and working class women, which threw into sharper relief the growing awareness that sexuality is socially constructed. It has never been experienced or given the same meanings by women, or those in power, throughout history, across geographical or cultural boundaries, within different religions or other forms of social organization. Other feminists pointed to different, not unproblematic, relations with men, different consequences which arose from being a lesbian, different constraints and priorities which made 'choice' too often a hollow word. As the collective changed, slowly the content and awareness have changed too. But with the recognition of absences, of racism and heterosexism, also has come a period of time when no one really seems to know how to write about sexuality or who should do the writing.

Nowadays the 'how to get bigger and better orgasms and stay true to yourself' stories can be found in the pages of mainstream magazines. In *Spare Rib* understanding the complexity of our sexualities has led to fewer articles directly about sex. However, the impossibility of strictly dividing off sexuality from other areas of life means that you will find discussions of sexuality in many articles about other subjects. In this book I think immediately of articles on herpes, on pelvic inflammatory disease (PID), on addictions, on cancer, which could easily have come into this chapter.

Female sexuality is completely bound up in how we experience and treat our bodies, how we respond emotionally to being a woman in a woman-hating environment. Women have always been defined sexually in relation to men, through men, and with the ultimate aim of procreation. Feminism challenges this definition and in doing so raises the many other entwined issues which must be addressed.

Physical relationships and the disabled woman
Julie Mimmack
SR 86 September 1979

I am a tetraplegic – paralysed from the armpits downwards with partial movement in my arms and hands. I have some feeling in my legs and torso generally, but no voluntary movement. I am confined to a wheel-chair and am 24 years of age. My injury was caused by a car accident seven years ago and although the muscles which function are stronger than before, there have been no other physical improvements.

This article is related to my own personal experiences. I only claim to have part-knowledge of the physical and psychological aspects of sex and the disabled woman. Because obviously every disability and individual are so very different. But I am being as open as possible and, if nothing else, it gets something off my chest!

If a disabled woman is unable to go out to work, she is put at a great disadvantage, in terms of meeting people on a day-to-day basis. During weekdays when I see young people leaving and returning from work (especially women) I feel quite apart from that 'world out there'. Whatever activities a disabled female may take up, whether it be painting or an Open University degree, nobody can convince you that it is similar to being able-bodied within a normal work situation. This can make you feel inadequate both physically and mentally, especially if you worked prior to your disability. If you have a boyfriend/husband, it may be extremely difficult to 'tune in' on a discussion of his working day. And if you feel yourself disappearing into the corner of the room, this can be destructive. It helps considerably if you take an interest in your partner's career, even if it is just a case of making the appropriate noises! But equally *he* should take an interest in your daily activities.

Social encounters at parties or other functions are obviously varied. But in my experience they do follow certain patterns.

(a) Complete rejection

In such cases even eye-to-eye contact is impossible. People get embar-rassed, but sometimes they're just indifferent – you're written off. I ignore them back or, if I don't like their remarks, I speak back in kind. I've got a loud mouth and I'm not prepared to huddle away in corners. There've been a few feet I've run over with my wheelchair too.

(b) Over-enthusiasm

This may be caused by overdrinking or whatever. You may be treated as a 'plaything' or a 'novelty'. The fact that you may be the only wheelchair-bound guest can draw excess attention, not so much for your 'self' but your 'predicament'. This may only temporarily boost the old ego; if you should so want it boosted!

(c) Admiration

This can be beneficial or otherwise. Personally I have found this coming from older men (usually married) and those with heart-rending tales to tell; breakdowns, marital hang-ups, etc. (as if you haven't got enough of your own). Admiration also seems to make the female a target for 'religious salesmen'. Often, promises are made at the end of what may seem a fruitful evening. But will you ever see him again? Even if sincere at the time, parties can be a superficial basis for a relationship. There are many obstacles to come.

A sexual relationship can be extremely difficult. Especially if the disabled female lives at home with parents – as I do – and is of the age when hopefully she would be living independently, working and travelling. Parents can be over-protective, especially if you are dependent on them both physically and financially. They may interrogate your partner more than in normal circumstances; after all, you are more vulnerable to maltreatment. Nonetheless, you are unable to create your own atmosphere in such a situation – making coffee, or generally 'moving around'. There is also that first moment when 'bladder management' is revealed. It would seem that this is the real test. How will he react to a mature individual who wears plastic knickers and pads and requires help when going to the loo? Rejection on this count can be very grim and frustrating.

When/if your relationship passes the 'bladder test' the next hurdle is arranging a private meeting (place and time). 'Time' is a leading factor here because (a) a considerable amount of physical preparation is required, and (b) unexpected visitors or disturbances are impossible to cope with – the disabled party can't quickly get up, dress, wash. When sexually aroused, the heat can be taken out of the moment when your partner has to help you empty your bladder and carefully clean and position you. This can cause a mechanical barrier. On the other hand things can be taken in a light-hearted manner, which helps. During and after sexual intercourse, over-exhaustion can make the disabled woman feel inadequate. The mind may be very willing to try out new positions and experiences, but the body function can be that much weaker.

I would imagine that all of us (the disabled included) have sexual fantasies. Mine relate to spontaneous sexual behaviour – sex in a lift, in any room of the house and in numerous positions: on the floor, up against the wall or whatever takes the mind's fancy! This makes sense to me anyhow because a disabled person's life is greatly limited and rarely spontaneous.

A successful sexual relationship would seem impossible to define (whether disabled or not). If you are praised, there is always a feeling of doubt; no one can really convince you of sexual prowess when half your body isn't really *normal* – however this may be defined. You may also worry about your body shape. Many disabilities come equipped with drooping breasts, a thin-rib cage not to mention a lax tum, due to lack of muscle tone. You may compare your body shape with how it was prior to disability. And wonder whether your partner is comparing your body to someone else's. In either case, discussion can help.

The inability of the disabled person to be purely physical – showing body movement, posture, wearing revealing clothes – can be a great disadvantage within the so-called 'market place' (bloody terrible concept but nobody can deny that it still exists). Seeing such physical abilities in others can result in jealousy. To compensate in some way the disabled woman may find herself exaggerating and 'pushing' her personality in order to be noticed physically. This can prove exhausting. The degree of 'pushing' would seem to depend on the company you are with, and how relaxed the company is generally; how many barriers have been broken down, and so on.

'Is your partner a nurse-cum-nancy?' This concept annoys me on two counts: the way that it is put forward by many people implies a distinct prejudice against homosexuals, and that it is 'unnatural' for a male to take on the 'caring' role – caring goes against the male macho image. It would seem to be a recognised fact, from experience (sorry, no statistics as yet), that disabled men have a greater chance of pairing up with able-bodied women. Hopefully with greater sexuality equality, the introduction of more male nurses, and different attitudes, this will no longer be the case.

To conclude I would say that if barriers can be broken down and a relaxed relationship achieved, one of the greatest outcomes is *confidence*. Both in oneself and with others.

Julie Mimmack died in 1981. Her mother, Daphne, writes about her grief in chapter 7 of this book.

Taking control of our sex lives
Angela Hamblin
SR 104 March 1981

'I've got four sisters and I've never really talked to any of them about sexuality. I've certainly never talked to them about orgasms and what they're like for them. In fact, I don't think I've ever really talked to any other woman about it – which, now I come to think about it, seems absolutely incredible. . . . I wonder what other women feel. . . . I really do. . . . I'd love to know.'

FIGURE 28 Oral sex *Sue Beasley* (*SR 138* January 1984)

It's over ten years now since women in this country first began meeting together, in small consciousness-raising groups, to share and discuss our common experience as women. And yet, despite our greater freedom and openness with each other, many of us still find it difficult to talk about our own sexuality.

I know that for me this has been a particularly difficult area of my life to share with others and yet I have also found that if I do not share it I remain cut off from other women's experience; isolated in my own private struggles and conflicts. In an attempt to 'open things up' I asked a number of my women friends whether they would be prepared to talk to me about their sexuality. To my surprise and delight they all agreed and together we began to explore areas which were important to us.

What we discovered was that we had all individually been concerned to assert much greater control over our sex lives. We wanted to free ourselves from the limitations which patriarchal definitions had placed upon our sexuality. We wanted to discover more about our own bodies, responses and needs and to explore more open, less goal-orientated, forms of sexual pleasure.

We range, in age, from early twenties to early fifties and whilst some of us now relate sexually to women, others have become celibate or bisexual and some have chosen to remain in long-term relationships with men. But whatever our current situations all of us, at some time in our lives, have had sexual relationships with men and it was issues around power and control within them which we most felt the need to challenge.

One of the first, and perhaps most basic, assumptions we questioned was about definitions of what 'sex' is. We were all agreed that the widely accepted belief that *real* sex is 'penetration – followed by penile thrusting – and orgasm' had been both oppressive to us as women and, in many cases, had actively restricted the development of our own autonomous sexuality.

'In the past fucking was always seen as *the* sexual activity. . . . I objected to the way men related to parts of my body – seeing everything as a "lead-up" to fucking.'

When sex is defined in this way men embark upon a series of predetermined, goal-orientated steps designed as one woman put it 'to get me ready for penetration'. When we asked ourselves how far we felt *we* had determined what happened to us sexually it became clear that, within this definition of sex, there was little, if any, space or opportunity for us to find out what we wanted.

'When I think back on it I didn't determine anything . . . guys would go through this complete routine: kissing; hand down your back; hand on your bosom; hand on your vulva (kissing you all the time); then inside you and straight into fucking. There was never any pause. . . . I mean, I was never really given a chance . . . everything would follow on from what they did initially.'

Within this definition of sex it is also assumed that if a woman expresses an interest in sex she is conveying her willingness to engage in sexual intercourse. This, of course, may not be the case at all. She may simply desire physical closeness; she may want an open-ended exploration; she may wish to express herself sexually but have no desire for sexual intercourse.

'There used to be an awful conflict when *I* wanted to stop the sex. I was made to feel that I had to justify it . . . it was as if there was an obligation to continue – like, once I'd started I couldn't then say "No"; I should have said "No" at the beginning . . . guys were entitled to sex and if he didn't get it he wouldn't go out with me. . . . Now, all that makes me feel so angry.'

One of the effects of this, of course, is to limit the scope we have, as women, to express and explore our own sexuality.

'I used to be afraid of initiating sexual activity because once something started it very easily became out of control and that's very much to do

343

with penetration and male sexuality. . . . I'm putting more emphasis now on if I do initiate things, then I also have the right to stop them – any time I want to.'

Many of us found we had not given sufficient weight to our own feelings and misgivings and had often dismissed them as our own hang-ups.

'I used to think that those little niggles I got in my head when I felt uncomfortable in sex were because I felt guilty . . . religious parents . . . sex taboo . . . that sort of thing. I don't think it's guilt any more. I think it's very much to do with lack of control.'

Refusing to comply with these expectations, we found, was one of the first steps in taking control back into our own hands. For many of us, the first step in breaking out of these conditioned patterns and responses was to refuse penetration. This was not always easy.

'I felt there was a lot of pressure on me to have penetration. I felt that as soon as there was any physical contact – that was the starting point which would eventually end up with penetration and male orgasm and that would be it.'

The point at which a woman takes a stand and refuses to relate sexually on the basis of these old assumptions is usually a time of crisis for the relationship.

'I made it clear to him that either things changed or I would leave. I remember this as a time of hideous turmoil in our lives, night after night of crying, shouting, arguing, wondering, tormented by doubts: "Am I just a selfish bitch?" I never would have managed without knowing other women were going through the same things.'

It seemed that, in some ways, one of the hardest things was simply to make the men *listen* to what we were saying. All the time we found ourselves hitting up against their preconceived ideas of *what sex is*.

'It was really difficult and for a long time we were both incredibly confused . . . all the time he was hanging on to this "norm" of sex . . . what sex *means* – right, sex means *this* – you know, penetration three times a week. There's so much pressure to believe this from people all around you – *they're* normal and we're not.'

Some of the relationships did not survive this period of crisis, others came through it and grew stronger as a result.

When the men began to listen and accept responsibility for their own behaviour and the need to change, some sort of dialogue became possible.

In some cases the woman had the active support and encouragement of her women friends whilst others struggled on alone.

Nevertheless we found it needed considerable time and struggle to transform our relationships from a sexuality-based-on-penetration to a more female-centred sexuality. And where a long-term relationship existed, with already well-established patterns of interaction, change could sometimes seem impossible. In these situations most women felt that a complete break from sex, often for quite long periods of time, was necessary in order to have the time and space to 'unlearn' the automatic pattern of male control and female compliance which, for many of us, had become so ingrained.

These periods of celibacy not only provided us with a breathing space within which we could begin to dismantle some of the long-established destructive patterns, but also gave us the opportunity to discover more about ourselves and our own needs.

Masturbation was one important way in which we began to learn more about ourselves and our bodies and it was interesting to see how our feelings about it had changed over time and been influenced by feminism. Some of us, for instance, had always masturbated, often in a guilt-ridden and secretive way, whilst others had come to it much later in life as part of our own sexual self-discovery.

'I used to feel a lot of shame over masturbation and the remnants of it are still there – but what I feel much more now is that it's very important in terms of my own sexual autonomy – you know – if things go wrong in sex I can always pleasure myself – I'm not that dependent any more – in fact, what I've been feeling recently is: "How wonderful I am to be able to give myself so much pleasure." '

Some women described how they often felt 'distanced' from their own experience during sex with a partner. 'It's almost as though I'm standing back and watching,' was how one woman described it. Yet when she masturbated she experienced herself quite differently.

Another woman saw this problem as originating in the fact that as women we have been conditioned to see ourselves through men's eyes and therefore perceive ourselves as objects in sex rather than being in tune with our own subjective experience. This can sometimes lead us to 'perform' both for our partners and for ourselves and one woman described how this had prevented her from having orgasms during intercourse.

'I was so busy performing – undulating and moaning and all that – that I wasn't concentrating enough on my own body. I was too attuned to my partner's experience of me to be able to get the simple motion, friction, timing and concentration I needed for orgasm. Learning not to perform

345

with my husband, after so many years of dishonesty, was excruciatingly difficult and painful.'

She felt that for her masturbation had played a crucial part in breaking this pattern, and helped her to be more directly in touch with her own experiences.

'I know this all sounds incredibly mechanical. That's because I find it difficult to talk about my own sexuality openly, honestly, straightforwardly; keep track of all the different levels of experience and analysis; and still make it come out remotely resembling what the lived sexuality is like.
   But now I masturbate more purposefully, learning about myself, my body, my fantasies – also getting to know my bodily sensations and what my body needs.'

One of the most important areas of change, we found, *was* our growing recognition of the importance and emotional depth of our relationships with other women. Sometimes this was expressed sexually.

'Sex with women seems more simple and straightforward, in some ways more safe and in some ways more dangerous. I like the feeling of equality with a woman, and also there are no rules, no ritualised steps to go through, everything is possible.'

Yet sex with women seemed to bring with it its own problems, particularly, it seemed, fears about performance.

'I am often anxious beforehand about being able to give another woman orgasms, as well as general love and pleasure. I catch myself worrying about my performance and despise myself for that.'

One of the most valuable things to come out of this sharing of our experience was the realisation that there was no *one* way forward; no simple uniform solution. We were all actively engaged in reclaiming our own sexuality and taking control back into our own hands and yet the *means* by which each of us chose to do this remained diverse; reflecting our own individual personalities, herstories, past experiences, and current situations.
   If the ways forward were diverse there was certainly unanimity about what it was we were leaving behind. We no longer accepted the 'old assumptions' about what sex is.

'I reject categories like foreplay, the sexual act, afterwards – because they assumed that 'real' sex means penetration and orgasm.'

Once it had been firmly established between us and our partners that sexual intercourse did not have to be an essential part of heterosexual sexuality our feelings towards it began to change; since it was no longer obligatory we could now consider it simply as *one* of the options.

We were also no longer prepared to tolerate practices which in the past we may have unwillingly accepted in the belief that this constituted a 'fair' exchange or was some kind of 'open sexuality'. Being pressured into anal intercourse and oral sex with men was one of the things we found most objectionable.

'In the end I completely turned off sex altogether, so now I simply refuse to do things I don't like.'

We also rejected the more subtle forms of male control in which men have expropriated our orgasms in order to demonstrate either their own sexual skill or used them as 'evidence' of their own anti-sexism.

'A fair proportion of partners have been keen to use techniques other than penetration, although strangely, I have sometimes discouraged this. I think partly because some men have been so overkeen to 'give' me an orgasm I have felt like a performing animal and "turned off".'

None of us were now prepared to have sex with a man unless it was on our terms. This often involved *apparently* unrelated things like moving into our own rooms.

' "I will now only sleep with him in *my* bed, on my territory", said one woman. "It's strictly by invitation only," said another. "He has no 'rights' over my body and I don't fulfil any 'obligations'. It's surprising how many times we sleep together simply enjoying the closeness of each other's bodies without the need for anything more. But it's really important that we can each return to our own beds/own rooms/own space whenever we want. I know it certainly helps me to retain a sense of my own personal autonomy." '

Changing the basis upon which we're prepared to have sexual relationships with men has meant not simply trying to find new techniques for increasing our sexual pleasure but changing the balance of power and control within the relationship itself.

'I Think I'm Gonna Be Sick . . .'
Katina Noble
SR 119 June 1982

Mine is an open relationship
Non-monogamous and free.
How can we struggle for personal politics
Enslaved by jealousy?

I've never really liked 'couples'
So smug in their unwedded bliss
Stifled by insecurities
'Bill and I think *this* and *this*'.

We've no right to possess anybody
Saying 'Sorry, he's mine'
Of course you can love more than one person
It's natural! It's fine!

He stayed out last night – no problem
But – he's seeing her again today
'You mean – this is ongoing, not just lust in the dark?'
I smile in a feeble way

I'm strong enough to cope with this!
(Maybe they won't click)
He says she won't want to get involved. . . .
But I think I'm gonna be sick.

Friday night. They're in her bed now
Wonder if she's got a duvet?
Wonder if her thighs are thinner than mine?
Wonder how long he'll stay. . . .

Now come on! You know this is no threat
He's your lover – and your friend!
This is politically very right on
(But when is it going to end?)

. . . will they linger in her bed all morning
. . . a smile, a touch, a lick . . .
gaze at each other over boiled eggs and toast . . .
I think I'm gonna be sick.

Well, I try reading *The Politics of Sex in the Bourgeois
   Family in Patriarchal Structures Under Capitalism*
But that is no help at all
I try meditation, T'ai Chi . . . Valium
But all I do is bawl

Weep, whimper, sob
Gulp back the tears
Do you need a prescription for cyanide?
This could go on for years . . .

I won't fall into the old scenario:
'He's a bastard. She's a bitch.'
That game's built on dishonesty
But there's just one tiny hitch

My body cannot cope with this
Guts churning, head heavy and thick
Maybe there's something in celibacy
I think I'm gonna be sick

I haven't got all the answers
But I won't give in to this
I'd rather *face* feelings than sink into
Unthinking, monogamous bliss

It's light now. He's not back yet.
God, I hope it's over quick
Anyone got a bucket?
I *know* I'm gonna be sick!

The politics of sexuality and birth control
Sue O'Sullivan
SR 105 April 1981

The 1960s and 1970s were heydays for the pill and IUD. By the mid 1970s 'old-fashioned' barrier methods which women used had all but disappeared as popular choices. My own history bridged the year or so between the accepted use of older devices and the adoption of the new methods. In 1961, deciding I needed birth control meant being fitted with a diaphragm. I was never comfortable using or even thinking about my 'device', and not surprisingly got pregnant with it sitting in my bag, next to the bed. After an illegal abortion, I went straight on to the pill, determined never to get unwillingly pregnant again. I saw myself as unable to cope with something like the diaphragm. The pill was a 'god' send.

It seems to me that various developments came together in the early 1960s to ensure the uncritical widespread acceptance and use of the pill. The application of western technological and scientific knowledge to the 'problem' of birth control was of central importance. The motivation for new discoveries in this field did not come from women's demands, as there was no popular women's movement in the 1950s. The motivation came from the confidence of a male-dominated, profit-orientated belief in the power of science and technology to advance and protect the 'free

349

world'. In the 1950s USA government officials and agencies, politicians and financiers came together in support of population control ideas and methods. The book *Population Bomb,* which presented a picture of the world as a ticking time-bomb which, if set off, would result in a population explosion causing war and communism, illustrated America's conservative concern with the politics of population.

The pill and the IUD were always tied up with American population control programmes and were used on women in Third World countries and on Black and poor women inside the USA. At the same time powerful drug companies and doctors pushed the pill, and many women wanted it. Seemingly they had made a 'choice'. Why did so many of these women reject barrier methods of birth control and take up the pill and, to a lesser extent, the IUD?

During the late 1950s the hold of traditional sex morals was breaking down. Sex, divorce, motherhood, the family, youth, were all beginning to be seen as problems. No coherent alternative morality emerged, but the cohesion of the old one was weakening. In growing numbers women were being pressed with a changing triad of ideas, practices and institutions around sex, reproduction and marriage. The shakiness of the 'holy' trinity meant that each aspect jarred but didn't separate from the others. We neither had the practical methods nor the challenging ideas which would enable us to struggle to make breaks between whom we slept with and when, how we felt about it, if and when we'd have children and who'd care for them, and if and what we thought about marriage.

Our lives were changing, but were filled with confusion and ambivalence, not the least about sleeping with men and using birth control. Many of us who 'did it' still usually did so because of pressure and/or highly romantic expectations, and often continued to out of optimism and/or resignation. At the same time, we tended to be ill at ease with our bodies and lacked the most basic body knowledge. The 'myth of the vaginal orgasm' was untoppled but some of us knew more about sex from historical novelettes than from any prevailing psychological or physiological theories. We also knew at some level about birth control and often said we didn't want to get pregnant, but lots of us didn't use birth control. All this ambivalence and confusion about our bodies, men, reproduction, sex and marriage, affected negatively the possibility of controlling our own fertility.

Our use, misuse, or non-use of the then-available barrier methods of birth control (primarily the diaphragm, various creams or pessaries, the cervical cap in Britain and Europe, or demands for a male lover to use a condom) were reflected in the contradictions I've described. Women also were receiving increasingly strident messages from men that if they didn't 'put out' they were frigid, teases, old-fashioned, or just hadn't discovered how great it was to fuck! Women had not defined their own needs, but they were, as always, terrified of unwanted pregnancies.

So it wasn't surprising that when the pill came along, most heterosexual women welcomed it with open arms. The only difficulty was to get over the fear that if you took the pill and were unmarried you were announcing to every man who came along your 'availability'. On the other hand, the pill was easy to take, you didn't have to be familiar with your body, and it offered the surest way of avoiding pregnancy. We could *let* sex happen to us, but the successful use of barrier methods demanded much more than passivity. The pill, at least initially, didn't challenge this at all; sex was about 'doing it', but not about resolving in a pro woman way the contradictions we faced in sexual relations with men. The pill permitted a separation between sex and reproduction, but in favour of male penetration. However, contained within the so-called sexual revolution and the popularity of the pill was an eventual feminist critique and struggle.

It is true that women were not given any counter-information about the pill which might have affected their use of it. But even if we had had the known information about possible risks, would we, at that time in history, have rejected the pill in favour of the older barrier methods? In order to understand the complexity of how we felt about ourselves in relationship to birth control, we have to look at the different influences on women. Of course the profit motives of the drug and IUD companies were an integral part of what shaped our patterns of 'choice', as were our naive beliefs in the progressive and neutral nature of western science and technology. It is the companies and their 'tame' scientists who, more than anyone else, must bear the responsibility for the widespread use of the pill and IUD. Given women's oppression, our internalised self-hatred, and the lack of a collective challenge to our subordination to men, it's not hard to see why many of us were easily persuaded that we were being modern and rational in our use of the pill.

Twenty years after its introduction the pill's ascendancy as one of the most common forms of birth control in the west is over. In the years since the pill was introduced, extensive research has shown just how dangerous hormones can be for women. Serious short-term effects came to light to reveal far more than the initial talk of 'weight gains', 'headaches', and 'nausea'. Thrombosis and possible links with cancer began to look very real and members of the medical profession itself regarded the pill as a danger to women.

From the late 1960s, the growing impact of feminism, especially in relation to the demystification of doctors, drugs, and the whole idea of medicine as a form of social control and as a part of sexual, race and class divisions, meant that more women were looking critically at what the medical profession was telling them to do. For example, many women were disturbed by medical intervention in pregnancy and childbirth. Why had events which had previously been seen as healthy occasions been defined by the medical profession as illnesses to be managed? More women were open to the idea of using forms of contraception which they controlled and which had fewer, if any, side-effects. Consciousness-raising and feminist analysis of our sexuality were both a start to the long task of resolving some of the ambivalence and confusion we had felt about ourselves throughout the late 1950s and 1960s, and which I've suggested led to our uncritical use of the pill in the first place and to our abandonment of the 'messy', 'unreliable' barrier methods. The development of women's health groups and the proliferation of feminist health courses and literature helped women to learn about and like their bodies, to gather together information, and discuss the links between sexuality and birth control. The autonomy of the women's movement made it possible and necessary to assert the wholeness of women apart from men – and the nature of our needs and desires both in relationship to men and to one another. As more women became lesbians, I think it brought home even more sharply to heterosexual women that they were taking risks with their bodies *for* the men they related to, and they felt angry at the casual assumption that it was OK for women to pump pills into themselves for years on end.

So in this country, and even more in the USA, a significant number of women were scared and angry enough about the risks they were taking with the pill and the IUD to decide that any advantages of those methods were far outweighed by the risks. The alternative which many women turned to was initially the diaphragm. Then in 1977 Barbara Seaman published a popular and influential book in the USA called *Women and the Crisis in Sex Hormones* (Bantam Books). One short chapter was called 'Gone but not forgotten: the cervical cap'. Most people date the upsurge in interest in the cap from the publication of this book. Today in the USA there are 30,000 to 40,000 women who have been fitted with caps from a variety of mainly alternative clinics and institutions.

All of this throws up some interesting questions for us as feminists. We can't go around claiming that the older forms of barrier contraceptives represent some golden past of woman-controlled fertility. Technological advances in themselves are not bad and I would welcome new forms of birth control which were proved safe and effective – surely something not out of the reach of a woman-centred science and technology. Also we still have to ask whether the impact of feminism and self-help has significantly changed women's attitudes towards their bodies and towards birth control, compared with 20 years ago.

Now government agencies in the USA have restricted health clinics from fitting caps, in the name of possible unknown risks. There is no point in simply saying they've got it *all* wrong – even if we oppose the restrictions. It's a matter of the politics of the approach. In the USA we see that it is traditional, government-approved groups and institutions which will set up studies of the cap and evaluate information. The very structure which feminist-informed health care sprang up in opposition to will sit in judgment on a method of birth control which *feminists* introduced as an *alternative* to mainline medical choices. The head of the

National Institute of Child Health and Human Development, which will sponsor a three-year government (Food and Drug Administration)-approved study, responded to the anger of feminist health activists at the restrictions on the cap: 'The people who are complaining are the same ones who yelled at the FDA for not requiring more studies on tampons. Either they want the FDA to protect them or they don't.' It's exactly this sterile notion of 'either/or' which reveals the limitations of the FDA position. Yes, feminists are saying that tampons came under scrutiny only after serious health problems arose. The difference is that it's huge multinational companies who produce and market tampons, and make immense fortunes out of menstruation. They had, and have, no intrinsic motive to monitor or investigate their own produce unless they're forced to. On the other hand, women's health clinics would tend to have no profit motivation in fitting cervical caps; they're motivated by feminist politics and perspectives. If problems with the cap became apparent why would they want to cover them up? It's not feminist health workers who've been shoving pills down women's throats over the past 20 years, or injecting women with Depo-Provera. Here in Britain we welcome any studies which throw more light on the effectiveness or possible health risks of the cervical cap, but we also want to take into account the known benefits *for* a heterosexual woman of using a device which pumps *no* extra hormones into her body, which can be left in place for a longer period of time than a diaphragm and therefore can possibly be more conducive to a pleasurable sexual life, and which, in common with the diaphragm, may offer protection from infections brought to the cervix by other sources – primarily the penis.

A feminist approach to birth control would have to take into account the present range of options women have, the context in which those choices are made and what possible future developments we want to see. How do we most effectively present counter-information? How do we assess information from different sources? How can we make informed decisions and measure effectively the relative risks of various forms of birth control? One thing for certain is that we must counter arguments based on 'either/or' thinking. We may want the cap to be available without claiming that it is perfect. The politics of demanding the right to try a cervical cap from FPA clinics involves challenging the medical profession's preference for pushing the easiest and fastest-taught method, and its keenness for drugs and technology. After all, we must insist that birth control, like other health care, exists for us, not we for it.

Thanks to Diane St Clair and Marianne Godfrey for helping me to get this article together.

FIGURE 29 Strippers' revenge *Alison Fell* (*SR 16* October 1973)

Editorial
SR 116 March 1982

Dear *Spare Rib*,
I'm writing to renew my subscription. I really enjoy the magazine, except for one thing. Why is there so much on lesbians in it? Don't get me wrong, I'm not anti-gay. But they are in a minority, and if you want to reach more readers, surely you shouldn't publish so much about them. As it is, I can't show your otherwise excellent magazine to my mother, my neighbours or my workmates. Hoping you will accept this criticism as kindly meant.

In sisterhood,
Anon.

Dear Reader,
You are by no means the only reader to write to us in these terms though you put it more politely than many.

We do want to reach more readers, but why do you assume they will all be heterosexual? Some of them *will* be lesbians. Thousands of lesbians are longing to read material relevant to their lives, and not finding it anywhere.

We're often puzzled as to where all these pieces are that readers say we publish. The fact is that we have, in over a hundred issues, published no more than half a dozen features about lesbians! Is it perhaps our classifieds, where each month women advertise to meet or correspond with each other – hardly surprising in a world where lesbians are very isolated and have few places to meet? If it's not these ads, then it must be the occasional brief mention within feature articles, such as the one on hysterectomy in *SR 112*, where, among other women's views, one lesbian had a voice. Surely it's relevant to remind ourselves how it takes just that bit more courage to face going into hospital when you're going to have to answer awkward questions about contraception and 'intercourse' behind thin curtains in a ward of listening ears, or be visited by your lover who dare not show you any affection openly there – just at the time when you most need it. In *SR 105* a mother, writing about caring for her son with learning disabilities, mentioned she was a lesbian. Several readers complained – irrelevant, they said. One accused us at *Spare Rib* of creating false divisions, unnecessarily labelling people. Yet it's obvious how much more vulnerable that mother would be, because of her sexuality, in terms of keeping her son if the authorities wanted to place him in an institution. We cannot ignore these vital aspects of women's lives.

When women mention in passing in their articles that they have a male lover, we receive no complaints. *This* is not seen as irrelevant, or creating differences between women. It's not seen as problematic at all – it's only women's lesbian relationships we are asked to justify and be quiet about. Do you, as a heterosexual woman, ask yourself about why you're heterosexual; why, in the world at large, you never have to justify your heterosexuality in the way lesbians do? We want to question the assumption that heterosexuality is 'the norm'. A whisper – which is all *Spare Rib* has really given to lesbians over the years – can seem like a shout when all around is silent. No other nationally distributed magazine gives lesbians any kind of voice of their own – just the passing curious mention or derogatory comment. So when the word appears in *Spare Rib* it probably stands out a mile.

You also say that lesbians are a minority, but why's that? What real choice do women have over their sexuality when the world is so silent about lesbianism; where lesbianism is made to seem 'unnatural' (animals don't do it), immature (just a passing phase), or breaking the sacred rule that says sex is only for making babies and our only sexual function is to procreate? The world bombards girls and young women with heterosexual propaganda in every comic, magazine, television show and billboard. *Spare Rib* is, in fact, just the magazine where you'd expect to read a good deal about lesbians. Women caring for women – something central to women's liberation – takes many forms, and we need to show it in all its fighting spirit and passion. Supporting women in making choices is central to the movement.

Amongst the neighbours, friends, mothers and work colleagues that you are presuming to be heterosexual there will be many who are silenced lesbians, who are painfully pretending to be heterosexual because of people's opinions and because of the very real threats and losses (jobs, children, housing, community and social support) that lesbians still face. The end of discrimination against lesbians is still a very long way off but will inevitably bring with it more women choosing lesbianism.

The more we use the word in *Spare Rib* with pride and relevance, the more women will be able to choose it, or claim it as theirs, at last, with relief, no longer afraid to say what they are. The more articles we publish like 'Life is just a phase I'm going through' (*SR 115*) and the interview with Jackie Forster in this issue, the more we print on lesbian politics, the better. Breaking the silence can only help us understand the links between our lives, how all women's efforts to be liberated are connected, and how our efforts can be strengthened.

In Sisterhood,
Spare Rib collective

AIDS – an epidemic of hysteria
Susan Ardill
SR 153 April 1985

Most women would confess to having breathed an inner sigh of relief during all the recent AIDS hysteria: at least it's not us having to confront this nightmare. Women, and especially lesbians, are in the lowest risk categories for contracting the disease. (I've seen only one mention in the straight press that the 'gay plague' doesn't include lesbians). But, apart from the fact that some of us *will* confront AIDS, as friends, relatives, health workers, we also know by now that any issue which has the familiar ingredients of sex, disease, the media and the health system is bound to have a good many implications for feminists. We can't complacently avert our eyes.

The basic facts should be well known by now. AIDS is thought to be caused by a virus known as HIV; 90% of people exposed to this virus will probably not develop AIDS. There is a test (not fully reliable) which shows if someone has been exposed to the virus (their blood will contain an antibody to it). The other 10% may incubate the virus for six months to four years (during which time they may be unknowingly infectious) before symptoms arise of breakdown of the body's defences; then secondary illnesses such as pneumonia can set in and are usually fatal.[1]

In order to take hold, the virus must enter the bloodstream, either through transmission of blood (transfusions, cuts, wounds, shared needles) or absorption of the virus into blood from semen. The anus is a more likely site for such absorption than the vagina, as it has thinner walls and is more likely to tear during sex.

Although gay activists here have been fighting for increased funding for research and care for years, it's only when the disease threatens 'normal' people that it gets publicity. I was in Australia in November when the press erupted into an orgy of queer-bashing after several people were infected via blood transfusions. There were serious calls to charge

---

1. Two years later it is thought that a much higher percentage of those exposed to HIV *will* develop AIDS.

the donor with manslaughter. Women were urged to donate blood – when several such women revealed that they were lesbians they were turned away by staff obviously brain-addled by the 'gay disease' 'theories' propounded by the media. (Though I have heard mentioned the existence of a Lesbian Blood Pool in Los Angeles.)

Back in Britain I weathered the February storm with a strange sense of déjà vu, as AIDS plagued the Fleet Street boys, and their readers were stirred into action, armed, no doubt, with misinformation from the tabloids.

We had firemen wavering over mouth-to-mouth resuscitation (gay lives are cheap), cab companies refusing to pick up from gay clubs, airlines trying to ban AIDS sufferers from flying, cleaners fearful of working in a theatre with Gay Sweatshop; conditions in jails made even more intolerable with restrictions on prisoners' movements. Numerous 'fellow-workers' across the nation were reported to be 'panicking' at the thought of sharing offices with homosexuals. After a prison chaplain died, the District Health Officer was quoted in the Mirror as saying there was 'no point' in tracing his close contacts, 'there is nothing anyone can do for them.' British Airways (and how many other companies?) is reported to be considering making new staff sign a declaration stating whether they are homosexual or bisexual. Now that an air hostess ('a pretty young victim') has AIDS, another stewardess was quoted (*The Sun*, 6 March) as saying, 'Our biggest fear has been that *AIDS* would spread to the girls.' Why the *biggest* fear? Because it would demonstrate that AIDS is not some mystery associated with male homosexuality?

The media has planted its seeds well – underneath the new automatic suspicion that all homosexuals are diseased lurks the real message – homosexuality` is the disease. That illnesses can stand as metaphors, a focus of disgust for those who bear them, is nothing new for women who've suffered gynaecological and venereal diseases. It's pretty apparent that our mates the journalists are more concerned to protect the 'public' from homosexuality *per se* than with looking at ways to help AIDS sufferers.

Ironically, it seems that it's mainly this savage homophobia which makes AIDS newsworthy. The spread of AIDS has reached epidemic proportions in some parts of Central Africa and Haiti, suffered equally by heterosexual women and men. Four out of the six women in Britain who've developed AIDS are from African countries. Yet all non-gay sufferers, generally poor and Black, are virtually ignored. Structural racism may also be a contributory factor to the directions medical research takes. In a major feature in the *New York Native* (17 December 1984) Dr Jane Teas claimed that the Center for Disease Control in Atlanta, Georgia, is suppressing her hypothesis linking AIDS with the spread of African swine fever (also epidemic in Central Africa and Haiti). Although tests have shown some correlation, Teas say the CDC refuses to investigate any connection between the two diseases.

What chance do women have of getting AIDS? So far in Britain only six women have. But the Centre for Disease Control reports a study which showed that, in a group of women in steady sexual relationships with men who had the antibody, 35% also developed the antibody i.e. the virus had been transmitted. So women having relationships with men in high-risk groups, e.g. intravenous drug-users, or active bisexuals, should take some precautions – avoiding anal sex, using condoms, avoiding intercourse if there are any vaginal abrasions.

The female nurse who accidentally infected herself with a needle from an AIDS patient, was reported (*Sunday Mirror* 24 February) to have been given the 'chilling warning' never to have children for fear of passing on the disease. AIDS *can* be passed to a foetus from the mother, but how likely this is is unknown. Also unknown is the effect of a pregnancy on a woman with the antibody or the disease. Could it activate or exacerbate AIDS? As yet, no one has any answers.

One area where a number of lesbians are personally affected is that of self-insemination. Lesbian-organised artificial insemination networks in the USA, particularly on the West Coast, have been drastically affected by the spread of AIDS. Gay men had tended to be favoured as donors; there was more trust that lesbianism would not be used against mothers in later custody bids. In Britain now, where as many as 30% of gay men might carry the antibody to AIDS, they are being advised against donating sperm; conversely, it would seem wise for lesbians currently planning self-insemination not to use gay donors. The woman would definitely be at risk; whether a foetus conceived with AIDS-infected sperm would necessarily develop the disease is yet another open question.

Even if the furore over AIDS dies down, the spin-offs will no doubt continue to wreak havoc in many people's lives. The present climate of mounting heterosexism could lead to a concerted push against 'gay rights', which is bound to affect lesbians too – in housing, employment, anti-discrimination legislation, grants funding. There are signs of a more repressive atmosphere around sexuality generally. Suddenly, 'freedom' is a bit thinner on the ground, and 'normalcy' has some added power to its punch. Let's not let 'the normals' get away with it.

What do you want to know about AIDS?
Sue O'Sullivan
SR 175 February 1987

During the past six months or so, AIDS has acquired a 'cross-over' identity. What many 'experts', lesbians and gay men said all along is finally forming the basis of a significant amount of mainstream media and government health education material. The disease only manifested itself *first* (in many western countries) among male homosexuals. Now the reality is coming home – into the homes of the so-called 'bridging groups'

358

SEXUALITY AND WOMEN'S LIBERATION

of bisexuals, intravenous drugs users and prostitutes and into the previously sanctified homes of heterosexuals.

Condoms are the name of the game, and how the manufacturers must be profitably squirming. What an irony. For ages men have claimed that condoms ruined their pleasure – 'like wearing a raincoat'. Now fear transforms their use into the joys of protection. Nothing like a hint of death to gild the image (and use) of this particular device. It is interesting to speculate whether heterosexual women will now find it easier to demand that men use condoms as a protection against the mutually feared AIDS; will the birth rate fall where the naked penis is feared?

All the talk about heterosexually active people being at risk from AIDS has obscured the very positive position lesbians occupy presently. Concern about the wide spectrum of people who may get AIDS is a step in the right direction, but because many people (and almost 100% of the media) continue to collapse lesbianism into homosexuality, lesbians are targeted in the 'gay plague' backlash which continues to run concurrently with the 'new' knowledge that heterosexuals get the disease as well. Lesbianism is virtually invisible in any media coverage – serious or sensational – of AIDS. The importance of making it clear that lesbianism is the safest sexuality going at present is not to claim some moral superiority. Its importance lies in revealing the absurdity of the popular claim that male homosexuals brought AIDS on themselves by flying in the face of nature and religion (since when have the voices of reaction ever condoned lesbianism?). It is important also to claim a visibility *as lesbians* in all the discussions about choices of sexual practice.

But I believe that AIDS is an issue which affects us all; not through some moral imperative but materially and politically. What AIDS makes abundantly clear is that the demarcations between our lives as heterosexuals, prostitutes, etc. etc. are relatively fluid. Heterosexual women become lesbians, many prostitutes are lesbians, some lesbians sleep with men from time to time, intravenous drug use cuts across boundaries.

AIDS is an even more serious threat to the lives of many Africans where it affects mainly heterosexuals of both sexes. Because of the heterosexual pattern of infection there, many more babies are born with AIDS than is now the case in the west. One estimate (*AIDS and the Third World*, PANOS Dossier 1) says that, 'The experience and success of Africa's fight with AIDS will determine how the rest of the world goes. Africa is humanity's frontline.' They estimate that at least one million Africans, mostly in Central Africa, will probably die of AIDS in the next decade.

The poverty of many African countries and the flow of large numbers of people from the countryside to urban areas – both distinct legacies of imperialism – create a situation in which the struggle against AIDS is extremely difficult. 'The cost of treating ten American AIDS patients is greater than the entire budget of Zaire's largest hospital, where as many as half the patients admitted are found to be carrying the AIDS virus' (PANOS).

359

AIDS is a world-wide phenomenon which does not 'belong' to any particular group and cannot be 'blamed' on any particular group. A radical and feminist 'politics of AIDS' is still on the agenda in this country. What do *SR* readers think about it all? Would feminist involvement in AIDS work mean that time and energy were going into a non-feminist issue? Please let me hear from you – your ideas, opinions and feelings.

Round in a flat world
Tessa Weare
SR 78 January 1979

Everywhere I go, it goes before me, this round full womb. When I sit it nests heavily on my thighs; as I turn my body, my arms brush against it. My skin is unbelievably stretched into this large gourd, this drum, this container. The baby curled inside kicks at my ribs, my pelvis, each side of my body. In about two weeks it will be born.

When I walk into a room of people I see them noticing this protruding part of me first, and me second. The more honest stare at it with fascination as they talk to me, others glance furtively pretending they haven't noticed. Many are uneasy, some even physically withdraw from me.

Meanwhile in the London streets I'm surrounded by advertising hoardings: thin models displayed across their flat surfaces. And women in the streets, their hips encased in tight jeans, hip-hugging skirts. I find myself staring at their flat bellies, unable to imagine that mine once looked like theirs. And the men too: everyone with bones and protruding genitals. I feel out of place.

Sometimes it seems as if I have an invisible seal around my body that both protects me and pushes me apart from everyone else. This may have something to do with a basic emotion, reaching back to the days when fertility was worshipped, that makes people feel hushed and forced to contemplate life and death when they see a pregnant woman. But mostly I think it's because pregnancy has no place in the sexuality that pervades everything.

Once you are pregnant you are 'obviously' another man's property, and rape – physical or verbal – has so much to do with the threat of impregnating the innocent, the vulnerable, or with punishment for being available – and I'm not. So for a long time I've been free from sexual innuendos, grabs at my tits, attempted pick-ups. Men who walk up to me turn away from my womb with a mixture of guilt, fear and disgust on their faces. Strangely, once I was no longer bombarded with sexist sexual advances, it struck me how in one way they gave me a sense of power, of attractiveness, and more importantly, a sense that I existed.

I'm trying to describe this – the alienation of being round in a flat, square world – because it wasn't something I expected about being pregnant.

There were things that could have prepared me. I can remember when my women's group were out on the street collecting signatures against the Benyon Bill, how we all felt very nervous about asking pregnant women to sign. It seemed like a sacrilege, as if a pregnant woman, absorbed by the process of making life, would somehow be upset or insulted by any mention of terminating it. And worse, as if she suddenly had no personality, no opinions, apart from her pregnancy.

But because I was a feminist and my pregnancy was planned, I thought it would be different. I didn't identify with the pregnant woman I saw caught up in the present image of motherhood, just as before I became a feminist I had refused to admit I was oppressed. I expected to keep a personality that would be seen as separate from pregnancy, that my life would not be enveloped by a child coming in the way my mother's was.

I planned to revel in my new fecundity when it began to show. I would be round and graceful, brightly coloured and shining with new life. I would be proud, dignified, active, full of vibrant sexuality. So positive that I would disturb any man who might feel disgust and envy at my power to reproduce.

I read in books, feminist ones included, that a woman feels more sexual when she is pregnant; fears of contraceptive failure are banished, for instance. British Medical Association pregnancy handbooks now advise 'Don't deprive yourself, therefore, or your partner of the normal pleasures for a young couple. . . . Intercourse is quite all right at almost all times during pregnancy.' And most modern books and magazines are full of small nudges of encouragement – pregnant women look 'more feminine', have 'an added bonus of beauty', and so on.

However I suspect that much of the emphasis on 'sexiness' during pregnancy has more to do with keeping husbands happy than with any recognition of the potential of female sexuality.

I, at least, never found mine. On a physical level, yes, I could see the potential; sex was more spontaneous without contraception. And without any possibilty of pregnancy each time we made love it was more clearly a reaffirmation of our love for each other, or a fulfilment of our sexual needs. Also the growing womb stretches the vagina upwards, making it more sensitive and open.

At the same time I felt more clumsy as my womb grew (five months onwards). My breasts went through many stages of aching and being less sensitive. And the baby knocking on my womb as I made love was often distracting. But as sex for me takes place on both an emotional and a physical level, I don't see any of those 'facts' standing on their own.

Emotionally I sometimes felt alive and vibrating with a sort of 'expanding' energy. At other times I didn't feel sexual at all; I wanted to be an enclosed fruit, untouched and gently ripening. Mostly my sexual desire took place on a mental/emotional level, while my body dragged some way behind.

But I can't say whether any of these were/are my 'natural' female

361

feelings about pregnancy, because everything I did and thought about myself was so affected by the attitudes I encountered in women and men, poisoned as we all are by patriarchal capitalist values.

Long before it was showing, the men I knew responded to my pregnancy with a sigh of relief. I was no longer such a threat as a feminist because I'd proved that underneath I was merely a woman. In their relief was a disdain, conscious or not, for they now felt able to remove themselves from me, place themselves above me.

Many of them stopped flirting with me – I never realised how much flirtation was in our relationship until it stopped. Others saw it as a chance to make me into their mothers. A few tried not to be 'put off', but nevertheless couldn't hide their embarrassment. All of this increased my anger and resentment, and yet filled me full of a feeling of impotence, for my words lost their effect, ironically at a time when I was actually most potent.

As for my feminist friends and sisters, most of them have chosen not to have children (yet). Quite often I found that because they'd rejected that potential in themselves, they rejected it in me too. Some treated me with pity, some with amazement that I'd voluntarily chosen to increase my own oppression. Others dismissed it as totally irrelevant, boring even, they couldn't see what the 'fuss' was about. And they certainly weren't about to get into gossiping about pink and blue woollies, which is what pregnancy is about, isn't it?

A gap has definitely grown between me and my friends who don't want children. I'm not separable from my decision. My friendships now tend towards people with children, or people who are contemplating them.

My disappointment at these reactions tended to increase my rejection of my body as 'me', and at the same time increase my absorption with the strange and new thing that was happening to my body. I have always been slim; I found it hard to accept my body growing round, heavy and 'fat' as people insisted on calling it. My sexuality was connected to being 'sylph-like'.

Shulamith Firestone calls pregnancy 'barbaric'. As my womb grew I felt conscious that this attitude was deep in many of us. Some reactions were hard to take. I asked one woman whether she would like to feel the baby kicking. I watched her physically draw herself back, 'erg no,' she replied, disgusted. After this happened on several occasions I learned to be more cautious.

There is a tendency amongst women to reject aspects of our bodies that can be used against us, to oppress us. Often I heard women describe pregnancy and childbirth as ugly, embarrassing or even disgusting. Much of that goes back to men who find women ugly when they are pregnant. Who refuse to touch their wombs. Who hate to recognise that they too once came into this world, bloody and blue, out of a woman's stretching vagina.

I've experienced this attitude mostly from feminists and lefties, in particular those rooted in the middle class. Others, who criticise me for not being married, or for not having a steady home, seem far more accepting of the physical side of my pregnancy.

It's difficult to admit that I've been very depressed at times. The atmosphere around me crippled my desire to bring my feminism to bear on my pregnancy and to be proud of my womb as something vibrantly sexual. This is a society that puts slabs of concrete over the fertile earth, that destroys hundreds of lives in its lust for hard metals wrenched out of the earth. That kills, rapes, destroys. In this world pregnancy is not worshipped, it is merely necessary.

'Having a baby isn't an illness: it's a perfectly natural process which millions of women cope with successfully (Gwen Farrow, *Maternity and Mothercraft*, January/February 1978). In other words, pregnancy (and childbirth) should take place between clean white sheets. It should be hidden, delicately beneath pale floral maternity dresses. Women should learn to 'cope' with it, with a decent display of modesty, guilt and embarrassment. Rather than feeling pride in their bodies, they should limit expressions of happiness to the number of prams, cots, cribs and Mothercare babyclothes they buy. They should be pleased, happy, pretty, but above all not overly obsessed by it. And never forget their husbands.

If they stray from this path, the combined 'care' of the medical profession and the pressure of advertising ensure they don't wander too far. I tried to rebel against this NHS image of motherhood, but the only image I could find was that of the Great Earth Mother, deprived of her magic and evil, now merely the round, loving all-provider. She bakes, knits and sews, and sits in passive contentment, breeding. Feminists have picked up on this image from the hippy sixties and tried to present it more positively. I felt, for example, this ran through the pregnancy section of the American edition of *Our Bodies Our Selves*.

Although it is a more constructive image than the previous one, going back to women as primarily physical, earthy beings is no help to someone like me who wants to have an active, working, intelligent image of themselves when pregnant. I don't feel I can counter my rejection of my physicality by worshipping it. The thought brings out all my fears of being engulfed by my body, becoming only tits, cunt, womb and no me.

Yet I needed an image to give me a positive sense of myself, to stop me feeling defeated and sinking into depression. Often I've felt as if I was struggling with an unknown, without words to describe it.

Alone, of course, it's impossible to defeat this feeling, just as it's impossible to struggle without a context. If your feelings of oppression have no meaning and no expression to others, how do you know it's not just you that's wrong?

I've had much appreciated support during my pregnancy. From the stubbornness I learnt from feminism. From my lover and the things we struggled through and survived, from friends and sisters. And from my lovely mother. But all of us at times have been confounded by the patriar-chal hatred of the womb.

Over the last eight months I've had glimpses of what pregnancy could be. One time when the old woman next door knitted a jumper for the baby, she told me with a smile that it was the wrong colour as the baby would be a boy. She explained that it was riding high, not from side to side, and this made it a boy. But somehow in her excitement and enthusiasm about the coming child, and in her calm assurance in the complete naturalness of that event, I could feel how women, long before the medical profession took control away from us, had had a whole world of knowledge and folklore that gave meaning to pregnancy, that celebrated it, and were not scared or revolted by it.

And when my lover lies beside me and plays games with the baby in the womb, tapping out messages which it taps replies to, then we feel how wonderful the new life is, how real and exciting. We've felt it change from a small wriggling tadpole to someone firm and muscular, with actions that are strong and controlled. Now it is pushing downwards, and soon, like all ripeness, it will burst out.

Even one time sitting on the tube, in a carriage suddenly full of men facing me, the baby started to kick violently, as it often does when travelling. I sat there laughing to myself as my round gourd heaved and hiccupped while the men, so still and flat and embarrassed, seemed suddenly nothing: irrelevant and removed compared to the awe and freshness of new life.

But a major experience of pregnancy has been all the things I can't do. I can't or shouldn't smoke, drink, travel too far. I can't rent houses/flats (no one wants a baby), I can't get a job. It's hard to stay up all night, to stand through a show. So often I've felt unable to 'keep up'. And keeping up is what this society is all about. Because there isn't a positive image to counter all this, I've felt at times very deeply that I was a drag – or that the pregnancy was.

Imagining a society where pregnancy was made easy, desirable, delightful, where children were expected in all public places, I realise how far from that we are. At the moment we cannot talk of women having a genuine choice about the way they experience pregnancy or children.

I began by thinking I could take on sexist attitudes to pregnancy, but now I feel no one can have a 'feminist pregnancy' on their own. Like all aspects of our oppression, we can't leave pregnancy to personal solutions: we have to change the structures and attitudes that surround us.'

Tessa Weare has now changed her name to Tessa Goldhawk.

'Clitoral truth'
Margaret S. Chalmers
SR 39 September 1975

I have never had a climax.
No! I swear!
It's the clitoral truth.

RESOURCE AND BOOK LIST

The organizations and books in this section do not represent a comprehensive listing. National organizations have sometimes been listed which can provide you with local contacts. The general feminist and advice contacts may be able to give more specific information.

CHAPTER 1 DOWN THERE

Organizations

Endometriosis Association
65 Holmdene Ave
London SE24 9LD
(01 737 4764)

Herpes Association
41 North Rd
London N7 9DP
(01 737 4764)

Hysterectomy Support Group
11 Henryson Rd
Brockley
London SE4 1HL
01 690 5987

Older Feminist Network
c/o A Woman's Place
Hungerford House
Victoria Embankment
London WC2

Older Lesbian Network
c/o London Friend
274 Upper St
London N1 2UA
(01 359 7371)

Latin American Women's Right Services
Beauchamp Lodge
2 Warwick Crescent
London W2 7ND
(01 289 1601)

Liberation Network of People with Disabilities
c/o Townshend House
Green Lanes
Marshfield
Chippenham

Liverpool Sickle Cell Centre
Abercromby Health Centre
Grove St
Liverpool L77 7HT
(051 708 9370)

London Black Women's Health Action Project
Wickham House
10 Cleveland Way
London E1 4TZ
(01 790 2424)

London Community Health Resource
68 Chalton St
London NW1 1JR
(01 388 0241)

London Health Emergency
335 Gray's Inn Rd
London WC1
(01 833 2020)

Manchester Sickle Cell Centre
Monton St
Manchester 14
(061 226 8972)

Multi-Ethnic Women's Health Project
City and Hackney Community Health Council
210 Kingsland Rd
London E2 8EB
(01 739 6308)

National Council of Voluntary Organizations
26 Bedford Square
London WC1B 3HU
(01 636 4066)

Patients' Association
Room 33
18 Charing Cross Rd
London WC2
(01 240 0671)

RADAR
25 Mortimer St
London W1N 8AB
(01 637 5400)

Radical Nurses Group
20 Melrose Road
Sheffield 3
South Yorkshire

Sickle Cell Society
Green Lodge
Barretts Green Rd
London NW10 7AP

Sisters Against Disablement
c/o Women's Reproductive Rights Information Centre (WRRIC)
52–54 Featherstone St
London EC1

Socialist Health Association
195 Walworth Rd
London SH17 1R
(01 703 6833/01 701 4706)

Women and Medical Practice
666 High Rd
London N17
(01 885 2277)

Women in Medicine
34 Hunter House Rd
Sheffield S11 8TW
(0742 660470)

Women in Prison
444 Chiswick High Rd
London W4 5TT
(01 994 6474/1)

Women's Health and Hazards Group
c/o A Woman's Place
Hungerford House
Victoria Embankment
London WC1

Books

Bryan, Beverley, Dadzie, Stella and Scafe, Suzanne, *The Heart of the Race: Black Women's Lives in Britain*, Virago, 1985.

Campling, Jo (ed.), *Images of Ourselves: Women with Disabilities Talking*, Routledge & Kegan Paul, 1981.

Craig, Marianne, *Office Workers' Survival Handbook*, British Society for Social Responsibility in Science, 1981.

Doyle, Lesley, *The Political Economy of Health*, Pluto, 1979.

Faulder, Carolyn, *Whose Body Is It? The Troubling Issue of Informed Consent*, Virago, 1985.

Grewal, Kay, Landor, Lewis and Parmar, P. (eds), *Charting the Journey: An Anthology of Black and Third World Women's Writing*, Sheba, 1987.

Kenner, Charmian, *No Time for Women: Exploring Women's Health in the 1930s and Today*, Pandora, 1985.

Mitchell, Jeannette, *What Is To Be Done About Illness and Health?*, Penguin, 1984.

Prashar, Anionwu and Brozovic, *Sickle Cell Anaemia – Who Cares?*, Runnymede Trust, 1985.

Roberts, Helen, *The Patient Patients*, Pandora, 1985.

Rowe, Dorothy, *Living With the Bomb: Can We Live Without Enemies?*, Routledge & Kegan Paul, 1985.

Savage, Wendy, *A Savage Enquiry: Who Controls Childbirth?*, Virago, 1986.

Sickle Cell Society, *Pain in Sickle Cell Disease*, Sickle Cell Society Publications

Torkington, Protasia, *The Racial Politics of Health: A Liverpool Profile*, Merseyside Area Profile Group, 1983.

CHAPTER 3 EMTOIONAL MATTERS

Organizations

Afro-Caribbean Mental Health Association
48 East Lake Rd
London SE5 9QL
(01 737 3604)

Asha-Lambeth
Asian Women's Resource Centre
27 Santley St
London SW4 7QF
(01 274 8854)

Asian Women's Project
Community Psychiatric Nursing Dept
Highcroft Hospital
Eddington
Birmingham 23
(021 378 2211, ext. 4129)

Birmingham Women's Counselling and Therapy Centre
43 Ladywood Middleway
Birmingham B16 8HA
(021 455 8677)

Glasgow Women's Support Network
2 Queens Ave
Glasgow G4 9BW
(041 332 2541)

NAFSIYAT – The Inter-cultural Therapy Centre
278 Seven Sisters Rd
Finsbury Park
London N4 2HY

National Association of Mental Health (MIND)
22 Harley St
London W1N 2ED
(01 637 0741)

Womankind
Bristol Settlement
43 Ducie Rd
Barton Hill
Bristol BS5 0AX
(0272 556164)

Women and Mental Health Information and Support Group
29 Stanley Rd
Whalley Range
Manchester
(061 226 9757)

Women's Counselling and Therapy Service
Oxford Chambers
Oxford Place
Leeds LS1 3AX
(0532 455725)

Women's Therapy Centre
6 Manor Gardens
London N7
(01 263 6200)

Books

Eichenbaum, Luise and Orbach, Susie, *What Do Women Want?*, Fontana, 1983.

Ernst, Sheila and Goodison, Lucy, *In Our Own Hands: A Book of Self-Help Therapy*, The Women's Press, 1981.

Haddon, Celia, *Women and Tranquillisers*, Sheldon Press, 1984.

McNeill, P. McShea, M. and Parmar, P. (eds), *Through the Break: Women in Personal Struggle*, Sheba, 1987.

Mitchell, Juliet, *Psychoanalysis and Feminism*, Penguin, 1974.

Nairne, Kathy and Smith, Gerrilyn, *Dealing With Depression*, The Women's Press, 1983.

Rowe, Dorothy,` *Depression: The Way Out of Your Prison*, Routledge & Kegan Paul, 1983.

Sayers, Janet, *Sexual Contradictions, Psychology, Psychoanalysis and Feminism*, Tavistock, 1986.

Welburn, Vivienne, *Postnatal Depression*, Fontana, 1980.

White, Evelyn C., *Chain, Chain, Change: For Black Women Dealing With Physical and Emotional Abuse*, Seal Press (USA), 1986.

Women in Mind, *Finding Our Own Solutions: Women's Experience of Mental Health Care*, Mind Publications, 1986.

CHAPTER 4 BIRTH CONTROL: WHO CONTROLS?

Organizations

Brook Advisory Centre
153a East St
London SE17 2SD
(01 708 1234)

Family Planning Information Service
27–35 Mortimer St
London W1
(01 636 7866)

Women's Global Network on Reproductive Rights
PO Box 4098
Minahassastraat 1
1009 AB Amsterdam
Netherlands
(20 923900)

Women's Reproductive Rights Information Centre
52–54 Featherstone St
London EC1
(01 251 6332)

Books

Drake, Katia and Drake, Jonathan, *Natural Birth Control; A Guide to Contraception Through Fertility Awareness*, Thorsons, 1984.

Pfeffer, Naomi and Woollett, Anne, *The Experience of Infertility*, Virago, 1983.

Rakusen, Jill and Phillips, Angela (eds), *Our Bodies, Ourselves*, revised 2nd ed, Penguin, 1987.

Saffron, Lisa, *Getting Pregnant Our Own Way:A Guide to Alternative Insemination*, Women's Health Information Centre, 1986.

Shapiro, Rose, *Contraception: A Practical and Political Guide*, Virago, 1987.

CHAPTER 5 ABORTION AND FEMINISM

Organizations

British Pregnancy Advisory Service
Head Office
Austy Manor
Wooton Wawen
Solihull
West Midlands B95 6BX
(05642 3225)

National Abortion Campaign
70 Great Queen St
London WC2B 5AX

Northern Ireland Abortion Law Reform Association
c/o 7 Winetavern St
Belfast BT1 1JQ

Pregnancy Advisory Service
11–13 Charlotte St
London W1P 1HD
(01 637 8962)

Ulster Pregnancy Advisory Association
719a Lisburn Rd
Belfast BT9 7GU
(0232 667345)

Books

Frater, Alison and Wright Catherine, *Coping With Abortion*, Chambers, 1986.

Pipes, Mary, *Understanding Abortion*, The Women's Press, 1986.

Neustatter, Angela and Newson, Gina, *Mixed Feelings: The Experience of Abortion*, Pluto, 1986.

CHAPTER 6 THE SHAPE OF HEALTH

Organizations

Islington Women's Sports Club
c/o Gina Jones
115 Manor Rd
London N16
(01 800 0471)

Northern Outdoor Women
c/o 104 Ivygreen Rd
Manchester M21

Outdoor Women
c/o 93 Foulden Rd
London N16

Spare Tyre (Feminist theatre/organisation offering help/advice to women
with eating problems)
86–88 Holmleigh Rd
London N16 5PY
(01 800 9099)

Sportswoman Campaign
BCM Womansports
London WC1N 3XX
(01 769 0753)

Women's Sport Foundation
c/o Sheffield Poly GES
51 Broomgrove Rd
Sheffield S10

Books

Blue, Adrianne, *Grace Under Pressure? Women in Sport*, Sidgwick & Jackson,
1986.

Chernin, Kim, *Womansize: The Tyranny of Slenderness*, The Women's Press,
1983.

Chernin, Kim, *The Hungry Self*, Virago, 1986.

Coward, Rosalind, *Female Desire*, Picador, 1984.

Leigh, Dr Irene and Wohnarowska, Fenella, *Coping With Skin and Hair
Problems*, Chambers, 1985.

Orbach, Susie, *Fat Is a Feminist Issue I*, Arrow, 1978.

Orbach, Susie, *Fat Is A Feminist Issue II*, Arrow, 1984.

Root, Jane, *Pictures of Women: Sexuality*, Pandora, 1984.

Winterson, Jeanette, *Fit For The Future*, Pandora, 1986.

Women and Migraines, Order from Women and Migraines, 28 Norcott Rd, London N16 7EL, £1 including p+p.

CHAPTER 7 CRISIS

Organizations

Bristol Cancer Help Centre
Grove House
Cornwallis Grove
Clifton
Bristol

British Association of Cancer United Patients (BACUP)
121–123 Charterhouse St
London EC1M 6AA
(01 608 1661)

Cancer Link
46a Pentonville Rd
London N1
(01 267 8046

Mastectomy Association
26 Harrison St, London WC1
(01 837 0908)

Books

Bishop, Beata, *A Time to Heal*, Severn House Publishers, 1985.

Doyle, Lesley, et al., *Cancer in Britain: The Politics of Prevention*, Pluto, 1983.

Faulder, Carolyn, *Breast Cancer: A guide to its Early Detection and Treatment*, Virago, 1983.

Forbes, Alec, MD, *The Bristol Diet*, Century, 1984.

Gerson, Max, *A Cancer Therapy*, Totality Books, 1958.

Kidman, Brenda, *A Gentle Way With Cancer*, Century, 1983.

Kübler-Ross, Elisabeth, *On Death and Dying*, Tavistock, 1970.

Lorde, Audre, *The Cancer Journals*, Sheba, 1985.

McNeill, P. McShea, M. and Parmar, P., *Through the Break: Women in Personal Struggle*, Sheba, 1987.

Sontag, Susan, *Illness As Metaphor*, Penguin, 1983.

Thurnhurst, Colin, *It Makes You Sick: The Politics of the NHS*, Pluto, 1982.

CHAPTER 8 ACROSS BOUNDARIES

Organizations

African Women's Confederation
66 Chesterford Rd
London E12 6LB

Anti-Apartheid Movement Women's Committee
13 Mandela St
London NW1 0DW
(01 387 7966)

Baby Milk Action Coalition
34 Blinco Grove
Cambridge CB1 4TS
(0223 210094)

Change-International Reports of Women
29 Great St James St
London WC1N 3ES
(01 405 3601)

FORWARD (Foundation for Women's Health, Research and Development)
Africa Centre
38 King St
London WC2 8JT
(01 379 6889)

ISIS International: journal and newsletter
Via S. Maria d'ell Anima 30
00186 Rome
Italy

National Women's Network for Worldwide Solidarity
c/o War on Want
3 Castles House
1 London Bridge St
London SE1

(01 403 2266)

Women for a Nuclear Free and Independent Pacific (NFIP)
62 Purser House
London SW2 2JA
(01 674 6201)

Women's International Resource Centre and Links (WISER LINKS)
173 Archway Rd
London N6
(01 341 4403)

Books

El Daree, Asma, *Woman, Why Do You Weep? Circumcision and Its Consequences*, Zed, 1982.

Sa'adawi, Nawal el, *The Hidden Face of Eve*, Zed, 1980.

CHAPTER 9 DISCUSSING CHILDBIRTH

Organizations

Association of Breastfeeding Mothers
131 Mayow Rd
London SE26 4HZ
(01 778 4769)

Association for Improvements in the Maternity Services (AIMS)
163 Liverpool Rd
London N1
(01 278 5628)

La Lèche League
BM 3424
London WC1V 6XX
(01 404 5011)

Maternity Alliance
59–61 Camden High Street
London NW1 7LJ
(01 388 6337)

National Childbirth Trust
9 Queensborough Terrace
London W2 3TB
(01 221 3833)

Books

Larbie, Jo, *Black Women and the Maternity Services*, Health Education Council/National Extension College for Training in Health and Race, 1985.

Phillips, Angela, *Your Body, Your Baby, Your Life*, Pandora, 1983.

Reader, Fran and Savage, Wendy, *Coping With Caesarean and Other Difficult Births*, Macdonald, 1983.

CHAPTER 10 ADDICTING FORCES

Organizations

Alcohol Concern
305 Gray's Inn Road
London WC1X 8QF
(01 833 3471)

Alcoholics Anonymous
P.O. Box 514
11 Redcliffe Gardens
London SW10
(01 834 8202)

ASH (Action on Smoking and Health)
51/11 Mortimer Street
London W1
(01 637 9843)

Drugs, Alcohol and Women Nationally (DAWN)
Boundary House
91–93 Charterhouse St
London EC1 M6HR
(01 250 3284)

Release
169 Commercial St
London E1 6BW
(01 603 8654)

Standing Conference on Drug Abuse (SCODA)
1–4 Hatton Place
Hatton Gardens
London EC1N 8ND
(01 430 2341)

TRANX
17 Peel Rd
Harrow HA3 7QX
(01 427 2065)

Women's Alcohol Centre
254 St Paul's Road
London N1 2LU
(01 226 4581)

Books

Camberwell Council on Alcoholism, *Women and Alcohol*, Tavistock, 1980.

Health Education Council, *Women and Smoking: A Handbook for Action*, Health Education Council, 1986.

Jacobson, Bobbie, *Beating the Ladykillers: Women and Smoking*, Pluto, 1986.

McConville, Brigid, *Women Under the Influence*, Virago, 1983.

CHAPTER 11 SEXUALITY AND WOMEN'S LIBERATION

Organizations

College of Health Healthline Telephone Service
(01 981 2717) (01 980 7222) (0345 581151)
For up to date information on AIDS.
Outside London call the 0345 number and you will be charged at local rates.

Lesbian Line
BM Box 1514
London WC1N 3XX
(01 251 6911)

London Black Lesbian and Gay Centre
(01 885 3543)

London Lesbian and Gay Centre
69 Cowcross Street
London EC1M 6BP
(01 608 1471)

Lesbian and Gay Switchboard
(01 838 7324)

PACE (Project for Advice, Counselling and Education)
Services provided by lesbians and gay men
London Lesbian and Gay Centre
69 Cowcross Street
London EC1M 6BP
(01 251 2689)

Scottish AIDS Monitor
P.O. Box 169, Edinburgh
(031 558 1167)

Sigma (self-help group for heterosexuals in a relationship with a lesbian
or gay man)
BM Sigma
London WC1N 3XX

SPOD (Sexual and Personal Relationships of Disabled People)
286 Camden Road
London N7 0BJ
(01 607 8851/2)

Terence Higgins Trust
BM AIDS
London WC1N 3XX
Helpline (01 242 1010) Monday to Friday 7–10p.m.; Saturday and Sunday
3a.m.–10p.m.

Welsh AIDS Campaign
c/o Health Education Advisory Committee for Wales
Secretariat
Room 2003
Welsh Office
Cathays Park
Cardiff CF1 3NQ
(0222 823395)

Books

Boyd, C., *et al.* (eds), *Out For Ourselves: The Lives of Irish Lesbians and Gay Men*, Women's Community Press, 1986.

Cartledge, Sue and Ryan, Joanna (eds), *Sex and Love*, The Women's Press, 1983.

Feminist Review Collective, *Sexuality. A Reader*, Virago, 1987.

Kitzinger, Sheila, *Women's Experience of Sex*, Penguin, 1985.

Richardson, Diane, *Women and the AIDS Crisis*, Pandora, 1987.

Rights of Women, *Lesbian Mothers On Trial*, Rights of Women, 1984.

Rights of Women Lesbian Custody Group, *Lesbian Mothers' Legal Handbook*, The Women's Press, 1986.

Snitow, Stansell and Thompson (eds), *Desire: The Politics of Sexuality*, Virago, 1984.

Tatchell, Peter, *AIDS: A Guide to Survival*, Gay Men's Press, 1986.

Valverde, Mariana, *Sex, Power and Pleasure*, The Women's Press, Canada, 1985.

Vance, Carole S., *Pleasure and Danger: Exploring Female Sexuality*, Routledge & Kegan Paul, 1984.

FEMINIST PUBLICATIONS

Everywoman
34A Islington Green
London N1 8DU

Outwrite Women's Newspaper
Oxford House
Derbyshire House, London E2
(01 729 4575)

Spare Rib
27 Clerkenwell Close
London EC1R OAT
(01 253 9792)

Women's Review
1–7 Christina St
London EC2A 4PA
(01 739 4906)

WOMEN'S CENTRES

England

A Woman's Place
Hungerford House
Victoria Embankment
London WC2
(01 836 6081)

Bristol Women's Centre
44 The Grove
Bristol
(0272 293575)

Cambridge Women's Centre
49a Burleigh Street, Cambridge
(0223 313675)

Cleveland Women's Centre
St Mary's Centre
Corporation Road
Middlesbrough
Cleveland

Croydon Women's Centre
13 Woodside Green
London SE25 5EY
(01 656 2369)

Feminist Library
Hungerford House
Victoria Embankment
London WC2
(01 930 0715)

Lancaster Women's Centre
The Plough
Bryer St
Lancaster
(0524 63967)

Manchester Women's Centre
Pankhurst Trust
2–4 Oxford Road
Manchester M15AQ
(061 228 2028)

Norwich Women's Education and Resource Centre
50 Bethel Street
Norwich NR2 1NR
(0603 628130)

Oxford Women's Centre
35–37 Cowley Road
Oxford
(0865 245923)

Reading Women's Advice and Resource Centre
6 Silver St
Reading

Wesley House Women's Centre
70 Great Queen Street
London WC2
(01 430 1076)

Ireland

Belfast Women's Centre
18 Donegall Street
Belfast BT1
(084 243363)

Cork Women's Centre
24 Sullivan's Quay
(021 967660)

Derry Women's Centre
7–9 Artillery Street
(0504 267672)

Dublin Women's Centre
27 Temple Lane, Off Dame Street
Dublin 2
(01 710088)

Scotland

Edinburgh Women's Centre
61a Broughton Street
Edinburgh
(031 557 3179)

HEALTH INFORMATION

College of Health
18 Victoria Park Square
London E2 2PF

Consumer association with publications and information on orthodox and alternative medicine. Healthline is open from 6–10p.m. every day for recorded information on a range of health topics.
(01 980 4848)

Women's Health Information Centre (WHIC)
52–54 Featherstone Street
London EC1
(01 251 6580)
Has general information on most aspects of women's health. Also produces a large range of broadsheets on specific areas of women's health.

Women's Reproductive Rights Information Centre
52–54 Featherstone Street
London EC1
(01 251 6332)
Information and publications covering all areas of reproduction.

ALTERNATIVE HEALING

British Acupuncture Association and Register
34 Alderney St
London SW1

British Homoeopathic Association
27a Devonshire St
London W1

British Naturopathic and Osteopathic Association
Frazer House
6 Netherall Gardens
London NW3

Institute for Complementary Medicine
21 Portland Place
London W1N 3AF

National Institute of Medical Herbalists
Hatherley Rd
Winchester
Hampshire

National Institute of Medicinal Herbalists
School of Herbal Medicine
148 Forest Rd
Tunbridge Wells
Kent

Register of Traditional Chinese Medicine
7a Thorndean St
London SW18

Society of Homoeopaths
101 Sebastian Ave
Shenfield
Brentwood
Essex CM15 8PP

Traditional Acupuncture Society
11 Grange Park
Stratford-on-Avon
Warwickshire CV37 6XH

INDEX

24; herpes, 25–7; thrush, 20–3; trichomonas, 23–5; warts, 27

Vajpayee, Atal Bihari, 95

vegetarianism, 230–4

violence, patriarchal, 151

virginity, tests for immigrants, 94, 95

Voluntary Euthanasia Society, 270, 277

wages, 74, 205, 311, 315

Wales, 206

Warnock, Dame Mary, 188

Warnock Committee, 177, 178

warts, 27, 51

Well Pensioner Clinics, 75

Well Women's Clinics, 73, 129, 130

Western Samoa, 289

womb, *see* uterus

women's liberation movement: abortion, 190, 196–202, 206, 207; addictions, 318; birth control, 153; childbirth, 303; and the disabled, 125–8; health, 208–9; lesbianism, 338; 'mental illness', 147; organisation of feminist events, 71; surrogacy, 179; therapy, 134–5, 143

work: danger at, 119–25; disabled women, 339; working conditions and health, 74

working class: Black women, 77; rickets, 82; *Spare Rib*, 338; treatment for cancer, 273

World Health Organisation: baby foods, 288–9; clitoridectomy, 294, 295; DDT, 291; DP, 166; International Conference on Women and Health, 167

X-ray testing, 94, 95–6

Zaire, 360

Zimbabwe, 173

Pandora Press is a feminist press, an imprint of Routledge & Kegan Paul. Our list is varied – we publish new fiction, reprint fiction, history, biography and autobiography, social issues, humour – written by women and celebrating the lives and achievements of women the world over. For further information about Pandora Press books, please write to the Mailing List Dept. at Pandora Press, 11 New Fetter Lane, London EC4P 4EE, or in the USA at 29 West 35th Street, New York, NY 10001–2291

Some Pandora titles you will enjoy:

Natural Healing in Gynecology

Rina Nissim

"Natural Healing compels us to care for our health in an intelligent and truly preventative manner. It provides a wealth of healing alternatives from eastern and western cultures and critiques the limits of conventional western medicine giving us the power of choice.

Its friendly conversational style is a delight, as though a wise woman were guiding us through whatever problem we have and helping us figure out what to do.

An unusual and invaluable resource indeed"

Boston Women's Health Collective

0 86358 069 6

Birth and our Bodies

Paddy O'Brien

This practical and positive companion guide provides women with detailed physical and mental exercises to practise through pregnancy and birth.

Working chronologically from the time when a woman may not even be pregnant but hopes to conceive in the near future, right through to the birth itself, the guide provides a comprehensive exercise programme for relaxation, combating morning sickness, stage fright in the last few weeks of pregnanacy and for strengthening the pelvic floor muscles.

Illustrated with line drawings taken from 'life' both in the exercise classes which Paddy O'Brien runs, and at the time of the birth itself, BIRTH AND OUR BODIES helps mothers to stay in touch with a body, and in charge of it, when it seems in danger of being taken over by the baby. So, as well as maintaining and strengthening your muscles you get stronger and more supple emotionally.

This is a pocket-sized companion, easy to use at home, or at work – it encourages the participation of partners and can be used too whenever you have time to yourself.

This is a practical and positive guide to physical exercises, massages, and meditations for women.

£3.95   0 86358 047 5

Test-Tube Women

What Future for Motherhood?

Edited by Rita Arditti, Renate Duelli Klein and Shelley Minden

Genetic engineering, sperm banks, test tube fertilisation, sex selection, surrogate mothering, experimentation in the third world, increased technological intervention in childbirth – are we taking pregnancy and the birth process out of the dark ages or into a terrifying 'brave new world'?

Who controls it? Who benefits? The technological machine grinds on, in headline-grabbing leaps or in quiet developments in research laboratories; but what are the implications for women worldwide?

"Should be read from cover to cover by Winston and Peel, Steptoe and Edwards, and all concerned professionally, politically or personally with the processes of procreation" *Bernard Dixon in NEW SOCIETY*

£4.95   0 86358 030 0

Patient Patients

Helen Roberts

Nearly every woman will see in these pages a reflection of herself in her relationship with doctors. Sheila Kitzinger

"I would say that she is defrosting and just as the fridge always seems to drip a lot when it is defrosting, this lady was dripping a little when I saw her, but then all my ladies drip, so I'm quite used to that."—a psychiatrist of his patient.

"He's a right vet. . ."—a patient of her G.P.

"If it hadn't been for my G.P. I wouldn't be here today. He's a marvellous doctor because you can talk and he'll listen."

Women go to their doctors more often and take more medicine than do men, and they spend more time looking after other people's health than men do. Helen Roberts investigate the relationship between women and their doctors. What makes women ill? Are their families any help? What do women think of their doctors? And what are the doctors views of their women patients and doctors alike? Helen Roberts sets out to answer these and many other questions in her sensitive portrayal of women, 'the patient patients'.

0 86358 019 X